PHILIP'S

STRE
Oxfordshire

First published 1994 by

Philip's, a division of
Octopus Publishing Group Ltd
2–4 Heron Quays, London E14 4JP

Second colour edition 2002
First impression 2002

ISBN 0-540-08110-8

© Philip's 2002

OS Ordnance Survey®

This product includes mapping data licensed
from Ordnance Survey® with the permission
of the Controller of Her Majesty's Stationery
Office. © Crown copyright 2002. All rights
reserved. Licence number 100011710

Printed and bound in Spain
by Cayfosa-Quebecor

Contents

III **Key to map symbols**

IV **Key to map pages**

VI **Route planning**

VIII **Administrative and Postcode boundaries**

1 **Street maps** at 2½ inches to 1 mile

261 **Town maps** of Reading and Swindon

263 **Index** of towns and villages

264 **Index** of streets, hospitals, industrial estates, railway
stations, schools, shopping centres, universities
and places of interest

Digital Data

The exceptionally high-quality mapping found in this atlas is available as digital
data in TIFF format, which is easily convertible to other bit mapped (raster) image
formats.

The index is also available in digital form as a standard database table. It contains
all the details found in the printed index together with the National Grid reference
for the map square in which each entry is named and feature codes for places of
interest in eight categories such as education and health.

For further information and to discuss your requirements, please contact
Philip's on 020 7531 8440 or george.philip@philips-maps.co.uk

Key to map symbols

Motorway with junction number	(22a)
Primary route – dual/single carriageway	
A road – dual/single carriageway	
B road – dual/single carriageway	
Minor road – dual/single carriageway	
Other minor road – dual/single carriageway	
Road under construction	
Pedestrianised area	
Postcode boundaries	DY7
County and unitary authority boundaries	
Railway	
Railway under construction	
Tramway, miniature railway	
Rural track, private road or narrow road in urban area	
Gate or obstruction to traffic (restrictions may not apply at all times or to all vehicles)	
Path, bridleway, byway open to all traffic, road used as a public path	

The representation in this atlas of a road, track or or path is no evidence of the existence of a of a right of way

174
94

Adjoining page indicators

Railway station	Walsall		
Private railway station			
Bus, coach station			
Ambulance station			
Coastguard station			
Fire station			
Police station			
Accident and Emergency entrance to hospital			
Hospital	H		
Place of worship			
Information Centre (open all year)			
Parking	P		
Park and Ride	P&R		
Post Office	PO		
Camping site			
Caravan site			
Golf course			
Picnic site			
Important buildings, schools, colleges, universities and hospitals	Prim Sch		
Water name	River Medway		
River, stream			
Lock, weir			
Water			
Tidal water			
Woods			
Houses			
Non-Roman antiquity	Church		
Roman antiquity	ROMAN FORT		

Acad	Academy	Mkt	Market
Allot Gdns	Allotments	Meml	Memorial
Cemy	Cemetery	Mon	Monument
C Ctr	Civic Centre	Mus	Museum
CH	Club House	Obsy	Observatory
Coll	College	Pal	Royal Palace
Crem	Crematorium	PH	Public House
Ent	Enterprise	Recn Gd	Recreation Ground
Ex H	Exhibition Hall	Resr	Reservoir
Ind Est	Industrial Estate	Ret Pk	Retail Park
IRB Sta	Inshore Rescue Boat Station	Sch	School
		Sh Ctr	Shopping Centre
Inst	Institute	TH	Town Hall/House
Ct	Law Court	Trad Est	Trading Estate
L Ctr	Leisure Centre	Univ	University
LC	Level Crossing	Wks	Works
Liby	Library	YH	Youth Hostel

The dark grey border on the inside edge of some pages indicates that the ping does not continue onto the adjacent page

■ The small numbers around the edges of the maps identify the 1 kilometre National Grid lines

he scale of the maps on the pages numbered in blue
3.92 cm to 1 km • 2½ inches to 1 mile • 1: 25344

0		¼		½		¾		1 mile
0	250 m		500 m		750 m	1 kilometre		

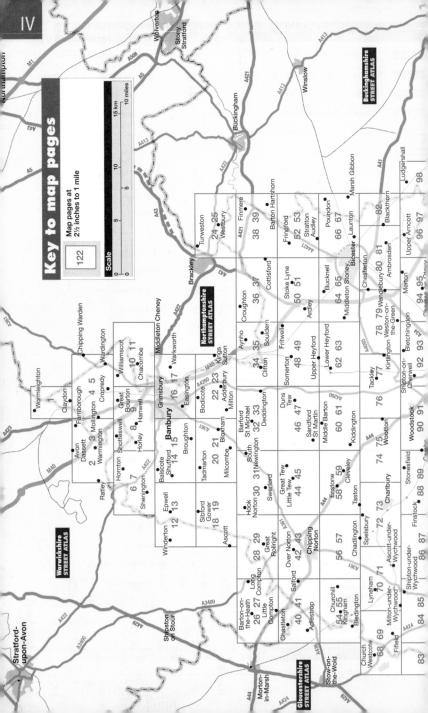

IV

Key to map pages

Map pages at
2½ inches to 1 mile

| 122 |

Scale

0   5   10   15 km
0   5   10 miles

Warwickshire
STREET ATLAS

Buckinghamshire
STREET ATLAS

Northamptonshire
STREET ATLAS

Gloucestershire
STREET ATLAS

Stratford-upon-Avon

Northampton

Wolverton

Stony Stratford

Buckingham

Winslow

Ludgershall

Wormleighton
Claydon
Chipping Warden
Wardington
Williamscot
Chacombe
Middleton Cheney
Warkworth
Kings Sutton
Turweston
Westbury
Finmere
Barton Hartshorn
Marsh Gibbon
Blackthorn

Farnborough
Mollington
Cropredy
Great Bourton
Grimsbury
Easington
Adderbury
Milton
Croughton
Aynho
Souldern
Fringford
Poundon
Upper Arncott

Avon Dassett
Shotteswell
Hanwell
Banbury
Bodicote
Barford St Michael
Deddington
Clifton
Somerton
Fritwell
Stoke Lyne
Cottisford
Bucknell
Middleton Stoney
Bicester
Chesterton
Wendlebury
Weston-on-the-Green
Ambrosden
Merton

Ratley
Horley
Broughton
Bloxham
South Newington
Duns Tew
Sandford St Martin
Upper Heyford
Lower Heyford
Ardley
Stratton Audley
Launton
Kirtlington
Bletchington
Shipton-on-Cherwell

Shenington
Epwell
Balscote
Shutford
Tadmarton
Milcombe
Middle Barton
Kiddington
Tackley
Wootton
Woodstock
Stonesfield
Stratford on Stour

Winderton
Sibford Gower
Ascott
Hook Norton
Swerford
Great Tew
Little Tew
Enstone
Cleveley
Taston
Charlbury
Finstock
Shipton-under-Wychwood

Barton-on-the-Heath
Long Compton
Little Compton
Great Rollright
Over Norton
Chipping Norton
Chadlington
Spelsbury
Ascott-under-Wychwood

Chastleton
Salford
Churchill
Kingham
Bledington
Lyneham
Milton-under-Wychwood

Church Westcote
Fifield
Adlestrop

Shipston on Stour
Moreton-in-Marsh
Stow-on-the-Wold

1				
2	3	4	5	
6	7	8	9	10	11
12	13	14	15	16	17
18	19	20	21	22	23	24	25
26	27	28	29	30	31	32	33	34	35	36	37	38	39
40	41	42	43	44	45	46	47	48	49	50	51	52	53
54	55	56	57	58	59	60	61	62	63	64	65	66	67
68	69	70	71	72	73	74	75	76	77	78	79	80	81	82
83	84	85	86	87	88	89	90	91	92	93	94	95	96	97	98

Twyford
Sonning
Caversham
Reading

Princes Risborough
Haddenham
Thame
Towersey
Henton

Chinnor
Bledlow Ridge
Kingston Blount
Beacon's Bottom
Stokenchurch

Henley-on-Thames
Wargrave
Shiplake
Tokers Green

Lower Assendon
Fawley
Middle Assendon
Nettlebed
Shepherd's Green
Sonning Common

Long Crendon
Shabbington
Tiddington
Wheatley
Cuddesdon

Teetsworth
Aston Rowant
Lewknor
Watlington
Brightwell Baldwin
Greenfield

Stoke Row
Nuffield

Whitchurch Hill
Pangbourne

Wormighall
Holton
Horspath
Garsington

Great Haseley
Stoke Talmage
Chalgrove
Brightwell Baldwin
Ewelme
Benson
Berrick

Crowmarsh Gifford
Cholsey
South Stoke
Woodcote
Goring

Horton-cum-Studley
Noke
Beckley
Stanton St. John
Kidlington
Yarnton
Marston
Oxford
Botley
North Hinksey
Kennington

Little Milton
Stadhampton
Berinsfield
Dorchester
Warborough
Long Wittenham
Brightwell-cum-Sotwell
Wallingford
Aston Tirrold
Aston Upthorpe
Blewbury
Moulsford

Aldworth

Sandford-on-Thames
Radley
Abingdon
Drayton
Culham
Sutton Courtenay
Didcot
Milton
Milton Hill
Upton
Chilton
West Ilsley

Freeland
Cassington
Wolvercote
Eynsham
Sutton
Stanton Harcourt
Cumnor
Northmoor
Wootton
Appleton
Marcham
East Hanney
Steventon
Harwell
East Hendred
Ardington
Wantage
Grove
West Hanney
Denchworth
Letcombe Regis

North Leigh
Witney
South Leigh
Ducklington
Standlake
Curbridge
Brize Norton
Aston
Cote
Bampton
Hinton Waldrist
Buckland
Charney Bassett
Stanford in the Vale
Kingston Bagpuize
Garford
Longworth
Sparsholt
Childrey
Letcombe Bassett

Minster Lovell
Crawley
Black Bourton
Langford
Clanfield
Littleworth
Faringdon
Great Coxwell
Longcot
Baulking
Uffington
Woolstone

Burford
Shilton
Carterton
Alvescot
Filkins
Lechlade on Thames
Kelmscott
Buscot
Watchfield
Shrivenham
Bourton
Ashbury
Bishopstone

Taynton
Great Barrington
Westwell
Eastleach Martin
Southrop
Highworth
Swindon
Baydon

Berkshire STREET ATLAS
Wiltshire STREET ATLAS

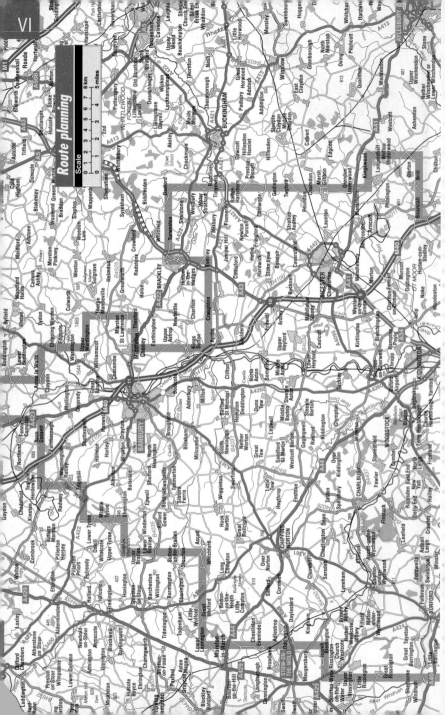

VI

Route planning

Scale

0 1 2 3 4 5 6 7 8km
0 1 2 3 4 5 miles

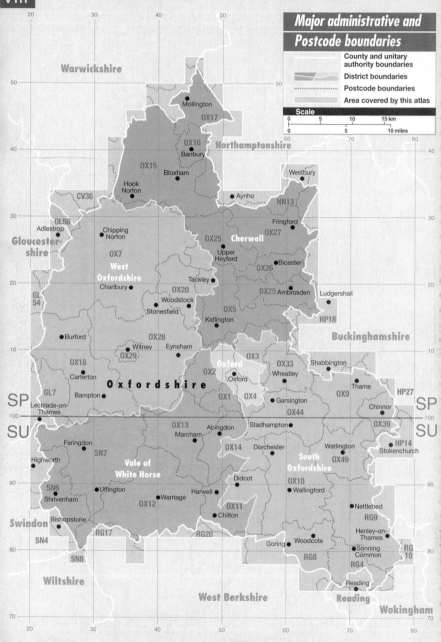

Warwickshire

Northamptonshire

Gloucester-
shire

Buckinghamshire

Wiltshire

West Berkshire

Wokingham

Major administrative and
Postcode boundaries

County and unitary
authority boundaries
District boundaries
Postcode boundaries
Area covered by this atlas

Scale
0   5   10   15 km
0   5   10 miles

Mollington
OX17
OX16
Banbury
OX15
Bloxham
Hook
Norton
CV36
Aynho
Westbury
NN13
Fringford
OX27
GL56
Adlestrop
Chipping
Norton
OX7
OX25
Cherwell
Upper
Heyford
OX26
Bicester
West
Oxfordshire
Charlbury
OX20
Tackley
OX25 Ambrosden
Ludgershall
GL
54
Woodstock
Stonesfield
OX5
Kidlington
HP18
Burford
OX28
Witney Eynsham
OX3
Shabbington
OX18
OX29
OX33
Wheatley
Thame
Carterton
Oxfordshire
OX2
Oxford
OX9
HP27
GL7
Bampton
OX1 OX4
Garsington
OX44
Chinnor
Lechlade-on-
Thames
OX39
SU
HP14
Stokenchurch
Faringdon
SN7
OX13
Marcham
Abingdon
Stadhampton
Highworth
Vale of
White Horse
OX14
Dorchester
Watlington
South
Oxfordshire
OX49
SN6
Shrivenham
Uffington
Wantage
OX12
Harwell
Didcot
OX11
Chilton
OX10
Wallingford
Nettlebed
RG9
Bishopstone
RG17
RG20
Goring
Woodcote
Henley-on-
Thames
Sonning
Common
RG
10
SN4
RG8
RG4
SN8
Reading

Oxford

Swindon

Reading

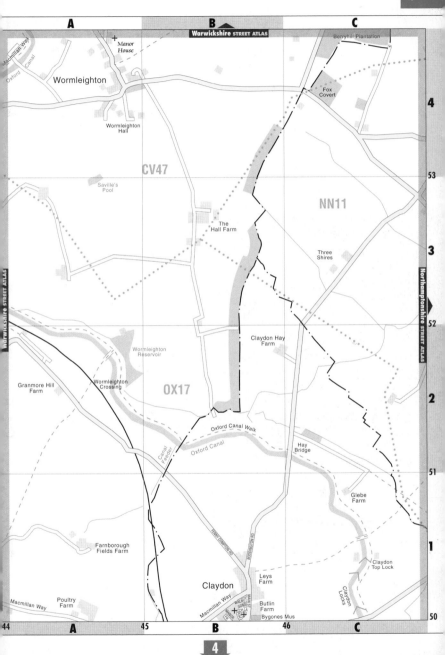

Berryhill Plantation

Manor House

Wormleighton

Fox Covert

4

CV47

53

Saville's Pool

NN11

The Hall Farm

Three Shires

3

Claydon Hay Farm

52

Wormleighton Reservoir

OX17

2

Granmore Hill Farm

Wormleighton Crossing

Oxford Canal Walk

Hay Bridge

Canal Feeder

Oxford Canal

51

Glebe Farm

Farnborough Fields Farm

1

Claydon Top Lock

Macmillan Way

Poultry Farm

Leys Farm

Claydon

Butlin Farm

Claydon Locks

Macmillan Way

Bygones Mus

50

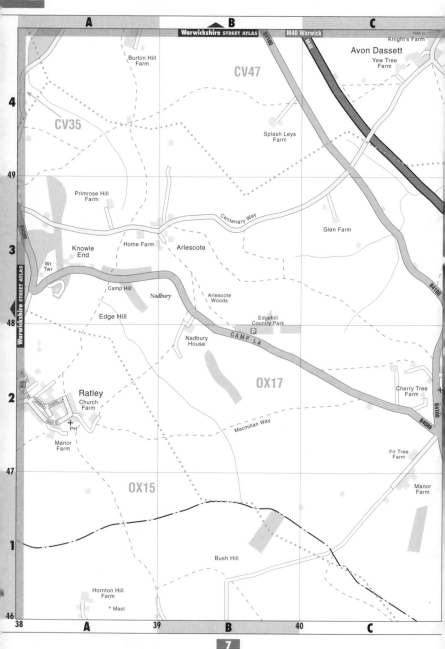

Warwickshire STREET ATLAS

M40 Warwick

PARK CL

Knight's Farm

Avon Dassett

Yew Tree Farm

CV47

Burton Hill Farm

CV35

Splash Leys Farm

Primrose Hill Farm

Centenary Way

Glen Farm

Knowle End

Home Farm

Arlescote

Wr Twr

Camp Hill

Nadbury

Arlescote Woods

Edge Hill

Edgehill Country Park

Nadbury House

CAMP LA

OX17

Cherry Tree Farm

Ratley

Church Farm

CHAPEL LA

HIGH ST

PH

Macmillan Way

Fir Tree Farm

Manor Farm

OX15

Manor Farm

Bush Hill

Hornton Hill Farm

Mast

Warwickshire STREET ATLAS

4

49

3

48

2

47

1

46

38

A

39

B

40

C

A
B
Warwickshire STREET ATLAS
C
A423 Southam

+ AVON CARROW

Stonewold

Dassett Fields

Windmill Lodge Farm

PH

HEYDONS TERR

Sourland Pool

Butchers Arms (PH)

Park Lodge

CV47

+ Farnborough

4

Farnborough Hall

The Rookery

Oak Hill

49

Farnborough Park

M40

Obelisk

Tile Barn

Southam Rd

A423

3

Markhamhole Spinney

Mollington Wood

Keepers Cottage

College Farm

Macmillan Way

48

* Mast

MOLLINGTON LA

VILLAGE RD

CHAPEL ST

PH

COURT LA

CHURCH LA

SCOTT CL

Warmington

OX17

ROUNDHILL RD 1
SCHOOL HILL 2
TINKER'S LA 3
THE ROW 4

BETTONY

MAIN ST

THE HOLT

LOWER FARM LA

2

Warmington Wood

MARCH RD

Deddington Hill

The National Herb Ctr

47

BANBURY RD

Warmington Fox Covert

The Wobbly Wheel (PH)

Angel Piece

1

B4100

Valley Farm

M40

46

41
A
42
B
43
C

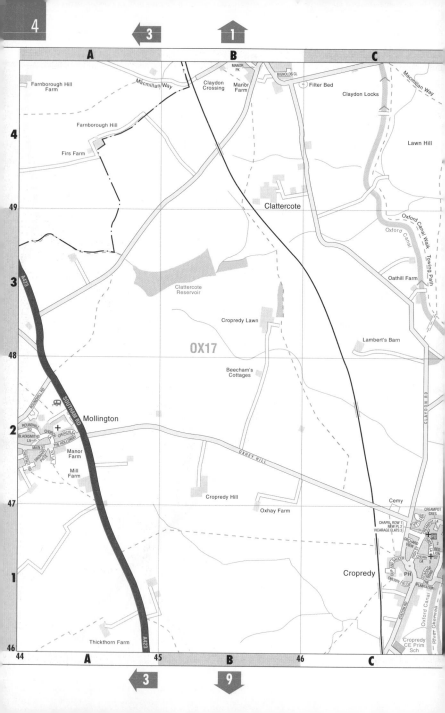

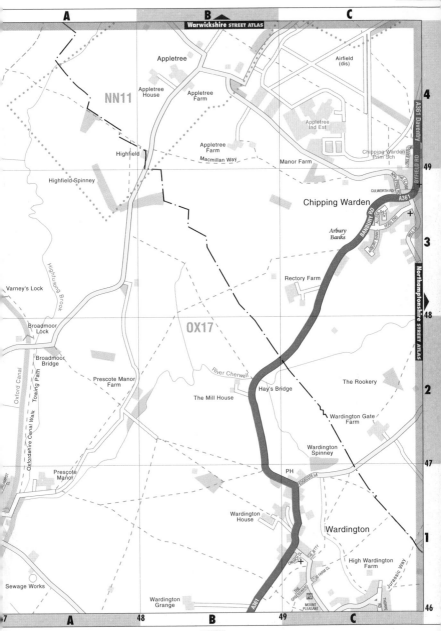

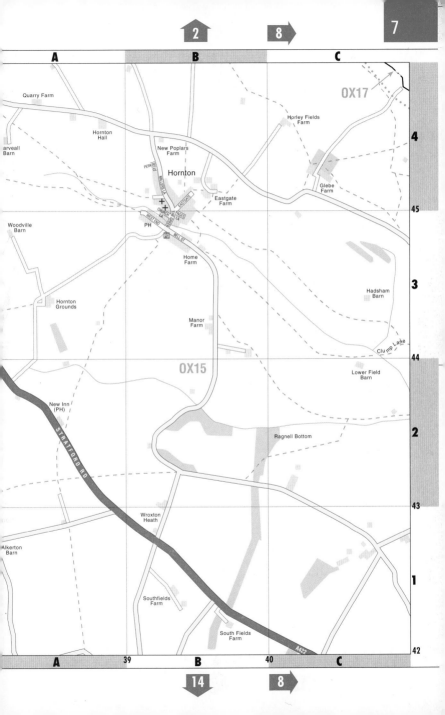

OX17

OX15

Quarry Farm

Horley Fields
Farm

arveall
Barn

Hornton
Hall

New Poplars
Farm

Glebe
Farm

PERKINS
CL

MILLERS LA

Hornton

Eastgate
Farm

CASTLEGATE

Woodville
Barn

CHURCH
WEST END

THE LA

PAGES

WEST END

PH

Pd

BELL ST

Home
Farm

Hadsham
Barn

Hornton
Grounds

Manor
Farm

Clump Lane

Lower Field
Barn

New Inn
(PH)

STRATFORD RD

Ragnell Bottom

Alkerton
Barn

Wroxton
Heath

Southfields
Farm

South Fields
Farm

A422

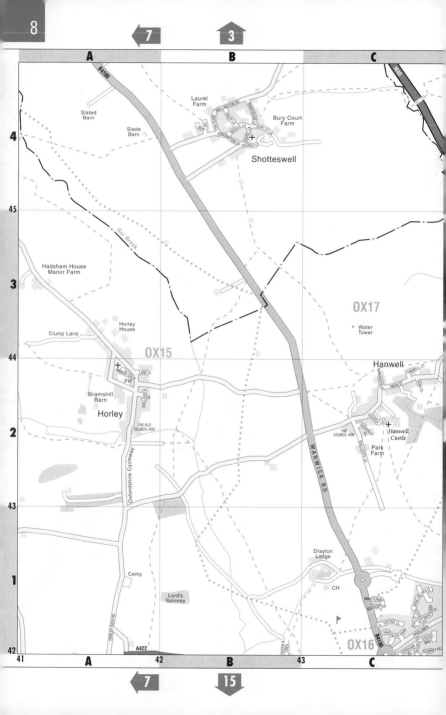

A
B
C

4

45

3

OX17

Water
Tower

44

OX15

Hanwell

2

WARWICK RD

Hanwell
Castle

43

1

Drayton
Lodge

CH

OX16

42

41
42
43

A
B
C

B4100

Slated
Barn

Slade
Barn

Laurel
Farm

Bury Court
Farm

CHURCH

Shotteswell

Sor Brook

Hadsham House
Manor Farm

Horley
House

Clump Lane

Bramshill
Barn

Horley

LANE CL

PH

MANOR ORCH

THE OLD
COUNCIL HOS

Oxfordshire Cycleway

HORLEY PATH RD

Cemy

Lord's
Spinney

A422

THE
COUNCIL HOS

Park
Farm

CHURCH LA

SPRINGSIDE

MAIN ST

HANWELL CT

PARK CL

WINSTON DR

ELLISON DR

QUEEN'S CRES

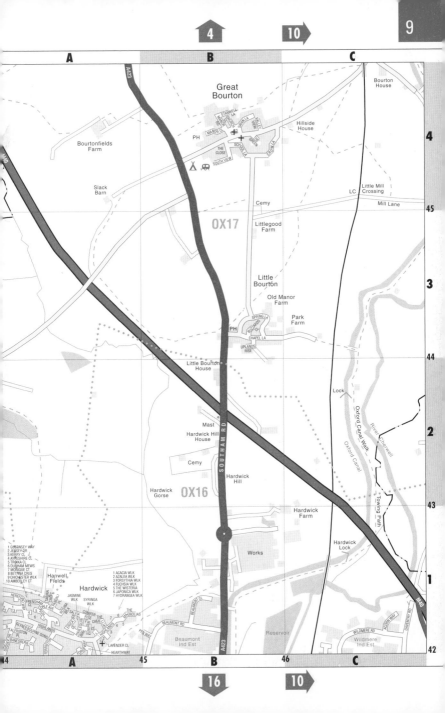

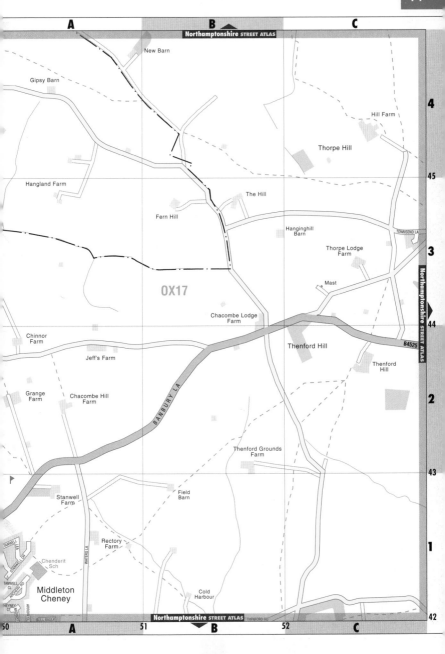

A

B

C

New Barn

Gipsy Barn

Hill Farm

4

Thorpe Hill

Hangland Farm

45

The Hill

Fern Hill

Hanginghill
Barn

TOWNSEND LA

Thorpe Lodge
Farm

3

OX17

Mast

Northamptonshire STREET ATLAS

Chacombe Lodge
Farm

44

Chinnor
Farm

Thenford Hill

B4525

Jeff's Farm

Thenford
Hill

Grange
Farm

Chacombe Hill
Farm

2

BANBURY LA

Thenford Grounds
Farm

43

Stanwell
Farm

Field
Barn

TANWELL

STANWELL DR

Rectory
Farm

WATERS LA

1

Chenderit
Sch

TANWELL CL

Middleton
Cheney

Cold
Harbour

BULL BAULK

THENFORD RD

42

50

A

51

B

52

C

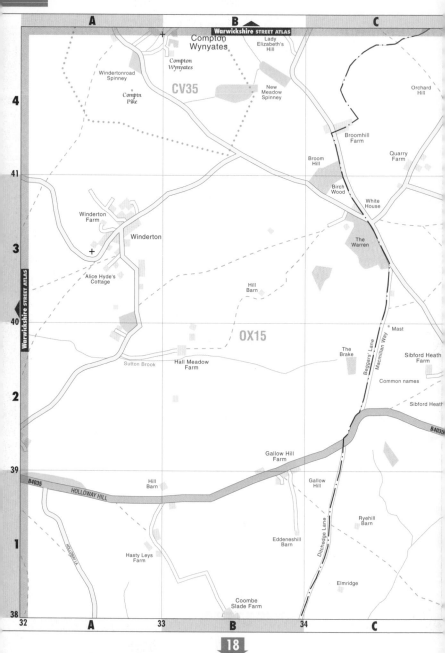

Compton
Wynyates

Lady
Elizabeth's
Hill

Compton
Wynyates

Windertonroad
Spinney

CV35

New
Meadow
Spinney

Orchard
Hill

Comptn
Pike

4

Broomhill
Farm

Quarry
Farm

Broom
Hill

41

Birch
Wood

White
House

Winderton
Farm

Winderton

The
Warren

3

Alice Hyde's
Cottage

Hill
Barn

40

Mast

Baggins' Lane

Macmillan Way

Sibford Heath
Farm

The
Brake

OX15

Common names

Sutton Brook

Hall Meadow
Farm

Sibford Heath

2

B4035

Gallow Hill
Farm

39

B4035

Hill
Barn

Gallow
Hill

HOLLOWAY HILL

Ditchedge Lane

Ryehill
Barn

1

Hasty Leys
Farm

Eddeneshill
Barn

Elmridge

Coombe
Slade Farm

38

32 **A** **33** **B** **34** **C**

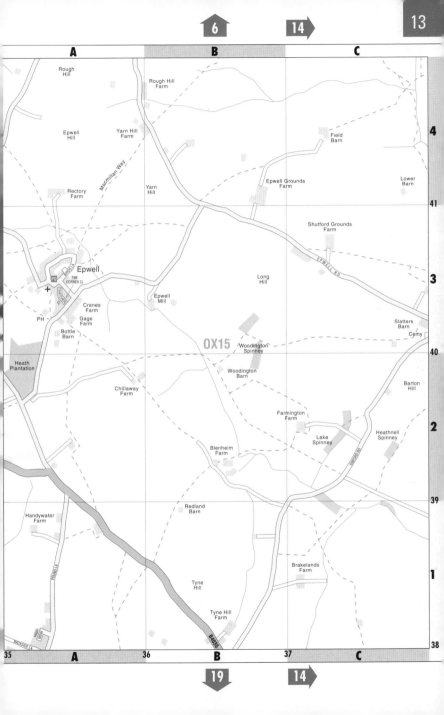

A B C

Rough
Hill

Rough Hill
Farm

Epwell
Hill

Yarn Hill
Farm

4

Field
Barn

Lower
Barn

Macmillan Way

Yarn
Hill

Epwell Grounds
Farm

Rectory
Farm

41

Shutford Grounds
Farm

Epwell

THE CORNER CL.

Long
Hill

EPWELL RD

3

Epwell
Mill

Cranes
Farm

PH

Gage
Farm

Slatters
Barn

Cemy

Bottle
Barn

OX15

Woodington
Spinney

40

Heath
Plantation

Woodington
Barn

Chillaway
Farm

Barton
Hill

Farmington
Farm

2

Lake
Spinney

Heathnell
Spinney

Blenheim
Farm

SHIPSTON RD

39

Redland
Barn

Handywater
Farm

Brakelands
Farm

1

POUND LA.

Tyne
Hill

Tyne Hill
Farm

B4035

HIGH

BACKSIDE LA.

38

35 A 36 B 37 C 38

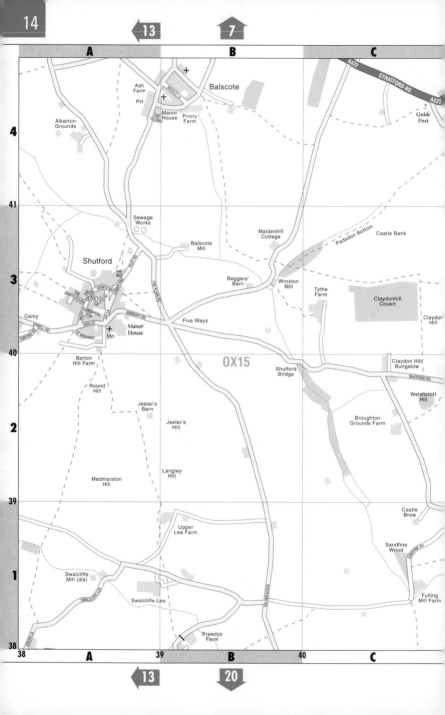

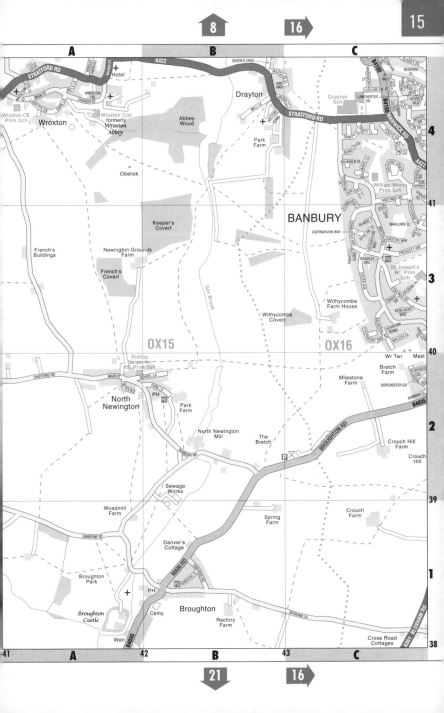

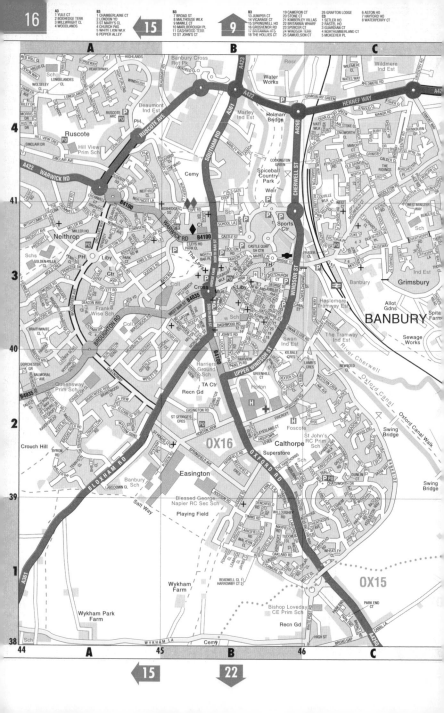

A   B   C

Overthorpe Hall
Overthorpe Prep Sch
BANBURY LA
The Carrdus Sch
B4525

BULL BAULK
CHURCH LA
HIGH ST
MANSION HILL
BARNETT RD
Libv
QUEEN ST
THE ACORNS DR

A422
A387
A422

11
A422

BLACKLOCKS HILL
Brinsall
WARKWORTH RD
Allot Gdns

4

Nethercote

A422 Brackley

MIDDLETON RD

PRINCETHORPE DR
The Willows
Home Farm

41

Ind Est
CROMBARTON RD

OVERTHORPE RD
Ind Est
THORPE DR
THORPE CL

The Bowling Green (PH)

Overthorpe

CHEYWODE

Longacre

+
Warkworth Farm

Warkworth House
THE COURTYARD

Warkworth

ASTROP RD

Northamptonshire STREET ATLAS

3

Home Farm

Sewage Works

Grove Lodge

40

OX16

Jurassic Way

OX17

Warkworth Hall Farm

2

Blackpits Farm

Farthinghoe Stream

39

Towing Path
River Cherwell

Swing Bridge

Oxford Canal Walk

1

Oxford Canal
Grant's Lock

OX15

Sutton Lodge Farm

38

7   A   48   B   49   C

M40

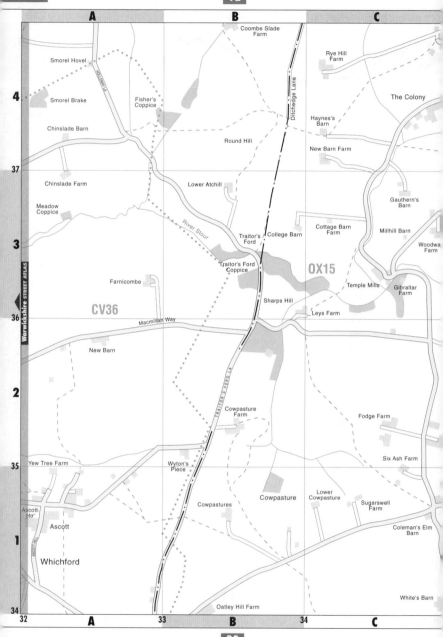

A B C

Coombe Slade Farm

Smorel Hovel

Rye Hill Farm

Ditchedge Lane

4

Smorel Brake

Fisher's Coppice

The Colony

Haynes's Barn

Chinslade Barn

Round Hill

New Barn Farm

37

Chinslade Farm

Lower Atchill

Gauthern's Barn

Meadow Coppice

Millhill Barn

River Stour

Cottage Barn Farm

Woodwa Farm

3

Traitor's Ford

College Barn

OX15

Traitor's Ford Coppice

Warwickshire STREET ATLAS

Farnicombe

Temple Mills

Gibraltar Farm

CV36

Sharps Hill

36

Macmillan Way

Leys Farm

TRAITOR'S FORD LA

New Barn

2

Cowpasture Farm

Fodge Farm

Six Ash Farm

35

Yew Tree Farm

Wyton's Piece

Cowpasture

Lower Cowpasture

Sugarswell Farm

Ascott Ho'

Cowpastures

Coleman's Elm Barn

Ascott

1

ASCOTT RD

Whichford

White's Barn

34

Oatley Hill Farm

32 A 33 B 34 C

19
14

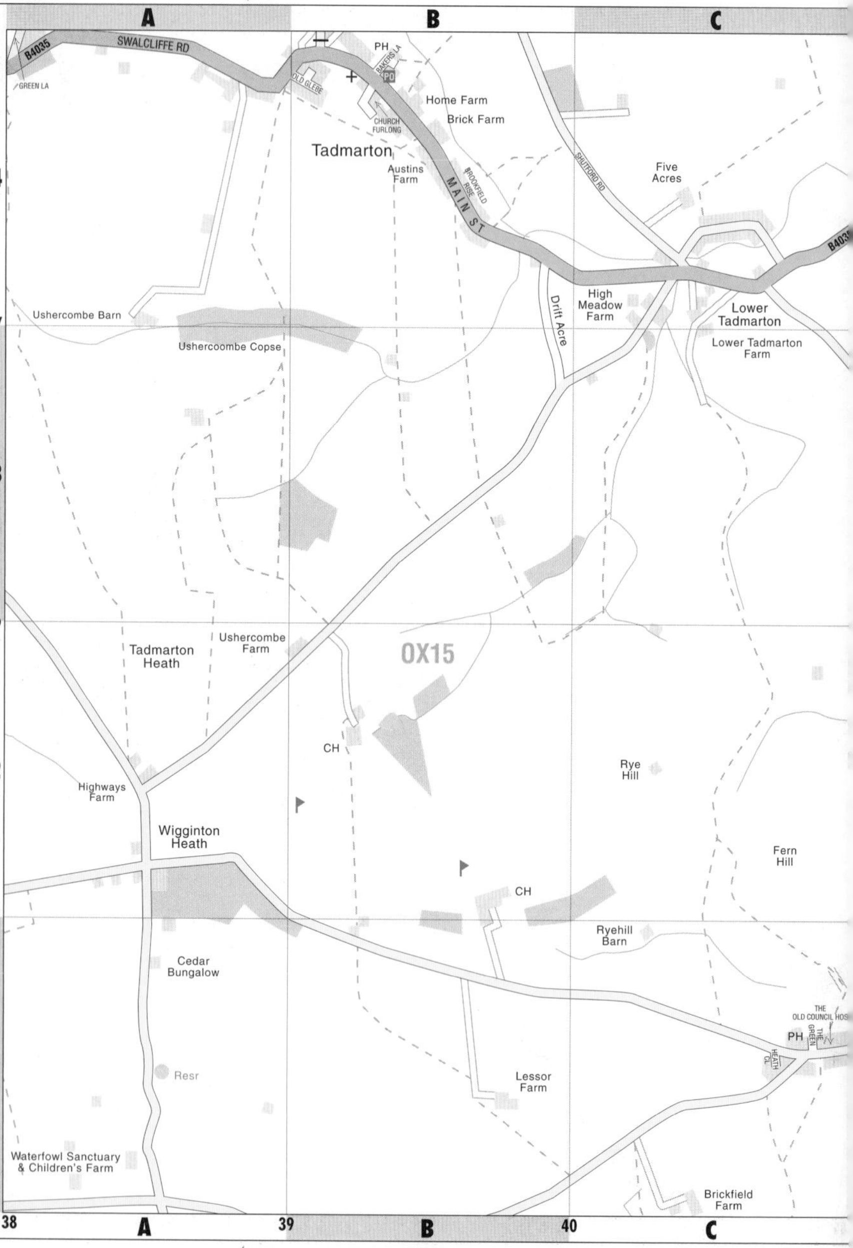

A

B

C

B4035

SWALCLIFFE RD

GREEN LA

PH

HALL GLEBE

CHURCH FURLONG

Home Farm

Brick Farm

Tadmarton

Austins Farm

Five Acres

MAIN ST

4

Ushercombe Barn

37

Ushercoombe Copse

High Meadow Farm

Drift Acre

Lower Tadmarton

Lower Tadmarton Farm

SPUTTING RD

B4035

3

Tadmarton Heath

Ushercombe Farm

36

OX15

CH

2

Highways Farm

Rye Hill

Wigginton Heath

Fern Hill

CH

35

Ryehill Barn

Cedar Bungalow

THE OLD COUNCIL HOU

PH

1

Resr

Lessor Farm

Waterfowl Sanctuary & Children's Farm

Brickfield Farm

34

38

A

39

B

40

C

19
31

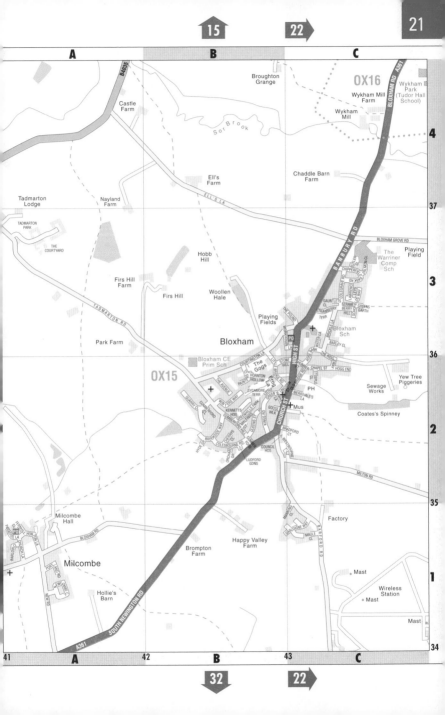

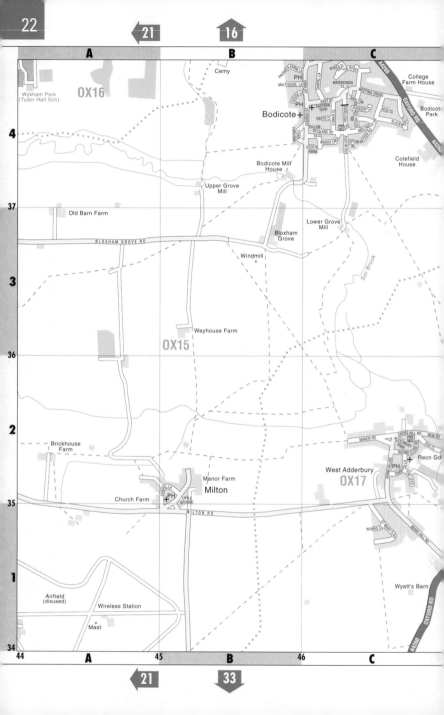

A **B** **C**

Wykham Park
(Tudor Hall Sch)

OX16

Cemy

PADDOCK FARM LA
RYDES PL
THE RYDES
PH
MALTHOUSE LA
CHAPEL LA
WATERCRESS
CL
EAST ST
WEEPING CROSS
EASTERN
TERR
College
Farm House

A4260

OXFORD RD

PH
CHURCH
DEERS CL
ROOKERY
WISE CL
MID

Bodicote
LIMES CL
SORELL RD
BLACKWO

Bodicot
Park

DILLON
CT
JANS RD
SEFTON
PL

4

WARDS CL
AUSTIN RD

Cotefield
House

DEER'S
FARM

Bodicote Mill
House

Upper Grove
Mill

Lower Grove
Mill

37

Old Barn Farm

BLOXHAM GROVE RD

Bloxham
Grove

Sor Brook

Windmill

3

Wayhouse Farm

OX15

36

2

Brickhouse
Farm

CROSS HILL RD
NEW RD
MANOR RD
DOG LA

ROUND CLOSE
PH
Recn Gd

West Adderbury

Manor Farm

OX17

Milton

CHURCH LA
PH
LITTLE
GROUND

35

Church Farm

MILTON RD

NORRIS CL
KEARS CL
THE LEYS

BERRY HILL RD

1

Airfield
(disused)

Wireless Station

Wyatt's Barn

Mast

OXFORD RD

A4260

34

44 **A** 45 **B** 46 **C**

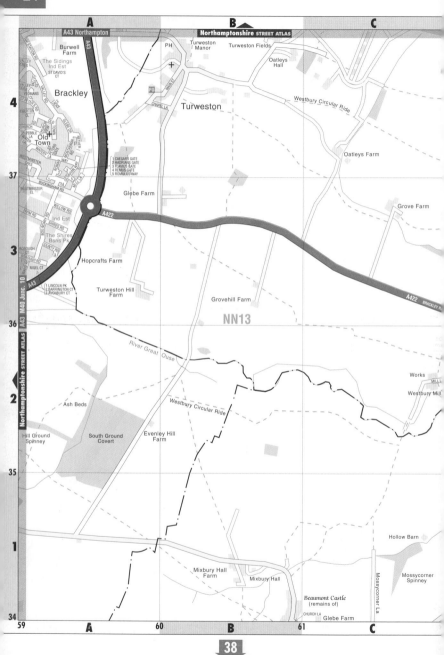

A43 Northampton

Burwell
Farm

The Sidings
Ind Est
ST DAVID'S
CT

Brackley

Turweston
Manor

Turweston Fields

Oatleys
Hall

Westbury Circular Ride

PH

PO

CHAPEL LA

Turweston

Oatleys Farm

Old
Town

1 CAESARS GATE
2 HADRIANS GATE
3 FLAVIUS GATE
4 REMUS GATE
5 ROMAN BRIDWAY

Glebe Farm

Grove Farm

BUCKINGHAM RD

WESTMINSTER
CL

WILLOW RD

Ind Est

The Shires
Bsns Pk

A422

Hopcrafts Farm

1 LINCOLN PK
2 BARRINGTON CT
3 AYLESBURY CT

Turweston Hill
Farm

Grovehill Farm

NN13

A422 BRACKLEY Rd

River Great Ouse

Works

MILL L

Westbury Mill

Ash Beds

Westbury Circular Ride

Hill Ground
Spinney

South Ground
Covert

Evenley Hill
Farm

Hollow Barn

Mossycorner
Spinney

Mixbury Hall
Farm

Mixbury Hall

Beaumont Castle
(remains of)

CHURCH LA
Glebe Farm

Mossycorner La

Northamptonshire STREET ATLAS

A43 Junc. 10

M40 Junc. 10

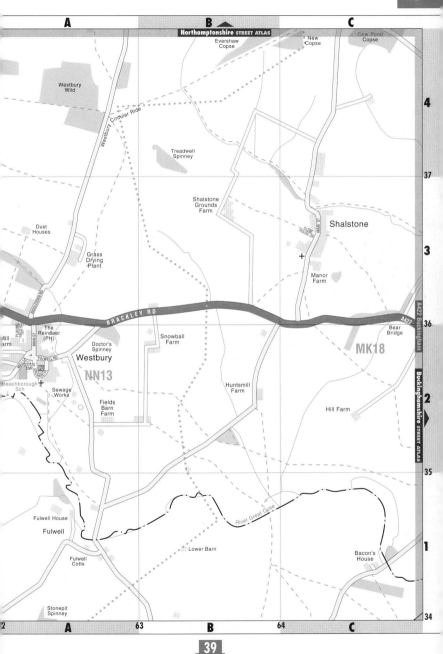

4

37

3

36

35

1

34

A   63   B   64   C

A422 Buckingham

Buckinghamshire STREET ATLAS

Westbury Wild

Evershaw Copse

New Copse

Cow Pond Copse

Westbury Circular Ride

Treadwell Spinney

Shalstone Grounds Farm

GLEBE HOUSE DRI

MAIN ST

Shalstone

Dust Houses

Grass Drying Plant

Manor Farm

Mill Farm

BUCKLEBURY RD

BRACKLEY RD

A422

Bear Bridge

The Reindeer (PH)

PLAYING FIELDS

MAIN ST

Doctor's Spinney

Snowball Farm

MK18

FULWELL RD

Westbury

NN13

Beachborough Sch

MILL CROFT DRI

Sewage Works

Fields Barn Farm

Huntsmill Farm

Hill Farm

Fulwell House

Fulwell

River Great Ouse

Lower Barn

Bacon's House

Fulwell Cotts

Stonepit Spinney

39

CV36

Cooper's Coppice
Oak Coppice

Wolford Wood

Rectory Farm

Barton Firs

Old Covert

Stanford Brook

Stanford Bridge

Wolford Lodge

Hopyard Coppice

BARTON RD

Home Farm

Gravels Barn

Barton House

Four Shire House

Gravels Coppice

Barton-on-the-Heath

Rainbow Farm

CAMDEN CL

The Four Shire Stone

Rectory Farm

Heath Farm

GL56

Brick Kiln Barn

Oakhouse Farm

Kitebrook Farm

Kitebrook

Brookend House

Kitebrook House

Salter's Well Farm

Kitebrook-End Farm

Middle Brookend Farm

The Bung

Rigside

Stuphill Covert

Tithe Barn

Grove Farm

BREWERY ROW

Sewage Works

Inn

Little Compton

POOL CLOSE COTTS

DEERHURST CL

Chastleton Glebe

The Grove

Durham's Farm

A3400 Stratford-upon-Avon

Kings Brake Farm

Harrow Hill

Harrow Hill Barn

Harrow Hill Farm

SHIPSTON RD

Nethercote Brook

Mill Farm

BARTON RD

Sewage Works

Coates House

Coates Barn

Craw Bridge

Long Compton

MALTHOUSE LA

VICARAGE LA

BROAD ST

EAST ST

THE BUTTS

The Compton District Prim Sch

CV36

Vicarage Barn

BARNCROFT

The Red Lion Hotel

WEAVERS COTTS

Fullbrook

Barton First Grove

Hill Farm

Ashby Farm

Hill Barn

Barton Hill

Barton Far Grove

GL56

Neakings

Macmillan Way

South Hill Farm

Wheelbarrow Castle

Hawton Farm

Slade Farm

Mast

Ashlea

Cemy

Oakham

OX7

Manor House

Langston Farm

WILLOW END

OAKHAM RD

Redlands Farm

Windmill Farm

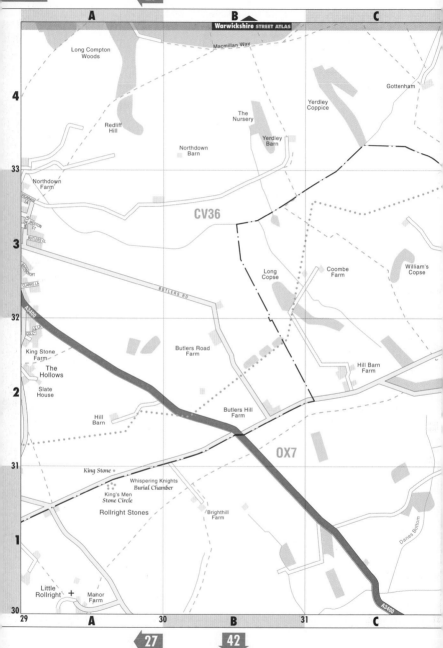

Long Compton
Woods

Macmillan Way

Gottenham

Yerdley
Coppice

The
Nursery

Redliff
Hill

Yerdley
Barn

Northdown
Barn

Northdown
Farm

VICARAGE LA

WESTON
CT

BUTLERS CL

CV36

SEDGECROFT

CLARKS LA

Long
Copse

Coombe
Farm

William's
Copse

A3400

BUTLERS RD

CLA LA
GULL

King Stone
Farm

The
Hollows

Butlers Road
Farm

Hill Barn
Farm

Slate
House

Hill
Barn

Butlers Hill
Farm

OX7

King Stone

Whispering Knights
Burial Chamber

King's Men
Stone Circle

Brighthill
Farm

Rollright Stones

Danes Bottom

Little
Rollright

Manor
Farm

A3400

A B C

Whichford Hill Barn

TRAITOR'S FORD LA

Halfway Lane

Fanthill Farm

CV36

Whichford Hill Farm

Mast

Brewery

BREWERY LA

OX15

Scotland End

Wychford Lodge Farm

Harwood House

33

Court Farm

Berryfield Farm

3

Fanville Head Farm

Hutton Grange Farm

32

Heath Farm Cottages

Great Rollright CE Prim Sch

Church End Farm

Heath Farm Bungalow

OX7

Church End

HOOK NORTON RD

CHURCH END

Rollright Heath Farm

2

HAMPLANDS

Manor House

HILL RD

D'OVERBROOK

THE GREEN

Great Rollright

Duckpool Farm

Manor Farm

HIGH ST

MIDDLE ROW

OLD FORGE RD

PO

PREW COTTS

Tyte End

Cardwell Farm

STONE ST

31

Sewage Works

River Swere

1

Limekiln Bungalow

Halt Farm

Walk Farm

Coldharbour Farm

30

29
19

A   **B**   **C**

Round Hill

Redlands Farm

Crushill Farm

Wks

Hook Norton CE Sch

Railway Farm

BRYMBO COTTS

4

Hook Norton

ORCHARD RD

HOLLYBUSH RD

IRONSTONE HOLLOW

AUSTIN'S ROW

STATION RD

Butter Hill

Sewage

East End

EAST END

Wks

Manor Farm

ROUND CLOSE RD

THE BOURNE

OLD SCHOOL

Cemy

Down End

33 Scotland End

SCOTLAND END

BREWERY LA

WETTING ST

PH

PARK RD

SOUTHROP RD

BEAN CRE

PARK RD

30

Down End

OX15

Park Farm

CROFT'S LA

Gilden Farm

Southrop

Grounds Farm

Cradle Farm

3

SWERFORD RD

Cradle House Farm

Highwood Farm

32

South Hill

Cradle Barn

2

South Hill Farm

Archell Farm

Swerford Park

East End

Swerford Park Farm

Church End

Between Towns

CHAPEL HILL

River Swere

OX7

ST MARY'S LA

Ash Hill Farm

Swerford

31

Grange Farm

A361

1

Coltscombe

BANBURY RD

Pomfret Castle

Hayes's Barn

Spring Farm

30

35   **A**   **36**   **B**   **37**   **C**

A361

29
44

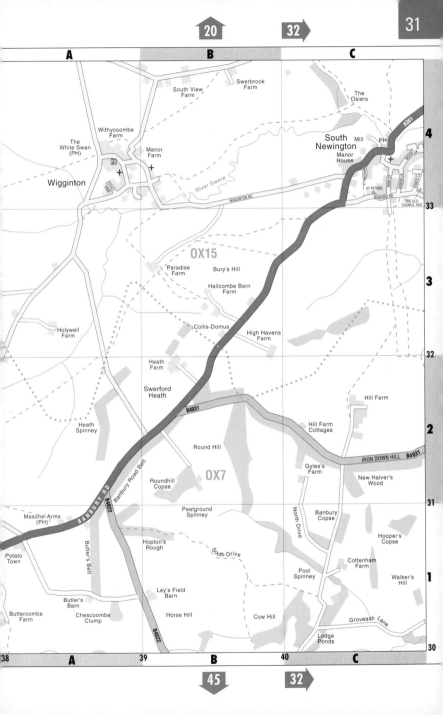

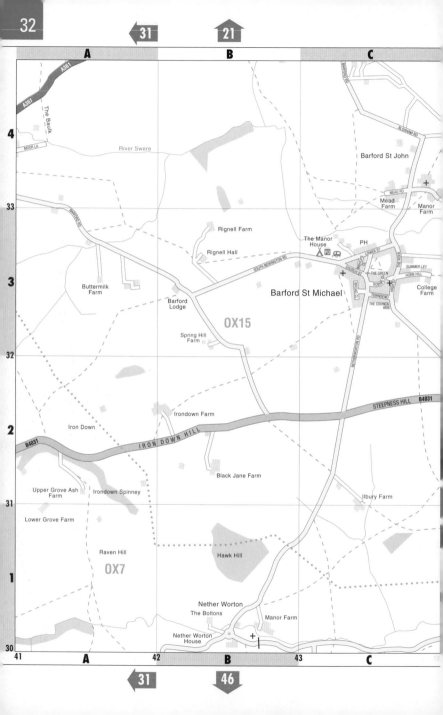

A   B   C

31   21

4

A361

The Bauk

MOOR LA

River Swere

BLOXHAM RD

Barford St John

33

BARFORD RD

MEAD RD

Mead
Farm

Manor
Farm

Rignell Farm

Rignell Hall

The Manor
House

PH

LEWELL ST

SOUTH NEWINGTON RD

SUMMER LEY

THE GREEN

HORN HILL

3

Buttermilk
Farm

Barford
Lodge

Barford St Michael

CHURCH ST

BRIAR LA

TOWNSEND

College
Farm

THE COUNCIL
HOS

OX15

32

Spring Hill
Farm

STEEPNESS HILL   B4031

2

Iron Down

Irondown Farm

IRON DOWN HILL

Black Jane Farm

Ilbury Farm

B4031

31

Upper Grove Ash
Farm

Irondown Spinney

Lower Grove Farm

1

Raven Hill

OX7

Hawk Hill

Nether Worton

The Boltons

Manor Farm

30

Nether Worton
House

41   A   42   B   43   C

31   46

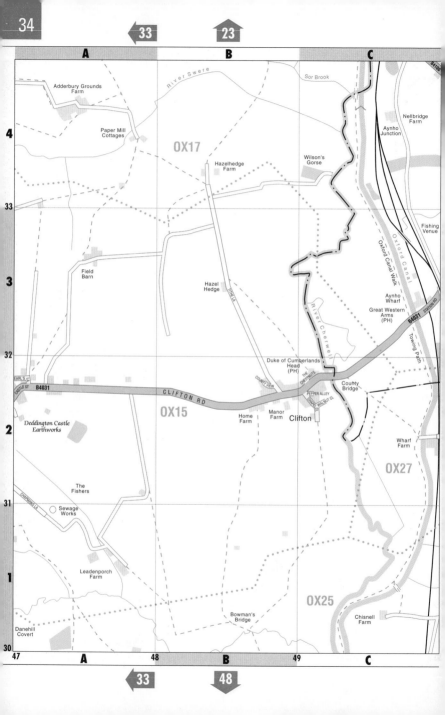

A B C

River Swere

Sor Brook

Adderbury Grounds Farm

Nellbridge Farm

4

Paper Mill Cottages

Aynho Junction

OX17

Wilson's Gorse

Hazelhedge Farm

Oxford Canal Walk

33

Fishing Venue

Field Barn

3

Hazel Hedge

Aynho Wharf

River Cherwell

Great Western Arms (PH)

B4031 STATION RD

Towing Path

32

Duke of Cumberlands Head (PH)

THE DIMS TWITS

EARL'S CL

Castle St

B4031

CLIFTON RD

County Firm

County Bridge

PEPPER ALLEY

WALNUT CL

OX15

Home Farm

Manor Farm

Clifton

Wharf Farm

Deddington Castle Earthworks

2

OX27

The Fishers

CHAPMAN'S LA

31

Sewage Works

1

Leadenporch Farm

OX25

Bowman's Bridge

Chisnell Farm

Danehill Covert

30

47 A 48 B 49 C

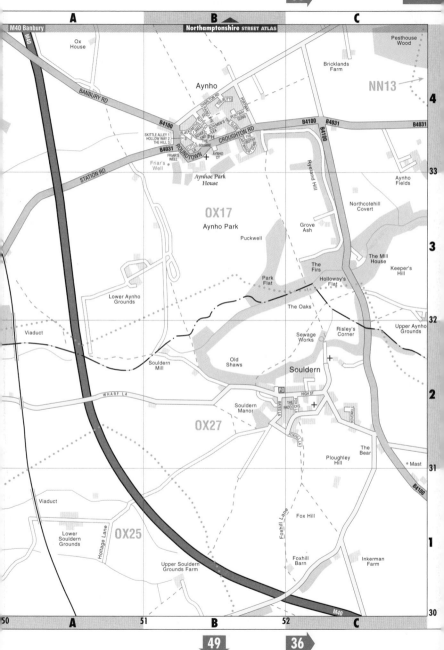

Northamptonshire STREET ATLAS

Key labels on map:

M40 Banbury
Ox House
BANBURY RD
B4100
Aynho
Bricklands Farm
Pesthouse Wood
NN13
CHARLTON RD
THE BUTTS
PORTWAY
CROUGHTON RD
B4100
B4031
B4031
SKITTLE ALLEY 1
HOLLOW WAY 2
THE HILL 3
BLACKSMITHS
WICKS
HOBB
SYDENHAM'S
CEA
STATION RD
PH
ROUNDTOWN
THE
LITTLE SQUARE
AYNHO CT
THE
BOTHY
Friar's Well
Aynhoe Park House
Ryeland Hill
Aynho Fields
OX17
Aynho Park
Northcotehill Covert
Puckwell
Grove Ash
The Mill House
Keeper's Hill
The Firs
Holloway's Flat
Park Flat
Lower Aynho Grounds
The Oaks
32
Viaduct
Sewage Works
Risley's Corner
Upper Aynho Grounds
Souldern Mill
Old Shaws
Souldern
WHARF LA
Souldern Manor
THE PADDOCKS
HIGH ST
FOX
RD
BOXWELL
OX27
FOXHILL LA
Ploughley Hill
The Bear
Mast
31
Viaduct
B4100
Lower Souldern Grounds
Hollage Lane
OX25
Foxhill Lane
Fox Hill
Upper Souldern Grounds Farm
Foxhill Barn
Inkerman Farm
M40

35

Northamptonshire STREET ATLAS

A — B — C

4

Warren
Farm

Home
Farm

Croughton
All Saints'
CE Prim Sch

Cemy

BRACKLEY RD

The Moors

The
Blackbird
(PH)

WHEELER'S RISE

HIGH ST

PO

PARK END

B4031

B4031

BLENHEIM

The Green

MILL LA

CHURCH LA

Croughton

Park End
Works

Ford

PORTWAY DR

Sewage
Works

NN13

SIXTH ST

Croughton
Mid Sch

33

Old Down
Pond

Old Down
Covert

Park
Farm

FIFTH ST

FOURTH ST

SIXTH ST E

Croughton
Elementary Sch

FIRST ST

Padbury's Bottom

Smanhill
Covert

New
Buildings

FOURTH
ST

THIRD ST

SECOND
ST

3

Middle
Covert

OX17

Masts

32

Upper Aynho
Grounds

2

Crook's
Firs

Ockley Brook

Pimlico
Farm

Thriftwood
House

OX27

31

B4100

Tower
Farm

Roundhill
Farm

Road under construction

A43

Lower
Rookery

Horwell
Corner

Round Hill

1

B4100

Horwell
Farm

Oxford
Lodge

Park
Farm
Wr
Twr

Hermitage
Belt

30

A43

Sharmans
Pit

53 — A — 54 — B — 55 — C

35

50

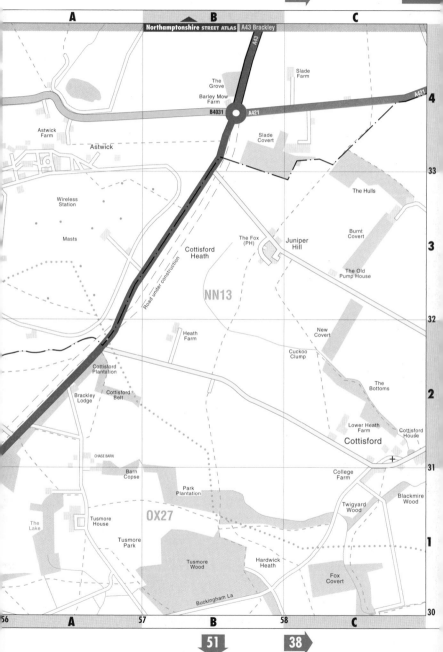

The Grove

Barley Mow Farm

Slade Farm

B4031   A421

A43

A421   4

Astwick Farm

Astwick

Slade Covert

33

Wireless Station

The Hulls

Masts

Burnt Covert

The Fox (PH)

Juniper Hill

3

Cottisford Heath

The Old Pump House

NN13

Road under construction

32

Heath Farm

New Covert

Cuckoo Clump

Cottisford Plantation

The Bottoms

Brackley Lodge

Cottisford Belt

2

Lower Heath Farm

Cottisford House

Cottisford

CHASE BARN

Barn Copse

College Farm

31

Park Plantation

OX27

Twigyard Wood

Blackmire Wood

The Lake

Tusmore House

Tusmore Park

Tusmore Wood

Hardwick Heath

Fox Covert

1

Buckingham La

30

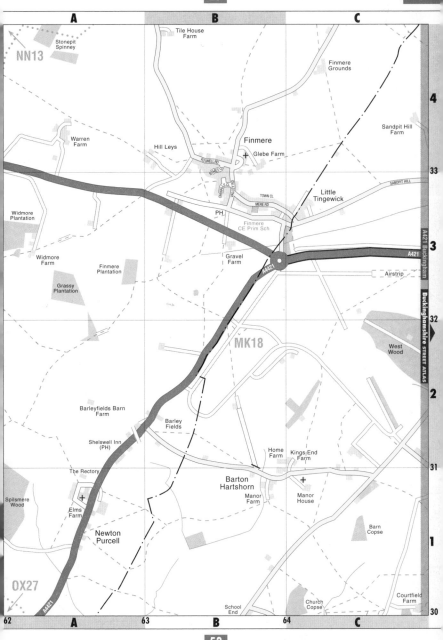

NN13

Stonepit
Spinney

Tile House
Farm

Finmere
Grounds

4

Warren
Farm

Hill Leys

Finmere

Glebe Farm

Sandpit Hill
Farm

BULWELL RD

33

SANDPIT HILL

Widmore
Plantation

CHURCH CL

STABLE CL

TOWN CL

**Little
Tingewick**

PH

MERE RD

Finmere
CE Prim Sch

Widmore
Farm

Finmere
Plantation

Gravel
Farm

A421 Buckingham

A421

3

A421

Airstrip

Grassy
Plantation

Buckinghamshire STREET ATLAS

32

MK18

West
Wood

2

Barleyfields Barn
Farm

Barley
Fields

Shelswell Inn
(PH)

Home
Farm

Kings End
Farm

31

The Rectory

**Barton
Hartshorn**

Spilsmere
Wood

Elms
Farm

Manor
Farm

Manor
House

Barn
Copse

**Newton
Purcell**

1

OX27

Barn
Copse

Courtfield
Farm

A421

School
End

Church
Copse

30

A   B   C

4

29

3

28

2

27

1

26

23   24   25

Glouestershire STREET ATLAS

GL56

OX7

New Town
Hogg's Barn
Cowley's Copse
Chastleton
THE LANE
Chastleton House
Harcomb House
Hill Farm
HORN LA
Horn Farm
Harcomb Wood
Diamond Way
Peasewell Wood
Chastleton Hill
Barrow House
Larch Plantation
Chastleton Barrow Fort
Hill Barn
Macmillan Way
Adlestrop Hill
Quarry (dis)
Pit (dis)
Hillside Farm
Peak Coppice
Fern Farm
Coomb Wood
Wayside
Outlands
The Naite
Evenlode Grounds Farm
Fern Drive
The Pheasantry
The Long Drive
Lower Farm
RICK ROW
MAIN ST
GLOUCESTER ST
STABLE COTTS
Adlestrop House
Manor Farm
Adlestrop
Diamond Way
Green Plantation
LAUNDRY COTTS
Adlestrop Park
Daylesford House
Daylesford Hill Farm
River Evenlode
Adlestrop Park Lodge
Baywell Wood
The Dell
A436 Stow-on-the-Wold
A436
SAWPITS LA
Oddington Lodge
A436
A44
A436

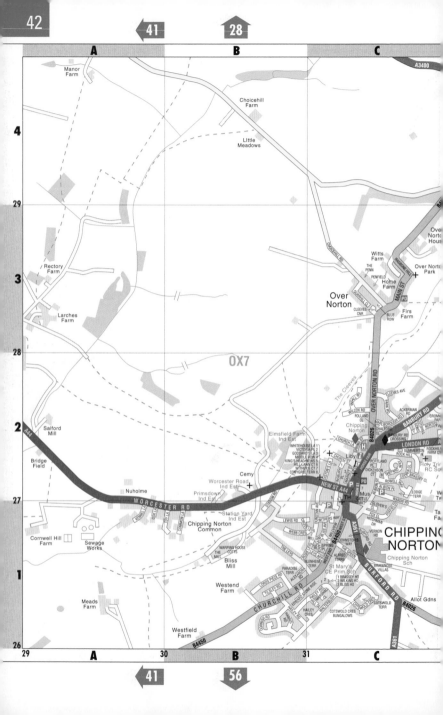

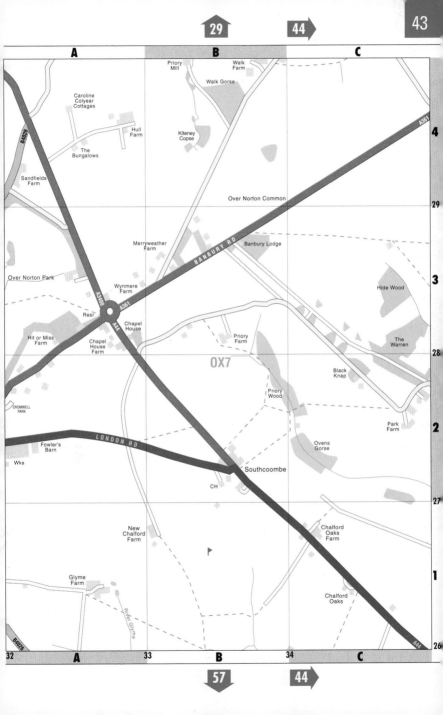

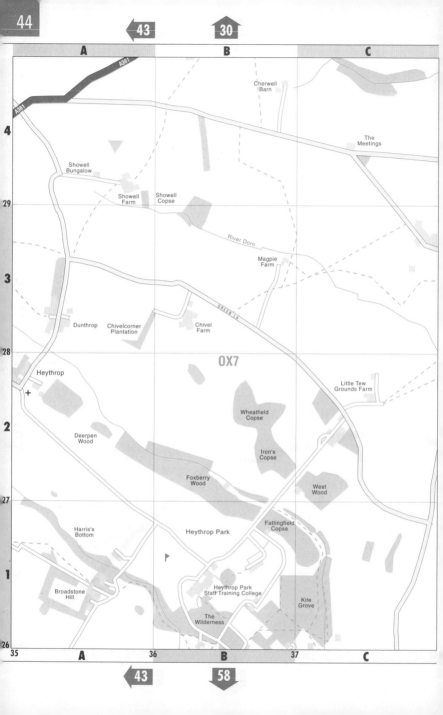

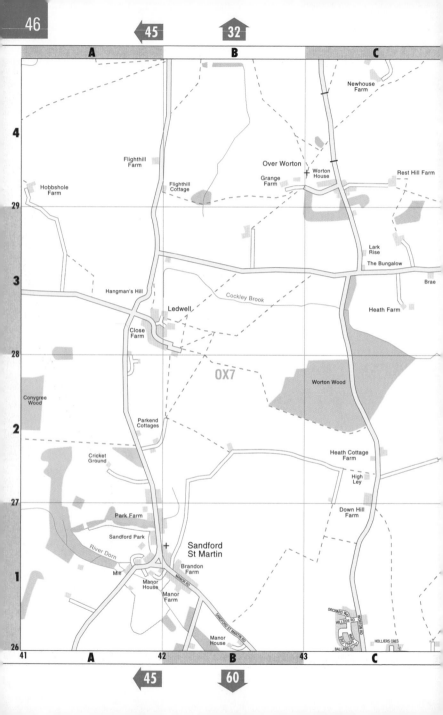

A B C

4

Newhouse
Farm

Flighthill
Farm

Over Worton

Worton
House

Rest Hill Farm

Hobbshole
Farm

Flighthill
Cottage

Grange
Farm

29

Lark
Rise

The Bungalow

Brae

3

Hangman's Hill

Cockley Brook

Ledwell

Heath Farm

Close
Farm

28

OX7

Worton Wood

Conygree
Wood

Parkend
Cottages

2

Heath Cottage
Farm

Cricket
Ground

High
Ley

27

Down Hill
Farm

Park Farm

Sandford Park

Sandford
St Martin

River Dorn

Brandon
Farm

1

Mill

Manor
House

Manor
Farm

ORCHARD RD
HILLSIDE RD
WORTON RD
SANDFORD ST MARTIN RD
MANOR RD

HOLLIERS CRES

26

Manor
House

BALLARD CL

41 A 42 B 43 C

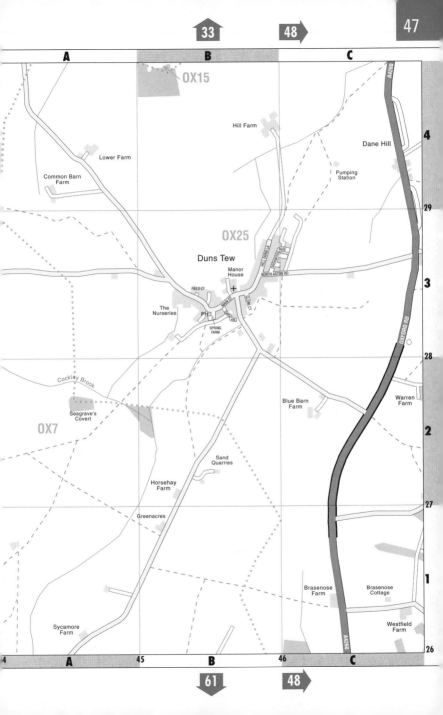

A
B
C

OX15

Hill Farm

Dane Hill

Lower Farm

Pumping
Station

Common Barn
Farm

OX25

Duns Tew

Manor
House

FIELD CT

NORTH ASTON RD

The
Nurseries

PH

SPRING
FARM

GLEBE CT

MAIN ST

Cockley Brook

Blue Barn
Farm

Warren
Farm

Seagrave's
Covert

OX7

Sand
Quarries

Horsehay
Farm

Greenacres

Brasenose
Farm

Brasenose
Cottage

Sycamore
Farm

Westfield
Farm

A4260

OXFORD RD

A4260

4
29
3
28
2
27
1
26

A   B   C

Coldharbour
Farm

Somerton
Lock

4   Dane Hill
Farm
Ram
Spinney

Manor House
Farm

Mill
Cottage

29   SOMERTON RD
The
Green   North Aston
Hall   Millhouse
Rectory
Farm

CH   THE HALL CL   North Aston
Farm

North
Aston   Towing Path   WHARF LA

VALLEY RD

ASHLE RD

CHURCH LA

Somerton   WIG   NUT RISE
The
Folly

MANOR

3   Jersey Manor
Farm

Oxford Canal Walk

Oxford Canal

River Cherwell

28   Hendon
Farm

MIDDLE ASTON RD

OX25

Warren
Copse   Warren
Lodge   Grange
Farm   Somerton
Crossing

2

Pig
Unit   Middle
Aston

27   Heyford Common
Lock

Middle Aston
House

Lakeside
Farm

1   The
Brambles

Dr Radcliffe's
CE Prim Sch

Allen's
Lock   OLD RECTORY 1
NEW COLLEGE SQ 2

FENTON   CHAPEL LA   NORTH SIDE   FIR LA

RISING
HILL   MILL LA   PH

26   Cow Lane   HIGH ST

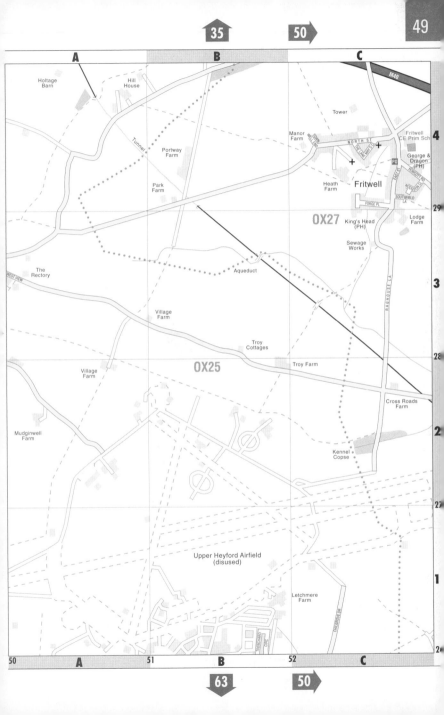

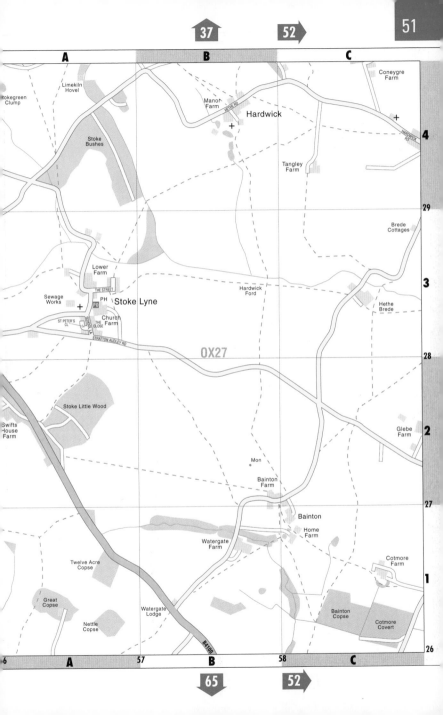

A
B
C

Coneygre
Farm

Stokegreen
Clump

Limekiln
Hovel

Manor
Farm

HETHE RD

Hardwick

4

HARDWICK RD

Stoke
Bushes

Tangley
Farm

29

Brede
Cottages

Lower
Farm

THE STREET

Sewage
Works

PH

PO

Stoke Lyne

Hardwick
Ford

3

Hethe
Brede

ST PETER'S
CL

SCHOOL

Church
Farm

THE CLOSE

STRATTON AUDLEY RD

OX27

28

Stoke Little Wood

Swifts
House
Farm

Glebe
Farm

2

Mon

Bainton
Farm

27

Bainton

Home
Farm

Watergate
Farm

Cotmore
Farm

Twelve Acre
Copse

1

Great
Copse

Watergate
Lodge

Nettle
Copse

Bainton
Copse

Cotmore
Covert

26

B4100

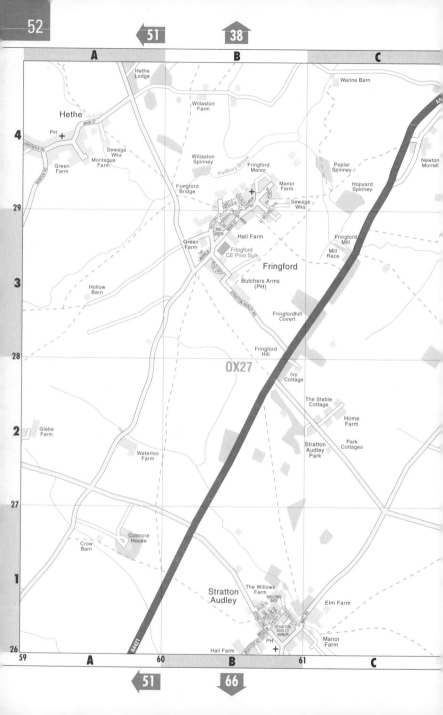

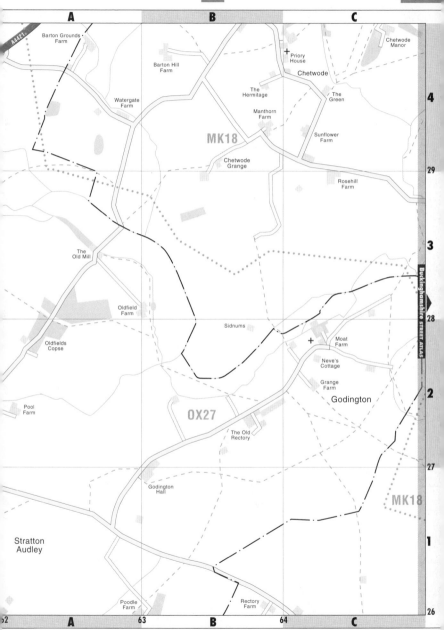

A
B
C

Barton Grounds Farm

A4421

Chetwode Manor

+ Priory House

Barton Hill Farm

Chetwode

The Hermitage

The Green

4

Watergate Farm

Manthorn Farm

MK18

Sunflower Farm

Chetwode Grange

29

Rosehill Farm

The Old Mill

3

Oldfield Farm

28

Sidnums

Moat Farm

Oldfields Copse

Neve's Cottage

+

Grange Farm

Pool Farm

OX27

Godington

2

The Old Rectory

27

Godington Hall

MK18

Stratton Audley

1

Poodle Farm

Rectory Farm

26

Buckinghamshire STREET ATLAS

40

A   **B**   **C**

Lower
Oddington

Oddington
House

Daylesford

The
Dell

Diamond Way

GL56

Daylesford
New Farm

New
Barn

Lower Oddington
Ashes

Bledington
Heath

River Evenlode

Bledington
Grounds

College
Farm

Glouestershire STREET ATLAS

B4450

Pebbly
Hill

OX7

ORCHARD
WAY

Hotel

Pebbly
Hill Farm

Mickland's
Hill

FIELD RD

Pebbly Hill
Barn

Banks
Farm

STOW RD

CHAPEL LA

MIDDLE
ORCH

Langston
Priory
Workshops

PH
Village
Farm

MAIN ST

Sewage
Works

Kingham

Hotel

B4450

Manor
Farm

Bledington
Sch

OLD BURFORD RD

Bledington Mill
Farm

Bledington

Oxfordshire Way

Westcote Brook

Westcote Brook

55
42

A   B   C

East Churchill
Grounds Farm

B4450

L Ctr

Bellpiece

4

B4450

Boulter's
Barn

OLD LONDON RD

Chadlington
Downs
Farm

Boulter's Barn
House

Sarsbank

25

BESBURY LA

Conduit Farm

Sarsgrove
Farm

Downs Hollow

3

Sars Brook

Sarsgrove
Wood

Dower House

The Barns
Plantation

CHESHIRE ROAD END RD

24

Sarsden Glebe

Parsonage Farm

OX7

Lowland
Barn

Iron Buildings

Sarsden Glebe
Farm

Nursery
Plantation

2

Home Farm

The
Belt

Squire's Clump
Tumulus

Kennels
Belt

23

Knollbury

1

Skew
Plantation

Fairgreen
Farm

Castle
Barn

Jubilee
Plantation

A361

CROSS'S LA

Blaythorne
Cottages

22

29   A   30   B   31   C

A361

B4026
Oldner House

Old Chalford
Farm

Old Chalford

Wychwood Way

4

Airfield
(disused)

Dean Buildings

Wychwood Way

25

East Downs

OLD LONDON RD

Chalford Green

3

Allens
Wood

Claridges Barn

Bury Hill

B4026

Galleypot Farm

24

OX7

Curdlehill
Farm

Green Lane

Wychwood Way

Spelsburydown
Farm

2

Hawk
Stone

Barley Hill

Little Hill

23

Barley Hill
Farm

CHIPPING NORTON RD

Barleyhill
Cottage

Upper Court
Farm

Chadlington

Dean
Manor

Spelsburydown
Farm

1

PH

Millend

ORCHARD
COTTS

STONESFIELD CL

QUARRY RD

EVERSLEY
CL

ASHCROFT
CL

RAWLINSON CL

CHURCH RD

Langston House

Dean

Lowlands
Farm

WEBBS CL

1 COLLEGE FARM
2 THE STOCKS

Dean Mill

Westend

SARSDEN CL

1

Chadlington
CE Prim

MANOR CL

Eastend

CHADLINGTON RD

34

22

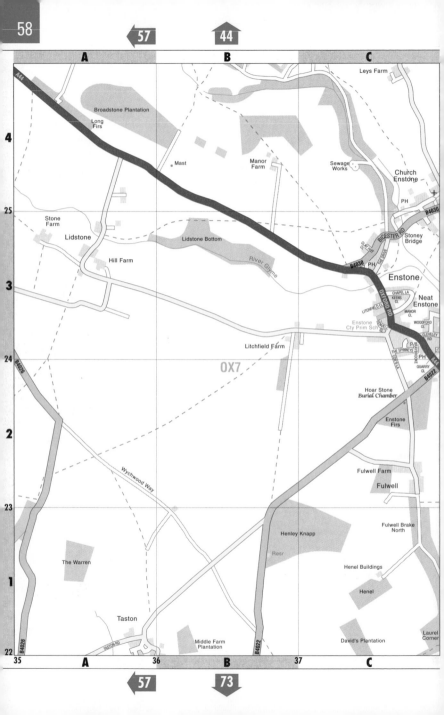

A B C

Leys Farm

Broadstone Plantation

Long Firs

4

Mast

Manor Farm

Sewage Works

Church Enstone

PH

B4030

25

Stone Farm

Lidstone

Lidstone Bottom

Hill Farm

River Glyme

OLD FORGE

THE DRIVE

BICESTER RD

B4030

PH

Stoney Bridge

Enstone

3

CHAPEL LA

KEENS CL

MANOR CL

Neat Enstone

WOODFORD CL

OXFORD RD

LITCHFIELD CL

CLEVELEY RD

Enstone Cty Prim Sch

24

Litchfield Farm

OX7

THE SPINNEYS

BEAUMONDE

B4022

PH

QUARRY CL

B414

Hoar Stone Burial Chamber

Enstone Firs

2

Fulwell Farm

Fulwell

Wychwood Way

23

Fulwell Brake North

Henley Knapp

Resr

Henel Buildings

1

The Warren

Henel

B4026

Taston

Middle Farm Plantation

David's Plantation

Laurel Corner

B4022

TASTON RD

22

35 A 36 B 37 C

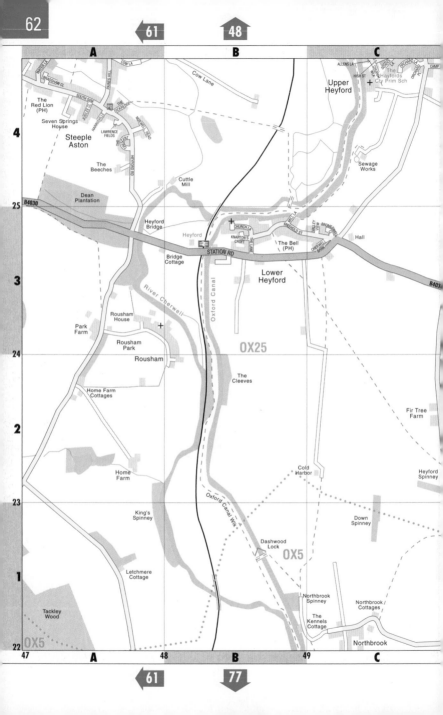

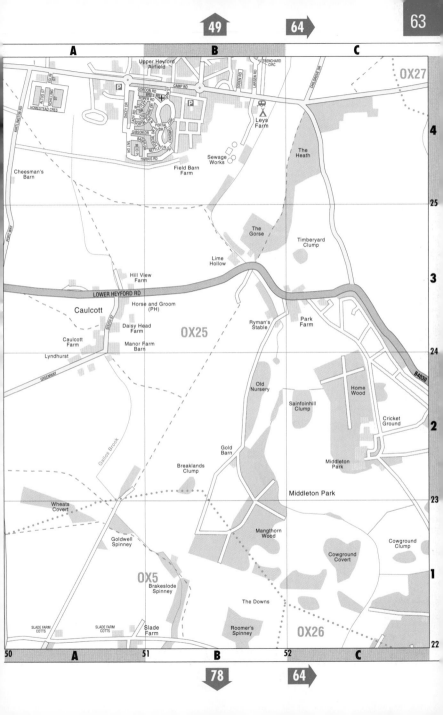

Manor Farm

Lower Farm

BANTON RD

Bucknell Manor Farm

Manor House

Bucknell

Lodge

Caversfield House

Caversfield

OX27

Home Farm

Hawkwell Farm

SPRINGFIELD RD
ELDERFIELD RD
OLD SCHOOL LA
THOMPSON DR

Bricknells Farm

CUCKOO CL
MANZEL RD

MARIGOLD WLK 1
SPEEDWELL CROFT 2
STONECROP LEYES 3
VERVAIN CL 4
BUTTERBUR GDNS 5

TAMARISK GDNS 6
SALLOW CL 7
THE MAGNOLIAS 8

A4095

JASMINE CR

Aldershot Farm

Lord's Farm

Bure Park Prim Sch

BANBURY RD

Cooper Sch

Gowell Farm

OX26

BICESTER

Woodfield

Sch

WALNUT CL

Himley Farm

HOWES LA

TAMAR CRES

Sch

BUCKNELL RD

THE APPROACH

WEST END WAY

Highfield

BLENHEIM DR

ROOKERY WAY

Brookside Prim /St-Edburg's CE Sch

Sports Ctr

Bicester Com Coll

St Mary's RC Prim Sch

NORTH ST

MANSFIELD RD

READING HO

WAYSIDE HO

NEW ST

Bicester North

MURDOCK RD

Longfields Prim Sch

Longfields CT

A4030

Bignell Belt

A4095

BOWMONT SQ

MIDDLETON STONEY RD

EVENLODE HO

THE WALLED GDNS

THE QUADRANGLE

Market

LONDON RD

B4100

Garth Park

Bicester Crossing

Whitelands Farm

ST MARY'S CL 1
LODDON CL 2
CHALVEY CL 3
COLNE HO 4
WINDRUSH CL 5
EVENLODE CL 6
CHERWELL CL 7
ALDBOURNE CL 8
WINTERBOURNE CL 9

King's End Services

B4030

Bicester Com

St Edburg's CE Prim Sch

Cemy

Liby

Mick's Trading Est

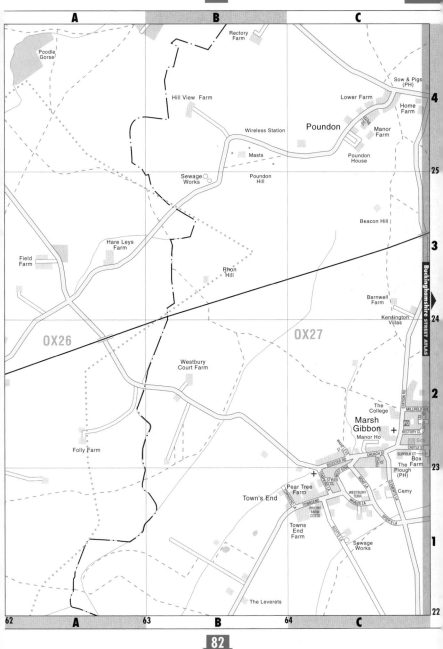

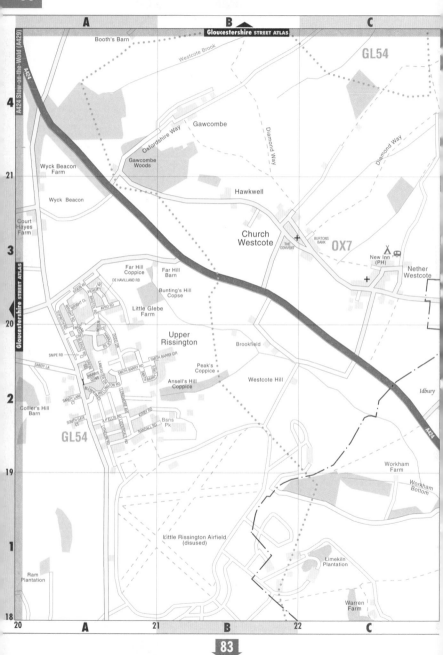

A   B   C

GL54

A424 Stow-on-the-Wold (A429)

Gloucestershire STREET ATLAS

Booth's Barn

Westcote Brook

4

Gawcombe

Oxfordshire Way

Diamond Way

Diamond Way

21

Wyck Beacon
Farm

Gawcombe
Woods

Hawkwell

Wyck Beacon

Court
Hayes
Farm

Church
Westcote

THE CONVENT

BURTONS
BANK

OX7

New Inn
(PH)

3

Nether
Westcote

Far Hill
Coppice

Far Hill
Barn

DE HAVILLAND RD

VICKERS RD

WRIGHT CL

AVRO RD

Bunting's Hill
Copse

Little Glebe
Farm

20

Upper
Rissington

Brookfield

SNIPE RD

SANDY LA

SMITH BARRY CIR

SMITH BARRY RD

Peak's
Coppice

Westcote Hill

SANDY LANE
CT

LANCASTER COMB

Ansell's Hill
Coppice

2

Collier's Hill
Barn

SOUTH GATE
CT

KIRBY RD

A P ELLIS CT

LONGMARSH DR

LOCKHEAD RD

RANDALL RD

LONDON RD

Bsns
Pk

Idbury

A424

GL54

19

Workham
Farm

Workham
Bottom

1

Little Rissington Airfield
(disused)

Limekiln
Plantation

Ram
Plantation

Warren
Farm

18

20   A   21   B   22   C

A
B
C

Diamond Way

Westcote Brook

Foscot

Foxcote Farm

Oxfordshire Way

River Evenlode

4

Bould Cottages

Bould

21

Bould Farm

Bould Wood

Foxholes Farm

Lower Farm

Foxholes

Chancellor's Oaks

Fifield Heath

Oak Copse

Foxholes Nature Reserve

Ash Strip

3

Roughborough Copse

Starveall Wood

OX7

Church Farm

Snow Hill

20

Idbury House

Herbert's Heath

Pheasant Pen

Home Farm Cottages

Idbury

Snow Hill Plantation

Home Farm

2

Jubilee

Hillside

The Dump

Coronation

19

The Banks

Fifield

Grange Farm

Bruern Grange

Grange Farm Cottages

Workham Farm

Merrymouth Inn

Brays

Crosswinds

1

Square Close

Little Hill

Patches

18

71
57

A **B** **C**

CROSS'S LA

Brookend

PH

Auburn House

Manor House

CHADLINGTON RD

Grove Farm

COUNCIL HOUSES 1
QUICKSET CL 2)

Spelsbury

BELL HILL

HORSE SHOE LA

SHOE LA

Colliron Brook

CHURCHILL RD

4

Greenend

Sewage Works

Little Wood

Wychwood Way

Greenhill Copse

Dean Grove

Coldron Mill

Glebe Farm

21

Lower Court Farm

River Evenlode

Oxfordshire Way

Catsham Bridge

Oxfordshire Way

3

Shorthampton Farm

Shorthampton

OX7

Ranger's March

Little Rookery

Water Lane

20

The Wilderness

Oxfordshire Way

Top Barn

Walcot Farm

Walcot

2

B4437

Walcot Quarter

Ranger's Lawn

Little Cranehill Copse

Rushy Bank

Jumpberry Corner

Ranger's Lodge

19

B4437

Chilson Hill

Top Brake

Church Brake

Cranehill Copse

Cranehill Lodge

1

Shock's Copse

Hazelwood Light

Cornbury Park

Deer Park

Knighton's Copse

Waterman's Lodge Farm

Hazelwood Copse

18

Stag's Plain

32 **A** **33** **B** **34** **C**

71
87

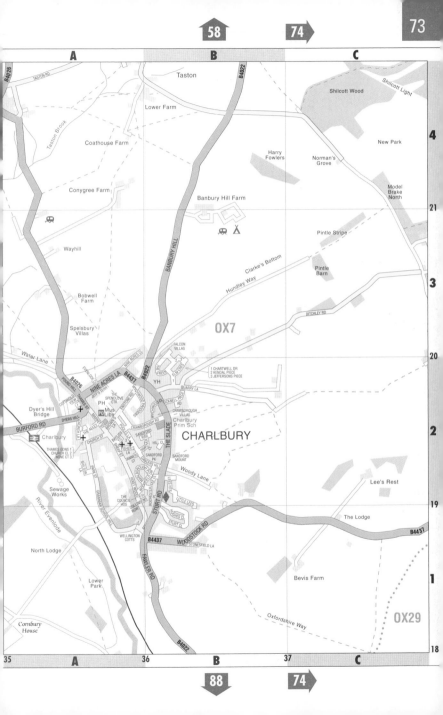

A   B   C

Old Grubbs

Dog Kennel Wood

TIMBER YARD COTTS

Ballhall Bottom

Pump Copse

Grimsdyke Farm

4

New Park

Kiddington Lodge

Kiddington Drive

The Lower House

Round Clump

Ditchley

Ditchley Park

Kiddington Lodge Plantation

21

Little Park

Little Park Plantation

Big Park

Out Wood

Model Farm

3

Model Farm Plantation

Hopyard Close

Rushy Bottom

OX7

OX20

Bottom Wood

Devils Pool

Spurnell's Well (Pump House)

20

Dustfield Farm

Devil's Pool

Kingswood Brake

Kingswood Bottom

Wood Farm

Ash Copse

Lodge Farm

Harry's Plantation

Kingswood Lane

Kingswood Farm

2

Sheer's Copse

B4437

Wychwood Way

Newbarn Farm

19

B4437

King's Wood

1

OX29

TORRFIELD RIDING

Callow Farm

Hill Barn Farm

18

38   A   39   B   40   C

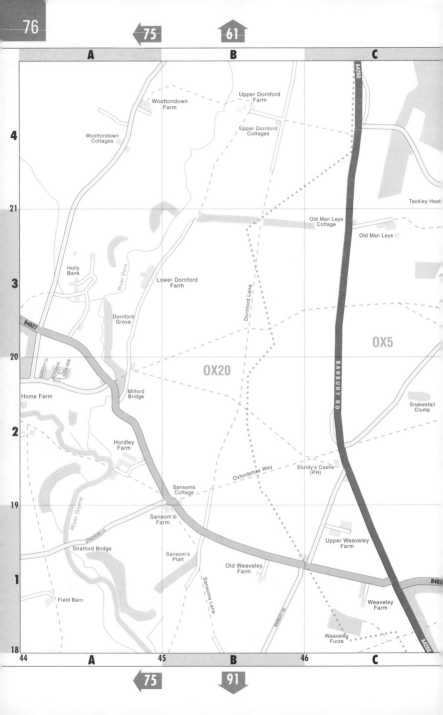

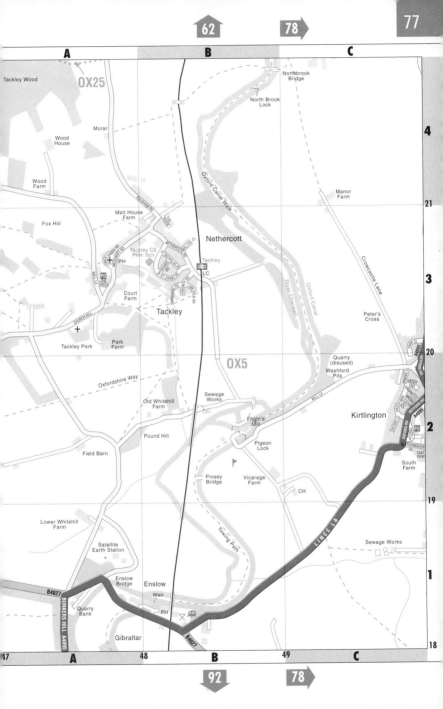

A
B
C

Tackley Wood

OX25

Morar

Wood House

Wood Farm

Fox Hill

Malt House Farm

ROUGHAN RD

Nethercott

Tackley CE Prim Sch

Tackley
LC

PH

BELL LA

NURSERY GREEN

NETHERCOTT RD

MILL LA CL

BICESTER RD

ST JOHN'S RD

LIME TREE CLOSE

CHURCH HILL

Court Farm

Tackley

Tackley Park

Park Farm

North Brook Lock

Northbrook Bridge

Manor Farm

Oxford Canal Walk

River Cherwell

Oxford Canal

Crowcastle Lane

Peter's Cross

Quarry (disused)

Washford Pits

OX5

Oxfordshire Way

Old Whitehill Farm

Sewage Works

MILL LA

Flight's Mill

Kirtlington

Pound Hill

Field Barn

Pigeon Lock

PARK CL

BICHESTER RD

A4095

CRESSWELL

POUND

HATCH RD

WATCH RD

OXFORD RD

HEYFORD RD

A4095

Lower Whitehill Farm

Satellite Earth Station

Pinsey Bridge

Vicarage Farm

CH

Towing Path

BLETCHINGDON RD

EAST VIEW

PO

South Farm

Sewage Works

LINCE LA

B4027

BUNKERS HILL A4095

Quarry Bank

Enslow Bridge

Enslow

Weir

PH

Gibraltar

B4027

47
48
A
B
49
C
18

4

21

3

20

2

19

1

79
65

B4030
A41

PINGLE DR

Recn Gd

McKay
Trad Est

B4100

The
Talisman
Bsns Ct

Bicester
Town

LONDON RD

Bicester Village
Ret Park

Foxey Leys
Copse

OXFORD RD

A41

Home
Farm

Gagle Brook

Langford
Park
Farm

Rodney
House

4

1 TUBBS YD
2 FORTESCUE DR
3 CHESTNUT CL

Chesterton
Lodge

GREEN LA

The Red
Cow
(PH)

TUBBS LA

Works

21

OX26

Wendlebury
Farm

Lodge
Farm

Promised
Land
Farm

LCs

3

Graven Hill

Bowler's
Copse

Depot

ORCHARD RD

Gravenhill
Wood

LC

LANGFORD LA

20

A41

Alchester
ROMAN TOWN
(site of)

OLD RECTORY

CHURCH LA

OX25

Red Lion
(PH)

Elm Tree
Farm

Langford Lane

2

FARRIER'S MEAD

Wendlebury

College
Farm

19

Merton
Grounds

1

M40

Astley
Bridge
Cottag

OX5

18

56
57
58

81
67

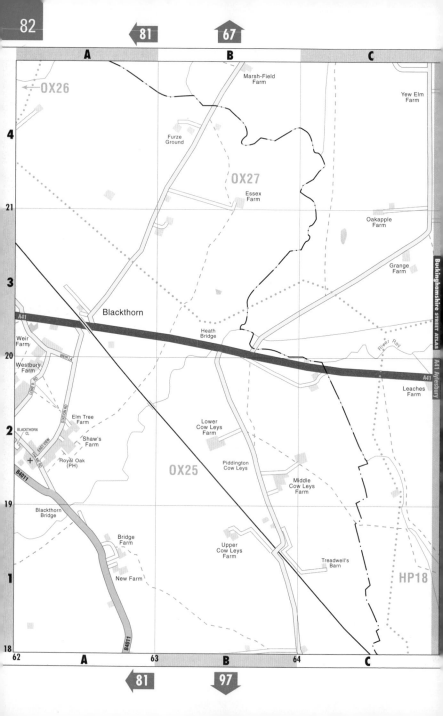

A   **B**   **C**

OX26

Marsh-Field Farm

Yew Elm Farm

4

Furze Ground

OX27

21

Essex Farm

Oakapple Farm

3

Grange Farm

A41 Blackthorn

Heath Bridge

River Ray

Weir Farm

20

Westbury Farm

A41 Aylesbury

Leaches Farm

Elm Tree Farm

2

BLACKTHORN CL

Shaw's Farm

Lower Cow Leys Farm

Royal Oak (PH)

OX25

Piddington Cow Leys

Middle Cow Leys Farm

B4011

19

Blackthorn Bridge

Bridge Farm

Upper Cow Leys Farm

Treadwell's Barn

HP18

1

New Farm

18

62   **A**   **63**   **B**   **64**   **C**

B4011

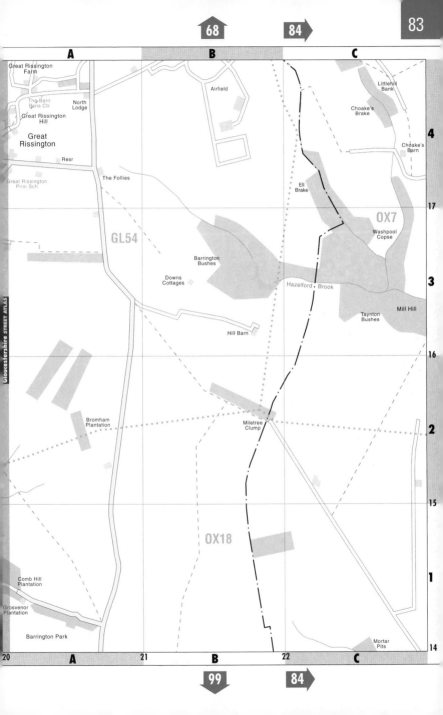

Great Rissington Farm

The Barn Bens Ctr

North Lodge

Great Rissington Hill

Great Rissington Hill

Great Rissington

Resr

Great Rissington Prim Sch

The Follies

GL54

Airfield

Barrington Bushes

Downs Cottages

Hill Barn

Littlehill Bank

Choake's Brake

Choake's Barn

Ell Brake

OX7

Washpool Copse

Hazelford Brook

Taynton Bushes

Mill Hill

Bromham Plantation

Miletree Clump

OX18

Comb Hill Plantation

Grosvenor Plantation

Barrington Park

Mortar Pits

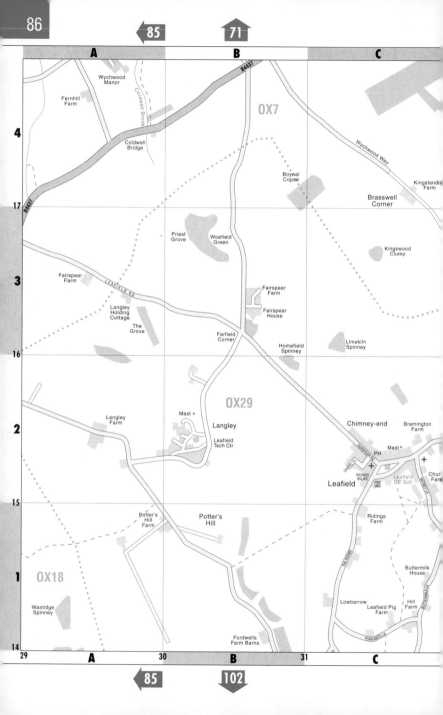

A   B   C

4

Wychwood
Manor

Fernhill
Farm

Coldwell Brook

OX7

Coldwell
Bridge

B4437

Wychwood Way

Boynal
Copse

Kingstandie
Farm

17

B4437

Brasswell
Corner

Kingswood
Clump

Priest
Grove

Woefield
Green

3

Fairspear
Farm

LEAFIELD RD

Fairspear
Farm

Fairspear
House

Langley
Holding
Cottage

The
Grove

Farfield
Corner

Homefield
Spinney

Limekiln
Spinney

16

Langley
Farm

Mast

Langley

Leafield
Tech Ctr

OX29

Chimney-end

Bramington
Farm

Mast

2

PH

FAIRSPEAR RD

CHAPEL LA

Leafield
CE Sch

Chur
Fare

THE RIDINGS

RIDINGS
BGLWS

Leafield

PO

WITNEY LA

15

Potter's
Hill
Farm

Potter's
Hill

Ridings
Farm

Buttermilk
House

1

OX18

THE RIDING

Wastidge
Spinney

Lowbarrow

Leafield Pig
Farm

Hill
Farm

BUTTERMILK LA

Fordwells
Farm Barns

PURRANS LA

14

29   30   31

A   B   C

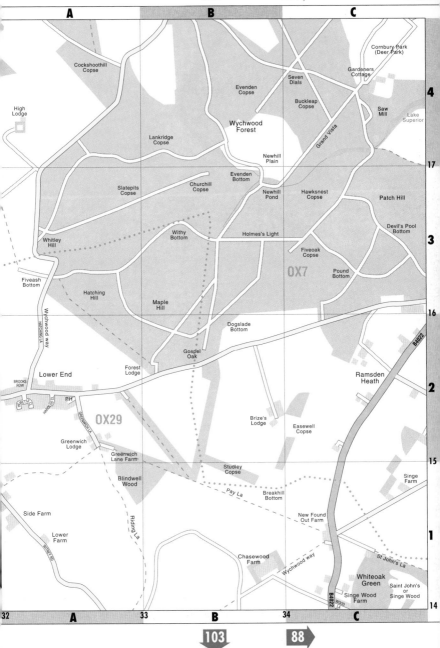

A   B   C

Cornbury Park
(Deer Park)

Cockshoothill
Copse

Gardeners
Cottage

Seven
Dials

Evenden
Copse

Buckleap
Copse

Saw
Mill

4

High
Lodge

Wychwood
Forest

Grand Vista

Lake
Superior

Lankridge
Copse

Newhill
Plain

17

Evenden
Bottom

Slatepits
Copse

Churchill
Copse

Newhill
Pond

Hawksnest
Copse

Patch Hill

Withy
Bottom

Holmes's Light

Devil's Pool
Bottom

Whitley
Hill

3

Fiveoak
Copse

OX7

Fiveash
Bottom

Hatching
Hill

Maple
Hill

Pound
Bottom

16

Dogslade
Bottom

B4022

Wychwood way

HATCHING LA

Gospel
Oak

Forest
Lodge

Ramsden
Heath

2

Lower End

BROOKS
ROW

PH

OX29

BARRETT'S LA
OXLEAN LA

GREENWICH LA

Brize's
Lodge

Easewell
Copse

Greenwich
Lodge

Greenwich
Lane Farm

15

Studley
Copse

Singe
Farm

Blindwell
Wood

Pay La

Breakhill
Bottom

Riding La

Side Farm

New Found
Out Farm

1

Lower
Farm

BURNEY RD

Chasewood
Farm

Wychwood way

St John's La

Whiteoak
Green

Saint John's
or
Singe Wood

Singe Wood
Farm

B4022

WOOD LA

32   A   33   B   34   C   14

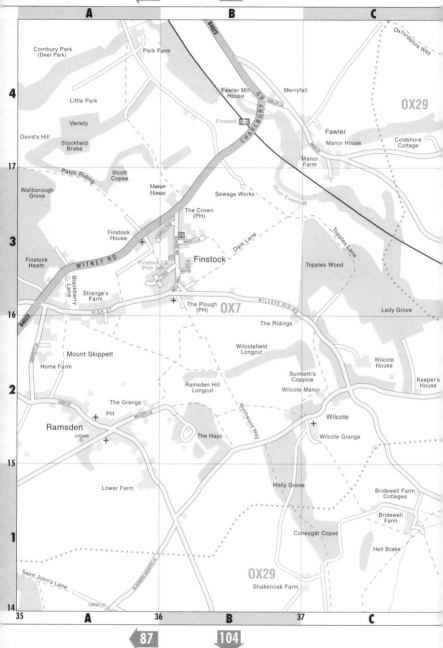

A   B   C

Oxfordshire Way

Cornbury Park
(Deer Park)

Park Farm

Fawler Mill
House

Merryfall

OX29

4

Little Park

Finstock

Fawler

Variety

Manor House

Coldshore
Cottage

David's Hill

Stockfield
Brake

CHARLBURY RD

FAWLER LA

Manor
Farm

BATH ST

17

Patch Riding

Illcott
Copse

Manor
House

Sewage Works

River Evenlode

Wallborough
Grove

The Crown
(PH)

Topples Lane

3

Finstock House

CHURCH RD

Dark Lane

Finstock

Topples Wood

WITNEY RD

Finstock CE
Prim Sch

MILL LA

Finstock
Heath

Blackberry
Lane

Strange's
Farm

HILL RISE

WELL HILL

MILES'S

Lady Grove

16

B4022

HIGH ST

The Plough
(PH)

OX7

WILCOTE RIDING

The Ridings

Mount Skippett

Home Farm

SKIPPETT LA

Wilcotefield
Longcut

Sumteth's
Coppice

Wilcote
House

Keeper's
House

2

HIGH ST

The Grange

WILCOTE LA

PH

Ramsden Hill
Longcut

Wilcote Manor

Wilcote

Ramsden

JORDANS
CL

The Hays

Wychwood Way

Wilcote Grange

15

Lower Farm

Holly Grove

Bridewell Farm
Cottages

Bridewell
Farm

1

BLACKLEYS/BLANTS LA

Coneygar Copse

Hell Brake

Saint John's Lane

OX29

TURLEY LA

Shakenoak Farm

14

35   A   36   B   37   C

Hill Barn Farm Cottages

Highfield Farm

White Horse (PH)

Liby

Farley Lane

North Farm

Ridings Farm

MAPLEWELL HO

Lower Farm

Spratt's Farm

Stonesfield Prim Sch

Stonesley Bottom

Stockey Bottom

Stockey Plantation

PEAKS LA

HIGH ST

Charity Farm

Stonesfield

PH

Oxfordshire Way

Wychwood Way

Notoaks Wood

Bagg's Bottom

Oaklands Farm

Oaklands Lodge

River Evenlode

KNOTT OAKS

STONESFIELD RD

Bridgefield Brake

Foxhole Barn

OX29

CHATTERLEY LA

West Close Farm

Bridgefield Bridge

Lower Riding Farm

Sewage Works

OX7

Ashford Mill Farm

Ashford Bridge

Whitehill Bridge

Lower Westfield Farm

Higher Westfield Farm

Ashford Mill Cottages

Whitehill Wood

Whitehill House

North Leigh Roman Villa (Remains Of)

Grintleyhill Bridge

Upper Riding Farm

Sturt Copse

Holly Court Farm

THE GREEN

Wychwood Way

Abel Wood

Highland View

East End

East End Farm

PH

A4095

91
77

A | B | C

4

A4095

Bakers
Lock

Oxford Canal

B4027

Bunkers Hill

Greenhill
Farm

STATION RD

VALPERTA CL

Chy

Cement
Works

Busby's
Spinney

17

Shiptonweir
Lock

Knapp's
Acre

Shipton-
on-
Cherwell

JEROME WAY

BIRCHWOOD DR

Weir

Oxford Canal

Oxford Canal Walk

Walnut Tree
Cottage

3

OX20

Shipton
Manor

Weirs

Hampton
Gay

Manor
Farm

Madam Hindes's
Spinney

BANBURY RD

Thrupp Wide

16

Manor
Farm

Thrupp Bridge

OX5

The Boat Inn
(PH)

CANAL RD

Oxford Canal

Lower
Farm

Home
Farm

2

Oxford Airport

Thrupp

The Jolly Boatman
(PH)

River Cherwell

Manor Farm

CHURCH LA

Sparrowgap
Bridge

15

Oxford Spires
Bsns Pk

BRIAR END

KIDLINGTON

Langford
Hall

LANGFORD LA

LAKESMERE

BANKSIDE

MARLBOROUGH
CT

THE MOORS

MEADOW VIEW

FREEBORN CL

ST MARY'S RD

SPINDLERS

1

GLEVE LANE CLOSE

Station Field
Ind Est

Cherwell
Bsns Ctr

BANBURY RD

MEAD WAY

1 WATTS WAY
2 KIDLINGTON CTR

FRANK COOK

FRANK BLO

Detention
Ctr

HAMPDEN
CL

School

P

P

Hampden
Farm

EVANS
LA

A44

SANDHILL

BEGBROKE LA

BROWEL DR

WILLOW WAY

FOXGLOVE RD

Roundham
Lock

LC

HEYFORD MEAD 2
CROWN RD 3

THE ROOKERY 1

CHAMBERLAIN
PL

BANBURY RD

A4260

P

BASSETT
WAY

BRAESIDE DR

OAK PL

14

47 | A | 48 | B | 49 | C

91
108

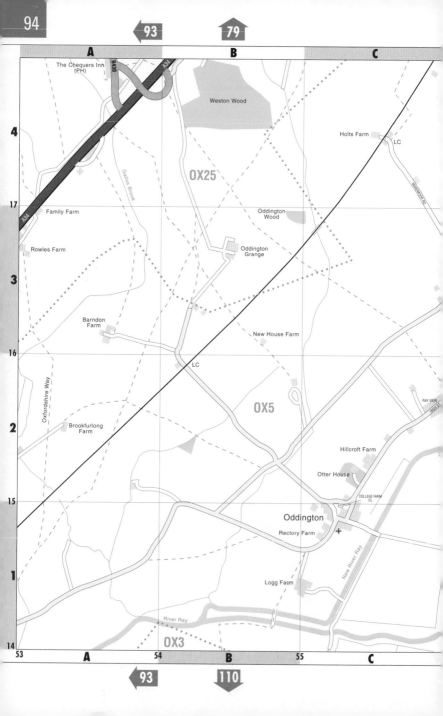

The Chequers Inn (PH)

B430

A34

Weston Wood

Holts Farm

LC

OX25

A34

Gallos Brook

Family Farm

Oddington Wood

Rowles Farm

Oddington Grange

Barndon Farm

New House Farm

LC

Oxfordshire Way

OX5

RAY VIEW

HIGH ST

Brookfurlong Farm

Hillcroft Farm

Otter House

COLLEGE FARM CL

Oddington

New River Ray

Rectory Farm

Logg Farm

River Ray

OX3

A   B   C

Sewage Works

West End
Farm

OUTMOOR
VIEW

PH

GULLEY
ROW

Merton

OX25

4

River Ray

17

Street Hill

3

M40

The
Homestead

Bridge House
Farm

Fencott Bridge

Mill Lane

Wks

BLACK BULL LA

Bull's
Lane

NEWGATE RD

Fencott

Pound Lane

Manor Farm

Charlton-on-Otmoor
CE Prim Sch

NOR FARM
BARNS

PH

OX5

Moor Lands

Murcott

LINE ACRES

16

Charlton-on-Otmoor

FIELD RD

PH

New River Ray

Pigeonhouse
Farm

2

PIGEONHOUSE LA

15

Ot Moor

Danger Area

1

OX33

14

6   A   57   B   58   C

A   B   C

4

River Ray

Astley Bridge Farm

The Plough (PH)

PALMER AVE

LC

LC

LC

PATRICK HAUGH RD

Upper Arncott

Arncott Hill

17

Depot

CH

OX25

LCs

Arncott Hill Farm

Arncott Wood

Depot

ARNCOTT WOOD RD

3

M40

Boarstall Lane

LC

LC

LC

LC

LC

16

New Park Farm

Red House Farm

Murcott

Marlake House

Latchmeads

OX5

Four Winds Farm

Oldhouse Spinney

2

Whitecross Green

Panshill Farms

Pans Hill

15

Manor Farm

Upper Panshill Farm

HP18

1

Whitecross Green Wood

Nature Reserve

OX33

14

Upper Wood

Oriel Wood

59   A   60   B   61   C

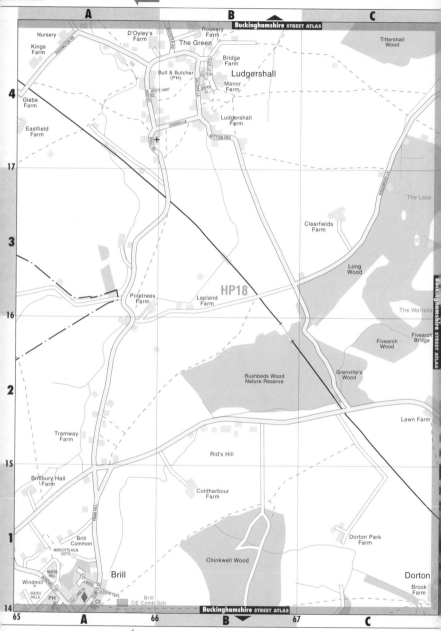

A **B** **C**

Tittershall
Wood

Nursery

Kings
Farm

D'Oyley's
Farm

Rookery
Farm

The Green

Bridge
Farm

Ludgershall

4

Bull & Butcher
(PH)

WHITE HART

Manor
Farm

Glebe
Farm

Eastfield
Farm

CHURCH LA

Ludgershall
Farm

BRILL RD

WOTTON END

17

The Lake

Clearfields
Farm

KINGSWOOD LA

3

Long
Wood

HP18

The Warrells

Poletrees
Farm

Lapland
Farm

16

Fivearch
Bridge

Fivearch
Wood

Grenville's
Wood

2

Rushbeds Wood
Nature Reserve

Lawn Farm

Tramway
Farm

15

Rid's Hill

Brillbury Hall
Farm

Coldharbour
Farm

1

Brill
Common

Dorton Park
Farm

NORCOTTS KILN
COTTS

TRAM HILL

NORTH
HILL

Brill

Chinkwell Wood

Dorton

Windmill

SOUTH
HILLS

PH

HIGH LAND DR

AVENUE RD

GODFREYS CL

Ct

Brill
CE Comb Sch

Brook
Farm

14

65 **A** 66 **B** 67 **C**

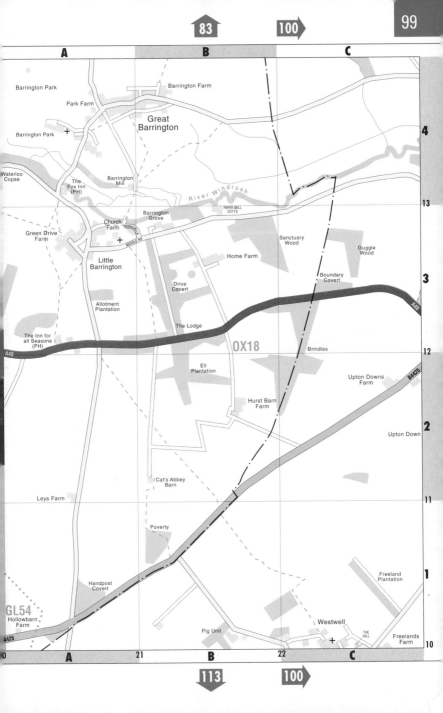

A   B   C

Barrington Park

Barrington Farm

Park Farm

Great
Barrington

Barrington Park

4

Waterloo
Copse

The
Fox Inn
(PH)

Barrington
Mill

River Windrush

13

Barrington
Grove

PAPER MILL
COTTS

Church
Farm

MINNOW LA

Green Drive
Farm

MIDDLE RD

Sanctuary
Wood

Guggle
Wood

Little
Barrington

Home Farm

Drive
Covert

Boundary
Covert

3

A40

Allotment
Plantation

The Lodge

The Inn for
all Seasons
(PH)

OX18

Brindles

12

A40

Ell
Plantation

Upton Downs
Farm

B4425

Hurst Barn
Farm

Upton Down

2

Cat's Abbey
Barn

Leys Farm

11

Poverty

Freeland
Plantation

1

Handpost
Covert

GL54

Hollowbarn
Farm

Pig Unit

Westwell

THE
HILL

Freelands
Farm

4425

10

0   A   21   B   22   C

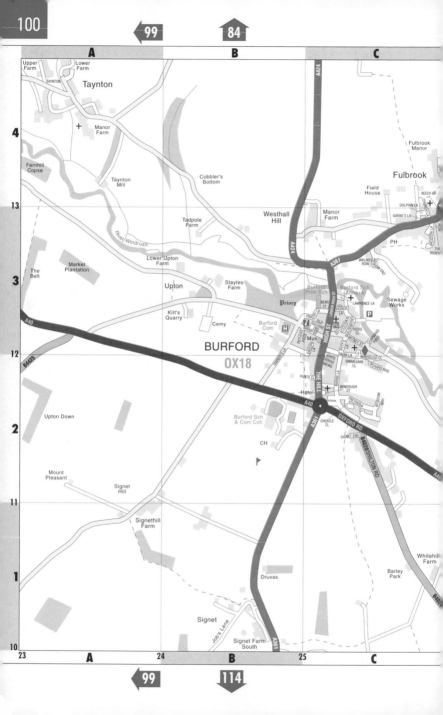

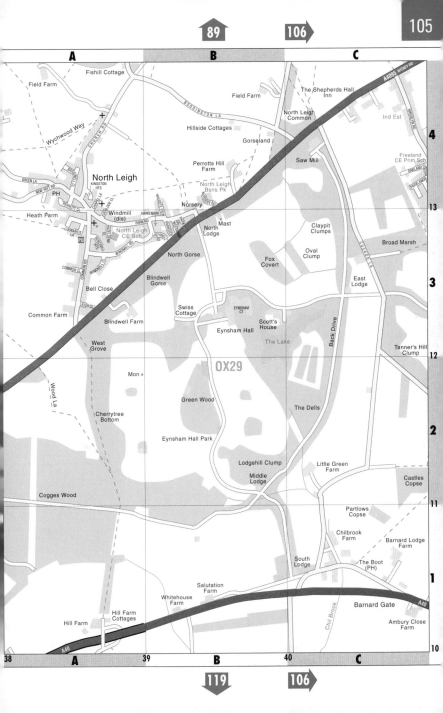

A B C

LOWER RD

HURDSWELL

Cook's Corner

4

Mill Farm

Allot Gdns

Pinsley Wood

OAKLAND CL
Freeland CE Prim Sch
PARKLANDS

Freeland

Cemy

CHURCH RD

13

Little Blenheim

Sewage Works

Church Hanborough

MANOR CL

PH

College Farm

PH

Whitehouse Farm

Dreydon House

PINKHILL HOUSE LA

3

Freeland House

Elm Farm

The Thrift

Goose Eye Farm

The Green

12

Lady Grove

New Barn Farm

River Evenlode

Vincents Wood

OX29

CUCKOO LA

2

Bowles Farm

City Farm

11

Eynsham Mill

Acre Hill Farm

New Wintles Farm

MILL LA

1

A40

A40

Evenlode Farm

Acre Hill House

Chil Brook

10

41 A 42 B 43 C

OX20

Burleigh Lodge

Bladon Heath

Burleigh Wood

Worton Heath

4

Hall Farm

St MICHAEL LA

Priory

SPRING HILL RD

Dolton Lane

Begbroke Wood

Burleigh Farm

13

River Evenlode

Spring Hill

OX5

Frogwelldown Lane

3

Works

12

Purwell Farm

OX29

CASSINGTON RD

Jericho Farm

YARNTON RD

2

Rectory Farm

Worton

The Elms

11

St Peter's CE Prim Sch

THE GREENS

ORCHARD CL

BELL LA

LYNTON LA

ST PETER'S CL

ELM RD

Cassington

P

CHURCH LA

ROUND LA

ROUSHAM HILL LA

Manor Farm

PH

ELMCROFT RD

MANOR CL

A40

MARLBOROUGH DR

1

OX2

Works

Whart Farm

CASSINGTON RD

TOLGATE LA

Marlborough Pool

River Thames or Isis

Oxfordshire Circular Walk

10

C4
1 ANDOVER CT
2 BLENHEIM CT
3 CLEVEDON CT
4 DORCHESTER CT
5 EXETER CT
6 FARNHAM CT
7 GUILDFORD CT
8 HERTFORD CT

Begbroke

Parker's Farm

Begbroke Hill

FERNHILL CL 1
MORRELL CL 2
BELGROVE CL 3

Sandy Lane Crossing

KIDLINGTON

Yarnton

College Farm

Kidlington Green Lock

Sewage Works

OX5

The Grapes Inn (PH)

Yarnton Lane Crossing

Gosford

Edward Feild Cty Prim Sch

Garden City

Stratfield Farm

Yarnton House
William Fletcher Cty Prim Sch

Little Blenheim

Hill Farm

The Paddocks

Stratfield Sports Gd

Frogwelldown Lane

Ickworth

Stratfield Brake

The Red Lion (PH)

Stonehouse Farm

Manor House

Mead Farm

Frieze Farm

OX29

Loop Farm

Swing Bridge

Peartree Hill

Oxey Mead

OX2

Duke's Lock

Motel

Service Area

P&R

Red Barn Farm Cottage

Sollershott

A40

Yarnton or West Mead

King's Weir

Pixey Mead

River Thames or Isis

Thames Path

King's Lock

Weir

Hotel

Manor Farm

NORTH WAY A40

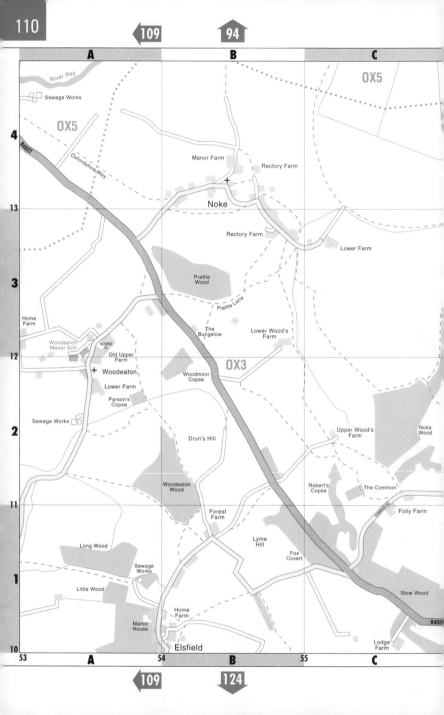

A   B   C

4

13

Horton-cum-Studley

3

12

OX33   **HP18**

2

11

1

Beckley

10

59   A   60   B   61   C

Old Arngrove

New Arngrove Farm

Warren Farm

Gardner's Barn

Tippens Copse

Nursery

Sermin's Copse

Studley Farm

Pasture Farm

Danes Brook

+ The Kings Arms (PH)

CHURCH LA

VENTFIELD CL

Studley Priory Hotel

PRIORY CL

Manor Farm

New Farm

Moors Farm

Sewage Works

CH

Studley Wood

Corner Farm

The Moat

Danesbrook Farm

Danes Brook

Moorbirge Brook

Oxfordshire Way

Menmarsh Guide Post

Moorbirge Bridge

Hell Coppice

York's Wood

Nature Reserve

Nature Trail

Oakley Wood

Shabbington Wood

Bernwood Forest

M40

M40

Buckinghamshire STREET ATLAS

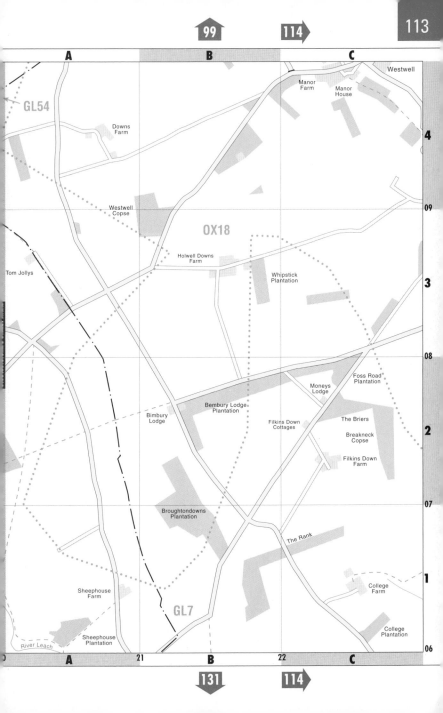

A
B
C

Westwell

GL54

Manor
Farm
Manor
House

Downs
Farm

4

Westwell
Copse

09

OX18

Holwell Downs
Farm

Whipstick
Plantation

Tom Jollys

3

08

Foss Road
Plantation

Moneys
Lodge

Bembury Lodge
Plantation

The Briers

Bimbury
Lodge

Filkins Down
Cottages

Breakneck
Copse

2

Filkins Down
Farm

Broughtondowns
Plantation

07

The Rank

1

Sheephouse
Farm

College
Farm

GL7

College
Plantation

Sheephouse
Plantation

06

River Leach

A
21
B
22
C

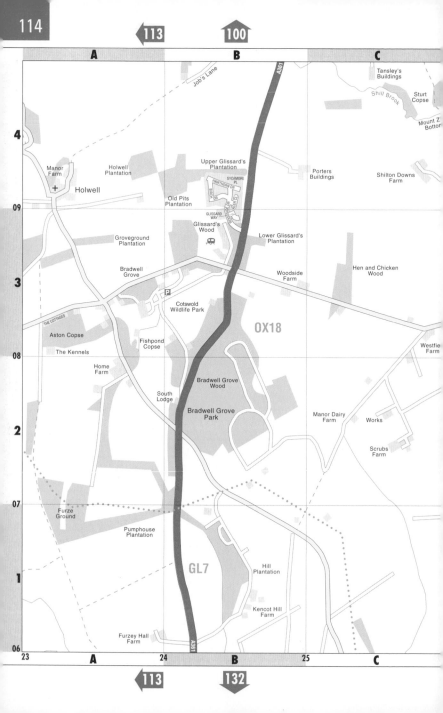

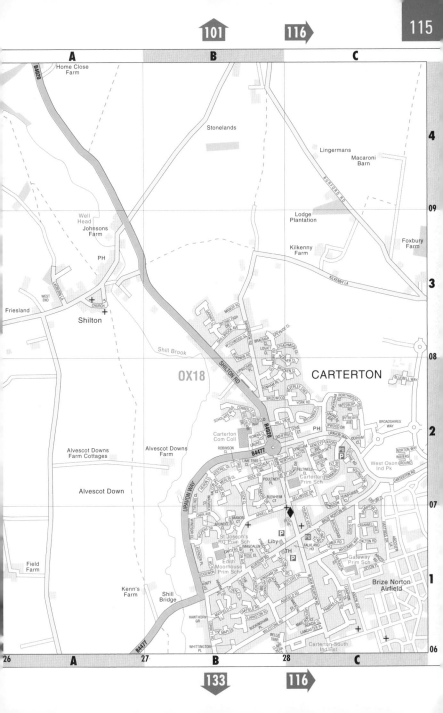

101
116

A **B** **C**

Home Close Farm

B4020

Stonelands

Lingermans

Macaroni Barn

4

BURFORD RD

Lodge Plantation

Well Head

Johnsons Farm

09

PH

Kilkenny Farm

Foxbury Farm

WEST END

PRIMROSE LA

CHURCH

Friesland

Shilton

KILKENNY LA

3

Shill Brook

OX18

SHILTON RD

MANOR RD

STONELEIGH DRI

WYCHWOOD AVE

GREENBROOK AVE

BRAEMAR CL

LOVATT CL

SPEYSIDE CL

STRATHMORE CL

RIVER CL

BRACKEN CL

CARTERTON

BLUEBELL WAY

08

B4020

ROWAN PL

BRIZEWOOD

EVERLEY CRES

YORK RD

NORTHWOOD

YATESBURY RD

Broadshires Way

SCHOLARS

COWLEY CL

CROSSWOOD WAY

HILL VIEW

DOVE

DOVETREES

PH

UPWOOD DR

UPAVON WAY

ODDHAM

NORTON WAY

WAVERS

2

Carterton Com Coll

ROBINSON CL

LIME TREE

LAUREL

ROWAN CL

NORTHFIELD RD

LYNEHAM

KESTREL CL

KIDLINGTON RD

FELTWELL PL

KENLEY CL

PUXFORD

EDGMOND

ELY CL

STANMORE

CARTERTON RD

West Oxon Ind Pk

Alvescot Downs Farm Cottages

Alvescot Downs Farm

Alvescot Down

UPAVON WAY

KESTREL CL

MERLIN CL

POULTNEY PL

FOX CL

BLENHEIM CT

BELLWOOD DR

HUMPHRIES

CRANWELL

SAMPTON

07

CARR AVE

ARUNDEL

MANOR

ARKELL AVE

BRIZ

WESTON RD

BRIGHTWOOD

MER RD

HASTINGS CL

ANDOVER

Field Farm

St Joseph's RC Prim Sch

Liby

FALKLAND HO

Gateway Prim Sch

HALTON RD

DEVON CL

ASHGROVE

CARTERS

MAGDALEN

ROSE CL

Edith Moorhouse Prim Sch

TH

P

Kenn's Farm

Shill Bridge

TRINITY

CLEAL

EDGEWOOD

LADYGROVE

BETJEMAN DR

Brize Norton Airfield

1

HAWTHORN GR

MAPLE

CAMPFIELD RD

MAYFIELD CL

CLARKSTON RD

ADERLEY RD

CAMP CL

PARRAS

CAMP RD

ANSON AVE

B4477

Carterton South Ind Est

WHITTINGTON PL

BUCKINGHAM

ACACIA CL

LANCASTER PL

MELKSHAM RD

BELLE TERR

CLARK CL

06

26 **A** **27** **B** **28** **C**

133
116

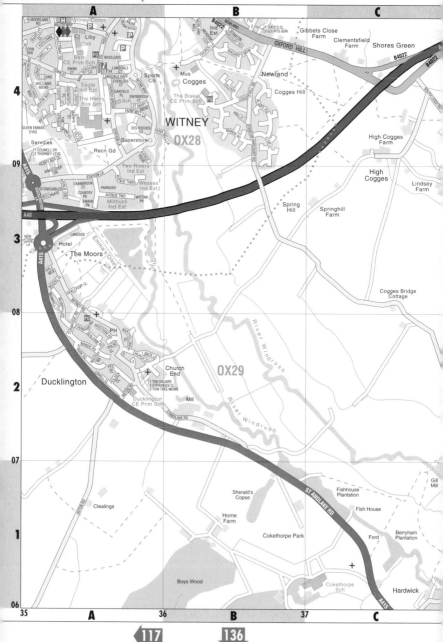

117
104

A
B
C

MOORLAND RD
WETHERBY
Witney Comm
B4022
Gibbets Close Farm
Clementsfield Farm
Shores Green
B4022

Liby Coll
Batt CE Prim Sch
WOOLGATE
LANGDALE CT
Langdale Gate
Sports Ctr
Mus Cogges
Newland
Cogges Hill
High Cogges Farm

Eagle Ind Est
The Henry Box Sch
SWINBROOK Sch
OAKFIELD PL
ST MARY
The Blake CE Prim Sch
High Cogges
Lindsey Farm

QUEEN EMMAS DYKE
DES ROCHES
FARM MILL
WITNEY
OX28
Superstore

Services
COLWELL DR
THORNEY LEYS
Recn Gd
Two Rivers Ind Est

STATION LA
CRANBROOK CT
COUNTRY PK
SWAIN PK
Millbuck Ind Est
AVENUE TWO
Wessex Ind Est
Spring Hill
Springhill Farm

A40
STONEGABLES
PARKSIDE
WITTAN PK

4
09
3
08
2
07
1
06

NEW CLOSE LA
Hotel
LAKESIDE
The Moors
Emma's Dyke
Cogges Bridge Cottage

A415
DALE WICK
CHATHOWY CL
River Windrush

PO
PH
BACK LA
CHURCH LA
Church End
OX29
River Windrush

Ducklington
POUND
LOVELLS
FEEL
1 THE SQUARE
2 STRAINGES CL
3 YEW TREE MEWS
Mill

ASTON RD
Ducklington CE Prim Sch
STANDLAKE RD

Gill Mill

Sherald's Copse
Fishhouse Plantation

Clealings
Home Farm
Fish House
Ford
Berryham Plantation

ST ANDLAKE RD
Cokethorpe Park

Boys Wood
Cokethorpe Sch
A415
Hardwick

35
A
36
B
37
C

A
B
C

A40

Green House Farm

Ash Plantations

Green Farm

Chil Brook

4

SOUTH LEIGH RD

Little Bartlett's

Kimber's Brake

Furzy Breach

Glebe House

09

CHAPEL RD

CHURCH END

Church End

Church End Farm

Margery Cross

The Masons Arms (PH)

South Leigh

Horman's Farm

Station Farm

Limb Brook

Warners

3

STATION RD

CHAPEL RD

Moor Lane

STATION HARDWICK RD

08

OX29

Blue Barn House

College Farm

Rushy Common

Tar Wood

2

Tar Farm

07

Tar Farm Cottages

Blue Barn

River Windrush

Friar's Farm

1

Hardwick Farm

Standlake Brook

B4449

06

A
39
B
40
C

119
106

A   **B**   **C**

A40

Chil Brook

PH
ELM PL.
OLD WITNEY RD
FRUIT LANDS

GREEN'S RD
HANBOROUGH CL.
MARLBOROUGH PL.
DUNCAN
STRATFORD DR.
FALSTAFF CL.
MARLBOROUGH PL.

Twelve Acre Farm

BARTHOLOMEW CL.
WILLOWS EDGE
THORNBURY CL.

Bartholomew Sch

Eynsham Com Prim Sch

Paddock Close

CHILBRIDGE RD

Litchfield Farm

CLOVER PL.

MILL ST MEWS
NEWLAND ST
TANNERS LA

P

Libr

Thames

GRANGE MILL CL.
BLANKSTONE CL.

SWAN ST
ABBEY PL.

HIGH ST

ORCHARD CL.
BITTERELL

4

Chil Brook

Abbey Farm

1 THE TUER
2 THE SQUARE
3 CHURCH ST
4 SWANLANDS HO

Eynsham

OXFORD RD

09

B404

Oasis Pk

Southfield Cottages

Oakfield Ind Est

PINKHILL LA.

3

The Nunnery

Southfield Barn

Foxley Farm

08

OX29

Limb Brook

The Bungalow

2

Bell Bridge

Pinkhill Farm

07

University Cottages

Wei

Nicholls' Farm

Sutton Farm

Thames Path

1

Sutton Green

Cox's Farm

Beaumont House

River Thames or Isis

Sutton

BUTTS LA.
BURN CL.
DUCK END LA.

Lower Farm

Sewage Works

06

The Fox (PH)

OX2

41   **A**   42   **B**   43   **C**

119
138

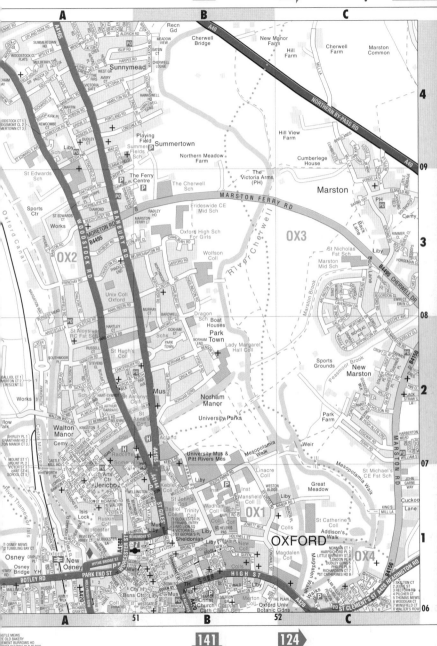

A B C

4

Pennywell Wood
Church Farm
Vicarage
Hill Farm
Wadley Hill
Sidlings Copse
Field Barn Cottage
Wick Copse

09

B4150
A40

OX3

Oxford City FC
Bayswater Brook
Wick Farm
Lower Farm
Crem

3

CLAYS
ALESWORTH GR 1
BROADHEAD PL 2
STOWFORD RD

NORTHERN BY-PASS RD

OXFORD

Stowford Farm

MARSH LA

08

B4150

New Marston Fst Sch
Headington
NORTH WAY

HIGH CROSS WAY
Barton
A40

Cemy
Ruskin Coll
1 HASTOE GRANGE
2 HEADLEY HO
3 RAYSON HO

The Roundway Sch

John Radcliffe
THE OLD STABLES
WILLIAM ORCHARD

2

HEADLEY WAY
St Joseph's RC Fst Sch
YH
Milham Ford City Girls Upper Sec Sch
H
Liby
St Andrews CE Fst Sch
A420
A40
A4142

Rye St Antony Sch
Emden Ho
The Sycamores

07

Headington Hill
Plater Coll
Cuckoo Lane
Headington Sch
LONDON RD
B4495
Headington Quarry
1 THE PARADE
2 LINDEN CT
Schs
QUARRY SCHOOL
HAROLD WHITE CL 1
KNIGHTS HO 2

Cuckoo Lane
HEADINGTON RD

1

A420
Brookes Univ Sports Complex
Cheney Sch
Oxford Brookes Univ
WINDMILL RD
B4495
Nuffield Orthopaedic Ctr
EASTERN BY-PASS RD
Liby
Carter CL
Slaymaker CL

GRANVILLE CT
OX4
New Headington
Park Hospl
H
Woodfarm Fst Sch
A4142
Shotover Trad Est

06

MORRELL AVE
Warneford
The Churchill
COLLISIDE CL
OLD RD
1 BRACEGIRDLE RD
2 CHILLINGWORTH CRES
3 FORESTERS TOWER

53 A 54 B 55 C

125 112

A   B   C

Wood Farm

HP18

Clearsale   Hursthill

Waterperry Common

4

Bernwood Forest

Commonleys Farm

09

Waterperry Wood

Polecat End

Drunkard's Corner

Park Farm House

Park Farm

3

Oxfordshire Way

Polecat End Hollows

Marsh Copse

Parson's Farm

Ledall Cottage

08

Holton Wood

OX33

2

Buryhook Barn

Holton Brook

Keeper's Cottage

Warren Farm

Pond Farm

Warren Wood

Old Park Farm

07

Lyehill Quarries (dis)

BURYHOOK CNR

Cottage Copse

Warwick Close Farm

1

Recn Gd

Wheatley Park Sch

Holton

The Rectory

Holton Place

Liby

Sports Ctr

BARNS CL

John Watson Sch

Church Farm

Moat

Wheatley

Wheatley Campus (Brookes Univ)

Garden Copse

06

59   A   60   B   61   C

Moorbrige Brook

A40

A40

B4027

B4027

A40

125 144

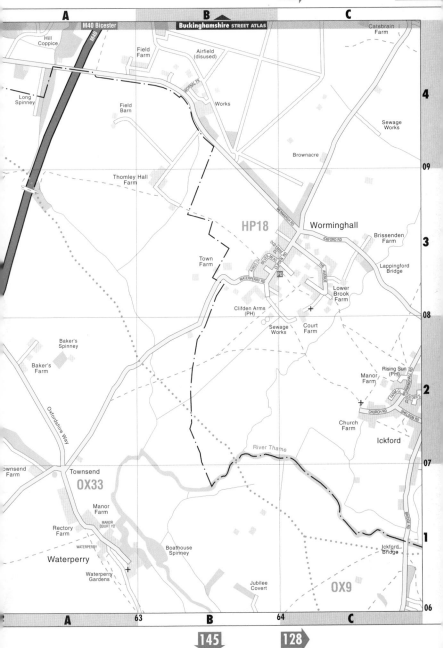

Buckinghamshire STREET ATLAS

A | **B** | **C**

M40 Bicester

Hill Coppice

Field Farm

Airfield (disused)

Catsbrain Farm

Long Spinney

Field Barn

WORNAL PK

Works

Sewage Works

4

Thomley Hall Farm

Brownacre

09

HP18

MENMARSH RD

Worminghall

ICKFORD RD

Brissenden Farm

3

Town Farm

OLD LONDON RD

CLIFDEN RD

MILL RD

THE AVENUE

Lappingford Bridge

WATERPERRY RD

PO

Clifden Arms (PH)

Lower Brook Farm

08

Sewage Works

Court Farm

Baker's Spinney

Rising Sun (PH)

Baker's Farm

Manor Farm

FRANKLINS

SHELDON RD

2

Oxfordshire Way

CHURCH RD

Church Farm

Ickford

River Thame

07

ownsend Farm

Townsend

OX33

BRIDGE RD

1

Manor Farm

Rectory Farm

MANOR COURT YD

Boathouse Spinney

Ickford Bridge

WATERPERRY

Waterperry

Waterperry Gardens

Jubilee Covert

OX9

06

A | 63 | **B** | 64 | **C**

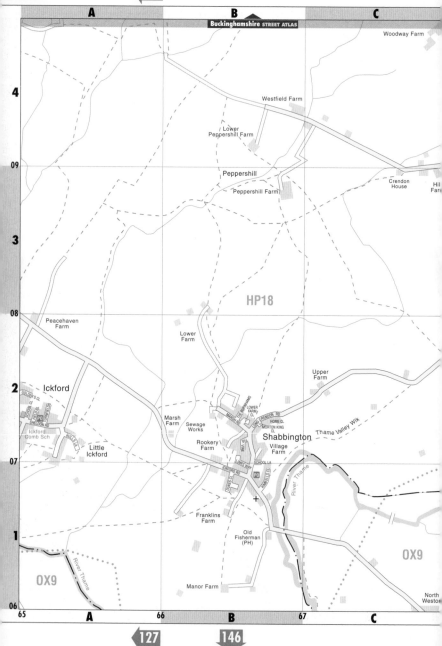

A   B   C

Buckinghamshire STREET ATLAS

Woodway Farm

4

Westfield Farm

Lower
Peppershill Farm

09

Peppershill

Crendon
House

Hil
Far

Peppershill Farm

3

HP18

08

Peacehaven
Farm

Lower
Farm

Upper
Farm

2

Ickford

Thame Valley Wlk

Marsh
Farm

LOWER
FARM
CL

CRENDON RD

HOME CL

Sewage
Works

MORTON KING
CL

Ickford
Comb Sch

Shabbington

Little
Ickford

Rookery
Farm

Village
Farm

07

LIMES WAY

SCHOOL LA

ICKFORD RD

PO

River Thame

Franklins
Farm

Old
Fisherman
(PH)

OX9

1

Manor Farm

OX9

North
Weston

06

65   A   66   B   67   C

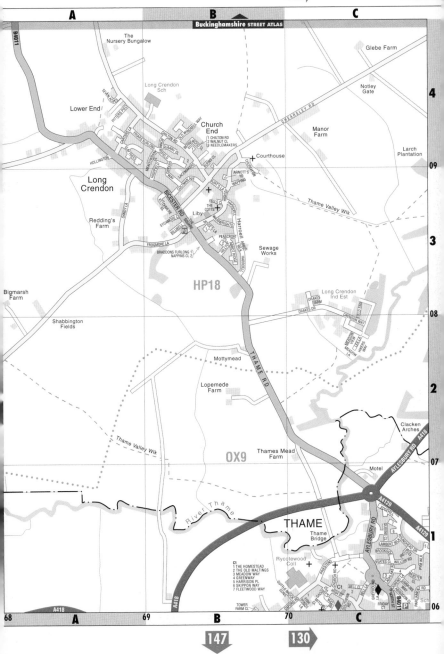

4

09

3

08

2

07

1

06

The Nursery Bungalow

Glebe Farm

Long Crendon Sch

Notley Gate

Lower End

Church End

Manor Farm

Larch Plantation

1 CHILTON RD
2 WALNUT CL
3 NEEDLEMAKERS

Courthouse

ARNOTT'S YD
WAPPING

Long Crendon

Redding's Farm

Liby

THE COTTS

Harroell

Sewage Works

BRADDONS FURLONG 1
NAPPINS CL 2

Peascroft

HP18

Bigmarsh Farm

Long Crendon Ind Est

DRAKES FARM

DRAKES DR

CRENDON WAY

Shabbington Fields

THAME RD

MEADOW VIEW

RIDGE WAY

MEADOW LA

Mottymead

Lopemede Farm

OX9

Thame Valley Wlk

Thames Mead Farm

Clacken Arches

Motel

AYLESBURY RD

A418

River Thame

A4129

THAME

Thame Bridge

AYLESBURY RD

A4129

Rycotewood Coll

C1 1 THE HOMESTEAD
2 THE OLD MALTINGS
3 MEADOW WAY
4 GREENWAY
5 HARRISON PL
6 SKIPPON WAY
7 FLEETWOOD WAY

FRIDAY CT

B4011

TOWER FARM CL

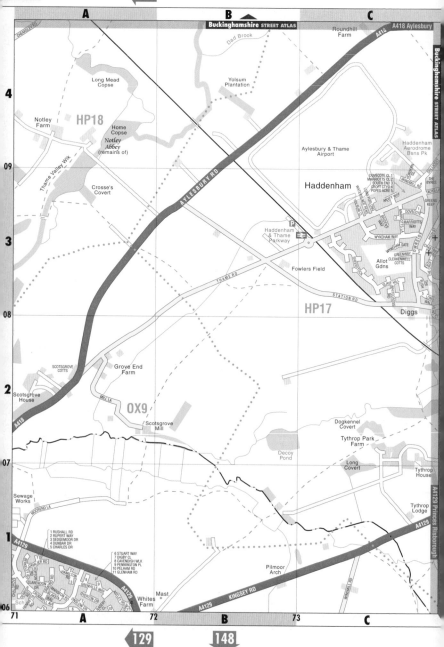

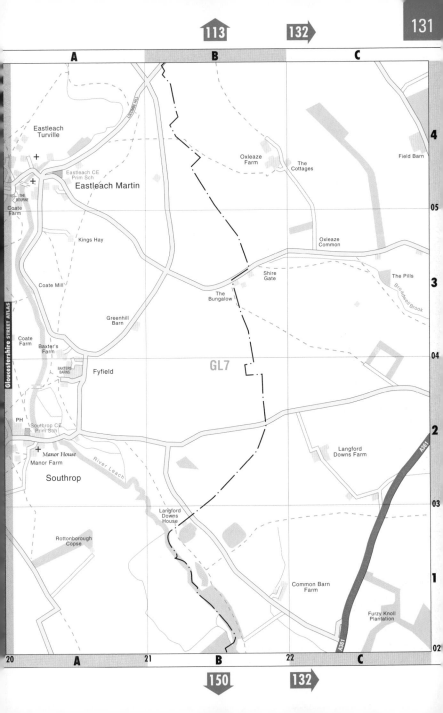

A
B
C

Eastleach Turville

+

Eastleach CE Prim Sch

+

THE BOURNE

Eastleach Martin

Coate Farm

Kings Hay

Coate Mill

Coate Farm

Greenhill Barn

Baxter's Farm

BAXTERS BARNS

Fyfield

PH

Southrop CE Prim Sch

+

Manor House

Manor Farm

Southrop

River Leach

Rottonborough Copse

Oxleaze Farm

The Cottages

Field Barn

Oxleaze Common

The Pills

Brockwell Brook

The Bungalow

Shire Gate

GL7

Langford Downs Farm

A361

Langford Downs House

Common Barn Farm

Furzy Knoll Plantation

A361

4

05

3

04

2

03

1

02

20
A
21
B
22
C

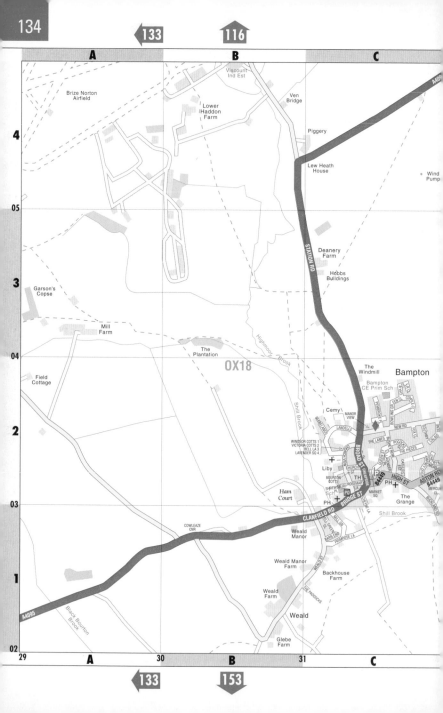

A B C

Stanton Harcourt CE Prim Sch

Chapel & Pope's Tower

Blackditch

Stanton Harcourt

4

Stanton Harcourt Ind Est

STEADY'S LA Steady's Farm

MANOR COTTS

Cemy

OX2

Tawney's Farm

05

Pimm Farm

Gravel Pits

Linch Hill Cottages

3

Whitle Copse

Elms Farm

Payne's Farm

West End

Stoneacres Lake

The Ferryman Inn

Bablock Hythe

Linch Hill Leisure Park

04

Lower Farm

OX29

Thames Path

River Thames or Isis

Towing Path

Mar

2

Mount Pleasant

CHAPEL LA

Watkins Farm

Manor Farm

Pencots

Long Meado

Long

OX13

Pinnocks Farm

Ferryman Farm

03

Brook Farm

The Dun Cow (PH)

Clarks Farm

GRATTON CL

Northmoor

STANDLAKE RD

The Red Lion (PH)

Church Farm

Rectory Farm

Eaton Plantation

Fairacre Farm

NORTHMOOR PK

1

Northmoor Lock

Ash Copse

Weir

02

41 A 42 B 43 C

139
122

A B C

TUDOR CT
B4044
EYNSHAM RD
B4044
WEST WAY
FIELD HO
A34
FERRY HINKSEY RD
New Botley

Nebles Farm Cottages
A420

Dean Court

Botley

HAWTHORN
MAPLE CL
LARCH CL

Kings Meadow Ind Est
Bulstake Stream

4

Hid's Copse

HUT-COMBE FARM
STANVILLE RD

TOYNBEE CL
CHESTNUT RD
BEECH RD

MORE RD
LIME RD
ARNOLD'S WAY

Matthew Arnold Sch

North Hinksey Village

Raleigh Park

The Fold

Hinksey Stream

A34

Conduit House

PH

05

Chawley

Cumnor Hill

OX2

Dene House

Westminster Coll

VERNON AVE

Harcourt Hill

Long Copse

HURST LA

Playing Field

3

NORFOLK RD

Hurst Hill

04

Powder Hill Copse

2

Hen Wood

Chiswell House (Priory)

Chiswell Farm

CHILSWELL LA

Whitebarn

Youlbury Wood

Birch Copse

03

Youlbury Pond

Mast

Henwood Farm

Upper Youlbury Heath

Pickett's Heath Farm

OX1

West Gardens

Chiswell Farm Cottages

1

HENWOOD DR

Wootton Close

Mayo's Farm

Jarn Mound

Old Boars Hill

BOARS HILL

Boars Hill

BESSELS LEA

JARN WAY

BERKELEY RD

Oxford Preservation Trust

Yatscombe Copse

FOXCOMBE LA

MID COPSE RD

02

White Hill Farm
B4017

ORCHARD LA

Foxcombe Hall

47 A 48 B 49 C

139
159

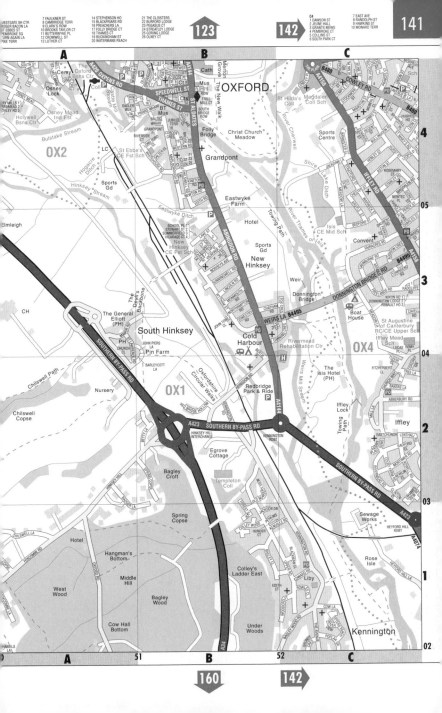

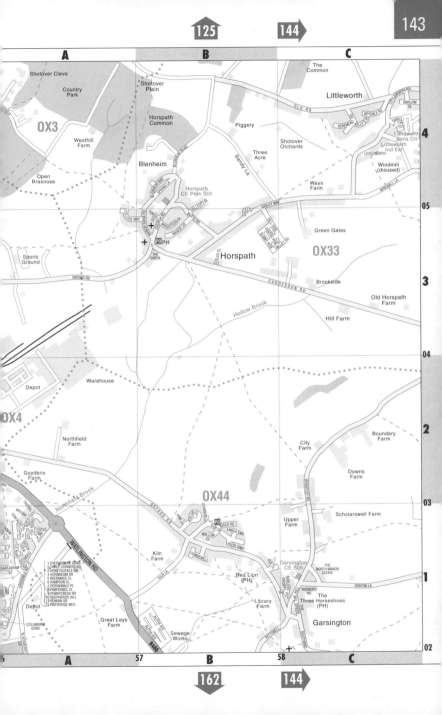

THAME

New Barn Farm

Whites Farm

Sewage Works

Lower Green Farm

Cotmore Wells

Westfield Farm

Quash Farm

Church Farm

Cotmore Wells Farm

1 GARDEN CITY
2 WALKER DR
3 LACEY DR
4 PEARCE WAY

Manor Farm

Towersey

Deans Farm

Uppe Greer Farm

Works

Works

Home Farm

Blackditch Farm

Nursery

The Copperlites

Cuttle Brook

Sydenham Hurst

OX9

Westbrook Farm

Thame Park

Square Covert

The Belt

Waterlands Farm

New Park

Brooklands

Hollier's Covert

Sea Pond Wood

Sydenham Grange Farm

Stocken Corner Covert

OX39

The Inn at Emmington (PH)

Manor Farm

Buckinghamshire STREET ATLAS

A B C

Bumpers

HP17

Ilmer

Grange Farm

Parkhill Covert

Manor Farm

4

Upper Farm

MANOR RD

05

OX9

North Mill Farm

3

Grovehill Farm

Penn Farm

HP27

Grovehill Covert

New Close Farm

Hinton Crossing Cottage

04

Down Covert

Cuttle Brook

Whites Close

New Close Farm Rd

Forty Green

Fortygreen Farm

Great Covert

Sewage Works

The Peacock (PH)

FORTY DR

2

Home Farm

OX39

Henton

03

College Farm

Manor Farm

Village Farm

OLD ORCHARD

Manor Farm

Emmington

Allnutt's Farm

1

Rectory

Church Covert

Westbrook Farm

Upper Farm

B 4009 LOWER ICKNIELD WAY

02

A 75 B 76 C

A 4445

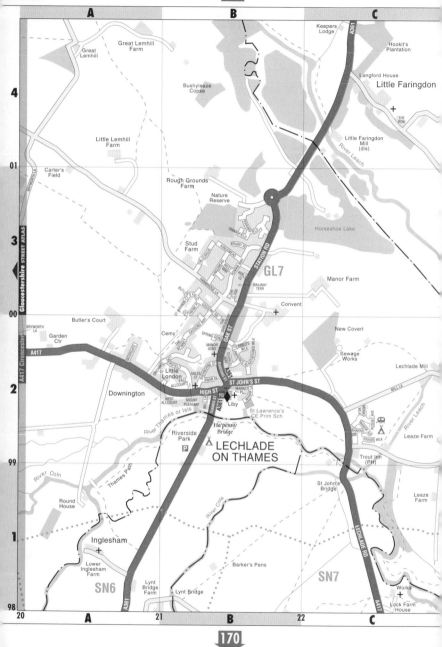

A   B   C

Tillingtons

4

Glebe
Farm

01

OX18

3

Langford Brook

GL7

00

Kelmscot Brook

2

Home
Farm

Kelmscott

Paradise Farm

The Plough
(PH)

Manor Farm

99

Kelmscott
Manor House

SN7

The
Anchor Inn
(PH)

1

Thames Path

River Thames or Isis

Philip's Farm
House

The Grange

Lock

Weir

98

A   B   C

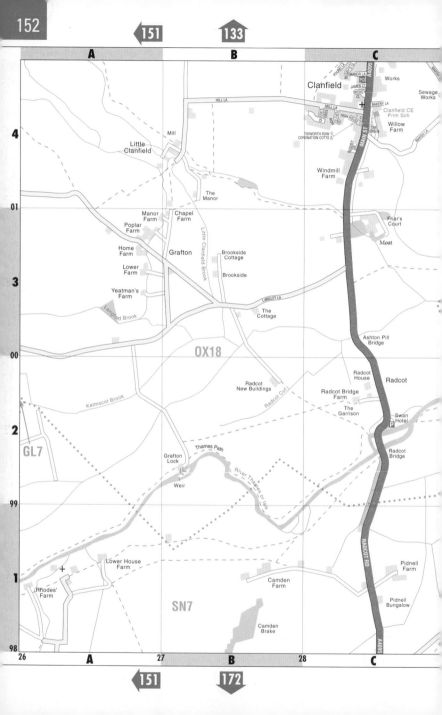

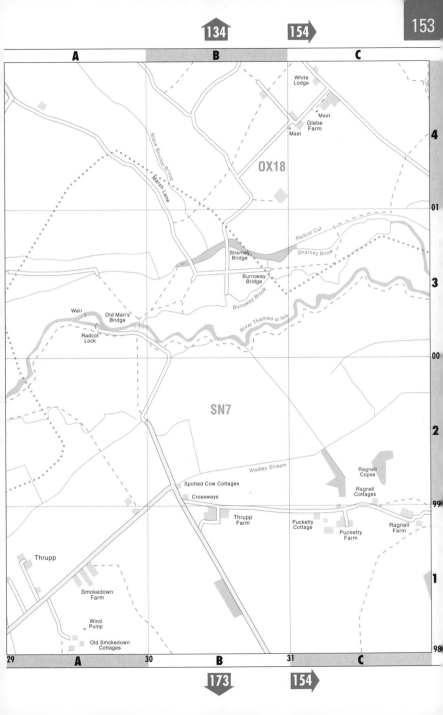

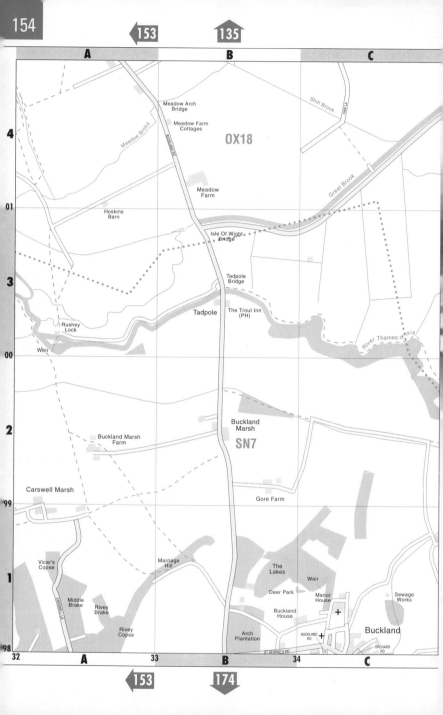

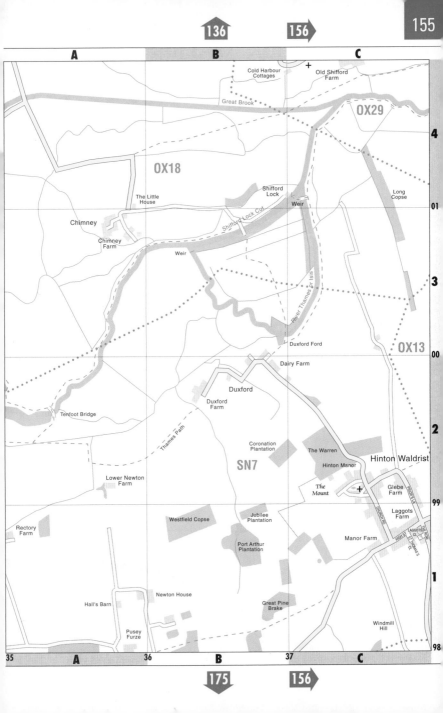

A
B
C

OX1

OX2

Lower England's Copse

Home Farm

Bessels Leigh

The Greyhound (PH)

The Cottage

Bessels Leigh Bank Wood

Wootton Bash Pk

THE ORCHARD

Radcliffe Lodge

Radcliffe House

Appleton CE Prim Sch

Bessels Leigh Common

Hull's Copse

New Copse

PH

PARK LA

Appleton

Colliers Copse

4

Hall

Holt Copse

Bessels Leigh Sch

The Field

01

Tubney Manor Farm

The Keepers House

Upwood Cottages

The Old Rectory

Great Park Farm

Dry Sandford Prim Sch

New Plantation

Triangle Plantation

Row Leigh La

3

THE RISE

A338

Upwood Park

Rowleigh House

Dry Sandford

Tubney Wood

Upwood Park

Manor Farm

White Hart Wood

00

Brushwood Farm

Blackgate La

Parsonage Moor

OX13

HONEYBOTTOM LA

Tubney Wood

Hitch Copse

String Lane

Cothill House Sch

COTHILL RD

Woodside

The Merry Miller (PH)

Cothill

2

Hitchcopse Farm

BLACKSMITHS LA

The Warren

99

Cothill Farmhouse

Mast

Sewage Farm

The Dog House Hotel (PH)

Oakley Park

Gozzard's Ford

OAKLEY HO

Grey Walls

Black Horse (PH)

1

Hylston

Buildings Farm

Black Horse Farm

Frilford Heath

CH

A338

Sheepstead Park

Sheepstead Folly

98

44
A
45
B
46
C

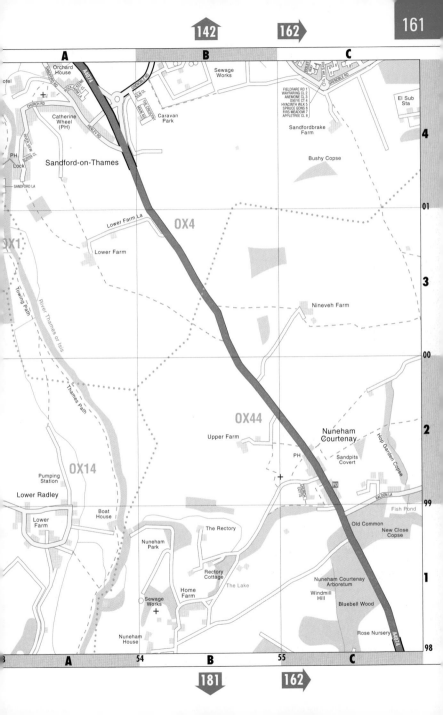

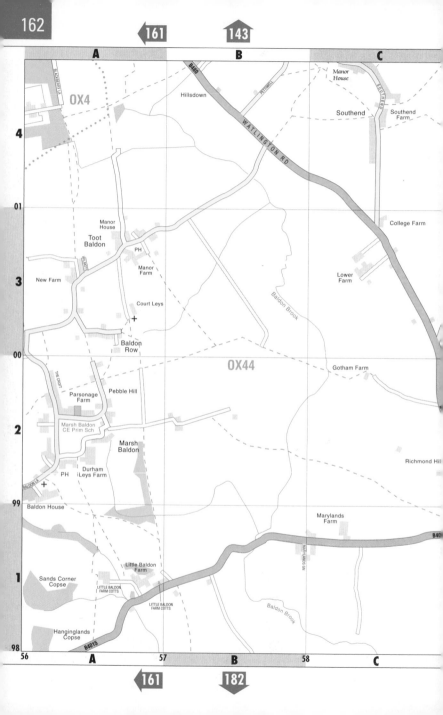

161
143

OX4

Hillsdown

Manor House

Southend

Southend Farm

WATLINGTON RD

B480

College Farm

Manor House

Toot Baldon

PH

Manor Farm

Lower Farm

New Farm

Court Leys

Baldon Brook

Baldon Row

OX44

Gotham Farm

THE CROFT

Parsonage Farm

Pebble Hill

Marsh Baldon CE Prim Sch

Marsh Baldon

Richmond Hill

BALDON LA

PH

Durham Leys Farm

Baldon House

Marylands Farm

B40

Sands Corner Copse

Little Baldon Farm

MARYLANDS GN

LITTLE BALDON FARM COTTS

LITTLE BALDON FARM COTTS

Baldon Brook

Hanginglands Copse

B4015

161
182

A   56   57   B   58   C

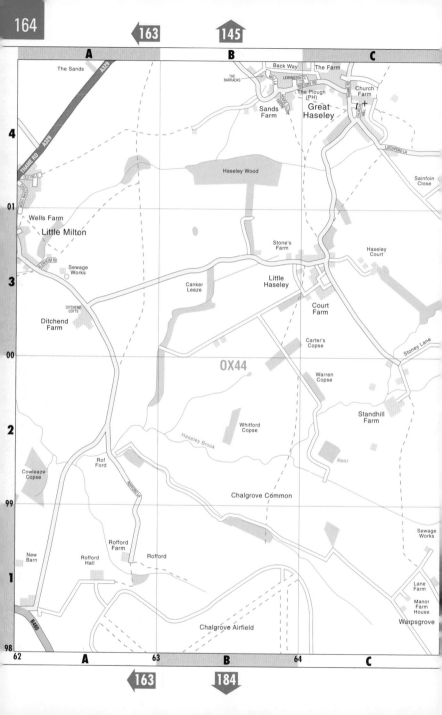

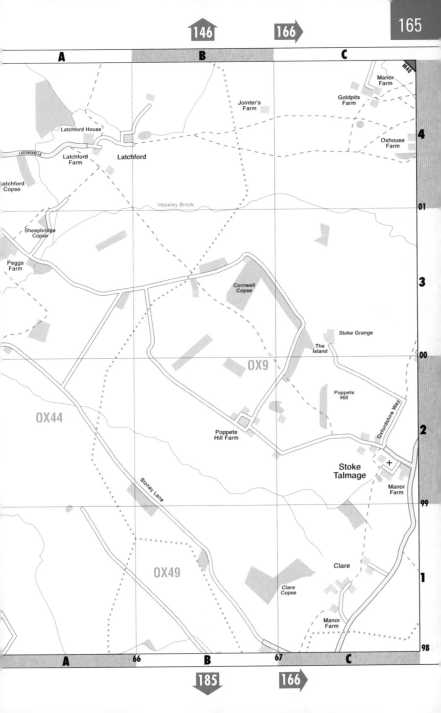

A B C

Tetsworth
Red Lion (PH)
The Green
PH
Judd's Lane
Tetsworth Prim Sch
Mount Hill Farm

MARSH END 1
CYGNET CL 2
THE MOUNT 3
PARKERS HILL 4
THE LAURELS 5

Dormers Leys

B4012

Attington Stud
Attington House

Copcourt

Harlesford House

Harlesford Farm

Upper Copcourt Farm

01

Oxfordshire Way

Haseley Brook

Wheatfield Cottages

Square Covert

3

B4012

Low Fai

Oxfordshire Way

Lower Farm

OX9

Adwell House Farm

BIX

BOT TREE LA

Adwell Farm

00

Glebe Farm

Wheatfield House

Adwell House

PH

GLEBE COTTS

Wheatfield Park

Adwell

Postcombe

Red Lion (PH)

Wheatfield Wood

Upper Farm

Bee Farr

2

Park Farm

Wheatfield

Adwell Cop

The Warren

99

Gilton Hill

Mill House

SALT LA

Netherc

1

Oxfordshire Way

The Salisbury Arms (PH)

Manor Farm

OX49

Oxfordshire Way

South Weston

Sewa Work

RECTORY LA

WESTON RD

98

68 A 69 B 70 C

A B C

Prospect Hill

SYDENHAM GR
Croton Ryder's
Farm Farm
Vears
Farm The Slades
PH +
PH
Musgrive
Sydenham Farm

HOLLIERS CL.

Vic

Sewell's Lane

4

Kingston
Stert

Manor
Farm Nursery
Chalford 01
Upper Chalford
Farm Kingston Stert
Farm

OX39 3

nheim
arm

00

OX9

BAKER'S
PIECE
HO

Moat
Manor

Lower Farm STERT RD OLD CROFT CL.

Town PH 2
Farm HIGH ST. B4009

Kingston
Blount Park La.

Aston Rowant
CE Sch Kingston
THE House
GREEN SCHOOL LA.

Home
Farm 99

Aston Park
Stud

OX49

Hope Lodge

Aston Rowant

The Croft
CHINNOR RD Woodway
Cottages

Woodway
Farm 1

Ridgeway

NETHERCROFT LA.

Sheepbrook
House

Swan's Way

98

Hotel
M40 BUTTS BRN. B4009 A40

A 72 B 73 C

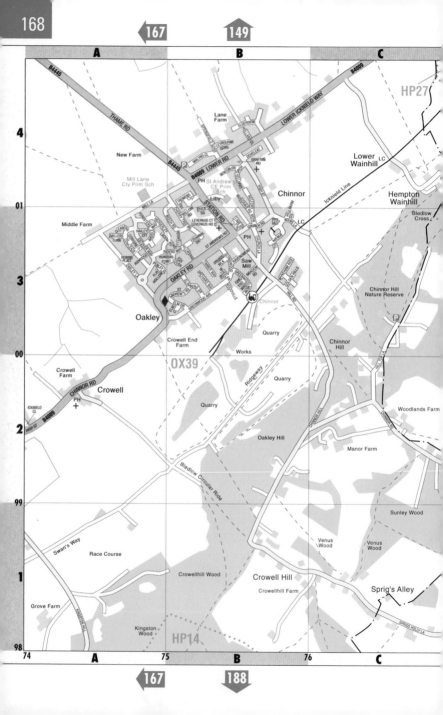

Bledlow

Frogmore Farm

ODDLEY LA

BLEDLOW RIDGE RD

BLEDLOW RD

Chiltern Way

Icknield Line

Midshires Way

Church Farm

The Warren

The Cop

Icknield Way Path

Home Farm

HP27

Thickthorne Wood

CH

Ridgeway

Parsonage Farm

Dean Plantation

LEE RD

Keeper's House

Lodge Hill

RIDGE LA

Bledlow Great Wood

Shimmell's Farm

Bledlow Circular Ride

Home Wood

OX39

HP14

Callow Down Farm

Chiltern Way

Frenche's Wood

Wigan's Farm

Beechgrove Farm

CRINGER RD

Harper's Farm

Lodge Hill Farm

Hedgerley Wood

Bledlow Ridge

Rout's Green

RANGER LA

THE STREET

Radnage Bottom Farm

CHAPEL LA

Daws Hill Farm

The Boot (PH)

SPRIGS HOLLY LA

CHURCH LA

Studmore Farm

4

01

3

00

2

99

1

98

A 77 78 B 79 C

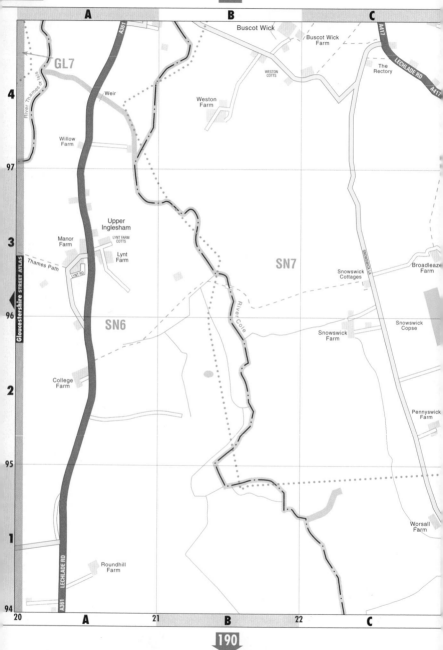

A B C

Buscot Wharf

P Buscot
PO

Kilmester Farm

Eaton Hastings 4

West Lodge

Taylor's Hill

LECHLADE RD

Stud Farm

Little Lake

97

Buscot House

SN7

The Lake

A417

ROADSIDE COTTS

Resr

Buscot Park

Canada Wood

Bury Hill

Cannon Hill

3

Cannonhill Wood

Old Wood

Black Plantation

Eaton Wood

Bushy Heath

Heath Farm

Resr

Longmead Plantation

Woodacre Wood

96

Oldfield Farm

Rowleaze Wood

Gorse Hill

2

Brimstone Farm

95

Coxwell Wood

Middle Leaze Farm

SN6

Fern Copse

1

B4019

Cuckoopen Plantation

B4019

Colleymore Farm

94

A 24 B 25 C

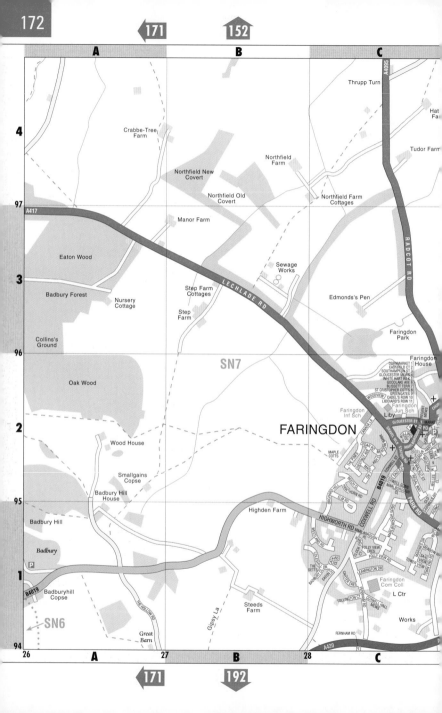

A   B   C

Barcote Manor

Carswell House

St Hugh's Sch

CASSWELL LA

St George's Rd

The Croft

The Lamb (PH)

Summerside

Bucklands CE Prim Sch

Orchard Cl

Summerside Rd

Buckland Rd

A420

4

Nursery Plantation

97

CH

Carswell Home Farm

Ashtree Farm

Lady Bushes

Stanford Road Cottages

Mount Pleasant Farm

Barcote Barn

BADGETT LA

Home Farm

Upper Ash Bed

Three Corner Clump

Broadmoor Cottage

3

Middle Ash Bed

Buckland Warren

Birch Hill

Sand Hill

Lower Ash Bed

96

Tagdown Barn

The Hideaway

SN7

Peat Bottom Wood

B4508

Long Plantation

2

Lower Tagdown Plantation

SANDY LA

Woodlands Farm Buildings

Rabbit Hill

Birch Hill

Sweet's Hill

Gainfield

Woodside Farm

Rectory Copse

Woodlands

Frogmore Brook

Coldharbour Farm

95

Hatford

Manorhouse Farm

Church Terr

Penstone's Barn

Little Hatford

Bow Rd

1

Laburnum Cottage

B4508

A417

Bow House

Bow Farm

94

B4508   A417

Bow

32   A   33   B   34   C

A
B
C

Buckland
Corner

Hinton
Corner

Cognells
Oaks

Pusey Common
Wood

Welmore
Farm

OX13

A420

Ayres's Common
Plantation

The
Roundabout

4

B4508

Birch
Plantation

97

Pusey
House

Park
Plantation

Lovell's
Court
Farm

Pusey

General
Downs
Plantation

Gimbro
Copse

Pusey
Lodge
Farm

3

+

Pusey
Farm

Turf Pits
Covert

Cherbury

Bushy
Cottages

96

SN7

Bushy
Barn

Gainfield
Cottages

2

Gainfield
Farm

OX12

95

BUCKLAND RD

Bedlam
Plantation

New
Barn

Hilltop
Farm

CHAPEL
LA

Eastfield
Farm

Minmere
Barn

PO
ORCHARD

BRIDLE PATH CL

BAGNFIELD

1

A
36
B
37
C

94

175 156

A   B   C

String Copse
PINE WOODS RD
A420
SPRING HILL
Middle Barn
HAYES AVE
CHERRY TREE CL
STONEHILL LA
SANDY LA
Blenheim Farm
Kingston Bagpuize House
PH
A420
Riding Centre
BULLOCKPITS LA
Nursery
LOWS POND LA
RACE FARM COTTS
RECTORY LA
Sewage Works
Race Farm

4

Bullockspits Farm

Lower Lodge Farm

97

SN7
New House
HANNEY RD
Plantation Barn

Newhouse Farm

Hunters Moon

Swannybrook Farm

Newhouse Cover

OX13

3

Cherbury Cottages

Cherbury House

Sheephouse Farm

96

Stanborough Covert

Ock Bridge

2
River Ock

LONG LONDON RD

95

Northfield Farm

OX12

Manor Farm

THE GREEN

Charney Bassett

Lyford Bridge

Lyford Grange

ORCHARD CL

Charney Wick

1
+

Lyford Manor

ALMSHOUSES

Poplars Farm

THE GREEN

Lyford

Manor Farm
+

94

Gallows Bridge

38   A   39   B   40   C

A415

A **B** **C**

Denys Farm

Resrs

4

Collin's Farm

Pickwick Farm

Dry Leys

Frilford

A415

Hamfield Barn

97

Comberley

Manor Farm

Fyfield Wick

3

A338

River Ock

Millets Farm

MILLETS FARM COTTS

MANOR FARM COTTS

Garford

Noah's Ark (PH)

90

College Farm

OX13

Garford Field

2

Nor Brook

9

Venn Mill

Childrey Brook

Common Barn

Letcombe Brook

OX12

1

9

41 **A** **42** **B** A338 **43** **C**

A   B   C

CH
Sherwood
Sheepstead Farm
Sheepstead House
Sheepstead Park
West Down La
Cow La

4

Josca's Prep Sch
Peads and Barnett's Farm
FORD LA
Fish Ponds

Orchard Farm

Peat Moor Lane

97

A415
A338

Denman Coll
Cemy
Kiln Copse

KINGS AVE
CHURCHILL WAY
THE
HOLLIES
TOWER LS
NEW RD
THE GAP
FRILFORD RD

HOWARD CORNISH RD
ANNIE
SWEET BRIAR
PH
20

HYDE COPSE
ORCHARD WAY
KEEPER CLOSE
Marcham CE Prim Sch
Marcham
PACKHORSE LA

Hyde Farm Nurseries

MARCHAM RD
A415

Sandford Brook

Manor Farm
Marcham Priory
MILL RD
PRIORY LA

Meadow Farm House

OX13

96

River Ock
Nor Brook
Childrey Brook

Marcham Mill
Weirs

5

Landmead Farm

1

OX14

44   A   45   B   46   C

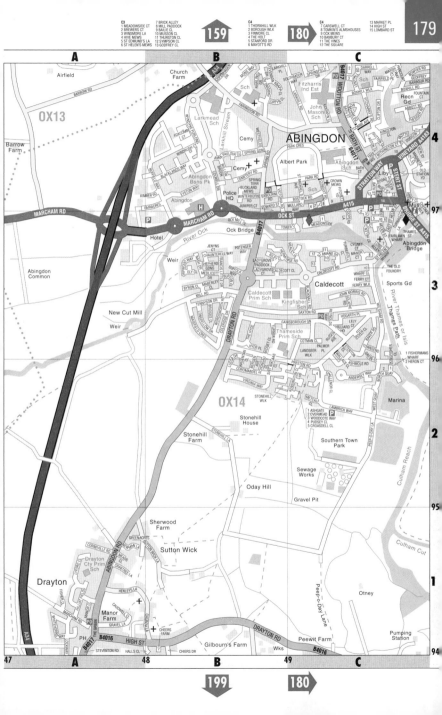

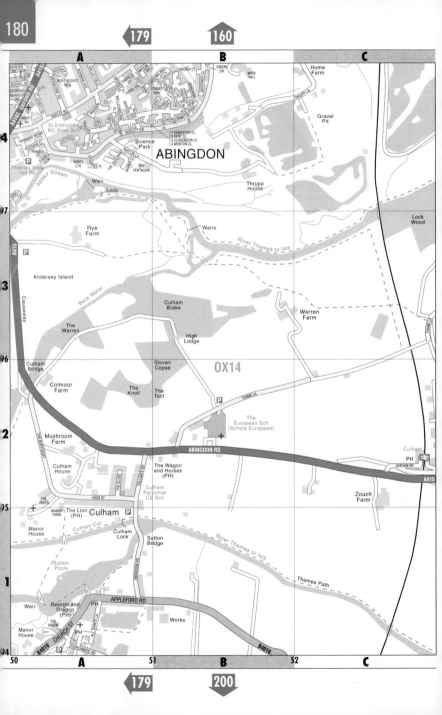

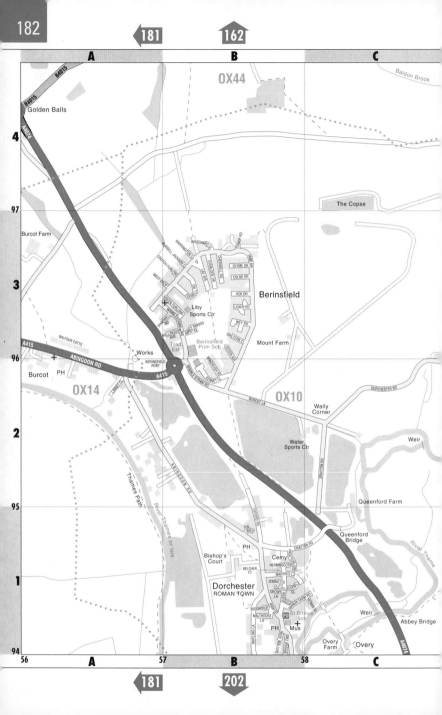

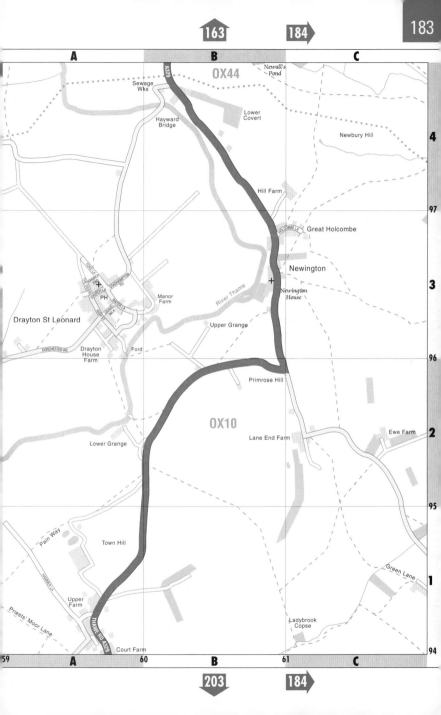

183
164

A   **B**   **C**

B480

Chalgrove Airfield

Hitchcox Poultry Farm

Newberry Hill

4

Monument Ind Pk

Chalgrove Field

Fox Covert

Hampden's Monument

97

Little Holcombe Covert

The Lamb (PH)

BOWER END
BROOKSIDE EST
HIGH ST
POPLAR FARM RD.

MAIN RD

Manor Farm

Mill House
THE RICKYARD

Langley Hall

QUARTERMAIN RD.

ADEANE RD.

SWINSTEAD CT.

FLEMMING AVE.

LANGLEY RD.

THE GUELDS

CHURCH LN.
ST MARK'S

FRENCH LAURENCE WAY

LUPTON RD.

MONDAY VERS RD.

FERN CL.

DITCHEND CL.

HASELEY LA.

CROMWELL CL.

Chalgrove

B480

Langley Field Farm

OX44

Chalgrove Com Prim Sch

CHURCH LN.

WILLOW
FRANKLIN CL.

Church Farm

Chalgrove Farm

3

BERRICK RD.

96

Southfield Barn

Hares Leap

Hollandside House

Cadwell La

Cadwell Farm

Cadwell Covert

2

OX49

OX10

Whitehouse Farm

95

Lonesome Farm

Manor Farm

Rumbolds Lane

Berrick Prior

1

Green Lane

Hollandtide Bottom

PH
Ivyhouse Farm

Berrick Salome

Rumbolds Farm

94

62   **A**   **63**   **B**   **64**   **C**

183
204

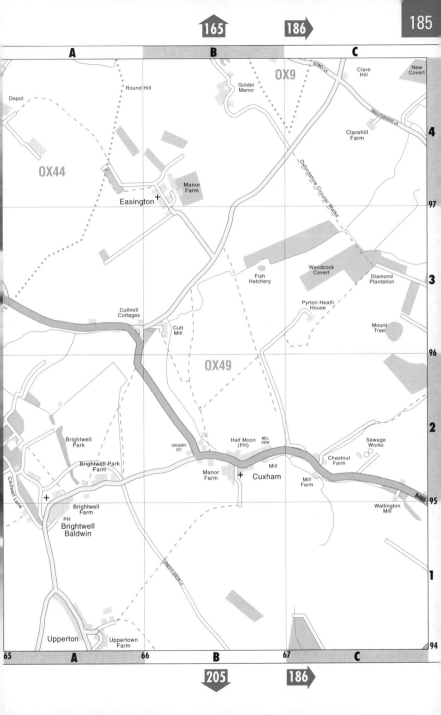

A B C

OX39

Kingston Grove

Grove Wood

High Wood

OX39

Crowell Wood

Collier's Lane

Lott Wood

Collier's Lane

Gurdon's Farm

Beechwood Shaw

4

M40

ASTON HILL

Aston Wood

Hawing Wood

Stockfield Wood

Hallbottom Farm

Hill Farm

97

Mast

Radio Station

Kiln Farm

OXFORD RD

Mallard's Court

Wood Farm

BOWLING GR 1
CHURCH PATH 2
LOWER CHURCH ST 3

Stokenchurch

3

M40

OXFORD RD

Hotel

Stokenchurch Jun Sch

1 CURZON GATE CT
2 BRITNELL CT
3 MILESTONE CL
4 FERNDALE CL
5 OLD SCHOOL CL
6 HART MOOR CL
7 FOWLERS FARM RD

North Remlets Wood

Hailey Wood

PH

CRICKET GR
COOPER'S COURT

Lib

Langleygreen Plantation

Independent Bsns Pk

CR Bates Ind Est

WYCOMBE RD

A4

96

Coopers Court Farm

HP14

Wallace Hill

Little Studdridge

CHILTERN WAY

Bissomhill Shaw

St Hugh's

Stokenchurch Inf Sch

SAUNDERS WOOD COPSE

2

MARLOW RD

95

Wellground Farm

Bowley's Wood

Studdridge Farm

Coombe Wood

Commonhill Wood

1

Penley Farm

Penley Wood

Commonhill Wood

Hartmoor Wood

94

74 A 75 B 76 C

A **B** **C**

4

Grange
Farm

Town
End

Radnage

Chiltern Way

Bledlow
Ridge

VIRGINIA
GONS

Bledlow
Ridge
Sch

PO

Andridge
Common

SPRIGS HOLLY LA

YOESDEN RD

CHURCH LA

TOWN END RD

Yoesden
Wood

FORD LA

SPRIGS HOLLY LA

Andridge
Farm

The Three
Horseshoes Inn
(PH)

BOTTOM RD

97

GRANGE FARM RD

BENNETT END RD

Bennett End

BEES LA

The Crown
(PH)

WHITE SQUARE LA

Radnage
CE Inf Sch

Bottom
Farm

3

Pophley's
Wood

Pophley's

The City

CITY RD

CHURCH LA

Pond
Farm

Waterend

RADNAGE COMMON RD

HP14

Ashridge
Farm

BAKER END RD

96

WELLERS END RD

Bottom
Wood

Eastwood
Farm

Bricks La

Beacon's
Bottom

The Mary
Towerton Sch

Studley Green
Farm

2

EASTWOOD RD

EAST END RD

ST FRANCIS RD

WYCOMBE RD

PH

Studley
Green

East Wood

Horsleys
Green

95

Moules Wood

BILLS LA

Thirds
Wood

OLD DASHWOOD HILL

A40 High Wycombe

Old House
Farm

Wycliffe
Centre

Fillington
Wood

A40

Gibbon's
Farm

1

MARLOW RD B482

Butterleys
Plantation

Dell's
Wood

Watercroft
Wood

M40

Dell's
Farm

BIGMORE LA

Penley Hollies

Bigmore
Farm

94

77 **A** 78 **B** 79 **C**

A B C

4

93

3

2

Wiltshire STREET ATLAS

91

1

90

20 A 21 B 22 C

Haresfield
BLACKWORTH
PINE FURLONG
FOLLY WAY
FOLLY DRI
FOLLY CL
DOWNS VIEW
THE MEWS
LECHLADE RD
KNOWLANDS
Northview Cty Prim Sch
ACROFT
CHASE CT
GREEN ACRE
HIGHWORTH
SHEEP
High St
Liby
Eastrop
Eastrop Grange
Southfield Prim Sch
Highworth Warneford Comp Sch
REDLANDS CL
STRAPS
A361 Swindon
B4000
A361
B4019

Lower Barn

Common Farm

Eastrop Farm

Wickstead Farm

Raglan's Wood

River Cole

B4019

Fresden Wood

Starveall Barn

Fresden Farm

SN6

Highmoor Copse

Round Robin Farm

Round Robin Wood

River Cole

EASTROP

1 MIDDLE HAINES CT
2 EASTVIEW TERR
3 GLEBE PL
4 STATION RD
5 CHURCH VIEW
6 ST MICHAEL'S AVE
7 CRICKLADE RD
8 THE ELMS
9 THE GREEN
10 SWINDON RD
11 MARKET PL.

The Buildings

SHRIVENHAM RD

Wrag Farm
CH

Friars Hill

B4508

B4508

Coombes Copse

River Cole

Bellingham Farm
Sevenhampton
THE REEMA HOS
BELLINGHAM LA

The Rookery

Sevenhampton Farm

Thorny Copse

New Covert

Little Coombes Copse

Friars Farm

Homegrown Copse

HIGHWORTH RD

Swan's Nest Copse

B4000

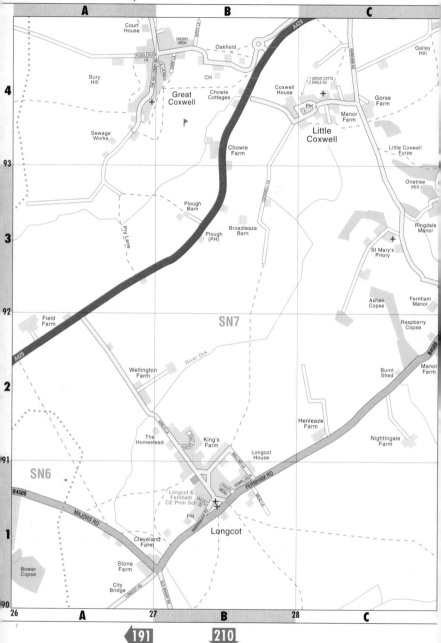

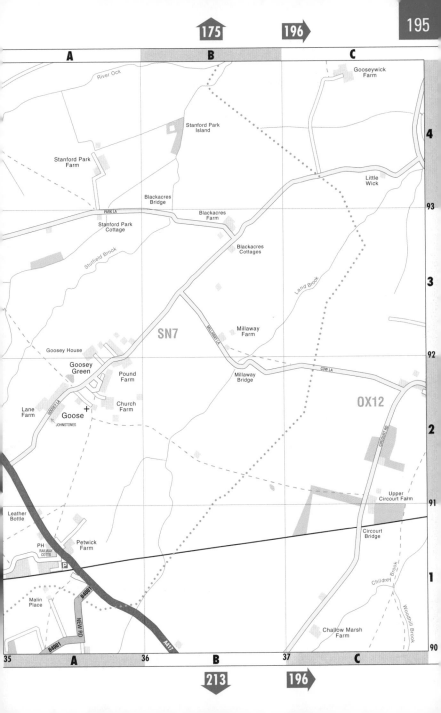

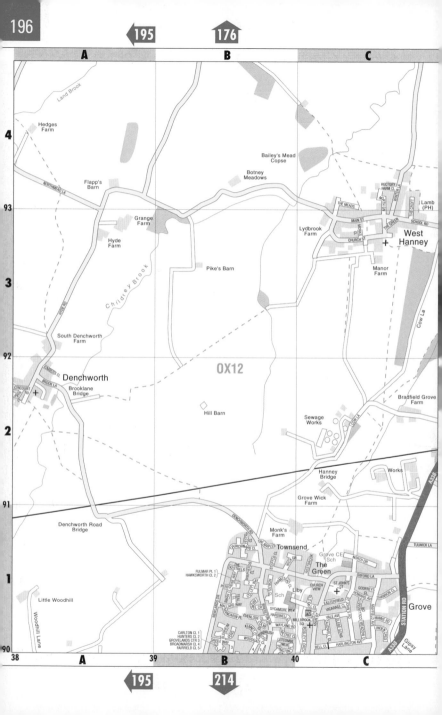

177
198
198

OX14

Drayton Copse

Steventon Field

Cow Common

Honeybottom
Boarding
Kennels

Barn Close
Farm

Goose
Willow

El Sub Sta

HANNEY RD

Orchard
Farm

Three
Elms

The
Views

OX13

Depot

Steventon

St Michael's
CE Prim Sch

Causeway
Farm

PH

Causeway
Crossing

Sewage
Works

LC   LC

Little
La

Steventon
Copse

VICARAGE RD

Ginge Brook

Hill Farm

OX12

Hill Barn

East Hendred Brook

Wood's
Farm

WOOD'S FARM RD

199
180

A **B** **C**

OX14

BROOK ST
B4016

CHURCH MILL RD

Abbey

Sutton
Courtenay

Cross Tree
Farm

CHURCH ST

OLD WALLINGFORD WAY

1 HILLYARD BARNS
2 THE NURSERY
3 HILLIERS CL

PH

COURTENAY CL

Hall

HOBBYHORSE LA

Gravel Pit

Nature
Reserve

Depot

Didcot
Power Station

Chy

A4130

MILTON RD

OX11

DIDCOT

Southmead
Ind Pk

CHURCHWARD

THE COBDEN
CTR

HAWKSWORTH
MOORBROOK
HARRIER

Sewage
Works

GOOCH

Didcot North
Junction

1 LAMBWITH STREAM
2 DUDWELL
3 DARI DR
4 ALPHIN BROOK
5 BLAKEHOPE BURN
6 NUNNEY BROOK

Easton's
Plantation

BASIL HILL RD
ROUGHPUTION
LYNCH RD

B4130

Didcot
Railway Ctr

Ladygrove
Park
Prim Sch

Didcot
Town FC
(Loop Meadow)

B4493

DRUIDS WLK 1
KING WLK 2
MEAD WLK 3
CASTLE WLK 4
BLAGROVE CL 5

NORTH RD

BRENDON CL 1
MALVERN CL 2
COTSWOLD PK 3
TOWER GDNS 4
WENLOCK CL 5

Didcot
Field

QUANTOCK
VIEW

Didcot
Parkway

Didcot
Junction

ANCHOLME CL 6
TYBURN GLEN 7

Stephen
Freeman
Prim Sch

ORDNANCE RD

Vauxhall
Barracks

GREAT WESTERN DR

FOXHALL RD

1 MACDONALD CL
2 SMITHS FARM LA
3 SAYERS DITCH
4 GLYN AVE

FREEMAN RD

MERRITT CL
MORRELL CL

BRASENOSE RD

CHURCHILL
CL

CHURCHILL RD

Recn
Gd

DUNSDEN WAY

Didcot
Girls Sch

BLAKES RD

Manor
Prim Sch

MILTON DR

GARTH RD

B4493

BROADWAY

Ind Est

Bridge
Farm

Manor
Farm

MANOR CL

CHURCH ST

Appleford

Appleford

Carpenters
Arms
(PH)

SINODUN
ROW

MAIN RD

Allot
Gdns

LC

Appleford
Crossing

B40

Hill Farm

Moor Ditch

OX14

199
218

A
B
C

Thames Path

River Thames or Isis

Long Wittenham
CE Prim Sch

PH

Fieldside

College
Farm

Inn.

HIGHLET

ST JOHN'S
ROW

Long
Wittenham

Mus

THE
CRESCENT

4

Moor Ditch

West Field

OX14

93

Bow Bridge

Westfield
Barn

Woodside
Farm

Pearith
Cottages

Westfield
Farm

Rose Hurst
Farm

3

Pearith
Farm

Wigbolds

Oxfordshire Circular Walks

92

Long
Wittenham
Wood

White Lees

Willington Down
Farm

LADY GR

Down Hill

White Lees
Farm

Ladygrove
Farm

2

Hopkins
Bridge

1 ROTHER GARTH
2 WEYCROFT
3 WANSBECK WOOD
4 DON CL
5 WINDBUSH MEWS

OX11

WEAVER
CROFT

Cow La

B4016

91

Bush Furlong

Hill View

Summerlees

A4130

1

ABINGDON RD

Hadden
Farm

CH

Field Farm

HADDEN HILL

A4130

B4016

90

A
54
B
55
C

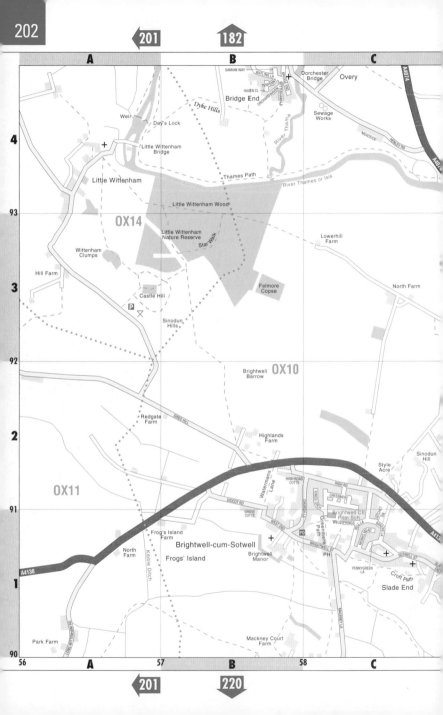

A | B | C

4

Parsonage Farm
Grace's Farm
WELLER CL
Home Sweet Home (PH)
Hare Hall
Bunkers
Scald Hill
Rumbolds Lane
CHAPEL LA
Roke
Roke Farm
Rumbold's Copse
93
OX49
The Horse and Harrow (PH)
Rokemarsh
THE SANDS
GROVE LA B400
Port Hill House
BRISK LA
B4009
Tidmarsh Lane
COTTESMORE LA
Windmill Farm
TYPP LA
3

WALLINGFORD RD
CEDARS
Fifield Farm
Cottesmore Farm
The Views
Shepherd's Hut (PH)
Hyde Shaw
92

BENSON WAY
BROOK ST
FIR TREES CL
PADDOCK CL
Benson
1 CROWN LA
2 ALDRIDGE CL
3 THE MOORLANDS
OX10
CYCLE LA
BRICK LA
Lower Farm
MARTIN'S BELT
BRITWELL RD
HAMPDEN WAY
CALLOW RD
Ewelme
BRIGHTWELL RD
GLEBE RD
ST HELEN'S AVE
2
SUFFOLK HO
WHIRLWIND WAY
Manor House
The Greyhound (PH)
Church Farm
Ewelme CE Prim Sch
THE CLOISTERS
DEVON CL
ANDERS RD
BLENHEIM PL
ANDERS RD
Fords Farm
BENSFIELD CL
Benson Airfield
ANDREW RD
LANCASTER RD
1 BLENHEIM PL
2 WESSEX RD
4 MERLIN CL
3 PUMA CL
91

DIAL CL
BATTLE RD
Rabbits Hill
Cow Common
Chiltern Way
BRICK LA
PO
Benson Com Prim Sch
BARBERRY WAY
BATTLE RD
Swan's Way
1
REVELL TAYLOR RD
GEOFFREY TAYLOR RD
WELLDOWN CL
ANTHONY HILL RD
HEADLEY LA
MICKEY RD
BOWER CL
Sewage Works
A4074
BEGGARSBUSH HILL
OXFORD RD
The London Road Inn (PH)
Mast
Gravel Pit
90
Marsh Wood
BLACK LA

62 | 63 | 64

A | B | C

A
B
C

4

93

3

92

2

91

1

90

The Old
Rectory
Lower
Farm
Cooper's
Farm House
The Priory
TURNER'S GN 1
HAMSTYLES 2
PH
Britwell
Salome
Heath
Plantation
Ashley's
Wood
OX49
Grove
Farm
Brightwell Grove
Home Farm
GROVE LA
Mon
Britwell Salome
House
Brockholes Lane
Brockholes
Covert
Mon
Icknield Way
North Farm
Ridgeway
Huntingland
Swan's Way
Icknieldbank
Plantation
Lower
Warren
Swyncombe Downs
RG9
Warren Bottom
Sliding Hill
OX10
The Nuttery
Lower Farm
Down Farm
Littleworth Hill
Lowerfarm
Cottages
BRINGSLA
POTTERS LA
Ladies Walk
Colliers Hill
Ewelme Downs
Colliers
Bottom

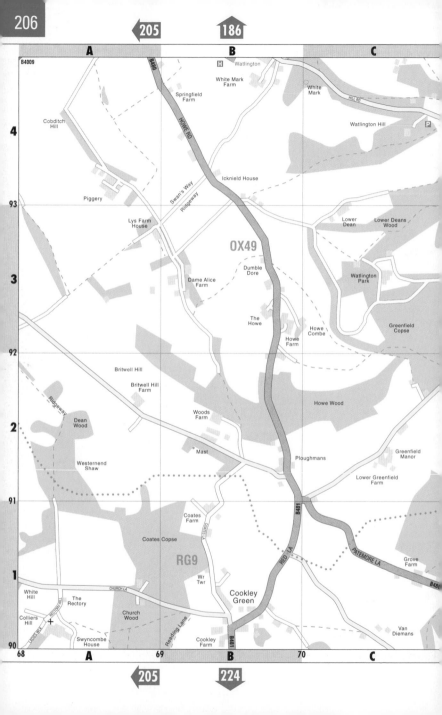

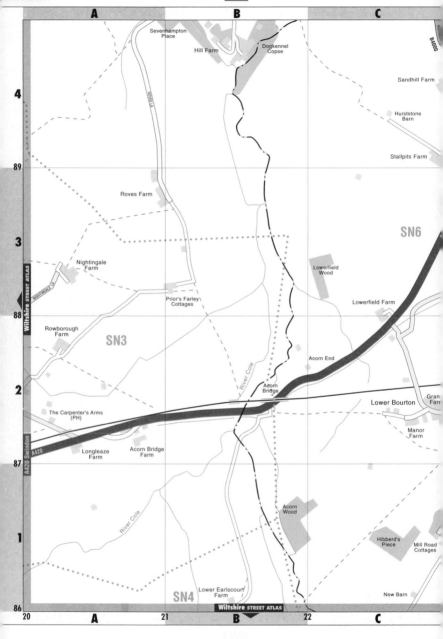

A   B   C

4

89

3   SN6

88

SN3

Sevenhampton
Place

Hill Farm

Dogkennel
Copse

Sandhill Farm

Hurststone
Barn

Stallpits Farm

Roves Farm

Lowerfield
Wood

Lowerfield Farm

Nightingale
Farm

Prior's Farley
Cottages

Acorn End

Rowborough
Farm

River Cole

Acorn
Bridge

2   Lower Bourton   Gran
Farr

The Carpenter's Arms
(PH)

Manor
Farm

87

Longleaze
Farm

Acorn Bridge
Farm

River Cole

Acorn
Wood

1

Hibberd's
Piece

Mill Road
Cottages

SN4   Lower Earlscourt
Farm

New Barn

86

20   A   21   B   22   C

NIGHTINGALE LA

A420 Swindon

A420

B4000

River Cole

Wiltshire STREET ATLAS

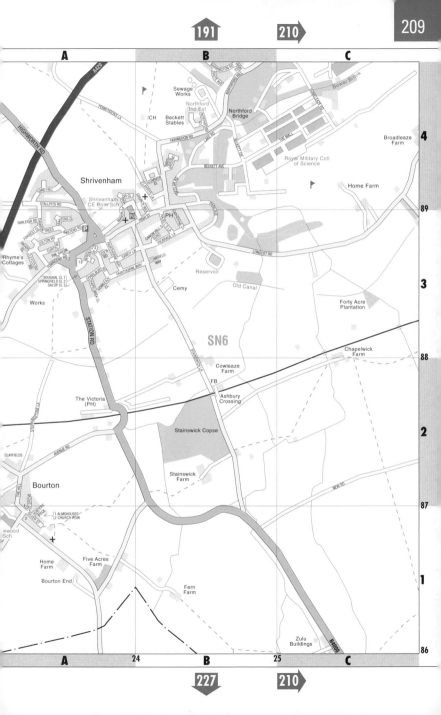

191
210

A   B   C

HIGHWORTH RD

A420

FARRINGDON RD

Sewage
Works

Northford
Ind Est

Bower Brook

TENNYSDOCKS LA

/CH

Beckett
Stables

Northford
Bridge

FARINGDON RD   LAKE RD

BECKETT RISE

THE MALL

Broadleaze
Farm

4

Shrivenham

Royal Military Coll
of Science

Home Farm

SAND HILL

STALLPITS RD

Shrivenham
CE Prim Sch

OX CL

BECKETT AVE

89

FARLEIGH RD

MARTENS CL

HIGH ST

TUCKER RD

CHURCH LA   +

PH

MARTENS CL

TOWNSEND RD   COXTON RD

P

CURTIS +

SANDY LA

STONEFIELD
WAY

PINEWOOD

CURTIS

THE GREEN

GIRSENG RD

SANDHILL
CT

VICARAGE LA

LONGCOT RD

Rhyme's
Cottages

CHARLBURY

CHAPEL RD

Reservoir

YOUGHAL CL 1
SPRINGFIELD CL 2
SALOP CL 3

CHAPEL BRICK CL

Cemy

Old Canal

3

Works

SN6

STAINSWICK LA

Forty Acre
Plantation

88

Chapelwick
Farm

STATION RD

Cowleaze
Farm

FB

The Victoria
(PH)

Ashbury
Crossing

STEPPINGSTONE LA

Stainswick Copse

2

CLAYFIELDS

AVENUE RD

NEW RD

87

Bourton

Stainswick
Farm

THE HILL

LIMES GROVE

1 ALMSHOUSES
2 CHURCH ROW

LONG ST

Home
Farm

Five Acres
Farm

ewood
Sch

Bourton End

Fern
Farm

1

Zulu
Buildings

B4000

86

A   24   B   25   C

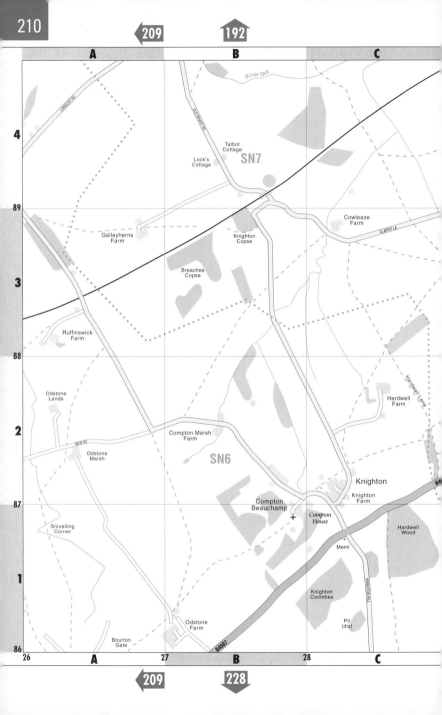

A **B** **C**

SN7

Ladycroft
Pond

Church's
Copse

Stutfield Brook

Fox Covert

Cross Bargain
Farm

Gabbits Copse

Featherbed Lane

Westcot Lane

South
Farm

4

Long Spinney
Copse

Round Spinney
Copse

Broadleaze
Farm

89

Kingston Common
Farm

3

Cemy

Fawler
Manor

Fawler

Kingston Lisle

88

HILL LANE

DROVE WAY

The Plough
(PH)

Manor Farm

North
Park

OX12

Georgesgreen
Farm

Hall
Place
Home
Farm

WEST ST

Star
(PH)

Sparsholt

WESTCOT LA

Westcot
Farm

CHURCH WAY

BLACKLANDS

BROADBROOK LA

SPARSHOLT RD

2

Kingston Lisle
Farm

Kingston Lisle
House

Green
Park

Westcot

Sparsholt Park

EASTMANTON LA

Kingston Lisle Park

B4507

87

Blowing Stone

The Warren

Oakbank
Plantations

Seven Acre Hill

B4507

BLOWINGSTONE HILL

Oakbank Barn

1

The Rides

Sparsholt Field

Kingstonhill Barn

Oxfordshire

Ridgeway

Circular Walks

Field Barn

Sheephouse Bottom

Clements Cottages

Lodge Farm

86

32 **A** **33** **B** **34** **C**

195 214

A • B • C

4

89

3

88

2

87

1

86

Lower Petwick

B4001

Hill House

A417

Garlands Cottage

Childrey Brook

Mill Lane

Petwick Stud Farm

Garlands Farm

Mill Farm

MARSH LA

Petwick Plantation

Coppice Leaze Barn

Aughton

WOODHILL LA

Pack Lane

NEW RD

Coppice Leaze Farm

West Challow

SILVER LA

Manor Farm

THE CURB

Wise's Farm

WOODHILL LA

A417

Challow House Farm

Fox Brake

Frethorne Stud

OX12

ORCHARD GORE

Manor House Farm

OLD SCHOOL LA

Cornhill Lane

EAST HILL RD

LOCKINGE RD

OLD GREY MARE LA

Pulpit Hill

Godfrey's Farm

ORCHARD FURLONG

CHURCH ROW

Cornhill Farm

East Challow CE Prim Sch

Eastmanton Farm

Childrey

ST LAWRENCE CL

WEST ST

Parsonage Farm

Dropshort Farm

ICKLETON RD

B4507

Veor Farm

DOG LA

HIGH ST

STOWHILL

Windmill Hill

The Ridgeway CE Prim Sch

WEST ST

HOTHOW WAY

The Hatchet (PH)

Antwicks Stud

Antwicks Manor

GREEN RD

Gallop

MIDDLEWAY BOTTOM

B4001

Cemy

Blandy's Farm

BASSETT RD

Letcombe Manor

Childrey Field

Letcombe Bassett Field

A • 36 • B • 37 • C

231 214

213 196

A B C

4

Woodhill Farm

Woodhill Cottages

Sewage Wks

89

Country Club

Woodhill Brook

Factory

Stockham Bridge

Stockham Farm

Fitzwaryn Sch

Recn Gd

CANAL CT

ROMAN RD

Works

Grove Bridge Farm

Elms Farm

STATION RD

A338

GIPSY LA

ST IVES RD

CHERRY TREE CL

MAYFIELD RISE

GROVE RD

WESTFIELD WAY 1
WILMOT WAY 2

3

Works

Canal Farm

Challow Park

East Challow

OGBOURNE CL 1
SEGSBURY CT 2
GROSVENOR PL 3
FRAMLANDS CL 4

CHALLOW RD

CANAL WAY

Stockham Prim Sch

SAXON PL

STOCKHAM PARK

STOCKHAM WAY

DEAN BUTLER

Belmont

SIMMONDS WLK

PLUMMER

BARWELL

BELMONT

LITTLEWORTH HILL

MOOR

Works

WORTHINGTON WAY

WILLOW WLK

LEONARD

THORNHILL

CROOK'S TERR

GROVE ST

HARCOURT WAY

HARCOURT RD

COURTENAY RD

HAMPDEN RD

UPTHORPE DR

CHARLTON VILLAGE

WEST

Charlton Cty Prim Sch

PALMERS

Charlton

88

Townsend

1 PARK TERR
2 HEDGE HILL RD
3 CHILDREY WAY
4 HILL CL
5 WINDMILL PL
6 HIGH VIEW

King Alfred's Sch W

NALDERTOWN

HAMCROFT

WEST HILL

GREENACRES DR

MARE

WHIPPS

LOCKS LA

LOCKS LA

OX12

MILL ST

LETCOMBE HO

MARKET PL

CAMEL CROSS

SEESON WAY

WALLINGFORD ST

Liby

Mus

Schs

BECKETT

ORMOND RD

B4507

CHARLTON RD

HALLETT'S

King Alfred's Sch E

CANGLE LA

HARCOURT

LETCOMBE CL

SPRINGFIELD RD

LARKDOWN

H

Wantage

2

B4507

Windmill Hill

Kirklands

ICKLETON RD

The Ham

PORTWAY

PORTWAY MEWS

B2
WILLOW LA

Allot Gdns

L Ctr

B4507

NEWBURY ST

B4494

1 CHARTER HO
2 THE GUILD HO
3 THREE PIGEONS CL
4 PARTRIDGE CL

ORCHARD WAY

Cemy

Chain Hill

WANTAGE

87

Bablakes Farm

Letcombe Brook

Resr

1 THE CLOISTERS
2 VICARS ROW
3 ALFRED ST
4 STIRLINGS RD
5 REGENT MALL
6 POST OFFICE LA
7 EAGLES CL

The Ark

Recn Gd

Chainhill House

Chain Hill Farm

Chain Hill

Resr

CHAINHILL RD

1

PH

POST OFFICE

ANVIL PADDOCK

Letcombe Regis

Letcombe Regis Field

MANOR RD

Manor Farm

Manor Road Farm

Wantage Field

86

Court Hill

Manor Farm

Gallops

Edgehill Springs

A338

B4494

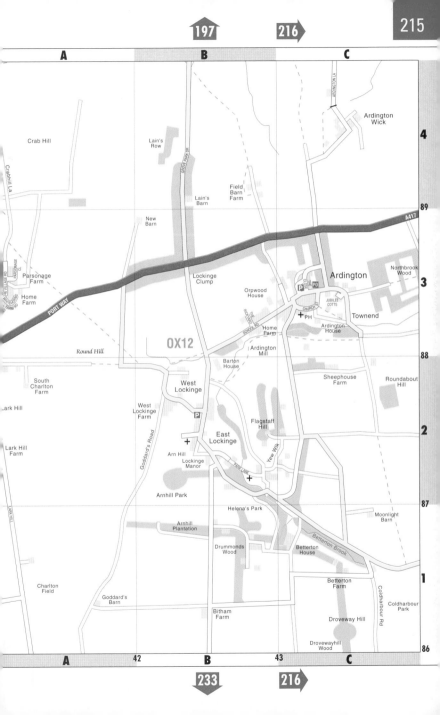

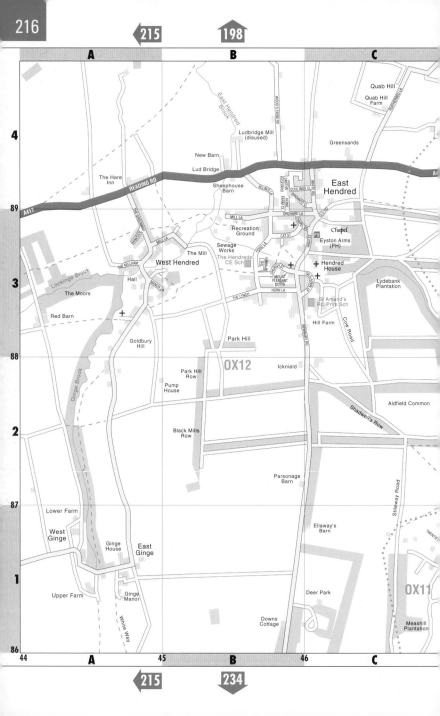

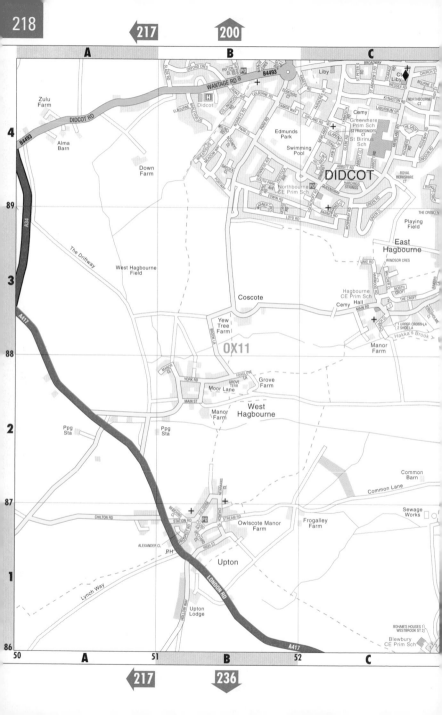

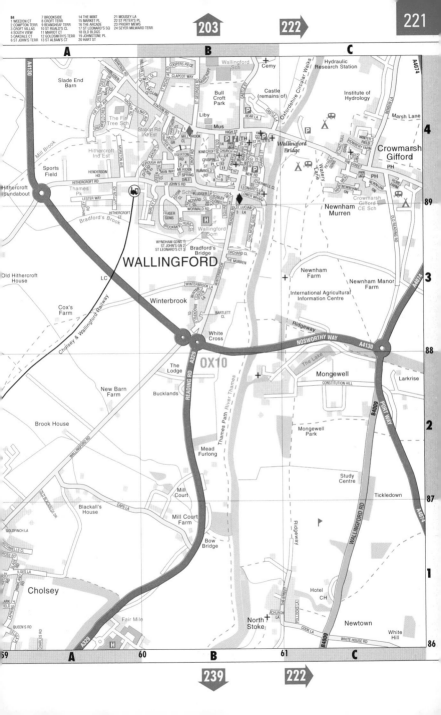

A **B** **C**

Marsh Wood

CLACK'S LA

Clack's Farm

Gould's Grove
Farm

Troy Cottage

4

Marsh
Lane

Shepherds
Cottage

Coldharbour Farm

Public Refuse
Tip

89

A4130

CROWMARSH HILL

Oakley
Wood

Hillview

A4130

Oakley Wood
Farm

Western View

3

Lonesome Farm

Swan's Way

NUFFIELD LA

Turners Court
Farm

Oakley Court

Blenheim Farm

Whitley
House

88

OX10

Cart Gap

Ridgeway

2

Sheepcot Farm

Oaken Copse

Woodhouse
Farm

Batchelor's Hill

Forest Row

87

Wicks Hill

Wicks Wood

Drunken Bottom

Pigtrough Bottom

1

Black Barn
Farm

Poors
Shaw

Poors Farm

Coblers Hill

Hailey
Compton

86

62 **A** **63** **B** **64** **C**

205
224

A · B · C

Ladies Walk
Jacob's Tent

Swans Way
GRINDON LA.

Ewelme Downs

Potter's Farm

Heriot's Plantation

4

Mogpits Wood

Ewelme Park

89

Harcourt Hill

Harcourthill Shaw

Goblins Glen

Chiltern Way

Ridgeway

Hogpen Shaw

May's Farm

OX10

Bury Knowle

3

Ambrose Farm

Oakengrove Copse

Warren Hill

88

BRIXTON HILL

GANGSDOWN HILL

RG9

Nuffield Place

Warren Hill

NUFFIELD HILL

Crown Inn (PH)

A4130

2

Morrell's Bottom

The White House

CH

Nuffield Common

Ridgeway

Nuffield

Timbers Farm

Little Common

87

Mongewell Woods

Howberry Lane

Heycroft Shaw

Ridgeway Farmhouse

Heath End

Woodmoorfield Shaw

1

Upper House Farm

Bixmoor Wood

Little Common

English Farm

86

A · B · C

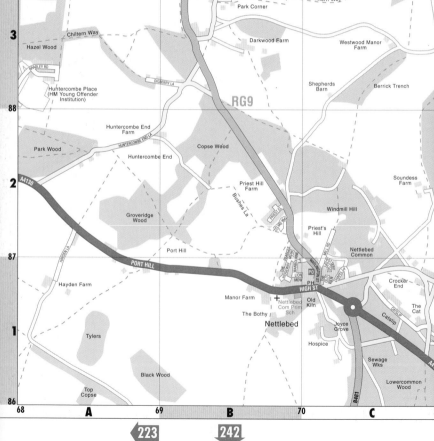

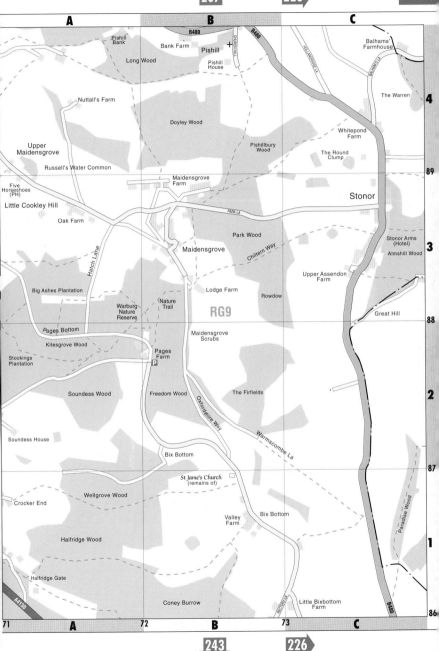

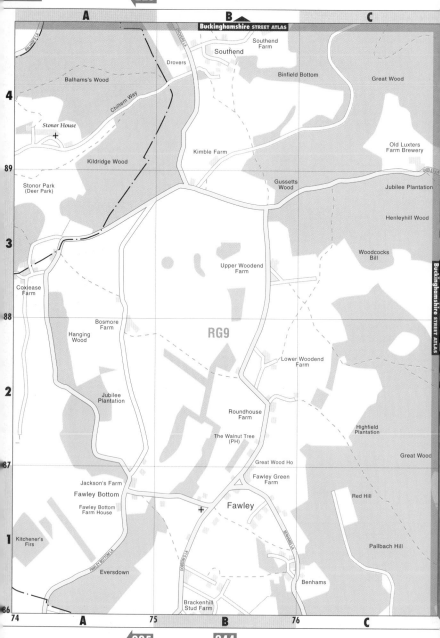

A   B   C

Buckinghamshire STREET ATLAS

Southend Farm

Southend

Drovers

Binfield Bottom

Great Wood

Balhams's Wood

4

Chiltern Way

Stonor House

Old Luxters Farm Brewery

Kimble Farm

Kildridge Wood

89

Stonor Park (Deer Park)

Gussetts Wood

Jubilee Plantation

Henleyhill Wood

Woodcocks Bill

3

Upper Woodend Farm

Coxlease Farm

88

Bosmore Farm

RG9

Hanging Wood

Lower Woodend Farm

2

Jubilee Plantation

Roundhouse Farm

Highfield Plantation

The Walnut Tree (PH)

Great Wood

87

Great Wood Ho

Jackson's Farm

Fawley Green Farm

Fawley Bottom

Red Hill

Fawley Bottom Farm House

Fawley

1

Kitchener's Firs

Pallbach Hill

Eversdown

Benhams

86

Brackenhill Stud Farm

74   A   75   B   76   C

Buckinghamshire STREET ATLAS

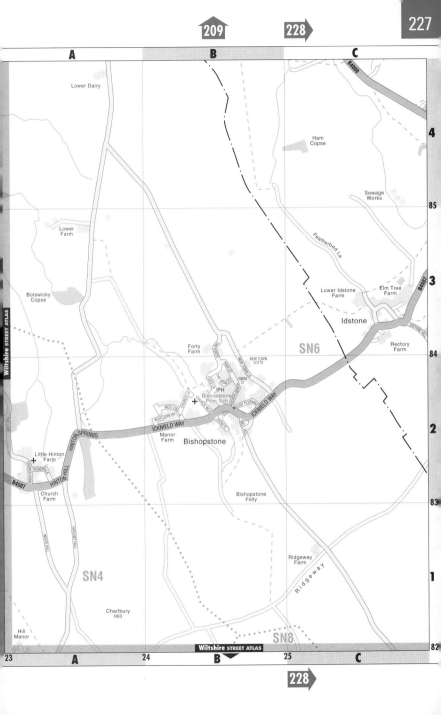

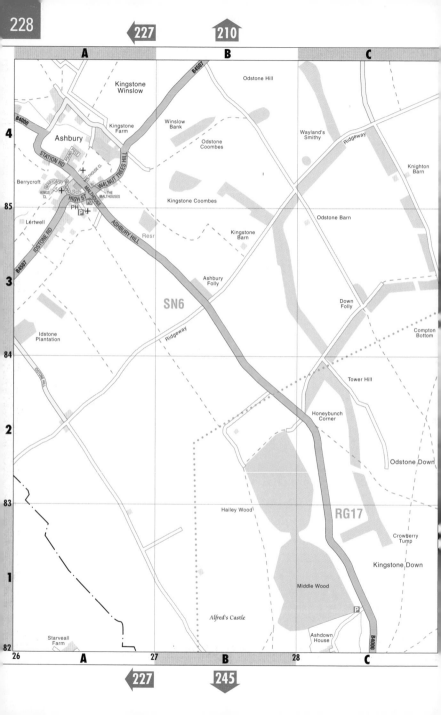

Ridgeway

SN7

Uffington Down

Long Plantaion

Woolstone Hill Barn

SN6

4

Pingoose Covert

85

Kingston Warren

Idlebush Barrow

OX12

Gallops

Kingston Warren Down

Gallops

3

Gallops

Woolstone Down

84

Compton Close

nighton Down

Gallops

2

Whit Coombe

Wellbottom Down

83

Gallops

Knighton Bushes Plantation

RG17

Lambourn Valley Way

Baldback Covert

1

Post Down

Parkfarm Down

Maddle Farm

Gallops

Postdown Border

Weathercock Hill

82

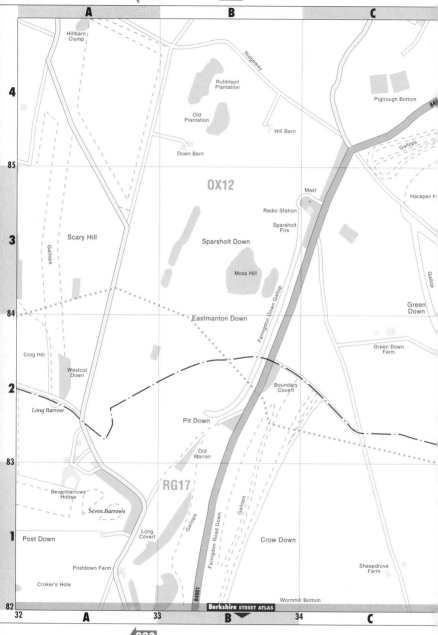

A
B
C

Sincombe Farm

B4001

B4001

Field Barn

Hackpen Hill

Gallop

Devil's Punchbowl

Letcombe Bassett Field

College Farm

Letcombe Brook

BASSETT RD

4

Gallop

MRS. LA.

BEECH LA.

HOLBORN HILL

Letcombe Bassett

The Yew Tree (PH)

Rectory Farm

85

Crowhole Bottom

Ppg Sta

Warren Farm East

Childrey Warren

Warren Farm West

Round Hill

Pitchpole

GRAMP'S HILL

BAYLIE'S LA.

3

Gallop

Folly Clump

Ridgeway

Smith's Hill Farm

Warren Down

OX12

Parsonage Hill

84

Greendown Farm

Gallop

Parsonagehill Barn

Rats Hill

Gallop

Flint Farm

2

Cockleberry Farm

83

Stancombe Hatts

North Plantation

Oxfordshire Circular Walks

RG17

1

Stancombe Farm

Lang Down

Nutwood Down

Poacher's Folly

Old Warren Wood

Stancombe Down

Nut Wood

82

35
A
36
B
37
C

231
214
231

A B C

4

85

3

84

2

83

1

82

38 39 40

Spike Lodge Farm
Field Barn
The Downs
Furzewick Farm
Wantage Down
The Ridgeway (YH)
Furzewick Down
Gallops
Pewit Farm
Black Bushes Barn
THE RIDGEWAY
Whitehouse Farm
Warborough Farm
Warborough Bottom
Castle Hill
Ridgeway
Segsbury Down
Segsbury Farm
Angeldown Farm
Angeldown Cottages
Upper Black Bushes
New Warren
Greenhill Down
OX12
Ashen Pen
Lattindown Farm
Black Bushes
Corpse Copse
Little Hall
Letcombe Bowers Farm
Pinal Wood
Bowers Wood
The Wilderness
Sparrow's Copse
South Plantation
Winterdown Bottom
Gallop
The Beeches

Gallop
COURT HILL RD
WARBOROUGH RD
MANOR RD
A338
B4494 CHAIN HILL RD

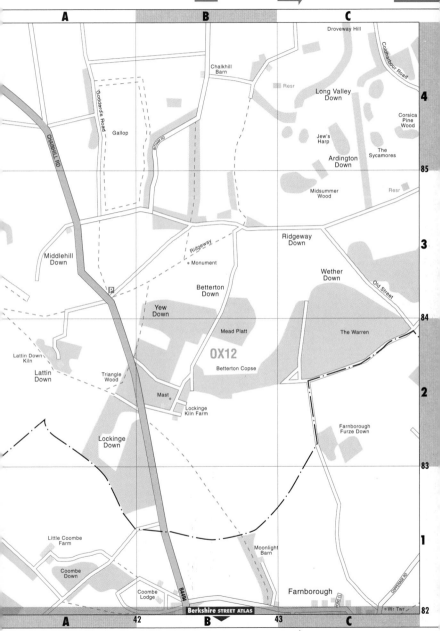

A B C

Droveway Hill

Coldharbour Road

Chalkhill Barn

Resr

Long Valley Down

4

Gurderds Road

Gallop

WITHAM RD

Corsica Pine Wood

Jew's Harp

The Sycamores

CHAINHILL RD

Ardington Down

85

Midsummer Wood

Resr

Middlehill Down

Ridgeway

Ridgeway Down

3

Monument

Wether Down

Old Street

Betterton Down

Yew Down

84

Mead Platt

The Warren

Lattin Down Kiln

OX12

Lattin Down

Betterton Copse

Triangle Wood

Mast

Lockinge Kiln Farm

2

Farnborough Furze Down

Lockinge Down

83

Little Coombe Farm

1

Moonlight Barn

Coombe Down

B4494

Coombe Lodge

Farnborough

COPPANS RD

Wr Twr

A B C

42 43 82

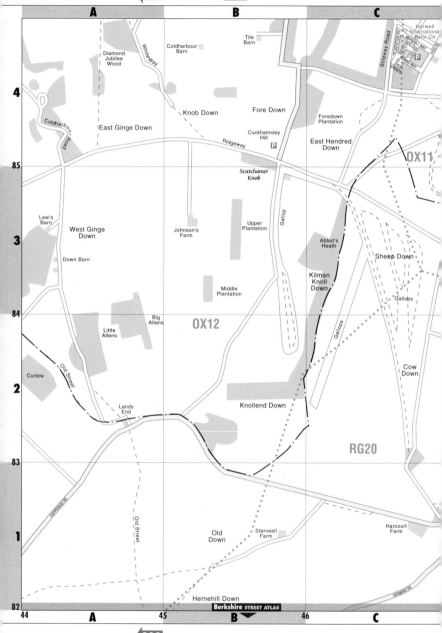

A B C

Harwell International Bsns Ctr

Stileway Road

Diamond Jubilee Wood

Whiteway

Coldharbour Barn

Tile Barn

4

Coldharbour Road

Knob Down

Fore Down

Foredown Plantation

East Ginge Down

Ridgeway

Cuckhamsley Hill

East Hendred Down

OX11

85

Scutchamer Knob

Lew's Barn

West Ginge Down

Johnson's Farm

Upper Plantation

Gallop

Abbot's Heath

Sheep Down

3

Down Barn

Kilman Knoll Down

Middle Plantation

Gallops

84

Big Allens

OX12

Gallops

Little Allens

Cow Down

Curlew

Old Street

2

Lands End

Knollend Down

RG20

83

Old Street

Copperage Rd

Old Down

Starveall Farm

Harcourt Farm

1

Old Street

Catmore Rd

Hernehill Down

82

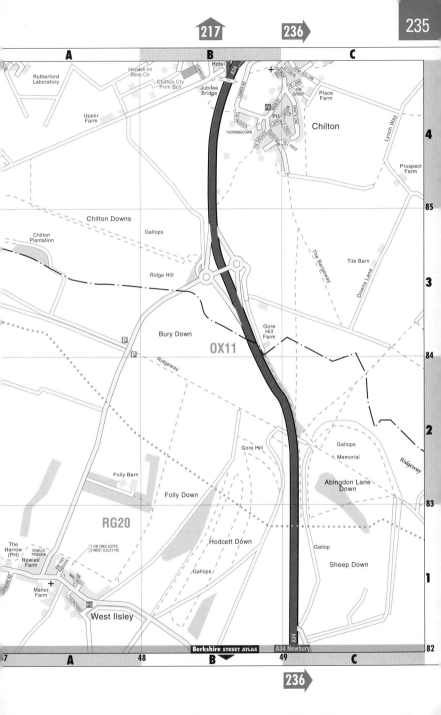

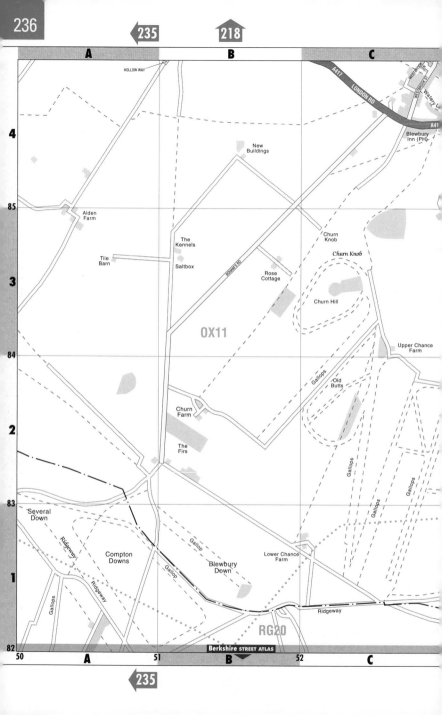

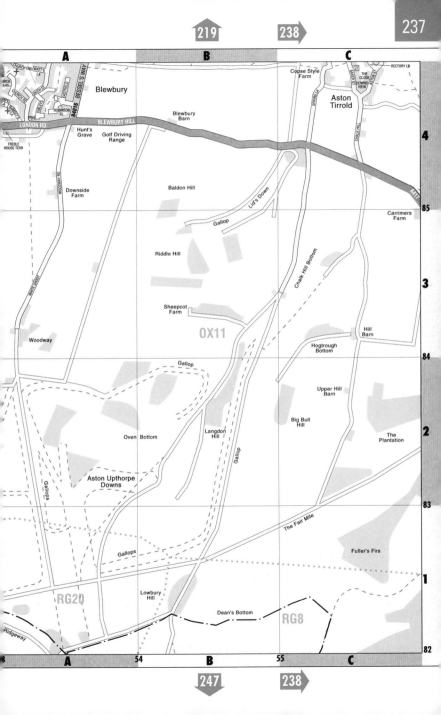

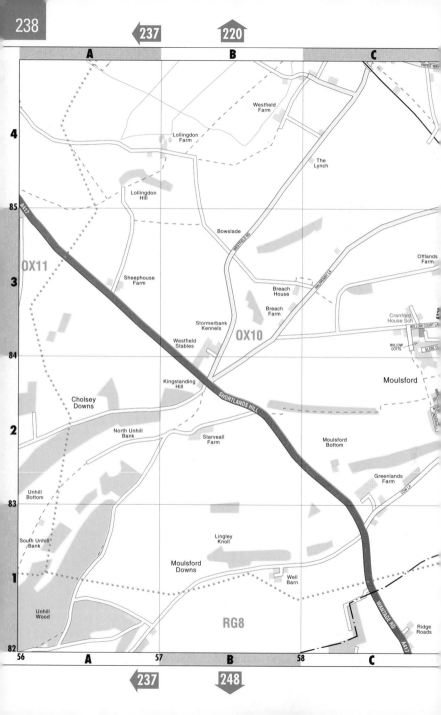

239
222

A B C

WHITE HOUSE RD
White House (PH)
The Cottage
PORT WAY
Stone Farm
PH
Hill Farm
Hailey
Meml
Cross Farm
CROSS CROSSER
WR CE
Larkstoke Stud
Swan's Way
Ipsden Farm
THE STREET
Ipsden
PO
NEWTOWN
Warren Hill
Warren Hill Farm
Zoo
Wellplace Farm
Wellplace
4

85
Ipsden House
Warrens Chase

OX10
Knapps Wichelo
GARSONS LA
Garsons Hill

3
Swan's Way
Kaffirs
Braziers Park
BRAZIERS LA
Braziers Cottages

Icknield Farm
84
Ouseley Barn
Ouseley Barn Cottages
Itchen Wood
The Bottom Farm House
Itchens Farm

2
Mile End Hill
RED LA
Hammond's Wood

Catsbrain Hill
83
Dean Farm
Woodcote Fruit Farm

SOUTH END RD
RG8
Upper Cadley's
Dean Wood
Langtree House
B471 RED LA
Massey's Pightle
A4074

1
Broad Street Farm
James Farm
Church Farm
Woodcote Cty Prim Sch
TIDMORE LA
GREENMOR
Langtree Sch

Lycroft's Shaw
BEECH LA
High Wood
Woodcote
PH
P
GORING RD
Liby
READING RD
B471
Beech Farm
82

62 A 63 B 64 C

A B C

4

85

3

84

2

83

1

82

68 A 69 B 70 C

Kate's Copse

Howberrywood Farm

Devil's Hill

Deadman's Lane

B481

Oxlands Bottom

Upper Shaw

Swan Wood

Highmoor Trench

English Lane

Oakingham Bottom

Newnham Hill

Nott Wood

Hall Farm

Highmoor Common Wood

Merrimoles

Highmoor

Newnhamhill Farm

Lower Highmoor

Stokerow Farm

Bush Wood

Little Farm

Highmoor Farm

The Dog & Duck (PH)

Holly Grove

The Crooked Billet (PH)

Church Farm

CHERRY TREE CL

NEWLAN

Highmoor Cross

Scotland

PO

ALMA GN

Witheridge Hill

Rising Sun (PH)

Stonehouse Farm

Vanalloys Bsns Pk

RG9

Padnell's Wood

Orchard Copse

Busgrove Wood

Clayhill Wood

Bear Wood

Satwell House Farm

Satwell

PH

Stag Hall

Greyhone Wood

Oveys Wood

Burnt Platt

Greyhone Plantation

RG4

Neal's Shaw

NEAL'S LA

Coldmoor Wood

Kibes

B481

Neal's Farm

Barn Farm

Great David's

Greatbottom Wood

Neal's Wood

ASHCROFT WY

WYFOLD CT

LIME AVE

The Grouse & Claret (PH)

Kingwood Common

Kingwood Kennels

Cheriton House

Hazel Grove

Littlebottom Wood

RG4

A B C

4

81

RG17

SN6

Starveall
Farm

Swinley
Down

Swinley
Copse

Harley
Bushes

Ashdown
Farm

Upper
Wood

Pumping
Station

Whiteshere

B4000

Bishopstone Downs

Idstone
Down

Botley
Bottom

3

Dean
Bottom

Botley
Copse

Russley
Park

THE
MEWS

80

Bailey
Hill

Goor Lane
Farm

SN8

Bailey Hill
Copse

2

Peaks Down

Hazelbury
Farm

GOOR LA

M4

79

Peaks
Wood

Bailey Hill
Farm

1

Gallop

THE
FINCHES

Baydon

THE
GREEN

Westfield
Farm

East Leaze
Farm

St Nicholas
CE Prim Sch

DOWNSMEAD

BAYDON RD

PO

FINCHES LA

Finche's
Farm

M4 Newbury

A 27 B 28 C

6 78

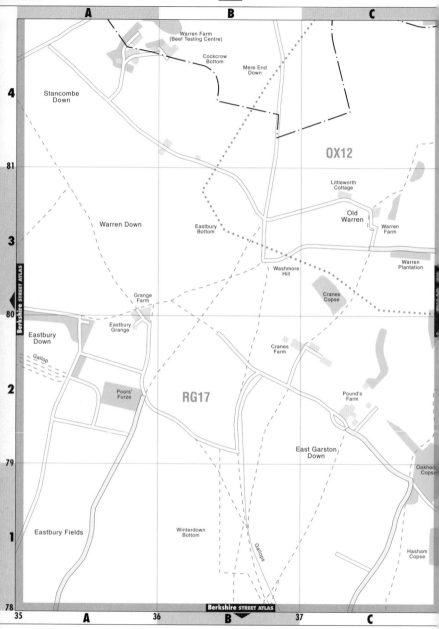

Warren Farm
(Beef Testing Centre)

Cockcrow
Bottom

Mere End
Down

Stancombe
Down

OX12

Littleworth
Cottage

Warren Down

Old
Warren

Warren
Farm

Eastbury
Bottom

Washmore
Hill

Warren
Plantation

Cranes
Copse

Grange
Farm

Eastbury
Down

Eastbury
Grange

Gallop

Cranes
Farm

Poors'
Furze

RG17

Pound's
Farm

East Garston
Down

Oakhed
Copse

Eastbury Fields

Winterdown
Bottom

Gallops

Hasham
Copse

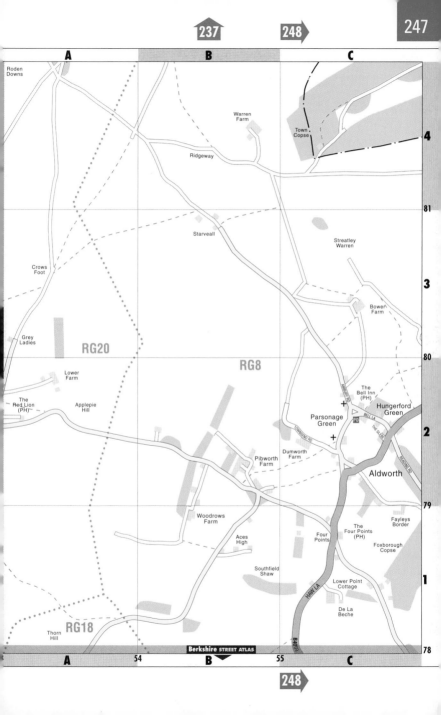

A **B** **C**

Roden
Downs

Warren
Farm

Town
Copse

Ridgeway

4

81

Starveall

Streatley
Warren

Crows
Foot

3

Bower
Farm

Grey
Ladies

RG20

RG8

80

Lower
Farm

The Bell Inn
(PH)

The
Red Lion
(PH)

Applepie
Hill

MARSH RD

BELL LA

Hungerford
Green

Parsonage
Green

THE GREEN

2

Pibworth
Farm

Dumworth
Farm

Aldworth

BEACHE RD

COMMON RD

Woodrows
Farm

Fayleys
Border

79

Four
Points

The
Four Points
(PH)

Aces
High

Foxborough
Copse

Southfield
Shaw

Lower Point
Cottage

1

HAW LA

De La
Beche

RG18

Thorn
Hill

B4009

78

A 54 **B** 55 **C**

A   B   C

Cow Common

Ham Wood

Thurle Down

Thurle Grange

4

Ridgeway
RECTORY RD

CH

Warren Farm

Lough Down

81

Stonefield Shaw

Lardon Chase

THE BULL M...

STREATLEY HILL B40...

P

Streatley CE Sch
HILL

THE LODGE

3

Kiddington Cottage

Common Wood

Westridge Copse

80

Westridge Barn

Westridge Green

RG8

As... Cops...

B4009

Lewingdon Wood

Mutton Copse

Westridge Manor Farm

2

Gould's Cottage

Bottom Barn

Wood Farm

Stitchens Green

Bennet's Woo... Farm

College Wood

Costrills Copse

79

Portobello Wood

Beechcroft Shaw

Benn... Wo...

READING RD

Southridge Pightle

Southridge Farm

Manor Farm

1

Pyghtle Cottage

Norcot Wood

Blackwood Cottages

Long Copse

Burnett's Copse

Black Wood

Growcroft Copse

Tombhill Shaw

78

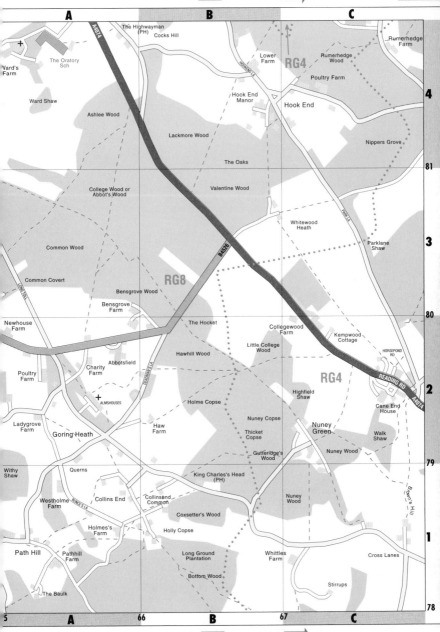

The Highwayman (PH)
Cocks Hill
Vard's Farm
The Oratory Sch
Ward Shaw
Ashlee Wood
Lackmore Wood
Lower Farm
RG4
Rumerhedge Farm
Rumerhedge Wood
Poultry Farm
Hook End Manor
Hook End
The Oaks
Nippers Grove
4

81
College Wood or Abbot's Wood
Valentine Wood
Whitewood Heath
Parklane Shaw
Common Wood
Common Covert
Bensgrove Wood
Bensgrove Farm
RG8
The Hocket
Collegewood Farm
Kempwood Cottage
3

80
Newhouse Farm
Abbotsfield
Charity Farm
ALMSHOUSES
Hawhill Wood
Little College Wood
Holme Copse
HORSEPOND RD
READING RD
RG4
Cane End House
Poultry Farm
Highfield Shaw
2

Ladygrove Farm
Goring Heath
Haw Farm
Nuney Copse
Thicket Copse
Nuney Green
Walk Shaw
Nuney Wood
79
Withy Shaw
Querns
King Charles's Head (PH)
Gutteridge's Wood
Nuney Wood
Brown's Hill
Westholme Farm
Collins End
Collinsend Common
Coxsetter's Wood
Holmes's Farm
Holly Copse
1
Path Hill
Pathhill Farm
Long Ground Plantation
Whittles Farm
Cross Lanes
The Baulk
Bottom Wood
Stirrups
78

A   B   C

4

Park
Farm

WYFOLD LA

Manor
Farm

COLLIERS LA

Peppard
Hill

CHURCH LA

RG9

Peppard
Hill
Peppard
Common

PEPPARD HILL

SPRINGWOOD LA

Wyfold
Grange

CHILTERN RD

HAZELMOOR RD

CHILTERN
BANK

Shiplake
Bottom

81

Wyfold
Wood

New Copse

Bishopswood
Sch

Sonning
Common

3

Withy
Copse

Common
Farm

WOODSIDE LA

THE CHARLET

HEARNS LA

Gallowstree
Common

Bishopswood
Farm

Sonning
Common
Prim Sch

Lib

COUNCIL
COTTS

The Crown &
Anchor
(PH)

READS LA

RG4

80

HOREPOND RD

Coldnorton
Shaw

Coldnorton
Wood

HAZELMOOR LA

Chiltern Edge
Com Sch

2

Cane End
Farm

WOOD LA

Oakridge
Farm

GALLOWSLEADE

Holly Tree
Farm

Kidmore End
CE Prim Sch

KENMORE LA

Vines
Farm

READING RD A4074

79

Madge Gray's
Wood

Highland
Wood

Kidmore
End

Curtis
Farm

PH

Cemy

Stocking
Shaw

CHALKHOUSE GREEN RD

Green Dean
Wood

Tankers Table
Farm

MILL LA

Cross
Farm

Kidmore
House

1

Hodmore
Farm

GREEN DEAN HILL

Bardolph's
Wood

Dyson's
Wood

Dysons Wood Lane

CHALKHOUSE
GREEN LA

Hodmore Farm
Cottage

Tinker's
Green

The Pack Horse
(PH)

A4074

78

A   68   69   B   70   C

A321 Henley-on-Thames

Mill Bank

WARGRAVE RD
MILL LA

P

Happy Valley

Temple Coombe Farm

Temple Coombe

Hatch Gate House

White Cottages

Cockpole Green

Kenton's Corner Cottage

The Old Hatch Gate (PH)

GOULDERS COTTS

WARREN ROW RD

The Druids Temple
Passage Grave

Thames Path

Hatchgate Farm

Worley's Farm

Crazies Hill CE Prim Sch

Sheephouse Farm

PO

81

Lower Bolney Farm

Penny's Lane

Hennerton House

Fairman's Wood

Crazies Hill

Bolney Court

Hennerton Backwater

CH

Maple Croft

Highfield

3

Kilnpits

RG9

River Thames

Wargrave Marsh

Gibstroude Farm

80

BOLNEY LA

BOLNEY RD

Lower Rivermead Farm

RG10

Berkshire STREET ATLAS

MANOR GROVE GATE
NURSERY
BRAMPTON CHASE
PH
LC
BASMORE LA

Shiplake

WILLOW LA

The Woodclyffes

A4155

STATION RD

OAKS RD

Lower Shiplake

THE CHESTNUTS

BADGERS WLK

Lashbrook

Towing Path

Wargrave Manor

BLAKES RD

2

BASKERVILLE LA

Lashbrook House

HIGHFIELD

HANOVER

79

White Gables

MILL LA

THE
WALLED
GDN

HILL LANDS

THE
WLK

VICTORIA RD

PO

Upper Wargrave

Lash Brook

Phillimore's Island

Thames Path

Borough Lake

STATION RD

River Loddon

Wargrave

PO
P
Liby
CHURCH ST
PH

B477
HIGH ST

SCHOOL LA

SCHOOL HILL

EMMA LA

SILVERDALE RD

Robert Piggott CE Inf Sch

1

Robert Piggott CE Jun Sch

Wargrave

A321

A321 Twyford

Berkshire STREET ATLAS

MUMBERY HILL

B477

78

A
78
B
79
C
77

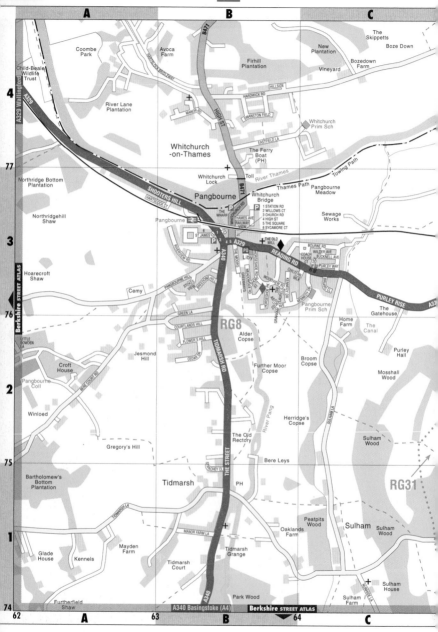

A B C

4

77

3

RG4

76

2

75

1

74

Greendean
Farm

Newell's
Copse

Currs
Copse

Trench Green

Pithouse Farm

BARDOLPH'S CL
ROKEBY DR

HARRIES VIEW
DYSONSWOOD LA

MULLENS
TERR

Tokers
Green

Dysons Wood
Farm

Chazey
Heath

CH

RUSSELL RD

Tanners
Lane
Farm

Newell's Lane

CH

Page's
Shaw

Pack Saddle
Inn
(PH)

BEECH RD

ELM RD

Tokers Green
Farm

Fox Hill
Farm

Middle
Farm

Pond Lane

Noke End
Shaw

Jacksons Lane

Farthingworth
Green

Shipnell's
Cottages

Rose Farm

Sandy Hill

SHEPHERDS LA

SILVERTHORNE DR

CARLTON RD

HILLTOP RD

GROVE FARM LA

CONISBOROUGH
WAY

MORECAMBE
AVE

BAMBURGH
CL

PINEWOOD
DR

Hemdean
Bottom

Grain Store

King's Hill

Chazey Wood

UPPER
WOODCOTE
RD

RICHMOND RD

WOODCOTE
RD

ST ANDREW'S RD

OAKLEY RD

Gravel Hill

CHAZEY RD

UPPER WARREN AVE

HARRAGE RD

HIGHMOOR RD

Caversham
Heights

The Warren

MAX
LENE

HALL
CL

THE WARREN

ST PETER'S HILL

Chazey Court
Farm

The
Chase

The Fishery

St Mary's
Island

River Thames

LAURENCE ALLISON
MEWS

WARREN
HOUSE CT

CLIFTON
PARK RD

WOODBURN
CT

A4074

Poplar Island

Appletree
Eyot

Upper
Large

Thames Path

Coombe
Bank

Thames Side Promenade

Rivermead
L Ctr

P

A329

OXFORD ROAD

STADIUM WAY

RG30

PANGBOURNE ST 1
LEDBURY CL 2
BRIDGEWATER CL 3
WESTBROOK RD 4
GORDON PL 5
BROUGHTON CL 6

WIGMORE LA

Little John's
Farm

THE PORTMAN
CTR

Reading West
Junction

RICHFIELD AVE

RG1

Wks

A329 Reading

Berkshire STREET ATLAS

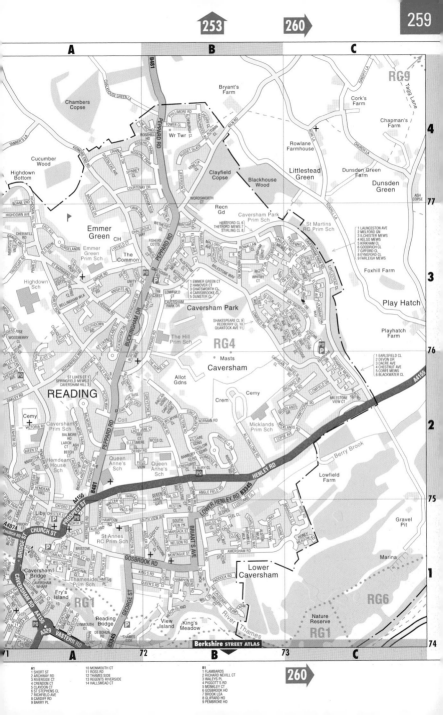

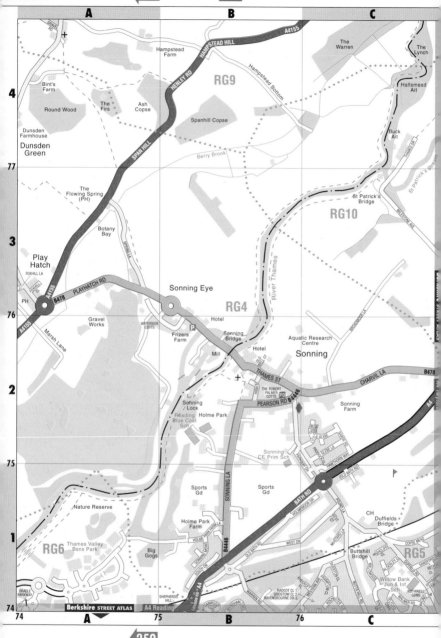

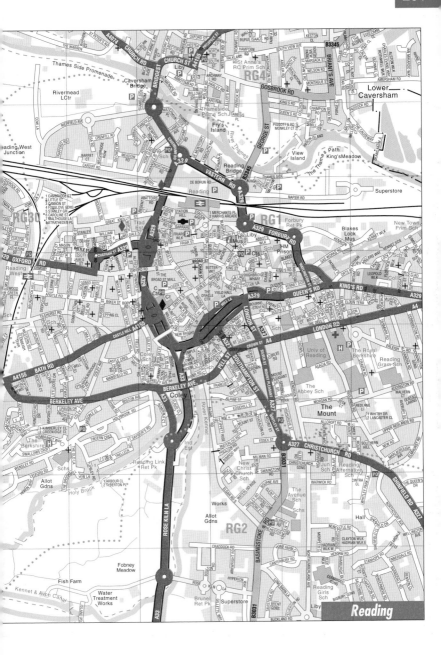

Reading

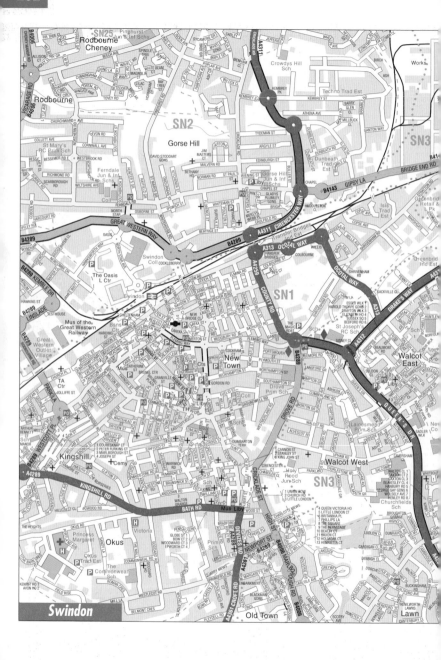

Swindon

Index

Church Rd 6 Beckenham BR2.........53 C6

Place name	**Location number**	**Locality, town or village**	**Postcode district**	**Page and grid square**
May be abbreviated on the map	Present when a number indicates the place's position in a crowded area of mapping	Shown when more than one place has the same name	District for the indexed place	Page number and grid reference for the standard mapping

Public and commercial buildings are highlighted in magenta. Places of interest are highlighted in blue with a star★

Abbreviations used in the index

Acad	Academy	Comm	Common	Gd	Ground	L	Leisure	Prom	Prom
App	Approach	Cott	Cottage	Gdn	Garden	La	Lane	Rd	Road
Arc	Arcade	Cres	Crescent	Gn	Green	Liby	Library	Recn	Recreation
Ave	Avenue	Cswy	Causeway	Gr	Grove	Mdw	Meadow	Ret	Retail
Bglw	Bungalow	Ct	Court	H	Hall	Meml	Memorial	Sh	Shopping
Bldg	Building	Ctr	Centre	Ho	House	Mkt	Market	Sq	Square
Bsns, Bus	Business	Ctry	Country	Hospl	Hospital	Mus	Museum	St	Street
Bvd	Boulevard	Cty	County	HQ	Headquarters	Orch	Orchard	Sta	Station
Cath	Cathedral	Dr	Drive	Hts	Heights	Pal	Palace	Terr	Terrace
Cir	Circus	Dro	Drove	Ind	Industrial	Par	Parade	TH	Town Hall
Cl	Close	Ed	Education	Inst	Institute	Pas	Passage	Univ	University
Cnr	Corner	Emb	Embankment	Int	International	Pk	Park	Wk, Wlk	Walk
Coll	College	Est	Estate	Intc	Interchange	Pl	Place	Wr	Water
Com	Community	Ex	Exhibition	Junc	Junction	Prec	Precinct	Yd	Yard

Index of localities, towns and villages

Abingdon 179 C4
Adderbury 23 A2
Adlestrop 40 B1
Aldworth 247 C2
Alvescot 133 B3
Ambrosden 81 B2
Appleford 200 C4
Appleton 158 A4
Ardington 215 C3
Ardley 50 B2
Ascott-under-Wychwood 71 B1
Ashbury 228 A4
Aston 135 C2
Aston Tirrold 237 C4
Avon Bassett 2 C4
Aynho 35 B4
Bampton 134 C2
Banbury 16 C3
Barford St Michael 32 C3
Barton-on-the-Heath ...26 C3
Baydon 245 C1
Beacon's Bottom ...189 B2
Beckley 111 A2
Begbroke 108 A4
Benson 204 A2
Berinsfield 182 B3
Berrick Salome ...184 A1
Bicester 65 B2
Bishopstone 227 B2
Bix 243 B4
Black Bourton ...133 C3
Blackthorn 82 A3
Bladon 91 B1
Bledington 54 B1
Bledlow 169 A4
Bledlow Ridge ...189 C4
Bletchingdon 93 A4
Blewbury 237 A4
Bloxham 21 B3
Bodicote 22 B4
Bourton 209 A2
Brackley 24 A4
Brightwell-cum-Sotwell 202 B1
Brill 98 A1
Britwell Salome ...205 C4
Brize Norton ...116 B2
Broughton 15 B1
Buckland 154 C1
Bucknell 65 A4
Burford 100 B3
Buscot 171 A4
Carterton 115 C2
Cassington 107 B1
Chacombe 10 C2
Chadlington 57 A1
Chalgrove 184 C3
Charlbury 73 B2
Charlton-on-Otmoor ...95 A2
Charney Bassett ...176 A1
Chastleton 40 B4
Checkendon 241 B2
Chesterton 79 C4
Childrey 213 B2

Chilson 71 C2
Chilton 235 C4
Chinnor 168 B4
Chipping Norton ...42 C1
Chipping Warden ...5 C3
Cholsey 221 A1
Church Westcote ...68 B3
Churchill 55 C3
Clanfield 152 C4
Claydon 1 B1
Clifton Hampden ...181 B2
Cockpole Green ...255 C4
Coleshill 191 A4
Combe 90 A3
Compton Wynyates ...12 B4
Cottisford 37 C2
Crawley 133 C2
Cropredy 4 C1
Croughton 36 B4
Crowmarsh Gifford ...221 C4
Cuddesdon 144 A2
Culham 180 A1
Cumnor 139 B3
Curbridge 117 B3
Cutteslowe 109 A1
Cuxham 185 B2
Deddington 33 C2
Denchworth 196 A2
Didcot 200 B2
Dorchester 182 B1
Drayton 179 A1
Drayton (Banbury) ...15 B4
Drayton St Leonard ...183 A3
Ducklington 118 A2
Duns Tew 47 B3
East Challow 214 A3
East Hagbourne ...218 C3
East Hanney 197 A3
East Hendred 216 C4
Eastleach Martin ...131 A4
Enstone 58 C3
Epwell 13 A3
Ewelme 204 C2
Eynsham 120 C4
Faringdon 172 C2
Farnborough (Berks) ...233 C1
Farnborough (Warks) ...3 C4
Fawley 226 B1
Fernham 193 A2
Fifield 69 B1
Filkins 132 B3
Finmere 39 B4
Finstock 88 B3
Forest Hill 125 C2
Freeland 106 A4
Fringford 52 B3
Fritwell 49 C4
Fulbrook 100 C4
Fyfield 157 B1
Garford 177 B3
Garsington 143 C1
Goring 249 B3
Great Bourton 9 B4
Great Coxwell ...192 B4

Great Haseley ...164 C4
Great Milton 145 A4
Great Rissington ...83 A4
Great Rollright ...29 A2
Great Tew 45 B4
Grove 196 C1
Haddenham 130 C3
Hailey 104 A3
Hampton Poyle ...93 A2
Hanwell 8 C2
Hardwick 51 B4
Harwell 217 C4
Henley-on-Thames ...244 A1
Hethe 52 A4
Highworth 190 A3
Hinton Waldrist 155 C2
Holton 126 B1
Hook Norton 30 A4
Horley 8 A2
Hornton 7 B4
Horspath 143 B3
Horton-cum-Studley ...112 A3
Ickford 128 A2
Idbury 69 A2
Ipsden 240 B4
Islip 109 C4
Kelmscott 151 B2
Kencot 132 C3
Kennington 160 C4
Kidlington 108 B4
Kidmore End 252 B2
Kingham 55 A2
Kings Sutton 23 C3
Kingston Bagpuize ...156 C1
Kingston Lisle 212 A2
Kirtlington 77 C2
Langford 132 B1
Launton 66 B1
Leafield 86 C2
Lechlade 150 B2
Letcombe Bassett ...231 C4
Lewknor 187 A4
Little Compton 26 C1
Little Coxwell 192 C4
Little Milton 164 A3
Little Tew 45 A3
Long Compton 27 C3
Long Crendon ...129 A3
Long Hanborough ...90 B1
Long Wittenham ...201 B4
Longcot 192 B1
Longworth 156 B2
Lower Basildon ...249 C1
Lower Heyford 62 B3
Lower Odington 54 A4
Ludgershall 98 B4
Lyneham 70 C3
Mapledurham ...257 C3
Marcham 178 B3
Marsh Gibbon 67 C2
Marston 123 C3
Merton 95 B4
Middle Barton 60 C4
Middleton Cheney ...11 A1

Middleton Stoney 64 A2
Milcombe 21 A1
Milton 199 B3
Milton (Banbury) ...22 B2
Milton Common ...146 A2
Milton-under-Wychwood 70 B1
Minster Lovell 102 C1
Mixbury 38 B4
Mollington 4 A2
Moulsford 238 C2
Murcott 95 C2
Nettlebed 224 B1
North Aston 48 A3
North Hinksey Village ...140 C4
North Leigh 105 A4
North Moreton 221 B4
North Newington ...15 A2
Northend 207 C3
Northmoor 138 B1
Nuneham Courtenay ...161 C2
Oddington 94 C1
Over Norton 42 C3
Oxford 123 C1
Pangbourne 256 B3
Piddington 97 C4
Poundon 67 C4
Purley on Thames ...257 A3
Radley 160 C2
Ramsden 88 A2
Ratley 2 A2
Reading 259 A2
Rotherfield Greys ...243 B1
Rotherfield Peppard ...253 A4
Salford 41 C3
Sandford-on-Thames ...161 A4
Shabbington 128 B2
Shalstone 25 C3
Shellingford 193 C4
Shenington 6 C1
Shepherd's Green ...243 A2
Shilton 115 A3
Shiplake 254 C1
Shipton-on-Cherwell ...92 A3
Shipton-under-Wychwood ...85 C4
Shotteswell 8 B4
Shrivenham 209 A4
Shutford 14 A3
Sibford Ferris 19 A4
Sibford Gower 19 A4
Somerton 48 C3
Sonning 260 C2
Sonning Common ...252 C3
Souldern 35 C2
South Hinksey 141 B3
South Leigh 119 B3
South Moreton 219 C3
South Newington ...31 C4
South Stoke 239 B2
Southend 226 B4
Southrop 131 A2
Sparsholt 212 C2
Spelsbury 72 C4
Stadhampton 163 B1

Standlake 137 B2
Stanford in the Vale ...194 C4
Stanton Harcourt ...138 A4
Stanton St John ...125 C4
Steeple Aston 62 A4
Steventon 198 C2
Stoke Lyne 51 A3
Stoke Row 241 C2
Stoke Talmage ...165 C2
Stokenchurch ...188 C3
Stonesfield 89 B4
Stonor 225 C3
Stratton Audley 52 B1
Streatley 249 A4
Sunningwell 159 C3
Sutton Courtenay ...200 A4
Swalcliffe 19 C4
Swerford 30 C2
Swinbrook 101 C3
Sydenham 167 B4
Tackley 77 B3
Tadmarton 20 B4
Tetsworth 166 A4
Thame 148 A4
Tiddington 145 C4
Tidmarsh 256 B1
Towersey 148 C4
Turweston 24 B4
Uffington 211 B4
Upper Arncott 96 C4
Upper Heyford 62 C4
Upper Inglesham ...170 A3
Upper Rissington ...68 B2
Upton 218 B1
Wallingford 221 B3
Wantage 214 C2
Warborough 203 A4
Wardington 5 C1
Wargrave 255 B1
Warmington 3 A2
Watchfield 191 C1
Waterperry 127 A1
Watlington 186 B1
Wendlebury 80 A2
West Hagbourne ...218 B2
West Hanney 196 C3
West Ilsley 235 A1
Westbury 25 A2
Weston-on-the-Green ...79 A1
Wheatley 144 A4
Whichford 18 A1
Whitchurch-on-Thames 256 B4
Wigginton 31 A4
Witney 118 B4
Woodcote 250 C4
Woodstock 91 A3
Woolstone 211 A2
Wootton 75 C3
Wootton (Oxford) ...159 A4
Worminghall 127 C3
Wroxton 15 A4
Wytham 122 A3
Yarnton 108 A3

A

A P Ellis Rd GL54 ......68 A2
Abberbury Ave OX4 ......142 A2
Abberbury Rd OX4 ......141 C2
Abbey Brook OX11 ......200 C2
Abbey Cl OX14 ......179 C4
Abbey Ctr OX14 ......180 A4
Abbey Pl Eynsham OX29 ......120 C4
  Oxford OX1 ......141 A4
Abbey Rd Banbury OX16 ......16 A4
  Oxford OX2 ......123 A1
  Watchfield SN6 ......191 C1
  Witney OX28 ......117 C4
Abbey St OX29 ......120 C4
Abbey Wlk OX1 ......123 A1
Abbey Woods Cl OX10 ......182 B3
Abbot Ridge HP18 ......129 B3
Abbot Wlk HP18 ......129 B3
Abbots Cl RG8 ......250 C4
Abbots Wlk GL7 ......150 B2
Abbots Wood E OX3 ......142 C4
Abbots Wood W OX3 ......142 C4
Abbotsmead Pl RG4 ......259 A1
Abbott Cl OX11 ......218 C4
Abbott Rd
  Abingdon OX14 ......179 C4
  Didcot OX11 ......218 C4
Aberaman RG4 ......258 C1
Abingdon & Witney Coll
  Witney Campus OX28 ......118 A4
Abingdon Bsns Pk OX14 ......179 B4
Abingdon Ct OX29 ......129 C1
Abingdon Coll OX14 ......159 C1
Abingdon Dr RG4 ......259 B3
Abingdon Hospl OX14 ......179 C2
Abingdon La OX29 ......117 A2
Abingdon Mus* OX14 ......179 C4
Abingdon Rd
  Carterton OX18 ......115 C2
  Clifton Hampden OX14 ......181 B2
  Culham OX14 ......180 B2
  Cumnor OX2 ......139 C2
  Didcot OX11 ......201 A1
  Dorchester OX10 ......182 B2
  Drayton OX14 ......179 A1
  Kennington OX1 ......141 B2
  Oxford OX1 ......141 B3
  Standlake OX29 ......137 B2
  Steventon OX13 ......199 A3
  Sutton Courtenay OX14 ......180 A1
Abingdon Sch OX14 ......179 C4
Ablett Cl OX4 ......142 A4
Abotts Mead OX10 ......239 A4
Abrahams Rd RG9 ......244 B2
Acacia RG9 ......244 B1
Acacia Cl OX18 ......115 C1
Acacia Gdns OX13 ......156 C1
Acacia Wlk Banbury OX16 ......9 A1
  Bicester OX26 ......65 C3
Acer Cl OX18 ......114 B4
Ackerman Rd OX7 ......42 C2
Acland Cl OX3 ......124 B1
Acland Hospl The OX2 ......123 B2
Acorn Cl OX26 ......65 C3
Acorn Way OX16 ......9 C1
Acre Cl OX3 ......142 C4
Acre Ditch OX15 ......19 A4
Acre End St OX29 ......120 C4
Acremead Rd OX33 ......143 C4
Adam Ct RG9 ......244 C1
Adderbury Ct OX17 ......23 A2
Adderbury Pk OX17 ......22 C2
Adderbury Chase
  RG31 ......257 A2
Addison Cres OX4 ......141 C3
Addison Dr OX4 ......142 B2
Addison Rd Banbury OX16 ......16 B2
  Reading RG1 ......259 A1
Adeane Rd OX44 ......184 B4
Adelaide St OX2 ......123 A2
Adkin Way OX12 ......214 B3
Adwell Sq RG9 ......244 B1
Akeman Ave OX25 ......81 B2
Akeman Cl OX5 ......78 A3
Akeman St OX29 ......90 A3
Alan Bullock Cl OX4 ......123 C1
Albermarle Dr OX4 ......214 B4
Albert Rd
  Henley-on-T RG9 ......244 C1
  Reading RG4 ......258 C2
Albert St Banbury OX16 ......16 B3
  Oxford OX2 ......123 A1
Albion Pl
  Chipping Norton OX7 ......42 C2
  Oxford OX1 ......141 B2
Albion St OX7 ......42 C2
Albury Cl RG30 ......258 B1
Albury View OX9 ......146 A3
Alchester Rd OX26 ......66 A1
Alchester Terr OX26 ......65 C1
Aldbarton Dr OX3 ......124 C2
Aldbourne Cl OX26 ......65 B1
Aldeburgh Cl RG4 ......259 B4
Alden Cres OX3 ......124 C2
Aldenham Cl RG4 ......259 B3
Alder Dr OX25 ......81 B2
Aldergate Rd OX26 ......65 B1
Alderley Cl
  Carterton OX18 ......115 B1
  Sonning RG5 ......260 C1
Aldrich Rd OX2 ......123 A4

Aldridge Cl OX10 ......204 A2
Aldsworth Ct OX28 ......117 C4
Aldworth Ave OX12 ......214 C3
Alec Issigonis Way OX4 ......142 B3
Alesworth Gr OX3 ......124 A3
Alexander Cl
  Abingdon OX14 ......160 A2
  Upton OX11 ......218 B1
Alexandra Rd OX2 ......122 C1
Alexandra Sq OX7 ......42 B1
Alfred St Oxford OX1 ......123 B1
  ❸ Wantage OX12 ......214 B2
Alfred Terraces OX7 ......42 C1
Alfredstone Pl OX12 ......214 C2
Alfriston Pl OX16 ......9 A1
Alice Smith Sq OX4 ......142 B1
Alison Clay Ho OX3 ......124 B3
Alister Taylor Ave OX10 ......204 B1
All Hallows Rd RG4 ......259 B2
All Saints CE Prim Sch
  Didcot OX11 ......201 A1
  Sutton Courtenay OX14 ......199 C3
All Saints Cl OX11 ......200 C1
All Saints La OX14 ......180 A1
All Saints Rd OX3 ......124 B1
All Soul's Coll OX1 ......123 B1
Allam St OX2 ......123 A2
Allder Cl OX14 ......159 C1
Allectus Ave OX26 ......81 B2
Allens La OX25 ......48 C1
Allens Orch OX17 ......5 C3
Alley The OX7 ......73 A2
Allin Cl OX4 ......142 A2
Allin's La OX12 ......216 B4
Allison Gdns RG8 ......257 B3
Allison Ho RG9 ......254 C4
Allnatt Ave OX10 ......221 B4
Allnut Cl OX49 ......186 A1
Alma Gn RG9 ......242 A2
Alma Pl OX4 ......141 C4
Almhouses OX28 ......104 B1
Almond Ave OX5 ......108 C3
Almond Dr RG4 ......259 C2
Almond Rd OX26 ......66 A1
Almshouses Bourton SN6 ......209 A1
  Charney Bassett OX12 ......176 B1
  Whitchurch-on-T RG8 ......251 A2
Alpha Ave OX44 ......143 B1
Alphin Brook OX11 ......200 C2
Alston Wlk RG4 ......259 B1
Altus St OX25 ......63 A4
Alvescot Rd OX18 ......115 B1
Alvis Gate OX16 ......15 C4
Ambassador Ave OX44 ......142 C2
Ambassador Ct ❼ OX26 ......65 C1
Amberley Ct OX16 ......9 A1
Ambleside Dr OX3 ......124 A2
Ambrose Rise OX33 ......144 B4
Ambury Rd RG8 ......241 A2
Amersham Rd RG4 ......259 B1
Amey Cres OX13 ......159 A3
Ammanford RG4 ......258 C2
Amory Cl OX4 ......142 B2
Amos Ct OX16 ......16 B3
Ampney Orch OX18 ......134 C2
Amwell Pl OX10 ......220 C1
Amyce Cl OX14 ......160 A1
Ancastle Gr RG9 ......244 B1
Anchome Cl OX14 ......160 A1
Anchor La OX11 ......220 A2
Ancil Ave OX26 ......66 B1
Andersey Way OX14 ......179 C2
Anderson Cl HP14 ......188 C2
Andersons Cl OX5 ......108 B4
Andover Cl Bicester OX26 ......66 A2
  Reading RG1 ......257 B1
Andover Ct OX5 ......108 C4
Andover La OX18 ......115 C1
Andover Rd OX10 ......204 B2
Andrew Rd OX10 ......203 A1
Andrews Ave NN13 ......36 C3
Andromeda Cl OX4 ......142 C1
Anemone Cl OX4 ......161 C4
Angelica Cl OX4 ......142 C1
Angle Field Rd RG4 ......259 A2
Anglesey Ct HP14 ......188 C3
Angus Cl OX16 ......16 A4
Anna Pavlova Cl OX4 ......142 A2
Anne Greenwood Cl
  OX4 ......142 A2
Annesley Cl OX5 ......93 A4
Annesley Rd OX4 ......142 A2
Ansell Way OX7 ......70 A1
Anson Ave OX18 ......115 C1
Anson Cl Marcham OX13 ......178 B3
  Wheatley OX33 ......144 A4
Anson Rd OX10 ......204 B2
Anson Way OX26 ......66 A2
Anthony Hill Rd OX10 ......203 A1
Anvil Cl SN7 ......194 C4
Anvil La OX12 ......214 A1
Anvil Paddock OX12 ......214 A1
Anxey Way HP17 ......130 B3
Apley Way OX18 ......117 C4
Apple Cl RG31 ......257 A2
Appleby Cl OX16 ......15 C4
Appleford Dr OX14 ......160 A1
Appleford Rd OX14 ......180 A1
Appleton CE Prim Sch
  OX13 ......158 A4
Appleton Rd
  Cumnor OX2 ......139 B2
  Longworth OX13 ......156 B2
Appletree Cl
  Sandford-on-T OX4 ......161 C4
  Sonning Common RG4 ......252 C3
Appletree Ind Est OX17 ......5 C4

Appletree Rd OX17 ......5 C3
Approach The OX26 ......65 B2
Apsley Rd OX2 ......123 A4
Arbury Banks OX17 ......1 C3
Arbury Cl OX16 ......16 C1
Arcade The Goring RG8 ......249 B3
  ❶❻ Henley-on-T RG9 ......221 B4
Archery Rd OX17 ......11 A1
Archway Rd ❷ RG4 ......259 A1
Arden Cl OX15 ......15 B4
Ardington La OX12,OX13 ......197 C1
Ardler Rd RG4 ......259 B1
Ardley Rd Ardley OX27 ......50 C1
  Middleton Stoney OX25 ......64 C2
  Somerton OX25 ......48 C3
Argentan Cl OX14 ......179 B2
Argosy Cl OX44 ......184 C3
Argosy Rd Benson OX10 ......204 B2
  Carterton OX18 ......115 C1
Argyle St OX4 ......141 C3
Aristotle La OX2 ......123 A2
Arkel Cl OX18 ......101 A4
Arkell Ave OX18 ......115 B1
Arkwright Rd OX26 ......66 A2
Arlington Cl OX18 ......115 C1
Arlington Dr OX3 ......123 C3
Armour Hill RG31 ......257 B1
Armour Rd RG31 ......257 B1
Armour Wlk
  Purley on T RG31 ......257 B1
  Reading RG31 ......257 B1
Armstrong Rd OX4 ......142 A1
Arncott Rd OX25 ......97 B4
Arncott Wood Rd OX25 ......96 C3
Arndale Beck OX11 ......201 A1
Arnold Rd OX4 ......141 C3
Arnold Way OX9 ......147 C4
Arnold's Way OX2 ......140 B4
Arnott's Yd HP18 ......129 B3
Arran Gr OX16 ......16 C3
Arrow Cl OX17 ......11 A1
Arthray Rd OX2 ......140 B4
Arthur Evans Cl OX13 ......159 A3
Arthur Garrard Cl OX2 ......123 A2
Arthur St OX2 ......123 A1
Arun Mews OX11 ......201 A1
Arundel Cl
  Carterton OX18 ......115 B1
  Kings Sutton OX17 ......23 C3
Arundel Pl OX16 ......15 C3
Ascott Hill OX36 ......18 A3
Ascott Rd OX7 ......85 B4
Ascott-under-Wychwood Sta
  OX7 ......71 B1
Ash Cl Faringdon SN7 ......172 C2
  Kidlington OX5 ......108 C4
  Watlington OX49 ......186 A1
Ash Copse RG4 ......259 C4
Ash Ct RG4 ......259 A2
Ash Gr Chesterton OX26 ......79 C4
  Oxford OX3 ......124 B2
Ash La OX25 ......81 B2
Ashburton La OX15 ......30 A3
Ashbury Hill SN6 ......228 A3
Ashbury with Compton
  Beauchamp CE Prim Sch
  SN6 ......228 A4
Ashby Ct OX14 ......160 B3
Ashby Rd OX26 ......65 B1
Ashcombe Cl OX28 ......118 A4
Ashcroft Cl
  Chadlington OX7 ......57 A1
  N Hinksey Village OX2 ......122 A1
  Reading RG4 ......258 C3
Ashcroft Rd OX16 ......16 B1
Ashdene Rd OX26 ......65 B3
Ashdown Way OX12 ......214 B4
Ashenden Cl OX14 ......159 C1
Ashfield Rd OX16 ......16 B1
Ashfields Cl OX12 ......197 B4
Ashfields La OX12 ......197 B4
Ashford Ave RG4 ......252 C3
Ashgate OX14 ......179 C2
Ashhurst Ct OX33 ......144 C4
Ashlee Wlk RG8 ......250 C4
Ashley Hill Pl RG10 ......255 C4
Ashlong Rd OX3 ......124 A3
Ashmole Pl OX4 ......142 C2
Ashmole Rd OX14 ......179 B1
Ashmolean Mus* OX1 ......123 B1
Ashridge OX39 ......168 A3
Ashridge Cl OX16 ......16 A3
Ashurst Way OX4 ......142 A2
Ashville Way OX4 ......142 C2
Aspen Cl OX26 ......65 C3
Aspen Sq OX4 ......142 C1
Asquith Rd OX4 ......142 A1
Astley Ave OX5 ......108 C3
Astley Rd OX9 ......130 A1

Aston St continued
  Oxford OX4 ......141 C4
Astrop Rd
  Kings Sutton OX17 ......23 C3
  Middleton Cheney OX17 ......17 C3
Atkinson Cl OX3 ......124 C3
Atkyns Rd OX3 ......142 C4
Atwell Cl OX10 ......203 A1
Atwell Pl OX3 ......124 B1
Aubrey Ct OX4 ......142 A2
Auburn Ct RG4 ......259 A1
Audlett Dr OX14 ......180 A4
Austen Wlk OX26 ......65 B1
Austin Dr OX16 ......15 C4
Austin Pl OX14 ......159 C1
Austin Rd OX15 ......22 C4
Austin's Way OX15 ......30 B4
Auton Pl RG9 ......254 C4
Autumn Cl RG4 ......259 B4
Autumn Wlk RG10 ......255 B1
Avenue Four OX28 ......118 A4
Avenue Ho OX4 ......258 B2
Avenue La OX4 ......141 C4
Avenue One OX28 ......118 A3
Avenue Rd Banbury OX16 ......16 C3
  Bourton SN6 ......209 A2
Avenue The Bloxham OX15 ......21 B2
  Chinnor OX39 ......168 B3
  Great Tew OX7 ......45 B4
  Kennington OX1 ......160 C4
  Wheatley OX33 ......144 B4
  Worminghall HP18 ......127 C3
Avenue Three OX28 ......118 A3
Avenue Two OX28 ......118 A3
Avery Ct OX2 ......123 A4
Avocet Way Banbury OX16 ......16 C2
  Bicester OX26 ......81 A4
Avon Carrow OX17 ......3 A4
Avon Cres OX26 ......65 B2
Avon Rd Abingdon OX13 ......159 B1
  Harwell OX11 ......217 B1
Avon Way OX11 ......200 C2
Avonbury Ct NN13 ......24 A3
Avro Rd GL54 ......68 A3
Awgar Stone Rd OX3 ......142 C4
Axis Rd SN6 ......191 C1
Axtell Cl OX5 ......92 B1
Aylesbury & Thame Airport
  HP17 ......130 A3
Aylesbury Rd
  Haddenham HP17,HP18 ......130 B3
  Thame OX9 ......130 B3
Aynho Ct OX17 ......35 B4
Aynho Rd OX17 ......23 B2
Ayrshire Cl OX16 ......9 A1
Ayrsparth Rd OX5 ......108 A3
Azalea Ave OX5 ......108 C3
Azalea Wlk OX16 ......9 A1
Azor's Ct OX4 ......142 A2

B

Bablock Hythe Rd OX13 ......139 A2
Back Hill OX17 ......16 B3
Back La Aston OX18 ......135 B2
  Ducklington OX29 ......118 A2
  Eynsham OX29 ......120 C4
  Long Compton CV36 ......28 A3
  Sibford Ferris OX15 ......19 A4
  Back Row GL56 ......40 B2
Back St OX7 ......166 A4
Backside La OX15 ......19 A4
Backsideans RG10 ......255 B1
Badbury Cl SN7 ......172 C1
Bader Dr OX25 ......63 A4
Badgemore La RG9 ......244 B2
Badgemore Com Sch
  RG9 ......244 B1
Badger Cl OX33 ......125 C2
Badger La OX1 ......141 A2
Badger Way OX16 ......16 C1
Badgers Copse OX14 ......160 C1
Badgers Rise RG4 ......259 A3
Badgers Wlk RG9 ......255 A2
Bagley Cl OX1 ......141 B1
Bagley Wood Rd OX1 ......160 B4
Bailey Cl OX12 ......214 B3
Bailey Rd OX4 ......142 B2
Bailie Cl ❽ OX14 ......179 C1
Bainton Rd Bucknell OX27 ......65 A4
  Hethe OX27 ......51 A4
  Oxford OX2 ......123 A3
Bakehouse La OX17 ......8 B4
Baker Ave OX10 ......204 B1
Baker Cl Benson OX10 ......204 B1
  Bicester OX27 ......66 A2
  Oxford OX3 ......124 C1
Baker Rd OX4 ......179 C3
Baker St OX11 ......237 C4
Baker's Ct OX29 ......90 A1
Baker's Piece OX39 ......168 C3
Baker's Piece Ho OX39 ......167 C2
Bakers La
  Brightwell-cum-S OX10 ......202 C1
  East Hagbourne OX11 ......218 C3
  Oxford OX4 ......141 C2
  South Newington OX15 ......31 C4
  Swalcliffe OX15 ......19 C4
  Tadmarton OX15 ......20 B4
Bakers Piece OX28 ......104 A1
Bakers Sq SN7 ......174 A3
Bakery La Clanfield OX18 ......152 C4
  Letcombe Bassett OX12 ......214 A1
Baldon La OX44 ......161 C2
Baldons Cl RG8 ......250 C4
Balfour Cotts OX14 ......182 A3

Balfour Rd OX4 ......142 C2
Balfour's Field RG8 ......241 B2
Balham's La RG9 ......225 C4
Ball La OX5 ......77 A3
Ballard Chase OX14 ......160 A2
Ballard Cl OX7 ......46 C1
Ballards Cl OX7 ......85 B4
Balliol Col OX15 ......77 B3
Balliol Coll OX1 ......123 B1
Balliol Ct OX2 ......123 A2
Balliol Dr OX11 ......219 A4
Balliol Rd Bicester OX26 ......65 C1
  Reading RG4 ......258 B2
Balmoral Ave
  Banbury OX16 ......15 C3
  Banbury, Crouch Hill OX16 ......15 C2
Balmoral Cl OX11 ......219 A4
Balmoral Way OX17 ......23 B3
Balmore Dr RG4 ......259 A2
Balmore Ho RG4 ......259 A2
Baltic Wharf OX1 ......141 B4
Bampton CE Prim Sch
  OX18 ......134 C2
Bampton Cl OX14 ......142 B2
Bampton Rd Aston OX18 ......135 B1
  Clanfield OX18 ......133 C1
  Curbridge OX18,OX29 ......117 A2
Banbury Bsns Pk OX17 ......23 B2
Banbury Cross Ret Pk
  OX16 ......16 A4
Banbury Ct ❿ OX14 ......179 C4
Banbury Gdns RG4 ......259 B2
Banbury Hill OX7 ......73 B3
Banbury La
  Kings Sutton OX17 ......23 C3
  Middleton Cheney OX17 ......10 C1
Banbury Mus* OX16 ......16 B3
Banbury Rd
  Adderbury OX17 ......23 A3
  Aynho OX17 ......35 A4
  Bicester OX26 ......65 C2
  Bloxham OX15 ......21 C3
  Chacombe OX17 ......10 B2
  Chipping Norton OX7 ......42 C2
  Chipping Warden OX17 ......5 C2
  Cuttleslowe OX2 ......109 A1
  Deddington OX15 ......33 C3
  Kidlington OX5 ......92 B1
  North Newington OX15 ......15 B2
  Over Norton OX7 ......43 B3
  Oxford OX2 ......123 A3
  Shipton-on-C OX5 ......92 A3
  Shutford OX15 ......14 A3
  Swerford OX7 ......30 B1
  Tackley OX20 ......76 C2
  Warmington OX17 ......3 A1
  Woodstock OX20 ......91 B4
Banbury Rd Crossing
  OX7 ......42 C2
Banbury Sch OX16 ......16 A2
Bandet Way OX9 ......148 A3
Banesberie Cl OX16 ......9 A1
Banjo Rd OX4 ......142 B3
Bank Cotts OX33 ......125 C2
Banks Furlong OX26 ......79 C4
Bankside Banbury OX16 ......16 C2
  East Hendred OX12 ......216 A3
  Kidlington OX5 ......92 B1
  Long Hanborough OX29 ......90 C1
  Oxford OX3 ......124 C2
Bannister Cl OX4 ......141 C4
Bannister Rd OX9 ......148 B4
Barbaras Mdw RG31 ......257 A1
Barberry Pl OX26 ......65 C2
Barbrook Cl RG31 ......257 B2
Barbury Dr OX12 ......214 B4
Barclose Ave RG4 ......259 B2
Barcombe Cl OX16 ......8 C1
Barcote La SN7 ......174 A3
Bardolphs Cl RG4 ......258 B4
Bardwell Ct OX2 ......123 B2
Bardwell Rd OX2 ......123 B2
Bardwell Terr OX26 ......65 C1
Barefoot Cl RG31 ......257 A1
Barford Rd Bloxham OX15 ......21 C1
  South Newington OX15 ......32 A3
Bargus Cl OX13 ......199 A2
Barksdale Ave NN13 ......36 C3
Barkus Way HP14 ......188 C3
Barley Cl Lewknor OX49 ......187 A4
  Sibford Gower OX15 ......19 A4
  Wallingford OX10 ......221 B3
Barley Hill Cty Prim Sch
  OX9 ......130 A1
Barleycott La OX1 ......141 B2
Barleyfields OX11 ......218 B4
Barlow Cl Milcombe OX15 ......21 A1
  Wheatley OX33 ......143 C4
Barn Bsns Ctr The GL54 ......83 A4
Barn Cl Denchworth OX12 ......196 C2
  Kidlington OX5 ......108 B4
Barn End OX18 ......134 C1
Barn La RG9 ......244 B1
Barn's Rd OX4 ......142 B2
Barnaco OX49 ......186 A1
Barnard Cl RG4 ......259 B3
Barnards Way OX12 ......214 C3
Barncroft
  Long Compton CV36 ......28 A3
  Wallingford OX10 ......221 B4
Barnes Cl OX11 ......218 C3
Barnes Rd OX11 ......218 C3
Barnet St OX4 ......142 A4
Barnett Rd
  Middleton Cheney OX17 ......17 C4
  Steventon OX13 ......198 C3

Barnett Way OX10 .....204 B1
Barnfield Cl OX12 .....175 C1
Barns Cl Cumnor OX2 ...140 A3
  Holton OX33 ....126 A1
Barns Hay OX3 ....123 C3
Barns Ho OX4 ....142 B2
Barns La OX18 ....100 C2
Baroma Way RG9 ....244 C1
Baronshurst Dr OX44 ..184 B3
Baronsmead RG9 ....244 B1
Barracks La Oxford OX4 142 A4
  Oxford OX4 ....142 B3
Barracks The OX44 .....164 B4
Barret Ct RG1 ....258 C1
Barrett St OX2 ....123 A1
Barrett's Way OX4 .....199 C3
Barrington Cl OX29 .....89 B4
Barrington Ave SN6 ...191 C1
Barrington Cl
  Berinsfield OX10 .....182 B3
  Oxford OX3 ....124 B1
  Witney OX28 ....117 C4
Barrington Ct NN13 .....24 A3
Barrington Rd SN6 .....209 B4
Barrow Hill Cl OX14 ...160 B1
Barrow La OX11 ....217 C4
Barrow Rd
  Abingdon OX13 ....179 A4
  Harwell OX11 ....217 C4
Barry Ave OX26 ....65 B2
Barry Pl **9** RG4 .....259 A1
Barthomew Ave OX5 ...108 A3
Bartholomew Cl
  Ducklington OX29 .....118 A2
  Eynsham OX29 ....120 B4
Bartholomew Rd OX4 ...142 B2
Bartholomew Sch OX29 120 B4
Bartholomew Tipping Way
  HP14 ....188 C3
Bartisa Rd OX26 ....65 C2
Bartlemas Cl OX4 ......142 A4
Bartlemas Rd OX4 .....142 A4
Bartlett Cl
  Wallingford OX10 .....221 B3
  Witney OX28 ....118 A4
Barton Cl OX17 ....23 C3
Barton Ho OX3 ....124 C2
Barton La Abingdon OX14 180 A4
  Oxford OX3 ....124 B2
Barton Rd
  Long Compton CV36,GL56 ...27 B4
  Oxford OX3 ....124 C2
Barton Village Fst Sch
  OX3 ....124 C2
Barton Village Rd OX3 124 B3
Barwell OX12 ....214 B3
Basil Hill Rd OX11 ....200 B2
Basildon Pk* RG8 .....249 B1
Baskerville La RG4 ....255 A2
Baskerville Rd RG4 ....252 C3
Basmore La RG9 ....255 A2
Basset Way OX5 ....108 C4
Bassett Ave OX26 ......65 C2
Bassett Rd
  Letcombe Bassett OX12 ..231 C4
  Oxford OX3 ....124 C2
Batchelors Row OX15 ...33 A2
Bate Collection of Historical
  Instruments * OX1 ...141 B4
Bateman St OX3 ....124 B1
Bates La OX4 ....35 B2
Bath Ct OX14 ....179 C4
Bath Pl OX1 ....123 B1
Bath Rd Banbury OX16 ..16 B3
  Sonning RG4 ....260 C1
Bath St Abingdon OX14 179 C4
  Oxford OX4 ....123 C1
Bath Terr OX26 ....65 C1
Batt CE Prim Sch OX28 218 A4
Batten Pl OX4 ....142 A1
Batting Cl HP14 ....189 C4
Battle Cl OX26 ....66 A2
Battle Rd Benson OX10 204 B1
  Oxford OX4 ....142 B3
Baulking La SN7 ....194 B1
Baulking Rd SN7 ......211 C4
Baxters Barns GL7 ....131 A2
Bay Tree Cl OX4 ....142 A2
Baydon Rd SN8 ....245 B1
Bayliss Rd RG10 ......255 B1
Baynes Yd OX7 ....73 A2
Bayswater Farm Rd
  OX3 ....125 A2
Bayswater Mid Sch OX3 124 C2
Bayswater Rd
  Oxford OX3 ....124 C2
  Stanton St John OX3 ..125 A4
Bayworth La OX1,OX13 .159 C4
Beach Pl OX3 ....124 C2
Beachborough Sch NN13 25 A2
Beaconsfield Rd OX16 ..16 B1
Beadnell Cl OX16 ......16 B1
Beagle Cl OX4 ....160 B1
Beagles Cl OX5 ....29 A4
Beale Park Wildlife Pk*
  RG8 ....249 C1
Beam Paddock OX18 ...135 A2
Beanacre Rd OX12 ......30 A3
Beanfurlong OX17 ......10 C2
Beanhill Cl OX29 ......118 A3
Beanhill Rd OX29 .....118 A3
Beansheaf Terr **3** OX10 221 B4
Bear Cl OX29 ....91 A3
Bear Close Flats OX20 ..91 A4
Bear Ct OX18 ....100 C3
Bear La
  North Moreton OX11 ...220 A4

Bear La *continued*
  Oxford OX1 ....123 B1
  Stadhampton OX44 ....163 B1
  Wallingford OX10 .....221 B4
Beargarden Rd OX16 ....16 B3
Bears Hedge OX4 ......142 A2
Beatrice Dr OX16 ....16 A3
Beauchamp La OX4 ....142 A2
Beauchamp Pl OX4 ....142 A2
Beaufort Cl
  8 Bicester OX26 .....66 A2
  Didcot OX11 ....218 C4
Beaulieu Cl OX16 ....16 C3
Beaulieu Ct OX13 ......159 C3
Beaulieu Mews OX11 ..201 A2
Beaumaris Cl OX16 .....15 C4
Beaumont Bldgs OX1 ..123 A1
Beaumont Pl OX1 .....123 B1
Beaumont Rd
  Banbury OX16 ....9 B1
  Oxford OX2 ....124 C2
Beaumont St OX1 .....123 B1
Bec Cl OX12 ....214 A1
Bec Tithe RG8 ....250 C2
Beckdale Cl OX26 ......65 A2
Becket St OX1 ....123 A1
Beckett Ave SN6 ......209 B4
Beckett St OX1 ....209 B4
Beckett Ho OX12 .....214 C2
Becketts Cl OX29 ......90 A1
Beckley CE Prim Sch
  OX3 ....111 A2
Beckley Cl RG8 ....250 C4
Beckley Ct OX3 ....111 A1
Becquerel Ave OX11 ..217 A1
Bedford Cl OX16 ....15 C4
Bedford St OX4 ....141 C3
Bedwells Heath OX1 ..140 B1
Beech Cl Faringdon SN7 172 C2
  Stokenchurch HP14 ...188 C2
  Watlington OX49 .....186 A1
  Wootton (Oxford) OX13 159 A4
Beech Cres OX5 ....108 C4
Beech Croft Rd OX2 ..123 A3
Beech La RG8 ....250 B4
Beech Rd Chinnor OX39 168 B3
  Eynsham OX29 ....120 C4
  Mapledurham RG4 ....258 B4
  N Hinksey Village OX2 140 B4
  Oxford OX3 ....124 B2
  Purley on T RG8 .....257 A1
  Thame OX9 ....147 B4
  Wheatley OX33 ....144 A4
  Witney OX28 ....117 C4
Beech Rise RG4 ....252 C3
Beechcroft OX16 ....16 B4
Beechcroft OX18 ......182 B1
Beeches The
  Deddington OX15 ......33 C2
  Goring RG8 ....249 A3
  Oxford OX3 ....124 C2
  Reading RG31 ....257 B2
Beechey Ave OX3 .....123 C2
Beechfield Cres OX26 ..16 B2
Beechgate OX28 ......118 A3
Beeching Cl OX14 ....218 B1
Beechwood OX4 ......142 A1
Beechwood Cl RG8 ...250 B3
Beesley Rd OX16 ....16 A3
Beeson Cl OX4 ....250 C4
Begbroke Cres OX5 ...108 A4
Begbroke La
  Begbroke OX5 ....92 A1
  Kidlington OX5 ....92 B1
Beggar's La OX13 .....156 B1
Beggarsbush Hill OX10 204 B1
Behoes La RG8 ....240 B1
Belbroughton Rd OX2 .123 B3
Belcher Ct OX10 ......182 B1
Belgrove Cl OX5 ......108 B4
Bell Cl Cassington OX29 107 B1
  Grove OX12 ....196 C1
  Thame OX9 ....129 C1
Bell La OX15 ....30 A4
Bell La Aldworth RG8 .247 C2
  Bampton OX18 ....134 C2
  Bicester OX26 ....65 C1
  Brightwell-cum-S OX10 202 C1
  Cassington OX29 .....107 B1
  Henley-on-T RG9 .....244 C2
  Lechlade GL7 ....150 B2
  Thame OX9 ....129 C1
  Wheatley OX33 ....144 A4
Bell Lodge **7** OX26 ....65 C1
Bell St Henley-on-T RG9 244 C1
  Hornton OX15 ....7 B3
Bell Street Mews RG9 244 C1
Bell's La OX15 ....30 A4
Bellamy Cl OX13 ......156 C1
Belle Terr OX18 ....115 B1
Belle Vue Rd RG8 ....254 B4
Bellenger Way OX5 ...108 B4
Bellingham La SN6 ...190 A1
Bellingham Wlk RG4 ..259 A3
Belmont OX12 ....214 B3
Belmont Mews OX9 ..147 C4
Belsyre Ct OX2 ....123 A2
Belvedere Rd OX4 ....142 A4

Ben Cl OX5 ....92 C1
Benares Gr RG9 ....242 A2
Benhams La RG9 ....226 B1
Benmead Rd OX5 ....92 C1
Bennett Cl OX17 ....10 C2
Bennett Cres OX4 ....142 B3
Bennett End HP14 ....189 B4
Bennett Rd SN7 ......172 C2
Bensgrove Cl RG8 .....250 C4
Benson CE Prim Sch
  OX10 ....203 C2
Benson Cl OX26 ....66 A2
Benson CM Inf Sch
  OX10 ....203 C2
Benson Com Prim Sch
  OX10 ....204 B1
Benson La Benson OX10 204 A1
Benson Rd Benson OX10 221 C4
Benson Pl OX2 ....123 B2
Benson Rd
  Abingdon OX14 ......159 C1
  Oxford OX3 ....142 B4
Bentley Cl OX16 ......115 C4
Benton Dr OX39 ......168 B4
Benwells OX39 ....168 B3
Bere Court Rd RG8 ...256 A2
Berens Rd SN6 ....209 A3
Bergamont Pl **4** OX4 142 C1
Bergen Ave OX14 .....179 B2
Berins Hill OX10 .....241 A3
Berinsfield Prim Sch
  OX10 ....182 B3
Berinsfield Rdbt OX10 182 A2
Berkeley Cl OX16 ......15 C4
Berkley Rd
  Sunningwell OX1 .....140 C1
  Thame OX9 ....130 A1
Berkshire Rd RG9 ....254 B4
Berner's Way SN7 ....173 A2
Bernewood Cl HP18 ..129 B4
Bernwood Rd
  Bicester OX26 ....65 C1
  Oxford OX3 ....124 C2
Berrick Rd OX44 .....184 B3
Berry Cl OX4 ....142 C2
Berry Croft OX14 ....159 C1
Berry Hill Rd OX17 ...27 C2
Berry La Blewbury OX11 219 A1
  East Hanney OX12 ...197 A3
Berrylands Rd RG4 ...259 A2
Berrymere Rd OX4 ...159 A4
Berrymoor Rd OX16 ...16 A3
Bertie Pl OX1 ....141 B3
Bertie Rd OX2 ....139 C3
Besbury La OX7 ....55 C3
Bessel's Way OX11 ..237 A4
Bessels Lea OX11 ....219 A1
Bessels Leigh Sch OX13 158 A4
Besselsleigh Rd OX13 ..
Bessemer Rd OX26 ....66 A1
Betony Way OX26 ......65 C2
Bettina Cres OX16 .....9 A3
Betty La OX1 ....141 B2
Between Towns Rd OX4 142 B3
Beverley Cl
  Abingdon OX14 ......159 C1
  Benson OX10 ....204 B2
Beverley Gdns
  Benson OX10 ....204 B2
  Blagrave RG4 ....258 B2
Beverley Cres OX18 ..115 C2
Blake CE Prim Sch The
  OX28 ....118 B4
Bevington Rd OX2 ....123 A2
Bhandari Cl OX4 .....142 A3
Bibury Cl OX28 ......117 B4
Bicester Com Coll OX26 65 B1
Bicester Com Hospl
  OX26 ....65 C1
Bicester Ho **7** OX26 ..65 C1
Bicester North Sta OX26 64 C2
Bicester Rd Bucknell OX27 64 C4
  Kidlington OX5 ......109 A4
  Launton OX26 ....66 B1
  Long Crendon HP18 ..129 B3
  Ludgershall HP18 .....98 B4
  Marsh Gibbon OX27 ...67 A4
  Middleton Stoney OX25 64 A2
  Stratton Audley OX27 ..66 B4
Bicester Town Sta OX26 80 C4
Bicester Village Ret Pk
  OX26 ....80 C4
Bickerton Rd OX3 ....124 B1
Biddel Springs SN6 ..190 A3
Biddlesden Rd NN13 ...25 A3
Bigmore La HP14 .....189 B1
Bignell View OX26 .....79 C4
Bignolds Cl OX17 ......4 A1
Bigwood Cl HP14 .....188 C3
Billwell HP18 ....129 B3
Bingley Gr RG5 ......260 C1
Binsey La OX2 ....122 C1
Binswood Ave OX3 ...124 B1
Birch Cl RG4 ....252 C2
Birch Dr OX18 ....114 B4
Birch Rd Ambrosden OX25 81 B2
  Garsington OX44 ....143 B1
Birches Cl RG8 ......250 C4
Birches The RG8 .....249 A3
Birchfield Cl OX4 ...142 C1
Birchwood Banbury OX16 16 B2
  Carterton OX18 .....115 C1
Birchwood Cl RG4 ...259 B3
Birchwood Dr OX5 ....92 A3
Bird Cl OX16 ....15 C3

Bird Wood Ct RG4 ....253 A2
Birdlip Cl OX28 ......103 B1
Birds La OX15 ....13 A3
Birmingham Yd OX10 .203 C2
Biscoe Ct OX33 ......144 B4
Bishop Carpenter CE Prim
  Sch OX15 ....15 A2
Bishop Kirk Pl OX2 ..123 A4
Bishop Loveday CE Prim Sch
  OX15 ....16 C1
Bishop's Wood OX44 .144 B2
Bishops Cl OX15 ....32 C3
Bishops Mdw OX29 ...89 B4
Bishops Orch OX11 ..218 C4
Bishopstone Prim Sch
  SN6 ....227 B2
Bishopswood Sch RG4 252 B3
Bishops Cl OX26 ......66 A2
Bitham Rd OX12 .....233 B4
Bitterell OX29 ....120 C4
Bix Comm RG9 ....243 B4
Black Bourton Rd
  Carterton OX18 .....115 C1
  Clanfield OX18 ......133 C1
Black Bull La OX5 .....95 B3
Black Croft OX12 ....214 B3
Blackberry La OX4 ...162 A4
Blackbird Assarts La
  OX7 ....88 A1
Blackbird Leys Rd OX4 142 B1
Blackburn Wlk OX26 ..66 A3
Blackditch OX29 .....138 A4
Blackfriars Rd **8** OX1 141 B4
Blackhall Rd OX1 ....123 B1
Blackhill La OX14 ....199 B2
Blackhorse La OX13 .158 C2
Blacklands OX12 .....212 C2
Blacklands Rd OX44 .204 A3
Blacklands Way OX14 179 B4
Blacklocks Hill OX17 ..17 A4
Blackman Cl OX1 ....141 C1
Blackmore Cl OX9 ...148 A4
Blackmore La RG4 ...253 A3
Blacknall Rd OX14 ...179 C3
Blacksmith Cl OX3 ...79 A1
Blacksmiths Hill OX17 35 B4
Blacksmiths La
  Charlton-on-O OX5 ....95 A2
  Mollington OX17 ....4 A2
Blacksmiths Mdw **17**
  OX4 ....142 C1
Blackstock Cl OX3 ...142 C4
Blackthorn Cl OX10 ..203 B1
Blackthorn Cl
  Blackthorn OX25 ......82 A2
  Oxford OX4 ....124 C2
Blackthorn Rd OX26 ..66 C1
Blackwater Cl RG4 ...259 C2
Blackwater Way OX11 201 A2
Blackwood OX11 ......22 C4
Blackworth SN6 ......190 A4
Bladon CE Prim Sch
  OX20 ....91 A1
Bladon Cl OX2 ....122 C4
Bladon Rd OX20 ......91 B2
Blaenant RG4 ....258 C3
Blaenavon RG4 ......258 C3
Blagrave Farm La RG4 258 B1
Blagrave Cl OX11 ....200 C1
Blagrave Ct OX11 ....218 A2
Blake Rd OX26 ....66 A2
Blake Way OX9 ......130 A1
Blake's Field OX11 ..200 B1
Blakehope Burn OX11 200 C2
Blakes Ave OX28 ....118 B4
Blakes Rd RG10 .....255 C2
Blandford Alley SN6 .190 A3
Blandford Ave OX2 ..123 A3
Blandford Rd OX5 .....92 B1
Blandy Ave OX13 ....156 C1
Blandy Rd RG9 ......254 B4
Blankstone Cl OX29 .120 B4
Blay Cl OX4 ....142 C2
Bleache Pl OX4 ......142 B3
Bledington St N OX7 ..54 B1
Bledlow Rd HP27 ....169 C4
Bledlow Ridge Rd HP27 169 B4
Bledlow Ridge Sch
  HP14 ....189 C4
Blencowe Cl OX27 ....65 C3
Blenheim NN13 ....36 A4
Blenheim Cl
  2 Kidlington OX5 ...108 C4
Blenheim Ct
  Bicester OX26 ....65 B2
  Cutteslowe OX2 .....123 A4
  Launton OX26 ....66 C1
  Witney OX28 ....117 C4
Blenheim Gdns OX12 196 B3
Blenheim Hill OX11 ..217 C4
Blenheim Orch OX3 ..106 A3
Blenheim Orch OX10 .197 A3
Blenheim Pal* OX20 ..91 A3
Blenheim Pl OX10 ...204 B1
Blenheim Rd
  Banbury OX16 ....16 C1
  Horspath OX33 ......143 B4
  Kidlington OX5 ......108 C4
  Lewknor OX49 ....186 A2
  Little Milton OX44 ..164 A3
  Reading RG4 ....259 A2
Blenheim Rise OX17 ..23 C3

Blenheim Terr
  Bletchingdon OX5 ....93 A4
  Chipping Norton OX7 ..42 C1
Blenheim Way
  Horspath OX33 ......143 B4
  Kingston Bagpuize OX13 156 B1
Blenheim La OX33 ...144 A4
Bleriot Rd GL54 ....68 A2
Blessed George Napier RC
  Sec Sch OX16 ....16 B2
Bletchingdon Parochial CE
  Sch OX5 ....93 A4
Bletchingdon Rd
  Bletchingdon OX5 ....78 A2
  Hampton Poyle OX5 ..93 A2
  Islip OX5 ....93 C1
Blewbury CE Prim Sch
  OX11 ....218 C1
Blewbury Hill OX11 ..237 A4
Blewbury Rd OX11 ...234 C1
Bliss Ho OX7 ....42 C1
Blissett Terr SN7 ....172 C2
Blomfield Pl OX2 ....123 A2
Blossoms Glade OX14 ..
Blounts Court Rd RG4 253 A3
Blowings The OX29 ..106 A4
Blowingstone Hill OX12 212 A1
Bloxham CE Prim Sch
  OX15 ....21 B2
Bloxham Grove Rd OX15 22 A3
Bloxham Rd Banbury OX16 22 A3
  Barford St M OX15 ...32 C4
  Bloxham OX15 ....21 A1
  Milcombe OX15 ....21 A1
  Wroxton OX15 ....21 C3
Bloxham Village Mus*
  OX15 ....21 C2
Blue Boar St OX1 ....123 B1
Blue Row OX7 ....42 C3
Bluebell Cl **8** OX26 ..65 C2
Bluebell Ct OX4 .....142 C1
Bluebell Ride OX1,OX14 160 C4
Bluebell Way OX18 ..115 C2
Blythe Pl OX26 ....66 A2
Boathouse Reach RG9 244 C1
Bobby Fryer Cl OX4 .142 C2
Bockett's Cnr OX18 ..102 A4
Boddington La OX29 .105 B4
Boddington Rd OX17 ..1 B1
Bodleian Liby * OX1 ..123 B1
Bodley Pl OX2 ....123 A4
Bodley Rd OX4 ......142 B2
Bohams Rd OX11 ....236 B3
Bolney La RG9 ....255 A3
Bolney Rd RG9 ......255 A3
Bolney Trevor Dr RG9 255 A2
Bolsover Cl OX29 ....90 A1
Bolton Rd OX16 ......16 B3
Bolton's La OX29 ...105 A3
Bonar Rd OX3 ....124 C1
Bonds La OX15 ....19 A4
Bones La RG9 ....254 A2
Bonham Pl OX18 ....115 B2
Bonn Sq OX1 ....123 B1
Bonnersfield HP18 ..102 B4
Book End OX29 .....103 B1
Boot St OX29 ....89 B4
Boreford Rd OX14 ..160 A1
Borough Ave OX10 ..221 B4
Borough Ct NN13 .....24 A3
Borough Rd NN13 ....24 A3
Borough Wlk OX14 ..159 C1
Borrowmead Rd OX3 124 A3
Bosley Cres OX10 ...221 B4
Bosley's Orch
  Didcot OX11 ....200 C1
  Grove OX12 ....196 C1
Bostock Rd OX14 ...179 C4
Boston Rd Bicester OX26 66 A2
  Henley-on-T RG9 ....254 C4
Boswell Rd OX4 .....142 B2
Bothy The Aynho RG10 35 B4
  Wargrave RG10 .....255 B1
Botley Cty Prim Sch
  OX2 ....122 B1
Botley Intc OX2 .....122 B1
Botley La OX2 ....122 C1
Bottle Square La HP14 189 B3
Bottom La RG8 ......241 A2
Bottom Rd HP14 ....189 C2
Boucher Cl OX12 ....214 B4
Boulevard The OX5 ...92 A1
Boulter Dr OX14 ....160 A2
Boulter St OX4 ......123 C1
Boults Cl OX3 ......123 C3
Boults La OX3 ......123 C3
Boundary Brook Rd OX4 142 A3
Boundary Cl OX20 ...91 B3
Boundary La RG4 ...258 C2
Bourlon Wood OX14 .159 B1
Bourne Cl Bicester OX26 65 B1
  Cutteslowe OX2 .....109 A1
Bourne La OX15 ......30 A4
Bourne Rd RG8 .....256 C3
Bourne St OX13 ....218 C4
Bourne The
  Eastleach Martin GL7 .131 A4
  Hook Norton OX15 ...30 A4
Bourton Cl Clanfield OX18 133 C1
  Reading RG30 ....257 C1
Bourton Cotts OX18 .134 C2
Bovewell OX6 ....35 C2

Bovingdon Rd OX18 .....115 C2
Bovington's Yd OX18 ...135 B2
Bow Rd SN7 ....174 C1
Bowbank Cl OX13 ......156 B2
Bower End OX44 ....184 B4
Bower Gn SN6 ....191 C1
Bowerman Cl OX5 ......108 B4
Bowers La HP14 ....189 B4
Bowfell Cl RG31 ......257 B1
Bowgrave Copse OX14 ..160 B1
Bowley Ho OX20 ....91 A3
Bowling Ct RG9 ....244 B2
Bowling Gn HP14 ......188 B3
Bowling Green Cl OX18 .134 C2
Bowling Green Farmhouse
 RG8 ....257 A3
Bowling Green La RG8 .257 A3
Bowmen's Lea OX17 ....35 B4
Bowmont Sq OX26 ......65 A1
Bowmont Water OX11 ..200 C1
Bowness Ave
 Didcot OX11 ....218 B4
 Oxford OX3 ....124 A2
Bowyer Rd OX14 ....179 C4
Box Tree La OX9 ......166 C2
Boxhedge Rd OX16 .....16 A3
Boxhedge Rd W OX16 ..16 A3
Boxhedge Sq OX16 .....16 A3
Boxhedge Terr ⊠ OX16 ..16 A3
Boxhill Rd OX14 ......179 C4
Boxhill Wlk OX14 .....179 C4
Boxwell Cl OX14 ......160 A1
Bracegirdle Rd OX3 ...124 C1
Bracken Cl
 Carterton OX18 ......115 B2
 Reading RG31 ....257 B1
Brackley Rd
 Croughton NN13 ....36 B4
 Westbury NN13 ....25 A3
Brackstone Cl RG4 ...259 B1
Bradburys The OX27 ...66 A4
Braddons Furlong HP18 .129 B3
Bradford Cl OX15 .....21 B4
Bradlands Way RG8 ...257 B3
Bradlands OX3 ....123 C4
Bradley Arc OX16 .....115 C3
Bradley Rd RG9 ......224 A3
Bradley's St RG8 .....241 A2
Bradmore Rd OX2 .....123 B2
Bradshaw Cl OX25 .....62 A4
Bradstock's Way OX14 .199 C3
Bradwell Rd RG31 ....257 B2
Brae Hill HP18 ....98 A1
Braithwaite Cl OX16 ..16 A3
Brake Hill OX4 ....143 A1
Bramber Cl OX16 ......15 C4
Bramber Mews RG4 ...259 C2
Brambling Way OX4 ...142 B1
Bramblings RG4 ......258 C3
Bramblings The OX26 ..66 A1
Bramley Cl OX12 .....197 A3
Bramley Cres RG4 ....252 C3
Bramley Hts OX28 ....117 C4
Brampton Chase RG9 ..255 A2
Brampton Cl OX14 ....159 C1
Brampton Dr OX18 ....115 C1
Brampton Rd OX3 .....124 C2
Bramshaw Rd RG30 ...268 A1
Bramwell Pl OX4 .....141 C4
Brandon Cl OX5 ......108 B4
Brantwood Cl OX16 ...16 A2
Brantwood Rise OX16 ..16 A2
Brasenose Bldg OX1 ..123 C1
Brasenose Coll OX1 ..123 B1
Brasenose Dr OX5 .....92 C1
Brasenose Driftway
 OX4 ....142 C3
Brasenose La OX1 ....123 B1
Brasenose Villas OX7 ..42 C1
Brashfield Rd OX26 ...65 C2
Brassey Cl OX7 ....42 C2
Brassey Ho OX7 ....42 C2
Braybrooke Cl OX7 .....58 C3
Braybrooke Gdns RG10 .255 B1
Braybrooke Rd RG10 ..255 B1
Braze La OX10 ....204 A3
Braziers La OX10,RG8 ..240 C3
Breedons Hill RG8 ....256 B3
Brenda Cl OX16 ....16 A2
Brendon Cl Didcot OX11 .200 B1
 Reading RG30 ....257 C1
Brent Ave OX11 ......200 C2
Brentford Cl OX11 ...220 C1
Brereton Dr OX12 ....196 B1
Bretch Hill OX16 .....15 C3
Brett Cl OX9 ....148 A4
Brewer Cl OX13 ......199 A2
Brewer St OX1 ....141 B4
Brewers Ct ⊠ OX14 ..179 C3
Brewery La OX15 .....29 C4
Brewery Row GL56 .....26 C1
Brewery St SN6 ......190 A3
Briaily HP14 ....189 B1
Briants Ave RG4 .....259 B1
Briar Cl Banbury OX16 .16 B1
 Kidlington OX5 ....92 B1
 Reading RG4 ....259 A3
Briar End OX5 ....92 B1
Briar Thicket OX20 ...91 B3
Briars Cl RG8 ....256 C3
Briarswood Cl HP14 ..188 C3

Briary Rd GL7 ....150 B3
Brice Rd OX25 ....63 B4
Brick Alley ⊠ OX14 ..179 C3
Brick Hill OX15 ......30 A3
Brick Row OX15 ....19 C4
Brickle La OX15 ......21 C3
Bricks La HP14 ......188 B2
Bridens Way HP17 ...130 C3
Bridewell Cl OX29 ...105 A4
Bridge Cl OX14 ......219 A4
Bridge End OX10 .....202 B4
Bridge Farm Cl OX12 .214 C4
Bridge Rd HP18,OX9 ..127 C1
Bridge St Abingdon OX14 .179 C3
 Bampton OX18 ....134 C2
 Banbury OX16 ....16 B3
 Islip OX5 ....109 C4
 Oxford OX2 ....123 A1
 Reading RG4 ....259 A1
 Witney OX28 ....104 A1
Bridge Street Mill Bsns Pk
 OX28 ....117 A2
Bridges Cl OX14 .....179 B3
Bridgewater Cl RG30 .258 B1
Bridle Cl OX16 ....16 C2
Bridle Path
 Charney Bassett OX12 .175 C1
 Woodcote RG8 ....250 C4
Bridle Rd RG8 ....250 C2
Bridus Mead OX13 ...219 A1
Bridus Way OX13 ....219 A1
Brierley Pl RG31 ....257 B2
Briggs Cl OX16 ......115 C3
Brigham Rd RG1 .....259 A1
Brightwell CE Prim Sch
 OX10 ....202 C1
Brightwell St OX10 ..202 C1
Brill CE Comb Sch HP18 .98 A1
Brill Cl RG4 ....259 A2
Brill Rd
 Horton-cum-S OX33 ..112 B3
 Ludgershall HP18 .....98 A4
Brimes Cl OX11 ......25 A3
Brinkburn Gr OX16 ...16 C4
Brinkinfield Rd OX44 .184 B4
Bristol Rd Bicester OX26 ..66 A2
 Upper Rissington GL54 ..68 A3
Bristow Ct RG4 .....259 C3
Britannia Cl OX18 ..115 C2
Britannia Hts ⊠ OX16 .16 B3
Britannia Rd OX16 ...16 B3
Britannia Wharf ⊠ OX16 .16 B3
British Telecom Mus*
 OX18 ....115 A3
Britnell Cl HP14 ....188 C3
Britwell Rd Didcot OX11 .200 C1
 Ewelme OX10 ....204 C2
 Watlington OX49 ....186 A1
Brixton Hill OX10 ...223 A2
Brize Norton Prim Sch
 OX18 ....115 B2
Brize Norton Rd
 Carterton OX18 ......115 C1
 Minster Lovell OX29 ..102 C1
Brizewood OX18 .....115 B2
Broad Cl
 Barford St M OX15 ....32 C3
 Kidlington OX5 ......108 B4
 N Hinksey Village OX2 .122 A1
Broad End OX15 ......16 C1
Broad Field Rd OX5 ..108 A4
Broad Gap OX15 ......16 C1
Broad Marsh La OX8 ..106 A3
Broad Oak OX15 .....122 C4
Broad St Abingdon OX14 .179 C4
 Bampton OX18 ....134 C2
 Banbury OX16 ....16 B3
 Long Compton CV36 ...27 C3
 Uffington SN7 ....211 B3
Broad Way SN7 ......211 B3
Broadbrook La OX12 .212 C2
Broadfields OX4 .....142 B1
Broadhead Pl OX13 ..124 A3
Broadhurst Gdns OX4 .142 A2
Broadmarsh Cl RG4 ..214 B4
Broadmoor La RG4,
 RG10 ....260 C2
Broadshires Way OX18 .115 C2
Broadwaters Ave OX9 ..147 C4
Broadway Didcot OX11 .218 C4
 Harwell OX11 ....217 C3
 Kidlington OX5 ......108 C3
Broadway Cl
 Harwell OX11 ....217 C3
 Witney OX28 ....103 B1
Broadway The OX4 ...95 A2
Broadwell Ct OX26 ...65 A1
Broadwell Rd GL7 ...132 B1
Brocklesby Rd OX4 ..142 A1
Brocks Way RG9 .....255 A3
Brode Cl OX14 ......160 A1
Brogden Cl OX4 .....140 C4
Brome Pl OX3 ....124 C2
Bromeswell Cl OX25 ..62 A4
Bromsgrove SN7 ....172 C2
Brook Cl HP18 ....98 B4
Brook Hollow OX10 ...91 A3
Brook La
 Denchworth OX12 ....196 A2
 Steeple Aston OX25 ..48 A4
 Thame OX9 ....129 C1
 West Hagbourne OX11 .218 B3
Brook Lea ⊠ RG4 ....259 B1
Brook Rd Bicester OX26 ..65 B2
 Great Tew OX7 ....45 B4
Brook St
 Aston Rowant OX49 ..167 C2

Brook St continued
 Benson OX10 ....204 A2
 Oxford OX1 ....141 B4
 Sutton Courtenay OX14 .200 A4
 Watlington OX49 ....186 A1
Brook Taylor Ct ⊠ OX1 .141 B4
Brook View OX44 ....143 A3
Brook Way OX29 ......90 A1
Brooke Rd OX16 ......16 A2
Brookfield Cl
 Milton-u-W OX7 ......70 A1
 Wallingford OX10 ...221 B3
Brookfield Cres OX3 ..124 A3
Brookfields Sch RG31 ..257 B2
Brookhampton Cl OX44 .163 B1
Brookhollow Wlk ⊠ OX4 .142 C1
Brooklyn Dr RG9 ....259 A3
Brookmead Dr OX10 .221 B3
Brooks Row OX26 .....87 A2
Brooksby Rd RG31 ...257 B1
Brookside
 Abingdon OX14 ......159 C1
 Cholsey OX10 ....220 C1
 Cuddesdon OX44 ....144 A1
 East Hanney OX12 ...197 A3
 Great Tew OX7 ....45 B4
 Harwell OX11 ....217 C4
 North Moor OX15 .....30 A4
 Oxford OX3 ....124 B1
 Thame OX9 ....129 C1
 ⊠ Wallingford OX10 .221 B4
 Watlington OX49 ....186 A1
Brookside Cl OX5 ....109 C3
Brookside Est OX44 ..184 B4
Brookside Prim/St Edburg's
 CE Sch OX26 ....65 C1
Broome Way OX16 ....16 C4
Broomfield Rd RG30 .258 A1
Broughton Castle*
 OX15 ....15 A1
Broughton Cl OX16 ..258 B1
Broughton Rd OX15,OX16 .15 C2
Broughtons Cl OX13 ..123 C3
Brown's La Charlbury OX7 .73 A2
 Woodstock OX20 ......91 A3
Browning Dr OX26 .....65 B2
Brownings Cl OX2 ....91 A3
Browns Cl OX2 ......140 A4
Bruern Rd OX7 ....70 A2
Brunel Cl OX16 ......258 B1
Brunel Cres OX12 ...196 B1
Brunel Dr RG5 ......260 C1
Brunel Rd OX11 .....218 B4
Brunswick Beck OX11 .200 C2
Brunswick Pl OX16 ...16 C3
Bryan Way OX12 ....214 C3
Bryant Pl RG8 ......257 A3
Brympton Cl OX11 ...201 A1
Bryon Ho OX26 ....65 C1
Bryony Cl OX4 ......143 A1
Bryony Rd OX26 ......65 C3
Bryworth La GL7 ....150 A3
Buchan Rd OX26 ......65 B2
Buchanan Rd OX25 ...96 C4
Buck Side OX4 ......141 C3
Buckingham Cl OX11 .219 A4
Buckingham Cres OX26 .65 A2
Buckingham Dr RG4 .259 A3
Buckingham Pl OX18 .115 B1
Buckingham Rd
 Bicester OX26 ....65 C2
 Brackley NN13 ....24 A3
Buckingham St ⊠ OX1 .141 B4
Buckland CE Prim Sch
 SN7 ....170 C4
Buckland Cl OX5 ....108 C4
Buckland Mews OX14 .179 B4
Buckland Rd
 Bampton OX18 ......154 B4
 Buckland SN7 ....170 C4
 Charney Bassett OX12 .175 C1
Buckler Pl OX4 .....142 A1
Buckler Rd OX2 .....123 A4
Bucknell Ave RG8 ...256 C3
Bucknell Rd OX26 ....65 C3
Buckner's Cl OX10 ..203 C2
Buckthorn La OX10 ..220 C1
Budd Cl OX20 ....91 A3
Bugloss Wlk OX26 ....65 B3
Bulan Rd OX3 ....142 C4
Bull Baulk
 Middleton Cheney OX17 .11 A1
 Middleton Cheney OX17 .11 A1
Bull Hill OX7 ....72 A4
Bull La OX18 ....135 C1
Bull Mdw The RG8 ..248 C3
Bull St OX18 ....135 C1
Bullingdon Cl OX10 .204 A1
Bullingdon Ave OX10 .141 C4
Bullmarsh Cl OX26 ...65 B3
Bullockspits La OX13 .176 B4
Bullring The OX15 ...33 C2
Bulls Cl GL7 ....132 B3
Bulls La OX10+HP18 .128 A2
 Kings Sutton OX17 ...23 C3
Bullsmead OX13 .....159 C3
Bullstake Cl OX2 ....122 C1
Bulrush Rd OX4 .....142 C1
Bulwarks La OX1 ....123 A1
Bunce's La RG8 .....251 A1
Bungalow Cl RG30 ..111 B1
Bunkers Hill OX5 .....77 A1
Buntings The OX26 ..66 A1
Bunyan Rd OX26 .....65 B2
Burbush Rd OX4 ....142 C3

Burchester Ave OX3 ..124 C2
Burchester Pl OX16 ..16 C4
Burcombe Way RG4 ..259 A2
Burcot la OX10 ......182 B2
Burcot Pk OX14 .....181 C3
Burdell Ave OX3 ....125 A2
Burditch Bank OX20 ..75 C3
Burdock Cl OX26 .....65 C2
Bure La OX11 ....201 A1
Bure Park Prim Sch
 OX26 ....65 B2
Burey Pl OX26 ....65 C1
Burford Com Hospl
 OX18 ....100 C3
Burford Lodge ⊠ OX18 .141 B4
Burford Rd
 Black Bourton OX18 ..133 C3
 Brize Norton OX18 ..115 C4
 Carterton OX18 .....115 B2
 Charlbury OX7 ....73 A2
 Chipping Norton OX7 ..42 C1
 Minster Lovell OX18,OX29 .102 B1
 Witney OX28,OX29 ..103 B1
Burford Sch & Com Coll
 OX18 ....100 C3
Burford Sch (Annexe)
 OX18 ....100 C3
Burford St GL7 .....150 B2
Burgan Cl OX4 ......142 B2
Burgess Mead OX2 ..123 A2
Burleigh Mews RG4 .259 B3
Burlington Cres OX3 .125 A2
Burlington Gdns OX16 .16 A3
Burnham Rise RG4 ..259 B4
Burnhams The HP18 .128 B2
Burns Cl HP18 ....129 B4
Burns Cres OX26 .....65 B2
Burns Rd OX16 ....16 A2
Burr Cl OX29 ....120 A1
Burr St OX11 ....217 C4
Burra Cl OX4 ....161 A4
Burrows Cl OX2 .....124 B2
Burrows Hill OX10 ..204 C2
Bursill Cl OX3 .....125 A2
Burswin Rd OX18 ...115 B3
Burt's La HP18 .....129 B3
Burton Cl OX14 .....179 B3
Burton Pl OX4 ......142 C2
Burtons Bank OX7 ...68 C3
Burwell Cl OX18 ....117 C4
Burwell Ct OX18 ....117 C4
Burwell Dr OX18 ....117 C4
Burwell Mdw OX28 ..117 C3
Bury Court La OX17 ..8 A4
Bury Croft Rd OX15 ..30 A3
Bury Mead OX29 ....138 A4
Bury St OX14 ....179 C3
Burycroft The OX14 .160 A4
Buryhook Cnr OX33 .126 B1
Buscot Dr OX14 ....160 A1
Buscot Ho* SN7 ....171 A4
Bush Furlong OX11 ..201 A1
Bushe The HP17 ....130 C3
Bushey Cl OX2 ......122 A1
Bushey Dr OX18 ....152 C4
Bushey Leys Cl OX3 .124 C3
Bushey Row OX18 ..134 C2
Butcher's Hill OX7 ...69 B2
Butcher's Row OX16 ..16 B3
Butler Cl Bloxham OX15 .21 C3
 Horspath OX33 ......143 B3
 Oxford OX2 ....123 A2
Butler's Field GL7 ..150 B3
Butlers Cl CV36 ......28 A3
Butlers Dr OX18 ....115 C1
Butlers Orch RG4 ...252 B2
Butlers Rd OX7 ......57 C2
Butlers Rd OX16,OX17 .28 B3
Butterbur Gdns OX26 .65 C2
Buttercup Sq ⊠ OX4 .142 C1
Butterly Rd HP14 ...188 C2
Buttermilk La OX29 ..86 C1
Buttermilk La OX29 ..86 C1
Butterworth Pl ⊠ OX4 .142 C1
Butterwyke Pl ⊠ OX1 .141 C4
Butts Cl OX17 ....35 B4
Butts Hill Rd RG5 ...260 C1
Butts La OX3 ....124 B4
Butts Rd Faringdon SN7 .172 C1
 Horspath OX33 ......143 B3
Butts The Aynho OX17 ..35 B4
 Long Compton CV36 ...27 C2
 Merton OX25 ....95 B4
 Standlake OX29 .....137 B2
Butts Way OX4 .....161 A4
Buttyman Way OX14 .214 A1
Buxton Ave RG4 ....258 C2
Buzzards Cl OX17 ....9 B3
Byeway The OX16 ....16 A1
Byfield Rd OX17 .....3 A3
Bygones Mus* OX17 ..1 B1
Byres The HP17 .....130 C3
Byron Cl OX14 ......179 A3
Byron Rd OX16 ....16 A2
Byron Way OX26 .....65 B2

C

Cadel's Row SN7 ....172 C2
Cadogan Cl RG4 ....259 B2

Cadogan Pk OX20 .....91 A3
Caernarvon Way OX16 .15 C3
Caesars Gate NN13 ..24 A3
Caius Dene OX18 ....134 C2
Calais Cl OX29 .....136 C3
Calcot Cl OX3 ......124 C1
Calcroft La
 Clanfield OX18 ......133 B1
 Kencot GL7 ....132 C2
Caldecott Cl OX14 ..179 B3
Caldecott Prim Sch
 OX14 ....179 B3
Caldecott Rd OX14 ..179 C3
Calder Cl OX16 ......16 C4
Calder Way OX11 ...201 A1
Caldicott Cl OX10 ..203 A3
Caleta Cl RG4 ......259 B3
Calthorpe Rd OX16 ..16 B3
Calthorpe St OX16 ...16 B3
Calves Cl OX5 ......108 B4
Cam Cl OX11 ....200 C1
Cambridge Terr ⊠ OX1 .141 B4
Camden Cl OX26 .....65 C2
Camel Cross OX12 ..214 B3
Camellias The OX16 ..9 A1
Cameron Ave OX14 ..160 B1
Cameron Ct ⊠ OX16 ..16 C3
Camp Ind Est OX9 ..146 A2
Camp La OX17 ....62 B4
Camp Rd OX25 ....63 B4
Campbell Cl OX26 ...65 C1
Campbell Rd OX4 ...142 A3
Campbells Cl OX20 ..91 B3
Campion Cl OX28 ...103 C1
Campion Cl
 Carterton OX18 .....115 C1
 ⊠ Sandford-on-T OX4 .142 C1
Campion Hall Dr OX11 .219 A4
Campion Pl OX26 .....65 B2
Campion Rd OX14 ...180 A4
Canada Cl OX16 ......16 B4
Canada La OX12 ....214 B4
Canal La OX15 ......16 C1
Canal Rd OX5 ....92 B2
Canal St Banbury OX16 .16 B3
 Oxford OX2 ....123 A1
Canal Way OX12 ....214 A3
Candy La OX13 .....159 A3
Cane La OX12 ......214 B4
Canning Cres OX1 ..141 C3
Cannons Field OX3 ..123 C3
Canon Hill's Gdns SN6 .209 B3
Canons Dr GL7 .....132 C2
Canterbury Cl OX16 ..17 A4
Canterbury Rd OX2 .123 A2
Capel Cl OX2 ....123 A4
Caps La OX10 ....221 A1
Captains Mill OX28 .104 A1
Cardiff Mews RG1 ..258 C2
Cardiff Rd RG1 .....258 C2
Cardigan St Oxford OX2 .123 A1
 Reading RG4 ....259 A1
Cardinal Cl Oxford OX4 .142 A2
 Reading RG4 ....259 B3
Cardinal Newman RC Mid
 Sch OX4 ....142 A3
Cardwell Cres OX3 ..124 A1
Carew Cl RG31 .....257 A2
Carey Cl OX2 ....108 C1
Cariad Ct RG8 ......249 A4
Carisbrooke Cl RG4 .259 B3
Carlesgill Pl RG9 ..254 C4
Carling Rd RG4 .....252 C3
Carlisle Rd RG31 ...257 A2
Carlton Cl OX12 ....196 B1
Carlton Rd
 Cutteslowe OX2 .....109 A1
 Reading RG4 ....258 C3
Caroline Ct OX20 ....91 A3
Caroline St OX4 ....123 C1
Carpenter Cl OX4 ..142 B1
Carr Ave OX18 .....115 C1
Carrdus Sch The OX17 .17 B4
Carse Cl OX14 ......160 A2
Carswell Cl OX18 ...115 C1
Carswell Circ OX25 ..63 B4
Carswell Com Prim Sch
 OX14 ....179 C4
Carswell Ct ⊠ OX14 .179 C4
Carswell La SN7 ....154 C1
Carter Cl OX3 ......124 C1
Carter Cres OX17 ...3 A3
Carters Cl OX18 ....115 C1
Carters La HP18 ....129 A4
Carterton Com Coll
 OX18 ....115 B2
Carterton Prim Sch
 OX18 ....115 C1
Carterton Rd OX18 .116 A2
Carterton South Ind Est
 OX18 ....115 C1
Cartwright Rd OX17 ..35 B4
Cassington Rd
 Cassington OX8 ....121 A4
 Eynsham OX8 ....120 C4
 Yarnton OX5 ....108 A3
Castle Cl Benson OX10 .203 C2
 Bicester OX27 ....65 C2
Castle Cres SN7 ....193 C4
Castle Fields OX27 ...50 A2
Castle La OX10 .....204 A4
Castle Mews ⊠ OX12 .214 B3
Castle Mill Rd OX2 ..122 C1
Castle Quay Sh Ctr OX16 .16 B3
Castle Rd Lewknor OX49 .186 A2
 Wootton OX20 ....75 C3
Castle Sq OX10 .....203 C2
Castle St Banbury OX16 .16 B3

Castle St continued
Deddington OX15 . . . . .33 C2
Oxford OX1 . . . . .123 B1
Steventon OX13 . . . . .198 C2
Wallingford OX10 . . . . .221 B4
Castle Wlk OX11 . . . . .200 C1
Caswell La OX18 . . . . .116 C3
Cat La Ewelme OX10 . . . . . .204 C2
Stadhampton OX44 . . . . .163 B1
Cat St OX12 . . . . .216 B3
Catharine Cl OX14 . . . . . . .160 C2
Catharine Ct SN6 . . . . .209 B3
Catherine St OX4 . . . . .142 A4
Catkins Cl SN7 . . . . .172 C1
Catmore Cl OX12 . . . . .214 B4
Catmore Rd RG20 . . . . .234 C1
Catsham La
Chadlington OX7 . . . . .72 B3
Chilson OX7 . . . . .72 B3
Catslip RG9 . . . . .224 C1
Catte St OX1 . . . . .123 B1
Cattle Mkt OX7 . . . . .42 C2
Catwell Cl OX4 . . . . .142 A3
Caudwell Cl
Drayton OX14 . . . . .179 A1
Grove OX12 . . . . .196 C1
Causeway Banbury OX16 . . . .16 C3
Bloxham OX15 . . . . .21 B1
Blechingdon OX5 . . . . .93 A4
Causeway The
East Hanney OX12 . . . . .197 A3
Reading RG4 . . . . .259 B1
Steventon OX13 . . . . .198 C2
Woodstock OX20 . . . . .91 A3
Causmans Way RG31 . . . . .257 B1
Cavalier Rd OX9 . . . . .130 A1
Cave St OX4 . . . . .123 C1
Cavell Rd OX4 . . . . .142 A3
Cavendish Dr OX3 . . . . .123 C3
Cavendish Pl OX27 . . . . .52 B1
Cavendish Rd
Cutteslowe OX2 . . . . .123 A4
Reading RG4 . . . . .259 B3
Cavendish Wlk OX9 . . . . . .130 A1
Caversham Hill RG4 . . . . . .259 A2
Caversham Park Dr
RG4 . . . . .259 B3
Caversham Park Prim Sch
RG4 . . . . .259 B3
Caversham Park Rd
RG4 . . . . .259 B3
Caversham Prim Sch
RG4 . . . . .259 A2
Caversham Rd RG4 . . . . . . .259 A1
Caversham Wharf RG1 . . . .259 A1
Cawley Rd OX17 . . . . .23 A3
Cawsam Gdns RG4 . . . . . . .259 B2
Caxton Cl RG30 . . . . .258 B1
Caxton Ct RG9 . . . . .244 C1
Cecil Aldin Dr RG31 . . . . . .257 B2
Cecil Sharpe Cl OX4 . . . . . .124 B1
Cedar RG9 . . . . .244 B1
Cedar Cl OX16 . . . . .16 B1
Cedar Cres OX9 . . . . .147 B4
Cedar Ct OX4 . . . . .142 B3
Cedar Dr Bicester OX26 . . . . .65 C2
Pangbourne RG8 . . . . .256 B2
Cedar Rd Faringdon SN7 . . .172 C2
N Hinksey Village OX2 . . . . . . .140 B4
Cedar Villa OX16 . . . . .16 A3
Cedar Wood Cres RG4 . . . .259 A2
Cedars The Benson OX10 . . .204 A3
Reading RG31 . . . . .257 B1
Celandine Pl ■ OX4 . . . . . . .142 C1
Celsea Pl OX10 . . . . .221 A1
Cemetery Rd
Abingdon OX14 . . . . .179 B4
Bicester OX26 . . . . .65 C1
Centaury Pl OX4 . . . . .143 A1
Centenary Bsns Pk RG9 . . .244 C1
Centre Rise OX33 . . . . .143 B3
Centre St OX16 . . . . .16 C4
Centremead OX2 . . . . .141 A4
Century Cl SN7 . . . . .173 A2
Chacombe CE Prim Sch
OX17 . . . . .10 C1
Chacombe Rd OX17 . . . . . . .10 C1
Chadlington CE Prim Sch
OX7 .57 B1
Chadlington Rd
Oxford OX2 . . . . .123 B3
Spelsbury OX7 . . . . .72 C4
Chaffinch Wlk OX4 . . . . . . .142 C1
Chainhill Rd OX12 . . . . .214 C1
Chalcraft Cl RG9 . . . . .254 B4
Chalfont Rd OX2 . . . . .123 A3
Chalford Cl OX7 . . . . .42 C2
Chalford Rd OX9 . . . . .167 A2
Chalgrove Com Prim Sch
OX44 . . . . .184 B3
Chalgrove Rd OX9 . . . . .130 B1
Chalgrove Way RG4 . . . . . .259 A3
Chalk Farm Rd HP14 . . . . . .188 B3
Chalk Hill
Aston Tirrold OX11 . . . . .237 C4
Henley-on-T RG9 . . . . .254 B3
Chalkhouse Green La
RG4 . . . . .253 A1
Chalkhouse Green Rd
RG4 . . . . .252 B2
Chalkhousegreen La
RG4 . . . . .259 A4
Challow Rd OX12 . . . . .214 A3
Chalmore Gdns OX10 . . . . .221 B3
Chalvey Cl OX26 . . . . .65 B1
Chamberlain Pl OX5 . . . . . . .92 B1

Chamberlaine Ct ■
OX16 . . . . .16 B3
Chambrai Cl OX14 . . . . .200 C4
Champion Rd RG4 . . . . .259 B1
Champion Way OX4 . . . . . . .142 A2
Champs Cl OX14 . . . . .160 B1
Chancel Way
Lechlade GL7 . . . . .150 B2
Marcham OX13 . . . . .178 B4
Chandler Cl OX18 . . . . .134 C2
Chandlers Cl
Abingdon OX14 . . . . .160 B1
Wantage OX12 . . . . .214 C2
Chandlings Manor Sch
OX1 . . . . .160 A4
Chapel & Pope's Twr*
OX7 . . . . .138 A4
Chapel Cl
Deddington OX15 . . . . .34 C2
Leafield OX29 . . . . .86 C2
South Stoke RG8 . . . . .239 B2
Chapel Dr OX25 . . . . .81 B2
Chapel End
Croughton NN13 . . . . .36 B4
Great Rollright OX7 . . . . .29 A2
Chapel Hill
Brize Norton OX18 . . . . .116 A2
Oxford OX1 . . . . .30 C2
Swerford OX7 . . . . .30 C2
Watchfield SN6 . . . . .191 B1
Chapel La Adderbury OX17 . . .23 A2
Benson OX10 . . . . .203 C2
Berrick Salome OX10 . . . . . . .204 A4
Bledington OX7 . . . . .54 B1
Bledlow Ridge HP14 . . . . .169 C1
Blewbury OX11 . . . . .237 A4
Bodicote OX15 . . . . .22 C4
Chalgrove OX44 . . . . .184 B3
Charney Bassett OX12 . . . . . .175 C1
Cropredy OX17 . . . . .4 C1
Enstone OX7 . . . . .58 C3
Fernham SN7 . . . . .193 A3
Great Bourton OX17 . . . . .9 B3
Hailey OX29 . . . . .104 A3
Kingham OX7 . . . . .55 A4
Little Tew OX7 . . . . .45 A3
Milton (Banbury) OX15 . . . . . . .22 B2
Nettlebed RG9 . . . . .224 C1
North Leigh OX29 . . . . .105 A4
Northmoor OX29 . . . . .138 B2
Oxford OX4 . . . . .142 A1
Ratley OX15 . . . . .2 A2
Salford OX7 . . . . .41 C3
Shipton-u-W OX7 . . . . .85 B4
Shotteswell OX17 . . . . .8 B4
Standlake OX29 . . . . .137 B2
Sutton Courtenay OX14 . . . . . .200 A4
Turweston NN13 . . . . .24 A4
Uffington SN7 . . . . .211 B4
Chapel Rd Ashbury SN6 . . . .228 A4
South Leigh OX29 . . . . .119 A3
Stanford in the V SN7 . . . . . . .194 C4
Chapel Row OX4 . . . . .4 C1
Chapel Sq
Deddington OX15 . . . . .33 C2
East Hendred OX12 . . . . .216 B3
Chapel St Bicester OX26 . . . .65 C1
Bloxham OX15 . . . . .21 C2
Hook Norton OX15 . . . . .30 A4
Oxford OX4 . . . . .141 C4
Warmington OX17 . . . . .3 A2
Watlington OX49 . . . . .186 A1
Chapel Way
Childrey OX12 . . . . .213 B2
N Hinksey Village OX2 . . . . . . .122 B1
Chapelwick Cl SN6 . . . . . . .209 A3
Chapmans La OX1 . . . . .34 A2
Chapmans Piece OX18 . . . .100 C3
Charbridge La OX26 . . . . . . .66 A1
Charbridge Way OX26 . . . . .66 A1
Charcroft Cl OX29 . . . . .118 A3
Charlbury Cl OX5 . . . . .92 B1
Charlbury Prim Sch OX7 . . .73 B2
Charlbury Rd Finstock OX7 . .88 B4
Oxford OX2 . . . . .123 B3
Shrivenham SN6 . . . . .209 A3
Charlbury Sta OX7 . . . . .73 A2
Charles Ct OX16 . . . . .16 B3
Charles Dr OX9 . . . . .130 A1
Charles Evans Way RG4 . . .259 B1
Charles Ho RG9 . . . . .254 C1
Charles Rd OX10 . . . . .239 A4
Charles St OX4 . . . . .142 A4
Charlton Cty Prim Sch
OX12 . . . . .214 C3
Charlton Pk OX12 . . . . .214 C3
Charlton Rd Aynho OX17 . . . .35 B4
Wantage OX12 . . . . .214 C3
Charlton Village Rd
OX12 . . . . .214 C3
Charlton-on-Otmoor CE Prim
Sch OX5 . . . . .95 A2
Charney Ave OX14 . . . . .160 B1
Charter Ho OX12 . . . . .214 C2
Charter Way OX10 . . . . .221 B4
Charterville Cl OX29 . . . . . .102 C1
Chartwell Dr OX7 . . . . .42 C1
Charvil La RG4 . . . . .260 C2
Chase Barn OX27 . . . . .37 A2
Chastleton Ho* GL56 . . . . . .40 A4
Chatham Rd OX1 . . . . .141 B3
Chatsworth Cl RG4 . . . . . . .259 B3
Chatsworth Dr OX16 . . . . . . .16 C2
Chatterpie La OX29 . . . . . . .89 C3
Chaucer Cl Bicester OX26 . . .65 B2
Reading RG4 . . . . .259 A3
Chaucer Ct OX10 . . . . .204 C2
Chaucer's La OX20 . . . . .91 A4
Chaundy Rd OX5 . . . . .77 B3

Chaunterell Way OX14 . . . .179 B3
Chawley La OX2 . . . . .140 A3
Chazey Cl RG4 . . . . .258 B4
Chazey Rd RG4 . . . . .258 B2
Cheapside OX18 . . . . .134 C2
Chearsley Rd HP18 . . . . .129 C4
Cheatle Cl OX14 . . . . .100 C2
Checkendon CE Prim Sch
RG8 . . . . .241 B2
Checker Wlk OX14 . . . . .179 C4
Chedworth Dr OX28 . . . . . . .117 C4
Cheers Farm OX14 . . . . . . .179 B1
Chelford Way OX4 . . . . .258 C2
Chelmscote Row OX17 . . . . .10 C4
Chelsea RG30 . . . . .257 C1
Chenderit Sch OX17 . . . . . . .11 A1
Cheney Ct OX17 . . . . .10 C1
Cheney La OX3 . . . . .124 A1
Cheney Rd OX16 . . . . .16 C4
Cheney St OX11 . . . . .124 A1
Cheney Wlk OX14 . . . . .159 C3
Chepstow Gdns OX16 . . . . . .15 C3
Chepstow Rd RG31 . . . . . . .257 B1
Chequers Pl
Cholsey OX10 . . . . .220 C1
Oxford OX3 . . . . .124 C2
Cherbury Gn OX12 . . . . .214 B4
Cheriton Pl RG4 . . . . .252 C2
Cherry Cl Kidlington OX5 . . . .108 C4
Reading RG4 . . . . .259 B4
Sandford-on-T OX4 . . . . .142 C1
Stratton Audley OX27 . . . . .52 B1
Warborough OX10 . . . . .203 A3
Cherry Fields OX17 . . . . .9 B3
Cherry Orch
Great Coxwell SN7 . . . . .192 B4
Highworth SN6 . . . . .190 A3
Cherry Orchard La SN6 . . . .190 A3
Cherry Rd OX16 . . . . .16 A4
Cherry St OX27 . . . . .52 B1
Cherry Tree Cl
Grove OX12 . . . . .214 C4
Kingston Bagpuize OX13 . . . . .176 B4
Stoke Row RG9 . . . . .242 A3
Cherry Tree Dr OX13 . . . . . .159 B1
Cherry Tree Rd OX39 . . . . . .168 B3
Cherrys Cl OX15 . . . . .21 B2
Cherwell Ave OX5 . . . . .109 A4
Cherwell Bank OX5 . . . . .62 C3
Cherwell Bsns Ctr OX5 . . . . .92 B3
Cherwell Cl
Berinsfield OX10 . . . . .182 B3
Reading RG4 . . . . .259 A3
Cherwell Sch The OX2 . . . . .123 B3
Cherwell St Banbury OX16 . . .16 C4
Oxford OX4 . . . . .123 C1
Cherwood House Cotts
OX27 . . . . .66 A4
Cheshire Dr OX25 . . . . .63 B4
Cheshire Rd OX9 . . . . .148 B4
Chester St Oxford OX4 . . . . .141 C4
Reading RG4 . . . . .259 A1
Chester Way OX16 . . . . .15 C3
Chesterton CE Prim Sch
OX26 . . . . .79 C4
Chestnut Ave
Faringdon SN7 . . . . .172 C2
Oxford OX3 . . . . .124 B2
Radley OX14 . . . . .160 C2
Reading RG4 . . . . .259 C2
Thame OX9 . . . . .147 B4
Chestnut Cl Bix RG9 . . . . . . .243 C4
Brize Norton OX18 . . . . .116 B2
Chesterton OX26 . . . . .80 A4
Launton OX26 . . . . .66 B1
Witney OX28 . . . . .104 B1
Chestnut Cotts RG8 . . . . . . .249 A3
Chestnut Ct ■ OX4 . . . . . . .142 B2
Chestnut Dr OX4 . . . . .71 A1
Chestnut End OX26 . . . . .65 C2
Chestnut Gr RG8 . . . . .257 B3
Chestnut Rd OX2 . . . . .186 A1
Chestnut Rd
Mollington OX17 . . . . .4 A2
N Hinksey Village OX2 . . . . . . .140 B4
Chestnut Tree Cl OX13 . . . .159 B1
Chestnuts The
Abingdon OX14 . . . . .160 B1
Deddington OX15 . . . . .34 C2
Kirtlington OX5 . . . . .78 A2
Shiplake RG9 . . . . .255 A2
Chetwode Banbury OX16 . . . .16 A4
Banbury,Cherwcllodur OX17 . . .17 B3
Chetwyn Mead OX18 . . . . . .134 C2
Cheviot Way OX16 . . . . .8 C1
Cheyne La OX18 . . . . .134 C2
Chibnall Cl OX44 . . . . .184 B3
Chichester Cl OX26 . . . . .65 C1
Chichester Pl OX18 . . . . . . .116 B3
Chichester Wlk OX16 . . . . . . .9 A1
Chiers Dr OX14 . . . . .179 B1
Chilbridge Rd OX29 . . . . . . .120 B4
Chilbrook OX11 . . . . .200 C1
Childrey Way
Abingdon OX14 . . . . .160 A1
East Challow OX12 . . . . .213 C2
Chilgrove Dr OX25 . . . . .49 C3
Chillingworth Cres OX3 . . . .142 C4
Chillingworth Rd OX3 . . . . .142 C4

Chilswell La
Sunningwell OX1 . . . . .141 A1
Wootton (Oxford) OX1 . . . . . . .140 C2
Chilswell Rd OX1 . . . . .141 B4
Chiltern App OX26 . . . . .65 C2
Chiltern Bank RG9 . . . . .252 C4
Chiltern Bsns Ctr OX4 . . . . .142 C2
Chiltern Cl Benson OX10 . . . .203 C3
Berinsfield OX10 . . . . .182 B3
Chalgrove OX44 . . . . .184 C3
Henley-on-T RG9 . . . . .254 A4
Chiltern Cres OX10 . . . . . . .221 A4
Chiltern Ct RG4 . . . . .259 A1
Chiltern Edge Com Sch
RG4 . . . . .252 C2
Chiltern End RG9 . . . . .254 B4
Chiltern Gdns OX49 . . . . . . .186 B1
Chiltern Gn OX9 . . . . .148 A4
Chiltern Nursery Training
Coll RG4 . . . . .259 A2
Chiltern Rd Reading RG4 . . .259 B2
Rotherfield Peppard RG9 . . . . .252 C4
Chiltern Ridge HP14 . . . . . . .188 B3
Chiltern Sculpture Trail*
HP14 . . . . .187 B2
Chiltern View
Little Milton OX44 . . . . .164 A4
Purley on T RG8 . . . . .257 B3
Tetsworth OX9 . . . . .166 A4
Chiltern Wlk RG8 . . . . .256 C3
Chilton Cl OX14 . . . . .160 A1
Chilton Cty Prim Sch
OX11 . . . . .235 B4
Chilton Rd
Long Crendon HP18 . . . . .129 B4
Upton OX11 . . . . .218 A1
Wallingford OX10 . . . . .221 B4
Chilwall Cl OX9 . . . . .148 A4
Chinalls Cl MK18 . . . . .39 B3
Chinnock Brook OX11 . . . . .200 C2
Chinnor Hill OX39 . . . . .168 C2
Chinnor Hill Nature
Reserve* OX39 . . . . .168 C3
Chinnor Rd
Aston Rowant OX49 . . . . .167 B1
Bledlow Ridge HP14 . . . . .169 B2
Thame OX9 . . . . .148 B3
Towersey OX9 . . . . .148 C3
Chipmunk Rd OX10 . . . . . . .204 B2
Chipperfield Park Rd
OX15 . . . . .21 B1
Chipping Norton Hospl
OX7 .42 C2
Chipping Norton Mus*
OX7 .42 C2
Chipping Norton Rd
Chadlington OX7 . . . . .57 A2
Hook Norton OX15 . . . . .30 A4
Chipping Norton Sch
OX7 .42 C1
Chipping Warden Prim Sch
OX17 .5 C4
Choicehill Rd OX7 . . . . .42 C3
Cholesbury Grange
OX3 . . . . .124 A2
Cholsey & Wallingford Rly*
OX10 . . . . .220 C2
Cholsey Cl OX4 . . . . .142 B2
Cholsey Prim Sch OX10 . . . .220 C1
Cholsey Sta OX10 . . . . .220 C1
Cholswell Cl OX13 . . . . .159 B2
Cholswell Rd OX13 . . . . . . .159 B1
Chorefields OX5 . . . . .92 B1
Choswell Spring OX4 . . . . . .142 C2
Chowns Cl OX9 . . . . .148 A4
Christ Church OX1 . . . . .123 B1
Christ Church Cath Sch
OX1 . . . . .141 B4
Christ Church Old Bldgs ■
OX1 . . . . .123 A1
Christchurch Cath*
OX1 . . . . .123 B1
Christchurch Ct OX16 . . . . . .16 C3
Christopher Rawlins CE Prim
Sch OX17 . . . . .23 A2
Church Ave
Henley-on-T RG9 . . . . .244 C1
Kings Sutton OX17 . . . . .23 C3
Church Cl Adderbury OX17 . . .71 B1
Ascott-u-W OX7 . . . . .71 A1
Benson OX10 . . . . .203 C2
Black Bourton OX18 . . . . .133 C3
Charlbury OX7 . . . . .73 A2
Cuddesdon OX44 . . . . .144 B2
Curbridge OX29 . . . . .117 B1
East Hagbourne OX11 . . . . . .218 C3
Frinfgord OX27 . . . . .52 B4
Great Bourton OX17 . . . . .9 B3
Islip OX5 . . . . .93 C1
Longcot SN7 . . . . .192 B4
Merton OX25 . . . . .95 B4
Rotherfield Greys RG9 . . . . . .243 B1
South Hinksey OX1 . . . . .141 A3
Wardington OX17 . . . . .5 C1
Church Cotts OX4 . . . . .161 C2
Church Cowley Rd OX4 . . . .142 A3
Church Cowley St James CE
Fst Sch OX4 . . . . .142 B2
Church End
Blewbury OX11 . . . . .219 A1
Croughton NN13 . . . . .36 B4
Drayton St L OX10 . . . . .183 A3
Great Rollright OX7 . . . . .29 A2
South Leigh OX29 . . . . .119 B3
Standlake OX29 . . . . .137 B2
Church Furlong OX15 . . . . . . .21 B1

Church Gn
Long Crendon HP18 . . . . .129 B4
Stanford in the V SN7 . . . . . . .194 C4
Witney OX28 . . . . .118 A4
Church Hill Chilton OX11 . . . .235 B4
Great Haseley OX44 . . . . .164 C4
Little Milton OX44 . . . . .163 C3
Stonor RG9 . . . . .225 B4
Tackley OX5 . . . . .7 A2
Warmington OX17 . . . . .3 A2
Church Hill Rd OX4 . . . . .142 A2
Church La Adderbury OX17 . . .23 A2
Aston Rowant OX49 . . . . .167 B2
Bicester OX26 . . . . .16 B3
Bicester OX26 . . . . .65 C1
Bishopstone SN6 . . . . .227 B2
Bledington OX7 . . . . .54 B1
Bledlow Ridge HP14 . . . . .189 C4
Bledlow Ridge, Radnage
OX39 . . . . .189 B4
Brightwell-cum-S OX10 . . . . . .202 C2
Burford OX18 . . . . .100 C3
Cassington OX29 . . . . .107 B1
Chacombe OX17 . . . . .10 C2
Chalgrove OX44 . . . . .184 B3
Charlbury OX7 . . . . .73 A2
Charlton-on-O OX5 . . . . .95 A2
Chinnor OX39 . . . . .168 B3
Chipping Norton OX7 . . . . .42 C2
Claydon OX17 . . . . .1 B1
Coleshill SN6 . . . . .191 A4
Croughton NN13 . . . . .36 B4
Crowmarsh G OX10 . . . . .221 B1
Drayton OX14 . . . . .179 A3
Drayton St L OX10 . . . . .183 A3
Ewelme RG9 . . . . .206 A1
Fernham SN7 . . . . .193 A2
Fulbrook OX18 . . . . .100 C3
Hailey OX29 . . . . .104 A3
Hampton Poyle OX5 . . . . .93 A2
Hanwell OX17 . . . . .8 C2
Harwell OX11 . . . . .217 C4
Hornton OX15 . . . . .7 B3
Horton-cum-S OX33 . . . . .112 A3
Islip OX5 . . . . .93 C1
Kirtlington OX5 . . . . .78 A2
Langford GL7 . . . . .132 B1
Longworth OX13 . . . . .156 A2
Lower Heyford OX25 . . . . .62 B3
Ludgershall HP18 . . . . .98 B4
Marston OX3 . . . . .123 C3
Middle Barton OX7,OX25 . . . . .61 A4
Middleton Cheney OX17 . . . . . .10 C1
Milcombe OX15 . . . . .21 A1
Mixbury NN13 . . . . .38 C4
Mollington OX17 . . . . .4 A2
Nuneham C OX44 . . . . .259 C4
Rotherfield Peppard RG9 . . . . .253 A4
Shilton OX18 . . . . .115 A4
Shiplake RG9 . . . . .254 C1
Shotteswell OX17 . . . . .8 B4
South Moreton OX11 . . . . . . .219 C3
Spelsbury OX7 . . . . .72 C4
Steventon OX13 . . . . .198 C2
Towersey SN9 . . . . .148 C4
Wallingford OX10 . . . . .221 B4
Watlington OX49 . . . . .186 A2
Wendlebury OX6 . . . . .80 A2
Weston-on-the-G OX25 . . . . . .79 B4
Witney OX28 . . . . .118 B4
Yarnton OX5 . . . . .108 A2
Church Mdw OX7 . . . . .70 A1
Church Mews RG8 . . . . .257 B3
Church Mill Cl OX29 . . . . . . .137 B2
Church Pas OX16 . . . . .16 B3
Church Path
Stanford in the V SN7 . . . . . . .194 C4
Stokenchurch HP14 . . . . .188 B3
Church Pl GL56 . . . . .54 A4
Church Rd
Appleton OX13 . . . . .158 A4
Ardley OX27 . . . . .50 B2
Benson OX10 . . . . .203 C2
Blewbury OX11 . . . . .237 A4
Brackley NN13 . . . . .24 A4
Chadlington OX7 . . . . .57 B1
Chinnor OX39 . . . . .168 B3
Cholsey OX10 . . . . .220 C2
Great Milton OX44 . . . . .145 A1
Hinton Waldrist SN7 . . . . .155 C1
Horspath OX33 . . . . .143 B3
Ickford HP18 . . . . .127 C2
Lewknor OX49 . . . . .187 A4
Long Hanborough OX29 . . . . .106 B4
Lower Odington GL56 . . . . .54 A4
Milton-u-W OX7 . . . . .69 A1
North Leigh OX29 . . . . .105 A4
Pangbourne RG8 . . . . .256 B3
Radley OX14 . . . . .160 C2
Reading RG4 . . . . .259 A1
Thame OX9 . . . . .129 C1
Weston-on-the-G OX25 . . . . . .79 A1
Wheatley OX33 . . . . .144 A4
Church Rise OX7 . . . . .88 B3
Church Row
Bishopstone SN4 . . . . .227 A2
Bourton SN6 . . . . .209 A1
Childrey OX12 . . . . .213 B2
Langford GL7 . . . . .132 B1
Church Sq OX15 . . . . .93 C1
Church Sch
Ardington OX12 . . . . .215 C3
Bampton OX18 . . . . .134 C2

Church St *continued*
Barford St M OX15 ....32 C3
Beckley OX3 ....111 A2
Bicester OX26 ....65 C1
Bladon OX20 ....91 A1
Bledington OX7 ....54 B1
Bloxham OX15 ....21 B2
Bodicote OX15 ....22 C4
Charlbury OX7 ....73 A2
Chipping Norton OX7 ....42 C2
Deddington OX15 ....33 C2
Didcot OX11 ....218 C4
Ducklington OX29 ....118 A2
East Hendred OX12 ....216 B3
Eynsham OX29 ....120 C4
Faringdon SN7 ....172 C2
Fifield OX7 ....69 A1
Henley-on-T RG9 ....244 B1
Idbury OX7 ....69 A2
Kidlington OX5 ....92 C1
Kingham OX7 ....55 A2
Marcham OX13 ....178 B3
Marsh Gibbon OX27 ....67 C2
Reading RG4 ....259 A1
Shellingford SN7 ....193 C4
Shipton-u-W OX7 ....85 B4
Somerton OX25 ....48 C3
Stokenchurch HP14 ....188 B3
Stonesfield OX29 ....89 B4
Sutton Courtenay OX14 ....180 A1
Upton OX11 ....218 B1
Wantage OX12 ....214 B2
Wargrave RG10 ....255 B1
Watlington OX49 ....186 A1
West Hanney OX12 ....196 C3
Wootton OX20 ....120 C2
Wroxton OX15 ....15 A4

Church Terr
Bicester OX26 ....65 C1
Stanford in the V SN7 .....174 B1

Church View
Ascott-u-W OX7 ....71 B1
Bampton OX18 ....134 C2
Banbury OX16 ....16 A2
Brackley NN13 ....24 A4
Carterton OX18 ....115 C1
Charlton-on-O OX5 ....95 A3
Freeland OX29 ....106 A3
Grove OX12 ....196 C1
Highworth SN6 ....49 B4
Stoke Row RG9 ....241 C3
Church View Rd OX28 ....117 C4
Church Villas OX11 .....237 A4
Church Way
N Hinksey Village OX2 .....122 B1
Oxford OX4 ....141 C2
Sparsholt OX12 ....212 C2
Church Wlk Adderbury OX16 ..16 B3
Bishopstone SN6 ....227 B2
Combe OX29 ....90 A2
Faringdon SN7 ....172 A2
Oxford OX2 ....123 A2
Shipton-u-W OX7 ....70 B1
Shrivenham SN6 ....209 B4
Upper Heyford OX25 ....62 C4
Churchfield RG9 ....223 B2
Churchfield La OX10 ....203 C2
Churchfields OX29 ......89 B4
Churchill CI Didcot OX11 .200 B1
Woodstock OX20 ....91 A3
Churchill Cres
Sonning Common RG4 ....252 C3
Thame OX9 ....148 A4
Churchill Dr OX3 ....124 B1
Churchill Gate OX20 ....91 B3
Churchill Hospl The
OX3 ....142 B4
Churchill Pl OX2 ....122 C4
Churchill Rd
Bicester OX26 ....65 C2
Chipping Norton OX7 ....42 B1
Didcot OX11 ....200 B1
Kidlington OX5 ....108 C4
Kingham OX7 ....55 A4
Churchill Way OX29 ....106 A4
Churchlea OX17 ....4 A2
Churchmere Rd OX14 ....180 A1
Churchward OX11 ....200 C2
Churchward Ct OX12 ....196 B1
Churchway RG20 ....235 A1
Chure The OX5 ....95 A2
Churchill OX11 ....201 A1
Cinnaminta Rd OX3 .....142 C4
Cinnamon CI OX44 ......184 B4
Circourt Rd OX12 ......195 C2
Circular Rd OX26 ....81 A3
Circus St OX4 ....141 C4
City Rd HP14 ....189 B3
Clack's La Benson OX10 .222 B4
Crowmarsh G OX10 ....222 B4
Clanfield CE Prim Sch
OX18 ....152 C4
Clanfield Cres RG31 ....257 B1
Clanfield Rd OX18 ......134 C1
Clapcot Way OX10 ......221 B4
Clare Terr OX18 ....115 B1
Clarence Pl OX12 ....216 C4
Clarence Rd RG9 ....254 B3
Clarendon CI OX14 .....180 A4
Clarendon Dr OX9 ....130 A1
Clark's Row OX1 ....141 B4
Clarks La CV36 ....28 A3
Clarkston Rd OX18 .....115 B1
Clay Bank OX5 ....30 A4
Clay CI RG31 ....257 A1

Clay Hut CI OX7 ....58 C3
Clay La OX5 ....204 B1
Claydon Ct 5 RG4 ......259 A1
Claydon Rd OX17 ....4 C2
Clayfields SN6 ....209 A2
Claymond Rd OX3 ....124 C2
Claypit La SN7 ....211 A4
Clayts La SN6 ....209 B4
Clays CI OX3 ....124 A3
Cleave The OX11 ....217 C4
Cleavers OX39 ....168 A3
Cleavers Sq 6 OX4 ....142 C1
Cleeve CI RG8 ....249 A4
Cleeve Down RG8 ....249 B4
Cleeve Park Cotts RG8 ..249 B4
Cleeve Rd RG8 ....249 A4
Cleeves Ave OX7 ....42 C2
Cleeves Cnr OX7 ....42 C2
Clematis Pl OX4 ....142 C1
Clement Burrows Ho 5
OX1 ....123 A1
Clements CI OX12 ....214 C3
Clements Gn OX11 ......219 C3
Clements La OX27 ....67 C1
Clements Mead RG31 ....257 A1
Clements Rd RG9 ....244 B2
Clerkenwell Cotts HP17 .130 C3
Clevedon CE Prim Sch
OX14 ....181 B2
Clevedon Ct OX5 ....108 C4
Clevedon Rd RG31 ......257 C2
Cleveland CI OX5 ....109 A4
Cleveland Dr OX4 ....142 B3
Clevelands OX14 ....160 A1
Cleveley Rd OX7 ....58 C3
Clewmede RG8 ....249 B4
Cleycourt Rd SN6 ......209 A3
Clifden Rd HP18 ....127 B3
Clifford Pl OX2 ....122 B4
Clifton Dr OX14 ....179 C4
Clifton Hampden CE Prim
Sch OX14 ....181 B2
Clifton Park Rd RG4 ....258 C2
Clifton Rd OX15,OX17 ....34 B2
Clifton Rise RG10 ......255 C1
Clinton CI OX4 ....141 C2
Clive Rd OX4 ....142 B3
Clock Tower Ct SN7 ....172 C1
Cloisters The
Ewelme OX10 ....204 C2
20 Oxford OX1 ....141 B4
Reading RG4 ....259 A2
1 Wantage OX12 ....214 B2
Clonmel CI RG4 ....259 B1
Close The
Ardington OX12 ....215 C3
Aston Tirrold OX11 ....237 C4
Benson OX10 ....203 C3
Chipping Warden OX17 ......5 C3
Great Bourton OX17 ....9 B4
Henley-on-T RG9 ....254 B4
Lechlade GL7 ....150 B3
Stanton Harcourt OX29 ...138 A4
Stoke Lyne OX27 ....51 A3
Woodcote RG8 ....250 C4
Closes The OX5 ....92 C1
Clover CI OX2 ....140 A3
Clover Mead OX26 ....65 C3
Clover Pl Eynsham OX29 .120 B4
Oxford OX4 ....142 C1
Coach House Ct RG8 ....256 C2
Coach La SN7 ....173 A2
Coach Way OX10 ....203 C2
Coalport Way RG30 .....257 C1
Coates La RG9 ....206 B1
Cobden Cres OX1 ....141 B4
Cobden Ctr The OX11 .....200 C2
Cochrane Rd OX10 ......204 B1
Cockcroft Rd OX11 .....218 C4
Cockington Gn OX16 .....16 C4
Cockpit CI OX20 ....91 A3
Cocks La OX13 ....159 B4
Cockshoot CI OX29 ....89 B4
Cockwell La SN7 ....192 B3
Cogges Farm Mus*
OX28 ....118 B4
Cogges Hill Rd OX28 ....118 B4
Coghill OX5 ....92 C1
Coker CI OX26 ....65 C1
Colborne Rd OX11 ......218 B4
Coldharbour CI RG9 ....254 B4
Coldicott St RG4 ....259 B1
Cole Ct OX11 ....200 C2
Colegrave Rd OX15 ......21 C3
Colemans Hill OX3 ......124 C2
Coleridge CI
8 Bicester OX26 ....65 B2
Oxford OX4 ....142 B3
Coleridge Dr OX14 ......179 B3
Colerne Rd OX18 ....115 C2
Coles La OX44 ....184 B4
Colesbourne Rd OX11 ...218 B4
Coleshill Dr SN7 ....172 C1
Colgrove Down OX2 .....140 A3
Collcutt CI OX33 ....143 B4
College CI Cholsey OX10 .220 C1
Holton OX33 ....126 B1
College Farm
Benson OX10 ....203 C2
Chadlington OX7 ....57 A1
College Farm CI OX5 .....94 C1
College Flats OX4 ......142 A1
College La
Long Compton CV36 ....28 A2
Oxford OX4 ....142 A1
College Sq OX13 ....156 A2
College The OX10 ......101 C2
College Way OX33 ......143 A3
Collett OX11 ....200 C2
Collett Way OX12 ......196 B1

Colley Wood OX1 ....141 B1
Collice St OX5 ....109 C4
Collier's La SN7 ....173 A2
Colliers La RG9 ....252 C4
Collingwood CI OX14 ...159 C1
Collingwood Rd OX11 ...218 B4
Collins St 8 SN7 ....211 A4
Collinsmith Dr OX12 ...196 C1
Collinsons Row OX7 .....73 A2
Collinwood CI OX3 .....124 C2
Collinwood Rd OX3 .....124 C2
Collyer Rd HP14 ....188 C2
Colmore La RG9 ....252 C4
Coln Rd OX11 ....217 A2
Colne CI Bicester OX26 ..65 B1
Grove OX12 ....196 B1
Colne Dr
Berinsfield OX10 ....182 B3
Didcot OX11 ....201 A2
Colonnade The RG31 ....257 B1
Colony Rd OX15 ....19 A4
Colterne CI OX3 ....124 A3
Coltman Ave HP18 ......129 B3
Colton Rd SN6 ....209 A3
Coltsfoot Sq 11 OX4 ...142 C1
Columbia Way OX12 ....214 B4
Columbine Gdns OX4 ...143 A1
Colville OX16 ....18 C3
Colville Wlk OX16 ....16 C4
Colwell Dr
Abingdon OX14 ....179 B4
Oxford OX3 ....125 A2
Witney OX28 ....117 C3
Colwell Rd OX10 ....182 B3
Colyton Way RG8 ....257 B3
Combe CE Prim Sch
OX29 ....90 A2
Combe Gate OX9 ....90 A2
Combe Rd Oxford OX2 ...123 A1
Stonesfield OX29 ....89 B4
Combe Sta OX29 ....90 A2
Combes CI SN7 ....173 A2
Comberwell OX44 ....143 B1
Comfrey Rd OX4 ....142 C2
Common CI
North Leigh OX29 ....105 A3
Shrivenham SN6 ....209 B4
Common La OX7 ....42 B1
Common Rd Beckley OX3 .110 C2
North Leigh OX29 ....105 A3
Compass CI 4 OX4 ......142 B2
Compton CE Prim Sch
OX29 ....27 C3
Compton Dr OX4 ....160 A1
Compton Terr 2 OX10 ..221 B4
Condor CI RG31 ....257 B2
Conduit Hill Rise OX9 ..147 C4
Conduit House* OX4 .....42 B2
Conduit Rd OX14 ....179 C4
Conifer CI OX2 ....140 B4
Conifer Dr Bicester OX26 .65 C3
Reading RG31 ....257 A1
Conifer Rise OX16 ....9 A1
Conigre OX39 ....168 A3
Conisboro Ave RG4 .....258 C3
Conisboro Way RG4 ....258 C3
Coniston Ave OX3 ......124 A2
Coniston Dr RG30 ......257 C1
Connaught Ho RG4 .....244 C2
Connolly Dr OX18 ......115 B2
Constable's Croft OX5 ..96 C4
Constitution Hill OX10 ..221 C2
Convent The OX7 ....68 B3
Conway Dr OX16 ....15 C3
Conway Rd OX13 ....159 B1
Conyger CI OX5 ....93 C1
Conygree Terr OX7 ......42 C2
Cook La OX10 ....221 C1
Cook's Hill OX15 ....14 C4
Cooks La OX7 ....41 C3
Coolidge CI OX3 ....124 B1
Coombe Hill Cres OX9 ..147 C4
Coombe The RG8 ....248 C3
Coombe Vale OX7 ....85 B4
Cooper CI
Chipping Norton OX7 ......42 C2
Wheatley OX33 ....143 C4
Cooper PI OX3 ....124 C2
Cooper Rd OX9 ....147 B4
Cooper Sch OX26 ....66 A2
Cooper's Court Rd HP14 .188 B3
Coopers Gate OX16 .....16 B4
Coopers Gn OX26 ....65 C3
Coopers La
Abingdon OX14 ....179 C3
Wantage OX12 ....214 C3
Coopers Piece OX10 ....221 B4
Coopers Pightle RG4 ...252 B2
Cope CI OX2 ....140 B4
Cope Rd OX16 ....16 B3
Copenhagen Dr OX14 ...159 B1
Copperage Rd OX12 ....234 A1
Copperfields RG4 ......258 C2
Coppice CI OX16 ....16 C2
Coppock CI OX3 ....124 C1
Copperfield CI OX12 ...214 B3
Copse Ave RG4 ....259 C2
Copse CI RG31 ....257 B2
Copse La OX3 ....124 A3
Copse Mead RG5 ....260 C1
Copse The
Abingdon OX14 ....160 B1
Wargrave RG10 ....255 C2
Copson La OX44 ....163 B1
Copthorne Rd OX5 .....108 B4
Corbett Rd OX18 ....115 B1
Cordrey Gn OX4 ....141 C2

Corfe Mews RG4 ....259 C2
Coriander Way 15 OX4 ..142 C1
Corn Avill CI OX14 .....160 B1
Corn Bar OX28 ....117 C4
Corn St OX28 ....118 A4
Corncrake Way OX26 ....66 A1
Corndell Gdns OX28 ....118 A4
Corner CI The OX15 ......13 A3
Corneville Rd OX14 .....179 A1
Cornfield CI OX28 ......117 C4
Cornhill La OX12 ....213 C3
Cornish Rd OX7 ....42 B1
Cornmarket
Faringdon SN7 ....172 C2
Thame OX9 ....147 C4
Cornmarket St OX1 .....123 B1
Cornwall CI RG31 ......257 A2
Cornwallis CI OX4 ......142 A3
Cornwallis Rd OX4 .....142 A3
Cornwell OX7 ....41 B2
Coromandel OX14 ....179 B2
Coronation Cotts OX18 .152 C4
Coronation La OX17 ......8 B4
Corpus Christi Coll OX1 .123 B1
Corunna OX4 ....142 C3
Cosford Gdns OX26 .....66 A2
Cosin CI OX4 ....142 A4
Costar CI OX4 ....142 B3
Cot's Gn OX5 ....92 B1
Cote Rd OX18 ....135 C2
Cothill House Sch OX13 .158 C2
Cothill Rd OX13 ....158 C2
Cotman CI OX14 ....179 C3
Cotmore CI OX9 ....148 A4
Cotmore Gdns OX9 .....148 A4
Cotshill Gdns OX7 ....42 C2
Cotswold CI
Minster Lovell OX29 ......102 C1
Sibford Ferris OX15 ......19 A4
Cotswold Cnr OX7 ....29 A2
Cotswold Cres
Chipping Norton OX7 ......42 C1
Marston OX3 ....123 C3
Cotswold Cres Bungs
OX7 ....42 C1
Cotswold Dene OX29 ...137 A3
Cotswold Mdw OX28 ....117 B4
Cotswold Pk OX11 ......200 B1
Cotswold Rd OX2 ....140 A3
Cotswold Terr OX7 ......42 C1
Cotswold View OX7 ......73 A2
Cotswold Way
Carterton OX18 ....115 B2
Reading RG31 ....257 B1
Cotswold Wildlife Pk*
OX18 ....114 B3
Cotswold Woollen Weavers
Mus* GL7 ....132 A3
Cottage Rd SN7 ....194 B4
Cottages The OX18 .....114 A3
Cottesmore La OX10 ....204 B3
Cottesmore Rd OX4 .....142 A2
Cotton Grass CI OX4 ...142 C1
Cotts The HP13 ....129 B3
Couching St OX49 ......186 A1
Coulings CI OX12 ......216 B4
Council Cotts RG4 ......252 A3
Council Hos
Bloxham OX15 ....21 B2
Great Bourton OX17 ....45 B4
Shiplake RG9 ....254 A1
Council Hos The
Barford St M OX15 ....32 C3
Charlbury OX7 ....73 A2
Hailey OX7 ....57 C4
Nettlebed RG9 ....224 B3
Council Houses OX7 ....72 C4
Council Houses The
OX7 ....91 B3
Country Pk OX28 ....118 A3
County Rd NN13 ....24 A3
County Trading Est OX4 ..142 C2
County View OX15 ....34 B2
Coupland Rd OX13 .....159 A3
Court CI Kidlington OX5 .108 B4
Shipton-u-W OX7 ....85 B4
Warmington OX17 ....3 A2
Court Close Rd OX9 ....148 C4
Court Dr OX10 ....203 A3
Court Farm Rd OX4 ....141 C2
Court Gdns RG8 ....249 B4
Court Hill Rd OX12 ....214 A1
Court Place Gdns OX4 ..141 C2
Court Rd OX12 ....214 A1
Court The OX14 ....159 C1
Courtenay CI OX14 .....200 A4
Courtenay Dr RG4 .....259 C1
Courtenay Rd OX12 ....214 C3
Courtfield Rd OX33 ....125 B4
Courthouse* HP18 .....129 B4
Courtiers Gn OX14 .....181 B2
Courtington La OX15 ....21 B3
Courtland Rd OX4 ......142 A2
Courtlands Hill RG8 ....256 B2
Courtlands Rd OX7 ......85 B4
Courts Gdns OX28 ......118 A4
Courtyard The
Banbury OX17 ....141 C2
Crawley OX29 ....103 B3
Tadmarton OX15 ....21 A3
Covent CI OX14 ....160 A2
Coverley Rd OX3 ....142 B4
Covert The OX20 ....91 B3
Cow La Denchworth OX12 .195 C2
Didcot OX11 ....201 A1
Grove OX12 ....196 B2
Kennington OX1 ....141 C1
Longworth OX13 ....156 B2

Cow La *continued*
Moulsford OX10 ....238 C2
Reading RG1 ....258 C1
Steeple Aston OX25 ....62 A4
Sutton Courtenay OX11 ...199 C1
Cowderoy Pl SN7 ....194 C4
Cowleaze OX39 ....168 A3
Cowleaze CI SN6 ......209 A3
Cowleaze Cnr OX18 ....134 B1
Cowley Rd Oxford OX4 ..142 C2
Cowley Junc OX4 ......142 C2
Cowley PI OX4 ....141 C4
Cowley Rd Oxford OX4 ..142 A1
Oxford, Littlemore OX4 ..142 A1
Cowper CI 2 OX26 ......65 B2
Cox La OX7 ....42 A1
Cox's Alley OX3 ....124 C2
Cox's Ct SN7 ....194 C4
Cox's La
Crowmarsh G OX10 ....222 A3
Stoke Row RG9 ....241 C3
Cox's Rd SN6 ....209 A3
Coxfield CI HP14 ....188 C2
Coxmoor CI OX7 ....54 C2
Coxwell Gdns SN7 ......172 C2
Coxwell St SN7 ....172 C1
Coxwell St SN7 ....172 C1
Cozens La OX7 ....54 C2
CR Bates Ind Est HP14 ...188 C3
Crabtree Cnr OX14 .....240 B4
Crabtree La OX14 ......179 A1
Crabtree Pl OX14 ......180 A4
Crabtree Rd
Haddenham HP17 ....130 C3
N Hinksey Village OX2 ...140 B4
Crafts End OX11 ....235 C4
Cranbourne Gdns RG30 .258 A1
Cranbourne Rd OX28 ...118 A3
Cranbrook Dr OX1 .....160 C4
Crane Furlong SN6 .....190 A4
Cranesbill Dr OX26 ......65 B3
Cranesbill Way OX4 ....142 C1
Cranford House Sch
OX10 ....238 C3
Cranham St OX2 ....123 A2
Cranham Terr OX2 ......123 A2
Cranleigh CI OX16 ......16 A2
Cranmer CI RG31 ......257 A2
Cranmer Rd OX4 ....142 C3
Cranston Ct 5 OX4 ....142 A2
Cranwell Rd OX18 .....115 C1
Craster Ct OX16 ....16 A2
Cratlands CI OX44 .....163 B1
Craufurd Rd OX4 ....142 C3
Craven Comm SN7 ......211 B4
Craven Way OX11 ......218 C4
Crawborough Rd OX7 ....73 B2
Crawborough Villas OX7 .73 B2
Crawley Mill Ind Est
OX29 ....103 B2
Crawley Rd OX29 ....104 A1
Crawshay Dr RG4 ......259 A4
Cray Ct OX11 ....200 C2
Craysleaze RG4 ....252 B2
Crazies Hill CE Prim Sch
RG10 ....255 C2
Creampot CI OX17 ....4 C1
Creampot Cres OX17 .....4 C1
Creampot La OX17 ....4 C1
Crecy Wlk OX20 ....91 B3
Cremyll Rd RG1 ....258 C1
Crendon Ct 4 RG4 .....259 A1
Crendon Way HP18 .....129 C2
Crescent CI OX4 ....142 B3
Crescent Ct OX4 ....142 B3
Crescent Rd Oxford OX4 .142 B3
Reading RG31 ....257 B1
Crescent The
Adderbury OX17 ....23 A3
Bicester OX26 ....65 B2
Carterton OX18 ....133 B4
East Hagbourne OX11 ....218 C3
Long Wittenham OX14 ....201 B4
Oxford OX2 ....123 A3
Sandford-on-T OX4 ......161 B4
Shiplake RG9 ....255 A2
Steeple Aston OX25 ......62 A4
Witney OX28 ....104 B1
Woodcote RG8 ....250 C1
Cress Hill Pl OX3 ....124 C2
Crest The
Bledlow Ridge HP14 .....189 C4
Reading RG4 ....259 B3
Crick Rd OX2 ....123 B3
Cricket Ground HP14 ...188 B3
Cricket Rd OX4 ....142 A3
Cricklade Rd SN6 ......190 A3
Cripley Pl OX2 ....123 A1
Cripley Rd OX2 ....123 A1
Crisp Rd RG9 ....244 B2
Crispin CI RG4 ....258 B3
Crispin Pl OX10 ....221 B4
Croasdell CI OX14 .....179 C2
Crockwell CI OX26 ......65 C1
Crockwell St CV36 ......27 C4
Croft Ave OX5 ....108 C4
Croft CI Merton OX25 ....95 B4
Oxford OX3 ....123 C2
Thame OX9 ....148 A4
Croft Cotts OX7 ....42 A1
Croft Ct OX7 ....73 B2
Croft Cl OX7 ....42 A1
Croft End OX12 ....214 A1
Croft La OX7 ....23 A2
Croft Rd Goring RG8 ...249 B3
Marston OX3 ....123 C2
Thame OX9 ....148 A4
Wallingford OX10 ....221 B4

Croft Terr 8 OX10 ...... 221 B4
Croft The
 Aston Tirrold OX11 ...... 219 C1
 Didcot OX11 ...... 218 C4
 East Hagbourne OX11 ...... 218 C3
 Haddenham HP17 ...... 130 C3
 Harwell OX11 ...... 217 C4
 Nuneham Courtenay OX44 ...... 162 A2
 Oxford OX3 ...... 124 B2
 West Hanney OX12 ...... 196 C4
Croft Villas 3 OX10 ...... 221 B4
Croft's La OX15 ...... 30 A3
Crofts The OX28 ...... 118 A4
Cromer Cl RG31 ...... 257 B1
Cromwell Ave OX9 ...... 130 A1
Cromwell Cl
 Chalgrove OX44 ...... 184 C3
 Faringdon SN7 ...... 173 A2
 Henley-on-T RG9 ...... 254 C4
 Marston OX3 ...... 123 C2
Cromwell Ct OX16 ...... 16 A4
Cromwell Dr OX11 ...... 219 A4
Cromwell Pk OX7 ...... 42 C2
Cromwell Rd
 Banbury OX16 ...... 16 A3
 Henley-on-T RG9 ...... 254 C4
 Reading RG4 ...... 259 A1
Cromwell St 12 OX1 ...... 141 B4
Cromwell Way OX5 ...... 109 A4
Cronshaw Cl OX11 ...... 200 C1
Crook's Terr OX12 ...... 214 B3
Crookdale Beck OX11 ...... 201 A2
Croom Cotts OX11 ...... 217 A4
Cropredy CE Prim Sch
 OX17 ...... 4 C1
Cross Ave OX10 ...... 204 B1
Cross Cl OX10 ...... 204 C1
Cross Hill Rd OX17 ...... 22 C2
Cross Keys Rd RG8 ...... 239 B2
Cross Leys OX7 ...... 42 C1
Cross Rd OX10 ...... 220 C1
Cross St OX4 ...... 141 C4
Cross Tree La GL7 ...... 132 A3
Cross's La OX7 ...... 56 C1
Crosslands OX27 ...... 52 B3
Crosslands Dr OX14 ...... 159 C1
Crossville Cres OX11 ...... 200 B1
Crossway OX7 ...... 60 C4
Crotch Cres OX3 ...... 124 A2
Crouch Hill Rd OX16 ...... 16 A2
Crouch St OX16 ...... 16 B3
Croughton All Saints' CE
 Prim Sch NN13 ...... 36 B4
Croughton Elementary Sch
 NN13 ...... 36 C3
Croughton Mid Sch
 NN13 ...... 36 C3
Croughton Rd OX17 ...... 35 B4
Crow La Great Bourton OX17 ...... 9 B4
 Wootton OX20 ...... 75 B4
Crowberry Rd OX4 ...... 142 C1
Crowell Rd OX4 ...... 142 B2
Crowmarsh Gifford CE Sch
 OX10 ...... 221 C4
Crowmarsh Hill OX10 ...... 222 A3
Crowmarsh Rd OX27 ...... 64 C3
Crown La Benson OX10 ...... 203 C2
 Dorchester OX10 ...... 182 B1
 South Moreton OX11 ...... 220 A4
Crown Mdw OX12 ...... 197 B4
Crown Mews OX14 ...... 179 C4
Crown Rd Kidlington OX5 ...... 108 A4
 Wheatley OX33 ...... 144 A4
Crown Sq Benson OX10 ...... 204 A2
 Wheatley OX33 ...... 144 A4
Crown St OX4 ...... 141 C4
Crown Wlk OX26 ...... 65 C1
Crowsley Rd RG9 ...... 255 A2
Crowsley Way RG4 ...... 252 C3
Croxford Gdns OX3 ...... 108 C3
Crozier Cl OX2 ...... 140 B4
Crumps Butts OX26 ...... 65 C1
Crutch Furlong OX10 ...... 182 B3
Cuckamus La OX29 ...... 105 A3
Cuckoo Cl OX17 ...... 65 C3
Cuckoo La
 Eynsham OX29 ...... 106 A2
 Freeland OX29 ...... 106 A2
Cuddesdon Cl RG8 ...... 250 C4
Cuddesdon Rd OX33 ...... 143 C3
Cuddesdon Way OX4 ...... 142 C1
Cues La SN6 ...... 227 B2
Culham Cl OX14 ...... 160 A1
Culham Parochial CE Sch
 OX14 ...... 180 A2
Culham Sta OX14 ...... 180 C2
Culkerne Cl OX14 ...... 160 A2
Cullerns The SN6 ...... 190 A3
Cullum Ho OX33 ...... 144 B4
Cullum Rd OX33 ...... 144 B4
Culworth Rd OX17 ...... 5 C3
Cumberford OX15 ...... 21 B2
Cumberford Cl OX15 ...... 21 B2
Cumberford Hill OX15 ...... 21 B2
Cumberland Rd OX4 ...... 142 A4
Cumberlege Cl OX3 ...... 123 C4
Cummings Cl OX3 ...... 124 C1
Cumnor CE Prim Sch
 OX2 ...... 139 C3
Cumnor Hill Cumnor OX2 ...... 140 A4
 N Hinksey Village OX2 ...... 140 A4
Cumnor Rd Cumnor OX2 ...... 139 B4
 Wootton (Oxford) OX1 ...... 159 A4
Cumnor Rise Rd OX2 ...... 140 B4
Cunliffe Cl OX2 ...... 123 B3
Cup & Saucer OX17 ...... 4 C1

Curbridge Rd
 Ducklington OX29 ...... 118 A2
 Witney OX28 ...... 117 C4
Curie Ave OX11 ...... 217 A2
Cursus The GL7 ...... 150 B3
Curtis Ave OX14 ...... 180 A4
Curtis Rd Kidlington OX5 ...... 92 C1
 Shrivenham SN6 ...... 209 A3
Curtiss Cl OX26 ...... 66 A3
Curtyn Cl OX14 ...... 179 B4
Curzon Gate Ct HP14 ...... 188 C3
Cuthwine Pl GL7 ...... 150 B3
Cutteslowe Fst Sch OX2 ...... 109 B1
Cutteslowe Rdbt OX2 ...... 109 A1
Cuttle Brook Gdns OX9 ...... 129 C1
Cuxham Rd OX49 ...... 186 A1
Cwmcarn RG4 ...... 258 C3
Cygnet Cl OX9 ...... 166 A4
Cygnet Ct OX14 ...... 179 C3
Cypress Gdns OX26 ...... 65 C3
Cyprus Terr OX2 ...... 122 C4

D

Dacey Dr OX25 ...... 63 A4
Dacre Ave RG4 ...... 259 C2
Daedings The OX15 ...... 33 C2
Dagdale Dr OX11 ...... 200 C2
Daimler Ave OX16 ...... 15 C4
Dairy Mdw OX33 ...... 177 B3
Dairyground The OX15 ...... 14 A3
Daisy Bank OX44 ...... 180 A4
Daisy Hill OX57 ...... 82 B3
Dale Cl Brackley NN13 ...... 24 A4
 Oxford OX3 ...... 141 A4
Dale Pl OX5 ...... 92 C1
Dale Wlk OX29 ...... 118 A3
Dalton Ave OX11 ...... 217 A2
Damer Gdns RG4 ...... 254 C4
Damson Trees SN6 ...... 209 A3
Dancers Hill OX7 ...... 73 B2
Danes Rd OX26 ...... 65 B1
Danesmoor OX16 ...... 16 A4
Danes La OX15 ...... 15 B1
Danvers Rd
 Broughton OX15 ...... 15 B1
 Oxford OX4 ...... 142 A2
Darcey Lode OX11 ...... 200 C2
Darell Rd RG4 ...... 258 C2
Darent Pl OX11 ...... 201 A1
Dark La
 Great Coxwell SN7 ...... 192 B4
 Reading RG31 ...... 257 B2
 Sunningwell OX13 ...... 159 C3
 Wargrave RG10 ...... 255 B1
 Wroxton OX15 ...... 15 A4
Darnell Wlk OX26 ...... 65 C2
Darrell Way OX14 ...... 159 C1
Dart Dr OX11 ...... 200 C2
Dart Rd OX11 ...... 159 B2
Dashwood Ave OX5 ...... 108 A3
Dashwood Mews OX5 ...... 77 C2
Dashwood Rd
 Banbury OX16 ...... 16 B3
 Oxford OX4 ...... 142 A2
Dashwood Rise OX5 ...... 47 B3
Dashwood Terr 11 OX16 ...... 16 B3
Datchet Gn OX10 ...... 202 C1
Daubeny Rd OX4 ...... 141 C3
Daubigny Mead OX18 ...... 116 B2
Davenant Ct 11 OX2 ...... 123 A4
Davenant Rd OX2 ...... 123 A4
Davenport Pl OX49 ...... 186 A1
Davenport Rd OX28 ...... 103 C1
Daventry Rd OX16 ...... 16 C4
David Nicholls Cl OX4 ...... 142 A2
David Walter Cl OX2 ...... 109 A1
Davis Cl OX33 ...... 115 C1
Davis Gdns OX7 ...... 65 C4
Dawls Cl OX7 ...... 71 A1
Dawson St 11 OX2 ...... 141 C4
Dawson St 11 OX4 ...... 141 C4
Day's La OX10 ...... 204 C1
Days Ground SN6 ...... 209 B4
De Bohun Rd RG1 ...... 259 A1
De Havilland RG RG4 ...... 68 A3
De Montfort Rd RG1 ...... 259 A1
De Vitre Pl OX12 ...... 214 B4
Deacon Way
 Banbury OX16 ...... 16 A3
 Reading RG30 ...... 258 A1
Deaconfield RG8 ...... 249 C2
Deadman's La RG8 ...... 251 B2
Dean Butler Cl OX12 ...... 214 B3
Dean Cl OX16 ...... 16 C4
Dean Court Rd OX2 ...... 140 A4
Dean Wood Cl RG8 ...... 240 C1
Deanfield Ave RG9 ...... 244 B1
Deanfield Rd
 Henley-on-T RG9 ...... 244 B1
 N Hinksey Village OX2 ...... 122 A1
Deans Cl OX26 ...... 65 C1
Deans Farm RG4 ...... 259 B1
Dearlove Cl OX14 ...... 159 C1
Dearne Pl OX11 ...... 201 A1
Deaufort Cl OX5 ...... 92 C1
Deddington Castle
 Earthworks* OX15 ...... 34 A2
Deddington CE Prim Sch
 OX15 ...... 33 C2
Deddington Hill OX15 ...... 33 C3
Deddington Rd OX15 ...... 33 C3
Deene Cl OX17 ...... 23 A2
Deer Park Rd OX28 ...... 117 B4

Deer Wlk OX4 ...... 142 C1
Deer's Farm OX15 ...... 22 C4
Deer's La RG8 ...... 241 B1
Deerhurst Ct GL56 ...... 26 C1
Deers Cl OX15 ...... 22 C4
Defiant Cl OX10 ...... 66 A2
Delafield OX HP14 ...... 188 C2
Delamare Way OX2 ...... 140 A4
Delapre Dr OX16 ...... 16 C4
Delbush Ave OX3 ...... 125 A2
Dell Rd RG31 ...... 257 B1
Delly Cl OX29 ...... 104 A4
Denbigh Pl RG1 ...... 258 C1
Denbigh Cl OX16 ...... 15 C1
Denbigh Rd OX30 ...... 130 A1
Denby Way RG30 ...... 257 C1
Denchfield Rd OX16 ...... 16 B1
Denchworth Rd
 Grove OX12 ...... 196 B1
 Wantage OX12 ...... 214 B3
Dene Hollow OX11 ...... 235 C4
Dene Rd OX3 ...... 142 B4
Dene Rise OX28 ...... 117 C4
Denefield Sch RG31 ...... 257 A2
Denman Cl OX13 ...... 178 B3
Denman's La OX2 ...... 139 C4
Denmark St OX4 ...... 141 C3
Denton Cl
 Abingdon OX14 ...... 180 A4
 N Hinksey Village OX2 ...... 140 A4
Denton Hill OX44 ...... 144 A1
Denton La
 Cuddesdon OX44 ...... 144 A1
 Garsington OX44 ...... 143 C1
Dents Cl OX3 ...... 124 A3
Derby Rd RG4 ...... 259 A2
Derwent Ave
 Didcot OX11 ...... 201 A1
 Oxford OX3 ...... 124 A2
 Reading RG30 ...... 257 C1
Derwent Cl OX13 ...... 159 B1
Derwent Rd OX26 ...... 65 A2
Des Roches Sq OX28 ...... 118 A4
Desborough Cres OX44 ...... 142 C2
Desmesne Furze OX3 ...... 124 B1
Devereux Pl 8 OX4 ...... 142 A2
Devil's Hill RG4 ...... 253 B3
Devon Cl OX10 ...... 204 B2
Devon Dr RG4 ...... 259 C2
Devon Pl OX18 ...... 115 C1
Devon Way OX16 ...... 16 A4
Devonshire Gdns RG31 ...... 257 B2
Dexter Cl OX16 ...... 16 B2
Diamond Ct OX2 ...... 123 A3
Diamond Pl OX2 ...... 123 A3
Dibleys OX11 ...... 237 A4
Dickens Ct Bicester OX26 ...... 65 B2
 Reading RG31 ...... 259 B1
Dickenson Ct OX4 ...... 142 C2
Dickredge The OX25 ...... 62 A4
Didcot Girls Sch OX11 ...... 200 B1
Didcot Hospl OX11 ...... 218 B4
Didcot Parkway Sta
 OX11 ...... 200 C1
Didcot Railway Ctr (Mus)*
 OX11 ...... 200 C1
Didcot Rd
 Brightwell-cum-S OX10 ...... 202 B2
 Harwell OX11 ...... 218 A4
 Long Wittenham OX14 ...... 201 B4
Dido Rd OX1 ...... 217 A1
Digberry La RG9 ...... 224 B3
Digby Cl OX9 ...... 130 A1
Digging La OX13 ...... 157 B1
Dillon Ct OX15 ...... 22 C4
Dirac Pl OX11 ...... 219 A4
Diston's La OX7 ...... 42 C2
Ditchend Cotts OX44 ...... 164 A3
Ditchley Rd OX7 ...... 73 C3
Dixon's Row OX12 ...... 214 C4
Dobson's La RG9 ...... 244 B4
Dodd Dr GL54 ...... 68 A2
Dodgson Rd OX4 ...... 142 B2
Dog Cl OX17 ...... 8 A1
Dog Kennel La OX7 ...... 85 B4
Doggett La Childrey OX12 ...... 213 B2
 Rotherfield Peppard RG9 ...... 252 B4
Doakenmeat La SN7 ...... 193 C4
Doily Cl OX15 ...... 30 A4
Dollicott HP17 ...... 130 C4
Dolphin La OX18 ...... 100 C3
Don Bosco Cl OX4 ...... 142 B3
Don Cl OX11 ...... 201 A2
Don Stuart Pl OX4 ...... 142 A4
Donegal Cl RG4 ...... 259 B2
Donkin Hill RG4 ...... 259 B2
Donnington Bridge Rd
 OX4 ...... 141 C3
Donnington Cl OX28 ...... 117 B4
Donnington Lodge OX4 ...... 141 C3
Donnington Mid Sch
 OX4 ...... 142 A3
Dora Carr Cl OX3 ...... 124 A3
Dorcas Rd OX16 ...... 17 A3
Dorchester Abbey Mus*
 OX10 ...... 182 B1
Dorchester Cres OX3 ...... 124 C1
Dorchester Cl OX14 ...... 160 A1
Dorchester Ct
 Cutteslowe OX2 ...... 123 A3
 4 Kidlington OX5 ...... 108 C4
Dorchester Gr OX16 ...... 15 C2
Dorchester Pl OX9 ...... 147 C4

Dorchester Rd
 Berinsfield OX10 ...... 182 C2
 Drayton St L OX10 ...... 183 A3
Doris Field Cl OX3 ...... 124 A2
Dormer Rd OX9 ...... 148 A3
Dormers The SN6 ...... 190 A3
Dorn Cl OX7 ...... 60 C4
Dorn View OX20 ...... 76 A2
Douglas Rd RG4 ...... 259 B1
Dove Ct 10 Bicester OX26 ...... 65 C1
 Carterton OX18 ...... 115 C2
Dove Gn OX26 ...... 65 A2
Dove House Cl OX2 ...... 122 C4
Dove La RG9 ...... 252 B4
Dovecote HP17 ...... 130 C3
Dovecote OX17 ...... 130 C3
Dovedale Cl RG4 ...... 258 C2
Dovehouse Cl OX29 ...... 120 C4
Doveleat OX3 ...... 168 B4
Dover Ave OX16 ...... 16 A4
Dovetrees OX18 ...... 115 C2
Down End OX25 ...... 63 B4
Down End OX35 ...... 30 A4
Downhill La OX29 ...... 104 A2
Downlands SN7 ...... 192 B1
Downs Cl OX11 ...... 217 C3
Downs Field Aldworth RG20 ...... 247 A2
 Didcot OX11 ...... 218 B4
 Standlake OX29 ...... 137 A3
 Witney OX29 ...... 103 A1
Downs The OX29 ...... 137 B3
Downs View
 Aston Tirrold OX11 ...... 237 C4
 Highworth SN6 ...... 190 A3
Downs Way Chilton OX11 ...... 234 C4
 Reading RG31 ...... 257 A2
Downside End OX3 ...... 125 A2
Downside Rd OX3 ...... 125 A2
Downsmead SN8 ...... 245 B1
Downsview Rd OX12 ...... 214 A4
Downsview Prim Sch
 RG31 ...... 257 B2
Doyley Rd Oxford OX2 ...... 141 A4
 Wallingford OX10 ...... 203 B1
Dr Radcliffe's CE Prim Sch
 OX5 ...... 48 A1
Dr South's CE Sch OX5 ...... 93 C1
Dragon Sch OX2 ...... 123 B2
Dragonhill Rd SN7 ...... 211 A1
Drake Ave OX11 ...... 218 B4
Drakes Dr HP18 ...... 129 C3
Drakes Farm HP18 ...... 129 C2
Dray's La RG9 ...... 253 A4
Draycott Rd OX13 ...... 156 B1
Draymans Croft 10 OX26 ...... 65 C1
Drayton Cty Prim Sch
 OX14 ...... 179 A1
Drayton Rd
 Abingdon OX14 ...... 179 B3
 Dorchester OX10 ...... 182 B1
 Sutton Courtenay OX14 ...... 199 C4
Drayton Sch OX16 ...... 15 C4
Dresden Way RG30 ...... 257 C1
Drewitts Cnr OX11 ...... 217 C4
Drift Ct OX4 ...... 142 C2
Drive The OX7 ...... 58 C3
Drivers La GL56 ...... 27 A1
Drove Acre Rd OX4 ...... 142 A4
Drove Way OX12 ...... 212 A2
Drovers La HP14 ...... 226 B4
Droveside OX10 ...... 220 C1
Druce Way OX4 ...... 142 C2
Druids Wlk Chinnor OX39 ...... 168 B3
Druid Cl OX11 ...... 200 C1
Dry La OX29 ...... 103 B2
Dry Sandford Prim Sch
 OX13 ...... 158 C3
Dryden Ave OX26 ...... 65 A2
Drylands Rd OX9 ...... 102 C1
Drysdale Cl OX14 ...... 160 C1
Duck End La OX29 ...... 120 B1
Duck La HP18 ...... 98 B4
Duck Sq OX39 ...... 168 B3
Ducklington CE Prim Sch
 OX29 ...... 118 A2
Dudgeon Dr OX4 ...... 142 A1
Dudley Cl RG31 ...... 257 A3
Dudley Ct OX2 ...... 123 A4
Dudley Gdns OX4 ...... 123 C1
Dudley La HP14 ...... 226 C4
Dudley Mews RG31 ...... 257 C1
Dudwell OX11 ...... 200 C2
Duffield Cl OX14 ...... 160 A1
Duffield Pl OX13 ...... 178 B4
Duffield Rd RG5 ...... 260 C1
Duke Of York Ave OX14 ...... 199 B2
Duke St Banbury OX16 ...... 16 C3
 Oxford OX2 ...... 141 A4
Dukes Cl HP18 ...... 128 B1
Dukes Rd OX5 ...... 108 C4
Dulas Cl OX11 ...... 200 C1
Dumbarton Way RG4 ...... 259 C3
Dunbar Dr OX9 ...... 130 A1
Duncan Cl OX29 ...... 120 B4
Duncan Gdns RG8 ...... 257 B2
Dundas Cl OX14 ...... 160 A4
Dunford Cl OX26 ...... 65 C1
Dunkin Cl OX16 ...... 16 C2
Dunluce Gdns RG8 ...... 256 C3
Dunmore Jun & Inf Sch
 OX14 ...... 159 C1
Dunmore La OX14 ...... 159 C1
Dunnock Way OX26 ...... 66 A1

Dunnock Way
 Sandford-on-T OX4 ...... 142 C1
 Wargrave RG10 ...... 255 C2
Dunsden Cl OX11 ...... 200 B1
Dunsomer Hill OX11 ...... 220 A4
Dunstan Ave OX7 ...... 42 C1
Dunstan Rd OX3 ...... 124 B2
Dunster Cl RG4 ...... 259 B3
Durant Way RG31 ...... 257 B2
Durham La OX29 ...... 107 B1
Durham Mews OX16 ...... 9 A1
Durford Cl Bicester OX26 ...... 66 A2
 Carterton OX18 ...... 115 C2
Dyer Straits OX12 ...... 234 C4
Dyers Hill OX7 ...... 73 A2
Dynham Pl OX3 ...... 124 B1
Dysonswood La RG4 ...... 258 C4

E

Eady Rd OX25 ...... 63 A4
Eagle Ind Est OX28 ...... 118 A4
Eagle La SN6 ...... 191 B1
Eagle Sq SN7 ...... 192 C4
Eagles SN7 ...... 172 C2
Eagles OX 7 RG2 ...... 260 B1
Earl St OX2 ...... 122 C1
Earl's La OX15 ...... 33 C2
Earlsfield Cl RG4 ...... 259 C2
Earlstoke Cl OX16 ...... 16 C4
Early Rd OX28 ...... 104 B1
Easington Gdns OX16 ...... 16 B2
Easington Rd OX16 ...... 16 B2
Eason Dr OX14 ...... 160 B1
East Allcourt GL7 ...... 150 B2
East Ave OX4 ...... 142 A4
East Challow CE Prim Sch
 OX12 ...... 213 C2
East Cl OX16 ...... 16 C4
East End OX15 ...... 30 A4
East Field Cl OX3 ...... 142 C4
East Hawthorn Rd OX25 ...... 81 B2
East Oxford Fst Sch
 OX4 ...... 141 C4
East St Banbury OX16 ...... 16 C4
 Bicester OX26 ...... 65 B2
 Bodicote OX15 ...... 22 C4
 Didcot OX11 ...... 219 A4
 Fritwell OX27 ...... 49 C4
 Long Compton CV36 ...... 27 C3
 Oxford OX2 ...... 123 A1
 Thame OX9 ...... 148 A4
East St Helen St OX14 ...... 179 C3
East View Blackthorn OX25 ...... 82 A2
 Kirtlington OX5 ...... 77 C2
East View Cl RG10 ...... 255 C1
East View RG10 ...... 255 C1
East Way RG31 ...... 199 A4
Eastbrook Cl OX25 ...... 97 C4
Eastchurch OX4 ...... 141 C2
Eastend OX11 ...... 196 C1
Eastern Ave OX4 ...... 142 A2
Eastern By-pass Rd
 OX4 ...... 142 C3
Eastern Ho OX4 ...... 142 A2
Eastern Terr OX15 ...... 22 C4
Eastfield OX11 ...... 237 A4
Eastfield Ct SN7 ...... 172 C2
Eastfield La
 Whitchurch RG8 ...... 256 B4
 Woodcote RG8 ...... 250 C3
Eastfield Rd OX28 ...... 104 A2
Eastgate OX15 ...... 7 B4
Eastleach CE Prim Sch
 GL7 ...... 131 A4
Eastman La OX12 ...... 212 C2
Eastrop Cty Inf Sch SN6 ...... 190 A3
Eastrop SN6 ...... 190 A3
Eastview Terr SN6 ...... 190 A3
Eastwood Rd
 Stokenchurch HP14 ...... 188 C2
 Witney OX29 ...... 103 B1
Eaton Cl SN7 ...... 172 C1
Eaton Ct OX2 ...... 123 B4
Eaton Rd OX13 ...... 139 A1
Ebbes La OX17 ...... 197 A2
Eccles Cl RG4 ...... 259 B1
Eden Croft OX14 ...... 160 A1
Eden Ct OX11 ...... 201 A1
Eden Dr OX3 ...... 124 A2
Eden Rd OX3 ...... 124 A2
Eden Way OX26 ...... 65 A1
Edencroft SN6 ...... 190 A4
Edenhall Cl RG31 ...... 257 B2
Edgar Milward Cl RG30 ...... 258 A1
Edgecombe Rd OX3 ...... 124 C2
Edgecumbe Cl OX17 ...... 5 C1
Edgehill OX9 ...... 129 C1
Edgehill Cty Pk* OX17 ...... 2 B3
Edgeway Rd OX3 ...... 123 C2
Edgeworth Dr OX18 ...... 115 B1
Edinburgh Cl OX16 ...... 15 C4
Edinburgh Dr
 Didcot OX11 ...... 200 A1
 Kidlington OX5 ...... 109 A4
Edinburgh Way RG4 ...... 15 C3
Edington Pl OX12 ...... 196 B1
Edington Rd OX28 ...... 117 B4
Edington Sq OX28 ...... 117 B4
Edith Ct OX14 ...... 141 B1
Edith Moorhouse Prim Sch
 OX18 ...... 115 B1
Edith Rd OX1 ...... 141 B4
Edmonds Ct OX11 ...... 218 B4

Edmund Halley Rd OX4 ....142 A1
Edmund Rd OX4 ....142 B3
Edmunds Rd OX16 ....15 C3
Edward Feild Cty Prim Sch
OX5 ....108 C4
Edward Rd OX1 ....141 C1
Edward St
Abingdon OX14 ....179 B4
Banbury OX16 ....6 C3
Edward Stone Rise OX7 ..42 B1
Edwin Ct OX2 ....122 C1
Edwin Rd OX11 ....218 B4
Egerton Cl NN13 ....24 A4
Egerton Rd Oxford OX4 ..142 A2
Wallingford OX10 ....221 B4
Eglin St OX25 ....63 A4
Eighteenth St OX11 ......217 A2
Eighth Ave OX3 ....142 C4
Eighth St OX11 ....217 A2
Elbourne OX11 ....218 B4
Elder Cl RG31 ....257 B1
Elder Way OX4 ....142 C1
Elderdene OX39 ....168 B4
Elderfield Cres OX11 ....235 B4
Elderfield Rd OX27 ....65 C4
Eldridge Cl OX14 ....159 C1
Eleanor Cl OX4 ....142 A2
Electric Ave OX2 ....141 A4
Eleventh St OX11 ....217 A1
Eliot Cl RG4 ....259 A2
Elizabeth Ave OX14 .....160 B1
Elizabeth Cl RG9 ....254 A4
Elizabeth Ct RG10 ......255 C1
Elizabeth Dr OX12 ......214 B3
Elizabeth Rd
Henley-on-T RG9 ....254 A4
Stokenchurch HP14 ......188 C2
Elizabeth Rise OX16 .....16 A2
Ell's La OX15 ....21 B4
Ellesmere Cl RG4 ....259 B2
Ellesmere Rd OX4 ....142 A2
Elliots Way RG4 ....259 A1
Ellison Dr OX17 ....8 C1
Elm Bridge Rdbt OX10 ...203 C2
Elm Cl Ambrosden OX25 ..81 B2
Bicester OX26 ....65 C2
Chinnor OX39 ....168 B3
Tetsworth OX9 ....166 A4
Wheatley OX33 ....144 B4
Witney OX28 ....117 C4
Elm Cres OX7 ....73 B2
Elm Ct Henley-on-T RG9 ..254 B4
Sonning Common RG4 ....252 C2
Elm Dr Chinnor OX39 .....168 B3
Garsington OX44 ....143 B1
Elm Gr Kidlington OX5 ...108 C3
Milton-u-W OX7 ....70 A1
Elm La OX25 ....81 B2
Elm Pl OX29 ....120 B4
Elm Rd Faringdon SN7 ...172 C2
Mapledurham RG4 ....258 B4
North Moreton OX11 .....220 A4
Wantage OX12 ....214 C3
Elm Tree Cl OX4 ....142 A2
Elm Tree Wlk OX13 ......159 B1
Elm Trees HP18 ....129 A4
Elmcroft RG8 ....249 B3
Elmhurst Rd RG8 ....249 B4
Elmleigh Ct RG4 ....259 B2
Elms Dr OX3 ....124 A3
Elms Par OX2 ....122 B1
Elms Rd Cassington OX29 107 B1
N Hinksey Village OX2 ...122 B2
Thame OX9 ....147 C4
Elms The Highworth SN6 ..190 A3
Langford GL7 ....132 B1
Elms Way RG9 ....224 B2
Elmscote Rd OX16 ....16 B1
Elmsfield Farm Ind Est
OX7 ....42 B2
Elmside SN7 ....193 A3
Elmstone Dr RG31 ....257 B1
Elmthorpe Rd OX2 ......122 C4
Elsfield Rd OX3 ....123 C3
Elsfield Way OX2 ....109 A1
Elsley Rd RG31 ....257 B2
Elstow Ave RG4 ....259 B3
Elstree Cl RG31 ....257 B1
Elswith Cl OX12 ....214 B4
Eltham Ave RG4 ....259 C3
Elton Cres OX33 ....144 B4
Elton Rd OX16 ....16 C1
Elvendon La RG8 ....250 B4
Elvendon Rd RG8 ....249 B4
Elwes Cl OX14 ....180 A4
Elwes Rd OX13 ....178 B3
Ely Cl Abingdon OX14 ...179 B3
Carterton OX18 ....115 C2
Emden Ho OX3 ....124 B2
Emma La RG10 ....255 C1
Emmanuel Christian Sch
OX4 ....142 A1
Emmens Cl RG8 ....241 B2
Emmer Green Ct RG4 ....259 B3
Emmer Green Prim Sch
RG4 ....259 A3
Emperor Gdns OX4 ......142 C1
Empstead Ct RG9 ....244 B1
Emey Cl OX14 ....160 B1
Enstone Airfield Complex
(Ind Est) OX7 ....59 B4
Enstone Cty Prim Sch
OX7 ....58 C3
Enstone Rd Charlbury OX7 ..73 A2
Little Tew OX7 ....45 A3

Enstone Rd continued
Middle Barton OX7 ....60 C4
EP Collier Prim Sch
RG1 ....259 A1
Epwell Rd OX15 ....13 C3
Eric Ave RG4 ....259 A3
Erica Cl Banbury OX16 ...9 A1
Oxford OX4 ....142 C2
Ermont Way OX16 ....16 C4
Ernest Rd OX11 ....218 C4
Ernicote Cl OX25 ....81 C2
Essex Rd OX9 ....148 A4
Essex St OX4 ....142 A4
Essex Way RG4 ....259 A1
Ester Carling La RG9 ...252 B4
Estover Way OX39 ......168 A3
Ethelhelm Cl OX14 .....160 B2
Ethelred Ct OX3 ....124 B2
Eton Cl OX28 ....118 B4
European Sch The
OX14 ....180 B2
Evans Cl OX29 ....120 C4
Evans Ct OX5 ....108 C4
Evans La OX5 ....108 C4
Evans Rd OX29 ....120 C4
Evans Yd 3 OX26 ....65 C1
Evelin Rd OX14 ....159 C1
Evelyn Cl OX2 ....140 A4
Evenlode OX16 ....16 A4
Evenlode Cl Bicester OX26 ..65 B1
Charlbury OX7 ....73 A2
Grove OX12 ....196 B1
North Leigh OX29 ....105 A3
Evenlode Cres OX5 ......92 A1
Evenlode Cl OX28 ....118 A4
Evenlode Dr
Berinsfield OX10 ....182 B3
Didcot OX11 ....200 C1
Long Hanborough OX29 ..90 A1
Evenlode Ho OX26 ......65 B1
Evenlode Pk OX14 ......160 A1
Evenlode Twr OX4 ......142 C1
Everard Cl OX3 ....124 B3
Eversley Cl OX7 ....57 A1
Evesham Rd RG4 ....259 A3
Ewart Cl OX26 ....65 B2
Ewelme CE Prim Sch
OX10 ....204 C2
Ewert Pl OX2 ....123 A3
Ewin Cl OX3 ....123 C3
Ewin Ct OX3 ....123 C3
Exbourne Rd OX14 .....179 B4
Exe Cl OX11 ....200 C1
Exeter Coll OX1 ....123 B1
Exeter Cl Didcot OX11 ..219 A4
5 Kidlington OX5 ....108 C4
Eylham RG4 ....257 A3
Eynsford Cl RG4 ....259 A1
Eynsham Com Prim Sch
OX29 ....120 C4
Eynsham Ct OX29 ......105 B3
Eynsham Rd
Cassington OX29 ....107 B1
Cumnor OX2 ....121 C1
N Hinksey Village OX2 ..140 A4
Eyot Pl OX4 ....141 C4
Eyre's La OX10 ....204 C3
Eyres Cl OX10 ....204 B2
Eyston Way OX14 ......179 B4

F

Faber Cl OX4 ....142 B1
Fair Cl OX26 ....65 C2
Fair Mile RG9 ....244 B2
Fair Mile Hospl OX10 ...221 A1
Fair View OX3 ....142 B4
Fairacres OX14 ....179 B4
Fairacres Rd
Didcot OX11 ....218 C4
Oxford OX4 ....141 C3
Fairfax Ave OX3 ....123 C2
Fairfax Cl Banbury OX16 ..16 A3
Reading RG4 ....259 A2
Thame OX9 ....148 A4
Fairfax Ctr OX5 ....108 C3
Fairfax Gate OX33 .....144 B4
Fairfax Rd
Chalgrove OX44 ....184 B3
Kidlington OX5 ....108 C4
Oxford OX4 ....142 C3
Fairfield OX10 ....220 C1
Fairfield Cl OX12 ....214 B4
Fairfield Dr OX28 ....117 C2
Fairfield Pl OX14 ....179 C4
Fairfield Rd RG8 ....249 B4
Fairfields OX29 ....136 C4
Fairford Rd RG31 ....257 B1
Fairford Way OX26 .....66 A2
Fairhaven Rd OX27 .....65 C4
Fairlawn End OX2 ......122 C4
Fairlawn Flats OX2 .....122 C4
Fairlawn Wharf OX14 ...179 C3
Fairlie Rd OX4 ....142 A2
Fairmile Ct RG9 ....244 B2
Fairspear Rd OX29 .....86 C2
Fairthorne Way SN6 ....209 A3
Fairview Est RG9 ....254 C4
Fairview Rd OX16 ......16 B2
Fairway The OX16 ......16 A3
Falcon Cl Banbury OX16 ..16 A2
Carterton OX18 ....115 B2
Oxford OX4 ....142 B1
Falcon Mead OX26 .....81 A4
Falcon Villas OX7 ....72 A3
Falkland Ho OX18 ....115 C1
Falkland Rd RG4 ....259 A1

Falkner's Cl OX17 ......23 A2
Fallow Way OX16 ....16 C1
Fallowfield Cl RG4 .....259 A2
Fallowfields OX26 ......65 C1
Falstaff Cl OX29 ....120 C4
Fane Cl OX26 ....65 B2
Fane Dr OX10 ....182 B3
Fane Ho 2 OX26 ....65 C1
Fane Rd OX3 ....123 C3
Fanshawe Pl OX4 ......142 C3
Fanshawe Rd OX9 .....148 A4
Faraday Ave OX11 .....217 A1
Faringdon Com Coll
SN7 ....172 C2
Faringdon Inf Sch SN7 .172 C2
Faringdon Jun Sch SN7 172 C2
Faringdon Rd
Appleton OX2 ....139 C1
Kingston Bagpuize OX13 ..156 C1
Shrivenham SN6 ....209 B4
Stanford in the V SN7 ..194 B4
Watchfield SN6 ....191 C1
Farleigh Mews RG4 ....259 C3
Farleigh Rd SN6 ....209 A3
Farley Cl OX29 ....89 B4
Farm Cl Aston OX18 ....135 C1
Chalgrove OX44 ....184 B3
Ickford HP18 ....127 C2
Kidlington OX5 ....92 C1
Purley on T RG8 ....257 B3
Sandford-on-T OX4 .....142 C1
Sonning Common RG4 ..252 C3
Farm Close La OX33 ...144 A4
Farm Close Rd OX33 ...144 A4
Farm Cotts OX5 ....93 A4
Farm St SN6 ....227 B2
Farm End Grove OX12 ..214 B4
Woodstock OX20 ....91 A4
Farm La OX29 ....103 B3
Farm Mill La OX28 .....118 A4
Farm Pl OX39 ....149 C1
Farm Rd Abingdon OX14 ..159 C1
Brackley NN13 ....24 A3
Goring RG8 ....249 B3
Henley-on-T RG9 ....254 C4
Farm Way OX16 ....16 C2
Farman Cres GL54 .....68 A2
Farmer Pl OX3 ....123 C2
Farmers Cl OX28 ....104 A1
Farmfield Rd OX16 .....16 B2
Farmhouse Cl OX29 ....138 A4
Farmhouse Mdw OX28 .117 C4
Farmhouse Mews OX49 386 A1
Farmiloe Cl RG8 ....257 B3
Farmington Dr OX28 ...117 C4
Farmoor Ct OX2 ....121 B1
Farmstead Cl OX12 ....196 B1
Farnborough Hall* OX17 ..3 C4
Farndon Rd OX2 ....123 A2
Farnham Ct 图 OX5 ....108 C4
Farnham Dr RG4 ....259 C2
Farrier's Mead OX4 ....80 A2
Farriers Cl OX27 ....52 B3
Farriers Mews OX14 ...180 A4
Farriers Rd OX7 ....60 C4
Farringdon Rd OX13 ...159 A1
Farthings The OX13 ...178 B4
Faulder Ave OX18 ......115 B2
Faulkner St 17 OX1 ....141 B4
Fawler La OX7 ....88 B4
Fawler Rd Charlbury OX7 ..73 B1
Uffington SN7,OX12 ....211 C3
Fawley Bottom La RG9 .226 A1
Fawley Cl OX12 ....214 B3
Fawley Ct* RG9 ....244 C3
Featherbed La
East Hendred OX12 .....216 C4
Milton OX14 ....199 A1
Mixbury NN13 ....38 B3
Feilden Cl OX29 ....118 A2
Feilden Gr OX3 ....124 A2
Fells Cl HP18 ....129 B3
Feltwell Cl OX18 ....115 C2
Fencott Rd OX5 ....95 A2
Fenlock Ct OX29 ....90 C1
Fenlock Rd OX29 ......90 C1
Fennel Way OX4 ....180 B4
Fenny Compton Rd OX17 ..1 B1
Fenway OX25 ....48 A1
Ferguson Pl OX14 .....180 B4
Fergusson Rd OX16 ...16 C4
Fermi Ave OX11 ....217 A1
Fern Glen RG31 ....257 B1
Fern Hill Rd OX4 ....142 C3
Fernbrook Rd RG4 .....258 C3
Ferndale Cl
Reading RG31 ....257 B2
Stokenchurch HP14 ....188 C2
Ferndale Prep Sch SN7 172 C2
Ferndale St OX14 ......115 C4
Ferndale St SN7 ....173 A2
Ferne Cl RG8 ....249 B4
Fernham Rd
Faringdon SN7 ....172 C1
Little Coxwell SN7 .....192 A2
Longcot SN7 ....192 B1
Shellingford SN7 ......193 B3
Fernhill Cl Kidlington OX5 ..108 B4
Milcombe OX15 ....21 A1
Tiddington OX9 ....146 A3
Fernhill Rd OX5 ....108 A4
Ferny Cl OX14 ....160 C2
Ferriston OX16 ....9 A1
Ferry Ct OX14 ....179 C3
Ferry Hinksey Rd OX2 .123 A1
Ferry La Goring RG8 ...249 B3
Moulsford OX10 ....239 A2
South Stoke OX10,RG8 ..239 A2

Ferry La continued
Wargrave RG10 ....255 B1
Ferry Mills OX2 ....141 A4
Ferry Pool Rd OX2 .....123 A3
Ferry Rd Oxford OX3 ..123 C2
Ferry Wlk OX14 ....179 C3
Fettiplace OX7 ....70 A1
Fettiplace Cl OX13 ....158 A4
Fettiplace Rd
Marcham OX13 ....178 B3
Oxford OX3 ....124 C3
Witney OX28 ....117 C4
Fewcott Rd OX27 ......49 C4
Fiddlers Hill OX7 ......85 B3
Fidlers Wlk RG10 ......255 C1
Field Ave OX4 ....142 C1
Field Cl Ickford HP18 ..128 A2
Kidlington OX5 ....108 C4
Kingston Bagpuize OX13 ..156 B1
Stonesfield OX29 ......89 B4
Yarnton OX5 ....108 A3
Field Ct OX25 ....47 B3
Field End
Long Crendon HP18 ...129 C3
Wargrave RG10 ....255 C1
Field Gdns
East Challow OX12 ....213 C3
Steventon OX13 ....199 A3
Field Ho OX2 ....140 B4
Field House Dr OX2 ...123 A4
Field La OX44 ....144 A2
Field Rd Kingham OX7 .54 C2
Murcott OX5 ....96 A3
Field St OX26 ....65 C1
Field The OX13 ....158 C3
Field View RG4 ....259 B3
Fielden Cl OX10 ....204 B1
Fielden Rd OX10 ......204 B1
Fieldfare Rd OX4 ......161 C4
Fieldmere Cl OX28 ....117 C4
Fieldside Abingdon OX14 .159 B1
East Hagbourne OX11 ..219 A3
Long Wittenham OX14 .201 B4
Upton OX11 ....218 B1
Fiennes Rd Banbury OX16 ..16 A3
Oxford OX4 ....142 A2
Fifteenth St OX11 .....217 A1
Fifth Ave NN13 ....36 C4
Fifth St NN13 ....36 C4
Fifth St E NN13 ....36 C4
Filkins Rd GL7 ....132 B1
Finch Cl OX3 ....124 B1
Finchdale Cl OX18 ....115 B2
Finches La SN8 ....245 C1
Finches The SN8 ......245 B1
Finchley La OX26 ......65 B1
Finham Brook OX11 ...200 C2
Finlay Ho RG9 ....244 C2
Finmere CE Prim Sch
MK18 ....39 B3
Finmore Cl 3 OX14 ....179 C4
Finmore Rd OX2 ......140 B4
Finsbury Pl OX7 ....42 C2
Finstock CE Prim Sch
OX7 ....88 B3
Finstock Sta OX7 .....88 B4
Fir Cl OX10 ....240 B4
Fir La OX5 ....93 A4
Fir Tree Ave OX4 .....221 A4
Fir Tree Cl OX13 ......156 C1
Fir Tree Cotts RG20 ..235 A1
Fir Tree Paddock RG20 ..235 A1
Fir Tree Sch The OX10 ..221 A4
Fir Trees OX1,OX14 ...160 C4
Fircroft Banbury OX16 ..16 B2
Bicester OX26 ....65 C3
Fircroft Cl RG31 ....257 B1
Firebrass Hill OX10 ...204 C3
Firs Cl OX7 ....54 A3
Firs Mdw 9 OX4 ......142 C1
Firs The Cuttleslowe OX2 ..123 A4
Wroxton OX15 ....15 A4
First Ave East Didcot OX11 ..200 B1
Oxford OX3 ....142 C4
First St Croughton NN13 ..36 C3
Harwell OX11 ....217 B1
First Turn OX2 ....122 C4
Firtree Cl OX16 ....9 A1
Fish Ponds La OX9 ....129 C1
Fisher Cl Banbury OX16 ..15 C4
Drayton OX14 ....179 A1
Fisher Row OX1 ....123 A1
Fisher's La OX7 ....73 A2
Fishermans Wharf
OX14 ....179 C2
Fishers Cl OX29 ....104 A3
Fishers Cotts RG4 ....259 B3
Fitchett Yd OX14 .....179 C4
Fitzcount Way OX10 ..203 B1
Fitzharris Ind Est OX14 ..179 C4
Fitzharry's Rd OX14 ..179 C4
Fitzharrys Sch OX14 ..159 C1
Fitzherbert Cl OX4 ....141 C2
Fitzwaryn Sch OX12 ..214 B3
Five Acre RG31 ....257 B1
Five Acres Cty Prim Sch
OX25 ....81 B2
Five Mile Dr OX2 ......109 A1
Fiveacres OX5 ....95 C2
Flambards 1 RG4 .....259 B1
Flatford Pl OX5 ....92 B1
Flavius Gate NN13 ....24 A4
Flatford Rd OX4 ....142 C1
Fleet Way OX11 ....219 A4
Fleetwood Way 7 OX9 129 C1

Fleming Cl OX26 ....65 B2
Fleming Dr OX7 ....60 C4
Flemings Rd OX20 .....91 B3
Flemming Ave OX44 ..184 B4
Fletcher Cl
Faringdon SN7 ....173 A2
Yarnton OX5 ....108 A3
Fletcher Rd OX4 ....142 C3
Flexney Pl OX3 ....124 B1
Flexneys Paddock OX29 138 A4
Flint Hollow OX39 .....168 A3
Flint St HP17 ....130 C3
Floral Cl OX12 ....214 C4
Florence Cl OX5 ....108 C4
Florence Park Rd OX4 .142 A3
Florey's Cl OX29 ......104 A3
Flowers Hill RG8 ......256 B2
Floyd's Row OX1 ......141 B4
Fludger Cl OX10 ....221 B4
Fogwell Rd OX2 ....122 A1
Foliat Cl OX12 ....214 C3
Foliat Dr OX12 ....214 C3
Folland Cl OX7 ....42 C2
Follets Cl OX5 ....108 A3
Followfields Cl 16 OX5 ..65 C1
Folly Bridge Ct OX1 ..141 B4
Folly Cl SN6 ....190 A4
Folly Cres Highworth SN6 ..190 A4
Watchfield SN6 ....191 C1
Folly Ct OX15 ....19 B4
Folly Dr SN6 ....190 A4
Folly Gn RG8 ....249 C3
Folly Orchard Rd RG8 ..240 C1
Folly View Cres SN7 ..172 C1
Folly View Rd SN7 ....172 C1
Folly Way SN6 ....190 A4
Ford La
Drayton St L OX10 .....183 A3
East Hendred OX12 ....216 B3
Garford OX13 ....178 A4
Ford's Cl HP14 ....189 C4
Fords Cl OX33 ....143 B3
Forest Cl Launton OX26 ..66 B1
Milton-u-W OX7 ....70 A1
Forest Hill RG30 ......257 C1
Forest Rd OX3 ....124 C2
Forest Side OX1 ....141 B1
Foresters
Beacon's Bottom HP14 ..189 B3
Chinnor OX39 ....168 A3
Foresters Twr OX3 ....124 C1
Forestry Hos OX49 ....207 A4
Forge Cl Benson OX10 ..203 C2
Horton-cum-S OX33 ...112 A3
Marsh Gibbon OX27 ...67 C2
Merton OX25 ....95 B4
Reading RG4 ....259 B1
Forge Pl OX27 ....49 C4
Forgeway OX16 ....9 A1
Forrest Cl SN6 ....209 A3
Forster La OX12 ....139 C2
Forsythia Cl OX26 ....65 C3
Forsythia Wlk OX16 ...9 A1
Fortescue Dr OX26 ...80 B4
Forties The OX44 .....145 A1
Fortnam Cl OX3 ....124 A2
Forty Gn HP27 ....149 C2
Forty The
Bishopstone SN6 ......227 B3
Cholsey OX10 ....220 C1
Foscote Private Hospl
OX16 ....16 B2
Foscote Rise OX16 ...16 C2
Fosseway The OX18 ..116 B2
Foster Rd OX14 ....159 C2
Fothergill Pl OX9 .....147 C4
Foudry Cl OX11 ......201 A1
Foundry St OX16 .....16 B3
Fountain Ct OX14 ....179 C4
Fourteenth St OX11 ..217 A2
Fourth Ave
Croughton NN13 ......36 C3
Oxford OX3 ....142 C4
Fourth St Croughton NN13 ..36 C3
Harwell OX11 ....217 A2
Fowler Rd OX16 ......16 C4
Fowler's Rd OX7 .....55 A2
Fowlers Farm Rd HP14 188 C2
Fox Cl Bampton OX18 .134 C2
Chipping Norton OX7 ..42 C1
Garsington OX44 ......143 B1
Hailey OX29 ....104 A2
Fox Cover OX39 ......168 B3
Fox Cres OX1 ....141 C3
Fox Furlong OX4 .....142 A1
Fox La Bicester OX26 ..65 B1
Middle Barton OX7 ...60 C4
Souldern OX6 ....35 C2
Wootton (Oxford) OX1,
OX13 ....159 B4
Foxborough Rd OX14 ..160 C1
Foxburrow La OX29 ...120 A1
Foxburrow La OX29 ...103 C2
Foxcombe Cl OX14 ...179 B4
Foxcombe La OX1 .....141 A1
Foxcombe Rd OX1 ...140 C1
Foxcroft Dr OX18 ....115 B1
Foxdown Cl OX5 .....92 C1
Foxfield OX7 ....42 C1
Foxglove Cl Bicester OX26 ..65 C2
🔲 Sandford-on-T OX4 ..142 C1
Foxglove La OX11 ....218 B2
Foxglove Rd OX5 .....108 A4
Foxhall Rd OX11 .....200 B1
Foxhill Cl RG4 ....260 A3
Foxhill La Reading RG4 ..259 C3
Souldern OX6 ....35 C2

Foxholes Nature Reserve*
OX7 .... 69 C3
Foxton Cl OX2 .... 108 C1
Foxtowns Gn OX5 .... 78 A3
Foxwell Dr OX3 .... 124 A3
Foxwood OX18 .... 135 C2
Foxwood Cl Aston OX18 .. 135 C2
Banbury OX16 .... 16 B1
Framlands Cl OX12 .... 214 A3
Framlingham Dr RG4 .... 259 C3
Frampton Cl RG5 .... 260 C1
Frances Rd OX7 .... 60 C4
Francis Little Dr OX14 .. 179 B3
Frank Cook Ct OX5 .... 92 C1
Frank Wise Specl Sch
OX16 .... 16 A3
Frank's La OX13 .... 198 C2
Franklin Cl
Chalgrove OX44 .... 184 B3
Kidlington OX5 .... 92 C1
Franklin Rd OX3 .... 124 A2
Franklyn Cl OX14 .... 159 C1
Fraser Ave RG4 .... 259 B3
Fraser Cl OX16 .... 16 C3
Fraser Gdns OX10 .... 221 B3
Frax Cl OX13 .... 156 C1
Frederick Rd OX4 .... 142 B2
Freeborn Cl OX5 .... 92 C1
Freehold St OX25 .... 62 B3
Freeland CE Prim Sch
OX29 .... 106 A4
Freelands Cotts OX33 .. 125 B4
Freelands Rd OX4 .... 141 C3
Freeman Rd OX11 .... 200 B1
Freemans Cl SN7 .... 211 B4
Freemans Rd OX15 .... 22 C4
French Cl OX28 .... 117 C4
French Laurence Way
OX44 .... 184 B3
Frenchay Rd OX2 .... 123 A3
Frensham Cl OX16 .... 9 A1
Frethern Cl OX18 .... 100 C2
Friar's Well OX17 .... 35 B4
Friars Cl SN6 .... 209 A3
Friars Furlong HP18 .... 129 A4
Friars Wharf OX1 .... 141 B4
Friars' Entry OX1 .... 123 B1
Friday Ct OX9 .... 129 C1
Friday La OX33 .... 144 A4
Friday St RG9 .... 244 C1
Frideswide CE Mid Sch
OX2 .... 123 B3
Friends Cl OX29 .... 89 B4
Frieze Way OX2,OX5 .... 108 C2
Frilford Rd OX13 .... 178 B3
Frilsham St OX14 .... 200 A4
Fringford CE Prim Sch
OX27 .... 52 B3
Fritwell CE Prim Sch
OX27 .... 49 C4
Fritwell Rd OX27 .... 50 A2
Frog La OX7 .... 70 A1
Frogmore La SN7 .... 194 C4
Frome Rd OX11 .... 217 B1
Fruitlands OX29 .... 120 B4
Fry Ct RG4 .... 259 A2
Frys Hill OX4 .... 142 C1
Fuchsia Wlk OX16 .... 9 A1
Fullbrook Cres RG31 .... 257 B2
Fullers Field OX44 .... 145 B1
Fullers Rd OX11 .... 219 C1
Fullwell Cl OX14 .... 159 C1
Fulmar Ct OX26 .... 66 A2
Fulmar Pl OX12 .... 196 B1
Fulwell Rd Finmere MK18 .. 39 B4
Westbury NN13 .... 25 A2
Furlong Cl OX4 .... 142 B2
Furlong Row OX18 .... 152 C4
Furlong The OX29 .... 137 A3
Furlongs The OX9 .... 147 B3
Fyfield Cl OX12 .... 214 C2
Fyfield Rd OX2 .... 123 B2

G

Gadge Cl OX9 .... 129 C1
Gainsborough Cres RG9 .. 254 B4
Gainsborough Gn OX14 .. 179 C3
Gainsborough Hill RG9 .. 254 B4
Gainsborough Rd RG9 .. 254 B4
Gaisford Rd OX4 .... 142 B2
Gales Ct GL7 .... 150 B2
Gall Cl OX14 .... 180 B4
Galley Field OX14 .... 180 A4
Gallowstree Rd RG9 .... 252 C4
Galpin Cl OX4 .... 142 A4
Galsworthy Dr RG4 .... 259 C3
Gangsdown Hill RG9 .... 223 C2
Gap The OX13 .... 178 B3
Gap Way RG8 .... 250 C4
Garde Rd RG4 .... 260 C2
Garden City OX9 .... 148 A4
Garden Cl Banbury OX16 .. 16 B4
Didcot OX11 .... 218 B4
Garden Ho OX4 .... 142 B3
Gardens Cl HP14 .... 188 C2
Gardens The
Radley OX14 .... 160 C2
South Stoke RG8 .... 239 B2
Gardiner Cl
Abingdon OX14 .... 180 B4
Wheatley OX33 .... 144 A4
Gardiner St OX3 .... 124 B1
Garford Cl OX14 .... 160 A1
Garford Rd OX2 .... 123 B3
Garne's La OX18 .... 100 C3
Garner Cl OX18 .... 115 B3
Garsington CE Sch
OX44 .... 143 C1
Garsington Rd OX4 .... 142 C2
Garsons La OX10,RG8 .... 240 C3
Garston Cl OX12 .... 214 C3
Garston Ct OX18 .... 116 A3
Garston La OX12 .... 214 C3
Garth Rd OX11 .... 200 C1
Garth The
N Hinksey Village OX2 .... 140 B4
Yarnton OX5 .... 108 A3
Garton End RG8 .... 250 B3
Gas La OX7 .... 85 B4
Gascoigne Way OX15 .... 21 C1
Gaskells End RG4 .... 258 B4
Gassons Mead OX18 .... 133 B3
Gassons Rd GL7 .... 150 B3
Gassons The GL7 .... 132 A3
Gassons Way GL7 .... 150 B2
Gatehampton Rd RG8 .... 249 B3
Gateley OX33 .... 143 B3
Gateway Prim Sch
OX18 .... 115 C1
Gathorne Rd OX3 .... 124 B1
Gatteridge St OX16 .... 16 B3
Gauntlets Cl OX15 .... 21 C3
Gaveston Gdns OX15 .... 33 C2
Gaveston Rd OX11 .... 217 C4
Gavray Dr OX26 .... 66 A1
Gaydon Cl OX18 .... 115 C2
Gaydon Wlk 2 OX26 .... 66 A2
Gayhurst Cl RG4 .... 259 B3
Gelt Burn OX11 .... 201 A1
Gentian Cl OX26 .... 65 B3
Gentian Rd OX4 .... 142 C1
Geoffrey Barbour Rd
OX14 .... 179 C4
Geoffrey Tuttle Dr
OX10 .... 204 B1
Geoffreyson Rd RG4 .... 258 C3
George Moore Cl OX4 .. 142 A3
George Rd HP14 .... 188 C3
George St Banbury OX16 .. 16 B3
Bicester OX26 .... 65 B2
Oxford OX1 .... 123 B1
Reading RG4 .... 259 A1
George Street Mews
OX1 .... 123 A1
Gerard Pl OX4 .... 142 B3
Germander Way OX26 .... 65 B3
Gibbs Cres OX2 .... 141 A4
Gibbs Rd OX16 .... 16 C4
Gibson Cl OX14 .... 160 A2
Gibson Dr OX25 .... 63 B4
Gidley Way OX33 .... 143 B4
Giernalls Rd OX29 .... 104 A3
Giffard Way HP18 .... 129 B4
Gifford Cl RG4 .... 259 C3
Giles Cl OX4 .... 142 A1
Giles Rd OX4 .... 142 B1
Gilkes Yd OX16 .... 16 A3
Gillett Cl OX16 .... 16 A3
Gillett Rd OX16 .... 16 A3
Gillians Way OX4 .... 142 A3
Gillott's Hill RG9 .... 254 B4
Gillott's Sch RG9 .... 254 A4
Gillotts Cl RG9 .... 254 A4
Gillotts La RG9 .... 254 B4
Ginge Cl OX14 .... 160 A1
Gipsy La
Great Coxwell SN7 .... 192 B4
Grove OX12 .... 214 C4
Oxford OX3 .... 124 A1
Reading RG30 .... 257 C1
Girdlestone Cl OX3 .... 124 B1
Girdlestone Rd OX3 .... 124 B1
Glade The RG8 .... 257 B2
Glades The OX26 .... 66 B1
Gladstone Ct OX3 .... 124 C2
Gladstone Rd OX3 .... 124 C2
Glamis Pl OX16 .... 15 C3
Glanville Gdns OX16 .... 16 A3
Glanville Rd OX4 .... 142 A4
Glebe Cl Ambrosden OX25 .. 81 B2
Moulsford OX10 .... 238 C3
Glebe Cotts
Aston Rowant OX9 .... 166 C2
South Stoke RG8 .... 239 B2
Glebe Ct OX25 .... 47 B3
Glebe Dr NN13 .... 24 A4
Glebe Gdns Grove OX12 .. 196 C1
Sonning RG4 .... 260 C2
Glebe House Dr MK18 .... 25 C3
Glebe La RG4 .... 260 C2
Glebe Pl SN6 .... 190 A3
Glebe Rd Cumnor OX2 .... 139 C3
Didcot OX11 .... 218 C4
Purley on T RG8 .... 257 A3
Stanford in the V SN7 .... 194 B4
Glebe Ride RG8 .... 249 A3
Glebe St OX4 .... 123 C1
Glebe The Aldworth RG8 .. 247 C2
Aynho OX17 .... 35 B4
Culham OX14 .... 180 A2
Cumnor OX2 .... 139 C3
East Challow OX12 .... 213 B3
Hook Norton OX15 .... 30 A4
Lewknor OX49 .... 187 A4
Rotherfield Peppard RG9 .... 242 C3
Standlake OX29 .... 137 B2
Wheatley OX33 .... 144 A4
Glebelands
Bampton OX18 .... 134 C2
Oxford OX3 .... 142 B4
Glen Cl OX27 .... 52 B1
Glenham Rd OX9 .... 148 A4
Glenmore Rd OX18 .... 115 B2
Glenrhondda RG4 .... 258 C3
Gliffard Ho 8 RG4 .... 259 B1
Glimbers Gr OX39 .... 168 B3
Glissard Way OX18 .... 114 B3
Glory Farm Sch OX26 .... 66 A2
Gloucester Court Mews
OX28 .... 104 A1
Gloucester La OX1 .... 123 A1
Gloucester Mews SN7 .. 172 C2
Gloucester Pl
Oxford OX8 .... 123 B1
Witney OX28 .... 104 A1
Gloucester St
Faringdon SN7 .... 172 C2
Oxford OX1 .... 123 B1
Glover's Cl OX7 .... 42 C1
Glovers Cl OX20 .... 91 B3
Glovers La OX17 .... 10 C1
Glyme Cl Abingdon OX14 .. 160 A1
Woodstock OX20 .... 91 A4
Glyme Dr OX10 .... 182 B3
Glyme Way OX29 .... 106 A4
Glympton Rd OX20 .... 75 C3
Glyn Ave OX11 .... 218 B4
Glyn Rd OX10 .... 203 B1
Glyncastle RG4 .... 258 C3
Glyndebourne Gdns OX16 .. 9 A1
Glynswood OX39 .... 168 B3
Gobles Ct OX26 .... 65 C1
Goddard's La OX7 .... 42 C2
Godfrey Cl 13 OX14 .... 179 C3
Godfreys Cl Brill HP18 .... 98 A1
Grove OX12 .... 196 C1
Godstow Cl RG5 .... 260 C1
Godstow Rd OX2 .... 122 C4
Godwyn Cl OX14 .... 179 C4
Goffe Cl OX9 .... 148 A4
Goggs The OX49 .... 186 A1
Golafre Rd OX14 .... 179 C3
Gold St OX44 .... 163 C3
Goldcrest Way OX26 .... 81 A4
Golden Cross OX1 .... 123 B1
Golden Hills OX39 .... 168 B3
Golden Rd OX4 .... 142 A4
Golden Villa Cl OX16 .... 16 A3
Golder's Cl HP18 .... 127 C2
Goldfinch La OX10 .... 221 A1
Goldsmith Cl 3 OX26 .... 65 B2
Goldsmith's La OX10 .... 221 B4
Goldsmith's Terr 12
OX10 .... 221 B4
Gooch OX11 .... 200 C2
Goodlake Ave SN7 .... 172 C2
Goodliffe Gdns RG31 .... 257 B2
Goodrich Cl RG4 .... 259 C3
Goodrington Cl OX16 .... 16 A3
Goodson Wlk OX3 .... 123 C2
Goodsons Ind Mews
OX9 .... 147 C4
Goor La SN8 .... 245 B2
Goose Gn OX15 .... 33 C2
Goose Green Cl OX2 .... 122 C4
Goose La OX15 .... 22 B4
Goose Wlk OX15 .... 21 B2
Gooseacre OX14 .... 160 C1
Goosey La SN7 .... 195 A2
Gordon Cl OX3 .... 123 C3
Gordon Dr OX14 .... 160 B1
Gordon Pl RG30 .... 258 B1
Gordon Rd OX25 .... 63 B4
Gordon St OX1 .... 141 B3
Goring & Streatley Sta
RG8 .... 249 B3
Goring CE Prim Sch
RG8 .... 249 B4
Goring Lodge 25 OX1 .... 141 B4
Goring Rd RG8 .... 250 C4
Gorse Leas OX3 .... 124 A3
Gorselands RG4 .... 259 A3
Gorton Playne OX7 .... 70 B1
Gorwell OX49 .... 186 A1
Gosbrook Ho 6 RG4 .... 259 B1
Gosbrook Rd RG4 .... 259 A1
Gosford Cl OX5 .... 108 C3
Gosford Hill Ct OX5 .... 108 C4
Gosford Hill Sch OX5 .... 108 C4
Goslyn Cl OX3 .... 124 B1
Gossway Fields OX5 .... 78 A2
Gott Cl OX27 .... 66 A3
Goulders Cotts RG10 .... 255 C4
Gouldland Gdns OX3 .... 124 A3
Goulds Villas OX16 .... 16 A3
Grafton Ho OX39 .... 168 B4
Grafton Lodge 26 OX16 .... 16 B3
Grafton Orch OX39 .... 168 B4
Graham Cl OX11 .... 237 A4
Graham Rd OX26 .... 65 B2
Grahame Ave RG8 .... 256 B3
Grammar School Hill
OX7 .... 73 A2
Gramp's Hill OX12 .... 231 C3
Grandison Ho RG9 .... 244 C2
Grandpont Pl OX1 .... 141 B4
Grange Ave RG9 .... 253 A4
Grange Beck OX11 .... 201 A2
Grange Cl Goring RG8 .... 249 A3
Highworth SN6 .... 190 A3
Grange Ct OX2 .... 140 A4
Grange Farm Rd HP14 .... 189 A4
Grange La OX15 .... 19 B4
Grange Mill Ct OX29 .... 120 B4
Grange Pk OX25 .... 48 A1
Grange Prim Sch The
OX16 .... 16 B2
Grange Rd Banbury OX16 .. 16 B2
Henley-on-T RG9 .... 244 C1
Oxford OX4 .... 142 A1
Grange The Kingham OX7 .. 55 A2
Reading RG4 .... 258 B3
Grangers Pl OX28 .... 104 A1
Grantham Ho OX2 .... 123 A2
Grants Mews 3 OX4 .... 141 C4
Granville Ct OX3 .... 124 A1
Granville Way OX26 .... 66 A1
Grasmere Ave RG30 .... 257 C1
Grass Hill RG4 .... 258 C2
Grates The OX4 .... 142 B2
Gravel Cl OX10 .... 203 C2
Gravel Hill
Henley-on-T RG9 .... 244 B1
Reading RG4 .... 259 A3
Sonning Common RG9 .... 252 C3
Gravel Hill Cres RG9 .... 252 C3
Gravel La Drayton OX14 .. 179 A1
Warborough OX10 .... 203 A4
Gravel Pits La OX5 .... 108 A3
Gravel Rd RG9 .... 253 C1
Gravel Wlk
Drayton St L OX10 .... 183 A3
Faringdon SN7 .... 172 C2
Graveney Dr RG4 .... 258 C2
Gravenhill Rd N OX26 .... 81 A4
Gravett Cl RG9 .... 254 B4
Grays Cl OX44 .... 184 B4
Grays Rd OX3 .... 124 A1
Great Barn* SN7 .... 172 A1
Great Clarendon St
OX2 .... 123 A1
Great Close Rd OX5 .... 108 B3
Great Haseley Ind Est
OX44 .... 145 B1
Great Mead OX1 .... 123 A1
Great Milton CE Prim Sch
OX44 .... 145 B2
Great Rissington Prim Sch
GL54 .... 83 A4
Great Rollright CE Prim Sch
OX7 .... 29 A2
Great Tew Prim Sch OX7 .. 45 B4
Great Western Dr OX11 .. 200 C1
Grebe Cl OX14 .... 179 C3
Grebe Rd Banbury OX16 .. 16 C2
Bicester OX26 .... 66 A1
Grebe Sq GL54 .... 68 A2
Green Cl Benson OX10 .. 204 A3
Bicester OX26 .... 65 C1
Didcot OX11 .... 218 C3
Steventon OX13 .... 198 C3
Wallingford OX10 .... 221 B4
Green Cnr OX28 .... 104 B1
Green Coll OX2 .... 123 A2
Green Dean Hill RG4 .... 252 B1
Green End Rd HP14 .... 189 C3
Green Farm OX17 .... 23 A2
Green Furlong OX10 .... 182 B3
Green Hill OX4 .... 143 A1
Green Hitchings OX44 .. 145 B1
Green La Banbury OX16 .. 16 B2
Bledlow Ridge HP14 .... 189 B3
Chesterton OX26 .... 79 C4
Ewelme OX10 .... 204 B2
Henley-on-T RG9 .... 254 B4
Little Tew OX7 .... 44 B3
Longworth OX13 .... 156 B1
Milton-u-W OX7 .... 70 A1
N Hinksey Village OX2 .... 140 A4
North Leigh OX29 .... 105 A4
Pangbourne RG8 .... 256 B3
Shiplake RG9 .... 254 A1
Sonning Common RG4 .... 252 C3
South Newington OX15 .... 31 C4
Stokenchurch HP14 .... 188 B3
Sunningwell OX13 .... 160 A3
Swalcliffe OX15 .... 14 A1
Uffington SN7 .... 211 B4
Upper Arncott OX25 .... 96 C4
Warborough OX10 .... 203 A4
Woodcote RG8 .... 250 C4
Woodstock OX20 .... 91 A4
Wootton (Oxford) OX13 .. 159 A3
Green N The OX10 .... 203 B4
Green Pl OX1 .... 141 B3
Green Rd Didcot OX11 .... 218 C4
Kidlington OX5 .... 108 C4
Oxford OX3 .... 124 C2
Green Ridges OX3 .... 125 A2
Green S The OX10 .... 203 B4
Green St OX4 .... 142 A4
Green The
Adderbury OX17 .... 23 A2
Alvescot OX18 .... 133 B3
Ascott-u-W OX7 .... 71 B1
Aston Rowant OX49 .... 167 B2
Barford St M OX15 .... 32 C3
Baydon SN8 .... 245 C1
Bix RG9 .... 243 C4
Bladon OX20 .... 91 A1
Cassington OX29 .... 107 B1
Chalgrove OX44 .... 184 B3
Charlbury OX7 .... 73 B2
Charney Bassett OX12 .... 176 A1
Charney Bassett, Lyford
OX12 .... 176 B1
Chesterton OX26 .... 79 C4
Chilton OX11 .... 235 C4
Chipping Norton OX7 .... 42 C1
Clanfield OX18 .... 152 C4
Culham OX14 .... 180 A2
Drayton OX14 .... 179 A1
East Hanney OX12 .... 197 A4
Fernham SN7 .... 193 A2
Fifield OX7 .... 69 B1
Fringford OX27 .... 52 B3
Garsington OX44 .... 143 C1
Great Bourton OX17 .... 9 B4
Great Milton OX44 .... 145 A1
Great Rollright OX7 .... 29 A2
Green The *continued*
Great Tew OX7 .... 45 B4
Highworth SN6 .... 190 A3
Hook Norton OX15 .... 30 A4
Hornton OX15 .... 7 B3
Horspath OX33 .... 143 B3
Horton-cum-S OX33 .... 112 A3
Launton OX26 .... 66 C1
Milcombe OX15 .... 20 C1
North Leigh OX29 .... 89 B1
Shrivenham SN6 .... 209 A3
Standlake OX29 .... 137 B2
Stanton Harcourt OX29 .. 138 A4
Steventon OX13 .... 199 A3
Sutton Courtenay OX14 .. 180 A1
Swalcliffe OX15 .... 19 C4
Tackley OX5 .... 77 A3
Uffington SN7 .... 211 B4
West Hanney OX12 .... 196 C3
Green's Rd OX29 .... 120 C4
Greenacres OX14 .... 179 A1
Greenacres Dr OX12 .... 214 B2
Greenacres La OX18 .... 135 B2
Greenfield Cres
Stonesfield OX29 .... 89 B4
Wallingford OX10 .... 221 A4
Greenfield Rd OX29 .... 89 B4
Greenfields OX25 .... 96 B4
Greenfinch Cl OX4 .... 142 C1
Greengates SN7 .... 172 C2
Greenheart Way OX13 .. 156 C1
Greenhill Ct OX16 .... 16 B2
Greenhills Pk OX15 .... 21 B2
Greenlands OX7 .... 70 A1
Greenleas Ave RG4 .... 259 A4
Greenmere OX10 .... 202 C2
Greenmere Prim Sch
OX11 .... 218 C4
Greenmore RG8 .... 250 C4
Greens Garth OX15 .... 21 C3
Greens Keep HP17 .... 130 C3
Greensward The OX17 .... 5 C1
Greenway
Haddenham HP17 .... 130 C3
Lower Heyford OX25 .... 63 A2
4 Thame OX9 .... 129 C1
Greenway The OX12 .... 216 A3
Greenways RG8 .... 256 B3
Greenwich La OX29 .... 87 A2
Greenwood Ave OX39 .. 168 B3
Greenwood Dr OX26 .... 65 A2
Greenwood Mdw OX39 .. 168 B3
Gregory Est OX49 .... 185 B2
Grenoble Rd Oxford OX4 .. 143 A1
Sandford-on-T OX4 .... 142 B1
Grenville Way OX9 .... 130 A1
Gresham Way RG30 .... 258 A1
Greycotes Sch OX2 .... 123 B2
Greygoose La GL56 .... 41 A3
Greyhound La OX9 .... 129 C1
Greys Cl OX16 .... 15 C3
Greys Ct RG9 .... 243 B2
Greys Hill RG9 .... 244 B1
Greys Rd RG9 .... 254 B4
Greystoke Rd RG4 .... 259 B2
Greystones Ct
Alvescot OX18 .... 133 B3
Kidlington OX5 .... 92 B1
Griffin Rd OX9 .... 148 B4
Griffiths Cl OX29 .... 138 B2
Griffiths Gdns OX27 .... 66 A4
Grimmer Way RG8 .... 250 C4
Grimsbury Dr OX16 .... 16 C4
Grimsbury Gn OX16 .... 16 C4
Grimsbury Sq OX16 .... 16 C4
Grindon La OX10 .... 205 A1
Grosvenor Pl OX12 .... 214 A3
Grosvenor Rd
16 Banbury OX16 .... 16 B3
N Hinksey Village OX2 .... 140 C3
Reading RG4 .... 259 B2
Grove CE Sch OX12 .... 196 C1
Grove Cotts
Brightwell-cum-S OX10 .. 202 B1
Little Coxwell SN7 .... 192 C4
Reading RG4 .... 259 A3
Grove Ct Deddington OX15 .. 33 C2
Oxford OX4 .... 142 A3
Grove Hill Highworth SN6 .. 190 A4
Reading RG4 .... 259 A2
Woodstock OX20 .... 91 A3
Grove La Ewelme OX10 .. 205 A3
Spelsbury OX7 .... 72 C4
Grove Park Dr
Ardington OX12 .... 215 B4
Grove OX12 .... 197 A1
Grove Rd Bladon OX20 .... 91 B2
Grove OX12 .... 214 C4
Harwell OX11 .... 217 B4
Henley-on-T RG9 .... 244 C1
Reading RG4 .... 259 A3
Sonning Common RG4 .... 252 C3
Grove St Banbury OX16 .... 16 B3
Cutteslowe OX2 .... 123 A4
Wantage OX12 .... 214 C3
Grove Terr OX11 .... 218 B2
Grove The
Abingdon OX14 .... 160 A1
Bourton SN6 .... 209 A2
Deddington OX15 .... 33 C2
Grovelands OX5 .... 108 B4
Grovelands Ctr OX12 .... 196 B1
Grovelands Rd OX3 .... 125 A1
Grundy Cl OX14 .... 180 A4
Grundy Cres OX1 .... 141 C1

Grunsell Cl OX3 ....124 B3
Guardian Ct **3** OX16 ....16 C3
Guelder Rd OX4 ....142 B1
Guernsey Way OX16 ....9 A1
Guild Ho The OX12 ....214 C2
Guildenford OX18 ....100 C3
Guildford Ct **7** OX5 ...108 C4
Gulley Row OX5 ....95 B4
Gullicote La OX7 ....8 C2
Gulliver's Cl OX15 ....8 A2
Gurden Pl OX3 ....124 C2
Gurl Cl OX3 ....124 C2
Gurney Cl RG4 ....258 B3
Gurney Dr RG4 ....258 B3
Gwyneth Rd OX4 ....142 A1
Gwynne OX RG31 ....257 B2

H

Hack La CV36 ....27 C4
Hackers La OX7 ....55 C2
Hadden Hill OX11 ....201 B1
Haddenham & Thame
  Parkway Sta HP17 ......130 C3
Haddenham Aerodrome Bsns
  Pk HP17 ....130 C4
Hadland Rd OX14 ....180 B4
Hadleigh Rise RG4 ....259 C2
Hadow Rd OX3 ....124 A2
Hadrians Gate NN13 ....24 A4
Hafod RG4 ....258 C3
Hagbourne CE Prim Sch
  OX11 ....218 C3
Hagbourne Rd OX18 ......250 C4
Hagbourne Rd
  Aston Tirrold OX11 ......219 B1
  Didcot OX11 ....219 A4
  East Hagbourne OX11 ...219 B1
Hailes Ave OX7 ....42 C1
Hailey CE Prim Sch
  OX29 ....104 A3
Hailey Cft OX39 ....168 A3
Hailey Cres OX7 ....42 C1
Hailey Rd
  Chipping Norton OX7 .....42 B1
  Witney OX28,OX29 ......104 A2
Haines Cl OX13 ....178 B4
Haldane Rd Oxford OX4 ..142 C1
  Reading RG4 ....258 C3
Hale Rd OX10 ....203 C3
Halfpenny La OX10 ....238 C3
Halifax Rd OX26 ....66 A2
Hall Cl OX49 ....186 A2
Hall Cl The OX25 ....48 A3
Hallett Cl OX12 ....214 C2
Halliday Hill OX3 ....124 A3
Halls Cl Drayton OX14 ...179 B1
  N Hinksey Village OX2 ..140 A4
Halls La OX12 ....197 A4
Hallsmead Ct **1** RG1 ..259 A1
Halse Water OX11 ....81 A1
Halton Rd OX18 ....115 C1
Ham La OX18 ....135 C1
Ham Rd OX12 ....214 B2
Hamble Dr OX14 ....160 A1
Hamble Rd OX11 ....201 A1
Hambleden Dr OX10 ......221 A4
Hambleside OX26 ....65 A1
Hambridge La GL7 ....150 B3
Hamcroft OX12 ....214 B3
Hamel The OX1 ....123 A1
Hamels La OX1 ....140 C1
Hamfield OX12 ....214 A2
Hamilton Ave RG9 ....244 C1
Hamilton Cl Banbury OX16 .16 C4
  Bicester OX26 ....65 C2
Hamilton Rd
  Cutteslowe OX2 ....123 A4
  Thame OX9 ....130 A1
  Wargrave RG10 ....255 C1
Hamlet The RG4 ....258 C2
Hamlyn Cl OX12 ....214 A1
Hammer La OX10 ....183 A1
Hammett Pl OX18 ....115 B1
Hammond's End RG8 .....241 A2
Hampden Ave OX9 ....147 C4
Hampden Cl
  Banbury OX16 ....15 C3
  Bicester OX26 ....66 A2
  Chalgrove OX44 ....184 B3
  Faringdon SN7 ....173 A2
Hampden Dr OX5 ....108 C3
Hampden Rd Oxford OX4 .142 B2
  Reading RG4 ....259 A1
  Wantage OX12 ....214 A2
Hampden Way OX10 .....204 C2
Hamplands OX7 ....29 A2
Hampstead Hill RG9 .....260 B4
Hampton Dr OX17 ....23 C3
Hamstyles OX49 ....205 C4
Hanborough Bsns Pk
  OX29 ....90 C1
Hanborough Cl OX29 .....120 C4
Hanborough Rd OX29 ....120 C4
Hanborough Sta OX29 .....90 C1
Handlo Pl OX3 ....124 C2
Hanney CE Prim Sch
  OX12 ....197 A3
Hanney Rd
  Kingston Bagpuize OX13 .176 B4
  Steventon OX13 ....198 B3
Hannis Rd OX7 ....42 B1
Hanover Cl OX7 ....73 B2
Hanover Ct RG4 ....259 B3

Hanover Gdns
  Bicester OX26 ....65 C1
  Wargrave RG10 ....255 C2
Hans Ave OX12 ....214 C3
Hanson Rd OX14 ....159 C2
Hanwell Ct OX17 ....8 C2
Hanwood Ct RG5 ....260 B1
Harberton Mead OX3 ....123 C2
Harbord Rd OX2 ....109 A1
Harborne Rd OX5 ....77 B3
Harcourt Cl RG9 ....244 B1
Harcourt Gn OX12 ....214 C3
Harcourt Hill OX2 ....140 C3
Harcourt Ho **5** OX26 ...65 C1
Harcourt Rd
  Stokenchurch HP14 .....188 C2
  Wantage OX12 ....214 C3
Harcourt Terr OX3 ....124 A1
Harcourt Way
  Abingdon OX14 ....159 C1
  Wantage OX12 ....214 C3
Harding Cl SN7 ....173 A2
Harding Rd OX14 ....179 B4
Hardings OX44 ....184 B3
Hardings Cl OX44 ....142 A2
Hardings Strings OX11 ...218 C4
Hardwell Cl OX12 ....196 B1
Hardwick Ave OX5 ....108 A4
Hardwick Pk OX16 ....8 C1
Hardwick Prim Sch OX16 .16 A4
Hardwick Rd Hethe OX27 .52 A4
  Whitchurch RGB 256 B4
Hardy Cl RG4 ....259 B1
Harebell Rd OX4 ....142 C1
Harecourt OX12 ....214 C2
Harefields OX2 ....109 A1
Harewood Rd OX16 ....16 C1
Harlech Ave RG4 ....259 B3
Harlech Cl OX16 ....15 C3
Harlequin Way OX16 .....16 C1
Harley Rd Oxford OX2 ...122 C1
  Reading RG4 ....259 A1
Harlington Ave OX12 ....196 A1
Harlow Way OX3 ....123 C4
Harmon Cl OX27 ....64 A3
Harold Hicks Pl OX4 ....141 C3
Harold White Cl OX3 ...124 C1
Harolds Cl OX29 ....124 B2
Harolds Cl OX29 ....87 A2
Harper Cl OX25 ....96 B4
Harpes Rd OX2 ....123 A4
Harpsden Rd RG9 ....254 C4
Harpsden Way OX2 ......254 C4
Harpsichord Pl OX44 ....123 C1
Harrier Pk OX11 ....200 B2
Harrier Rd OX14 ....66 A2
Harriers Ground Sch
  OX16 ....16 B2
Harriers View OX16 ......16 B2
Harris Gdns GL54 ....68 A2
Harris Rd OX25 ....63 B4
Harris's La OX13 ....156 B1
Harrison Pl **8** OX9 ...129 C1
Harrison's La OX20 ....91 A3
Harrisville OX25 ....62 A4
Harroell HP18 ....129 B3
Harrogate Rd RG4 ......258 C2
Harrow Rd OX4 ....142 C2
Harrowby Rd OX16 ....16 B1
Hart Ave SN7 ....172 C2
Hart Cl OX14 ....180 B4
Hart Moor Cl HP14 ......188 C2
Hart Pl OX26 ....66 A2
Hart St Henley-on-T RG9 .244 C1
  Oxford OX2 ....123 A1
Hart-synnot Ho OX2 ....123 A2
Hartley Cl OX3 ....203 A3
Hartley Ct OX2 ....123 A2
Harts Cl OX5 ....108 B4
Hartslock Bridleway
  RG8 ....256 B4
Hartslock Ct RG8 ....256 A3
Hartslock View RG8 .....249 C1
Hartslock Way RG31 .....257 B1
Harvest Pl RG10 ....255 C1
Harwell Cl OX14 ....160 A1
Harwell Int Bsns Ctr
  OX11 ....218 A2
Harwell International Bsns
  Ctr OX11,OX12 ....234 C4
Harwell Prim Sch OX11 ..217 B4
Harwell Rd OX14 ....199 C3
Harwood Rd OX11 ....218 C3
Haslemere Gdns OX5 ....109 A1
Haslemere Tramway Est
  OX16 ....16 C3
Haslemere Way OX16 .....16 B3
Hastings Cl OX16 ....15 C1
Hastings Dr OX18 ....115 C1
Hastings Hill OX7 ....55 C3
Hastings Rd OX16 ....15 C4
Hastoe Grange OX3 .....124 A2
Hatch Cl OX5 ....77 C2
Hatch End OX5 ....77 C2
Hatch Gate La RG10 .....255 C4
Hatch Way OX5 ....77 C2
Hatchet Hill SN4 ....227 A1
Hatching La OX9 ....42 A3
Hatfield Pits La OX29 ...104 B4
Hathaways OX33 ....144 A4
Havelock Rd OX4 ....142 B3
Haven Cl OX10 ....202 B4
Haven Vale OX12 ....214 C3
Havers Ave OX14 ....199 B1
Haw La Ardwell RG8 ....247 C1
  Bledlow Ridge HP14 ....189 C4
Hawke La OX15 ....21 B2

Hawke's La OX15 ....19 B4
Hawker Sq GL54 ....68 A2
Hawkins St **8** OX4 ...141 C4
Hawkins Way OX16 .....159 A3
Hawksmead OX26 ....81 A4
Hawksmoor Rd OX2 .....109 A1
Hawkswell Gdns OX2 ....123 B4
Hawksworth Cl OX12 ...196 B1
Hawthorn Ave
  N Hinksey Village OX2 ..140 B4
  Wallingford OX10 ......221 B4
Hawthorn Cres OX12 ....214 C4
Hawthorn Dr OX18 .....114 B4
Hawthorn Gr OX18 .....115 A3
Hawthorn Rd
  Eynsham OX29 ....120 C4
  Faringdon SN7 ....172 C2
Hawthorn Way
  Kidlington OX5 ....108 C4
  Sonning RG4 ....257 B4
Hawthorn Wlk **2** OX26 .65 C2
Hawthorne Ave OX13 ...159 B1
Hawthorne Cl OX15 ......18 C4
Hawthornes RG31 ....257 A2
Hawthorns The OX16 .....16 B2
Hayden La RG9 ....224 A2
Haydon Rd OX11 ....200 C1
Hayes Ave OX13 ....176 B4
Hayes Cl OX3 ....123 C2
Hayfield Rd OX2 ....123 A3
Hayford Ho **7** OX16 ...16 C3
Hayfords Cty Prim Sch The
  OX25 ....62 C4
Haynes Rd OX3 ....123 C3
Hayward Dr OX18 ......115 B1
Hayward Rd OX2 ....109 A1
Haywards Cl
  Henley-on-T RG9 ....244 B1
  Wantage OX12 ....214 C3
Haywards Rd OX14 .....199 A4
Hazel Ave OX7 ....147 C4
Hazel Cres OX5 ....108 C3
Hazel End OX44 ....143 A3
Hazel Gdns RG4 ....252 C3
Hazel Gr Bicester OX26 ..65 C2
  Stoke Row RG9 ....242 A1
  Wallingford OX10 ......221 B4
Hazel Rd
  N Hinksey Village OX2 ..122 B1
  Purley on T RG8 ....257 B2
Hazel Wlk OX5 ....108 C3
Hazeldene Cl OX29 ......105 A3
Hazeldene Gdns OX16 ....16 B2
Hazell's La SN6 ....209 A3
Hazells La GL7 ....132 A3
Hazelmoor La RG4 ......252 B2
Hazelnut Path OX1,OX14 .160 C4
Hazelrig Cl OX9 ....148 A4
Hazelton Cl OX9 ....147 C4
Hazelwood Cl RG31 .....257 B1
Headington Mid Sch
  OX3 ....124 A1
Headington Quarry CE Fst
  OX3 ....124 C1
Headington Rd OX3 ....124 C2
Headington Rdbt OX3 ...124 C2
Headington Sch OX3 ...124 A1
Headley Ho OX3 ....124 A1
Headley Way OX3 ......124 A2
Healey Cl OX14 ....179 B1
Hean Cl OX14 ....160 A1
Hearns La RG4 ....252 B3
Hearthway OX16 ....9 A1
Heath Cl Milcombe OX15 ..20 C1
  Oxford OX3 ....142 B4
Heath Dr RG9 ....254 A1
Heath La OX20 ....91 A1
Heathcote Ave OX16 .....16 C1
Heathcote Cl OX44 .....160 B1
Heather Cl
  Carterton OX18 ....115 B3
  Sonning Common RG4 ..253 A3
Heather Pl OX3 ....123 C2
Heather Rd Bicester OX26 .65 C2
Milton OX14 ....199 B3
Heathfield Ave RG9 ....254 A1
Heathfield Cl RG9 .....254 A1
Hedge End OX20 ....91 B3
Hedge Hill Rd OX12 ....213 C3
Hedgemead Ave OX14 ..160 B1
Hedgerley OX39 ....168 A3
Hedges The OX15 ....14 A4
Helen Rd OX2 ....122 C1
Hellebourine Cl OX4 ...142 C1
Helwys Pl OX5 ....92 B1
Hemdean Hill RG4 .....259 A2
Hemdean House Sch
  RG4 ....259 A2
Hemdean Rd RG4 ......259 A2
Hemdean Rise RG4 .....259 A2
Hemmingway Dr OX26 ...65 C2
Hemplands OX29 ....104 A3
Hempton Rd OX15 ....33 C2
Henderson Ho OX10 ....221 A4
Hendon Pl OX26 ....66 A2
Hendred Ho OX4 ....142 A3
Hendred St OX4 ....142 A3
Hendred Way OX14 ....160 A1
Hendreds CE Sch The
  OX12 ....216 B3
Hengest Gate OX11 ....217 C4
Hengrove Cl OX3 ....124 B2

Henley Ave OX4 ....142 A3
Henley Cl (Deanfield Bldgs)
  The RG9 ....244 B1
Henley Coll (Rotherfield
  Bldgs) The RG9 ....244 B1
Henley Dr SN6 ....190 A4
Henley Gdns **18** OX26 ..65 C1
Henley Rd
  Dorchester OX10 ......202 C4
  Reading RG4,RG9 ....260 B4
  Sandford-on-T OX4 .....161 A4
Henley St OX4 ....141 C4
Henley-on-Thames Sta
  RG9 ....244 C1
Henleys La OX14 ....179 A1
Hennef Way OX16 ....16 C4
Henor Mill Cl OX14 .....160 A1
Henrietta Rd OX9 ......130 A1
Henry Box Cl OX28 .....118 A4
Henry Box Sch The
  OX28 ....118 A4
Henry Rd OX2 ....122 C1
Henry Taunt Cl OX3 ....124 C3
Hensington Cl OX20 ......91 A2
Hensington Rd OX20 .....91 A3
Hensington Wlk OX20 ....91 B3
Henwood Dr OX1 ....140 A1
Herald Way **8** OX26 ...66 A2
Herbert Cl OX4 ....142 A4
Hereford Way OX16 ......9 A1
Heritage La OX7 ....71 A1
Herman Cl OX14 ....180 A4
Hermitage Rd OX14 ....179 C3
Hernes Cl OX2 ....123 A4
Hernes Cres OX2 ......123 A4
Hernes Rd OX2 ....123 A4
Heron Cl OX18 ....115 B2
Heron Ct Abingdon OX14 .179 C2
  Bicester OX26 ....66 A1
Heron Island RG4 ......259 B1
Heron Rd OX14 ....204 B2
Heron's Wlk OX14 ......159 C1
Herons Pl OX2 ....123 A4
Herringcote OX10 ......182 B1
Herschel Cres OX4 .....142 B2
Herschel Cl **6** OX4 ..142 B2
Herschel Ct Bicester OX26 .65 C2
  Reading RG4 ....259 B3
Hertford Coll OX1 .....123 B1
Hertford Ct **8** OX5 ..108 C4
Hertford St OX4 ....142 A4
Hethe Rd Cottisford NN13 .38 A2
  Hardwick OX27 ....51 B4
Hewett Ave RG4 ....258 B2
Hewett Cl RG4 ....258 B2
Hewetts Cl OX29 ....87 A2
Hewgate Ct RG9 ....244 C1
Heycroft OX29 ....87 A2
Heydons Terr OX17 ......3 C4
Heyford Cl OX3 ....137 B3
Heyford Hill La OX4 ...141 C1
Heyford Hill Rdbt OX4 .141 C1
Heyford Mead OX5 ......92 B1
Heyford Rd
  Kirtlington OX5 ....77 C2
  Middleton Stoney OX5 ...64 A2
  Steeple Aston OX25 .....62 A4
  Heyford Sta OX25 ......62 C3
Hicks Cl OX29 ....104 A3
Hid's Copse Rd OX2 ...140 A4
Higgs Cl OX11 ....219 A3
High Acres OX16 ....16 C2
High Cross Way OX3 ...124 C3
High Furlong OX16 ......16 A4
High House Cl OX18 ...152 C4
High Land Cl HP18 ......98 A1
High Mdw Reading RG4 .258 B2
  Sjbford Gower OX15 .....31 C1
High Rd Bexley OX3 ....111 A2
Brightwell-cum-S OX10 .202 C2
Brightwell-cum-S, Slade End
  OX10 ....203 A1
High Road Cotts OX10 ..202 B2
High St
  14 Abingdon OX14 ..179 C4
  Adderbury OX17 ....23 A2
  Ascott-u-W OX7 ....71 B1
  Ashbury SN6 ....228 A4
  Aston OX18 ....135 B2
  Aston Rowant OX9 .....167 C2
  Bampton OX18 ....134 C2
  Banbury OX16 ....16 B3
  Barford St N OX15 ......32 B3
  Benson OX10 ....203 C2
  Bishopstone SN6 ......227 B2
  Bloxham OX15 ....21 C3
  Bodicote OX15 ....22 B4
  Burford OX18 ....100 C3
  Chalgrove OX44 ....184 B4
  Charlton-on-O OX5 ......95 A2
  Charney Bassett OX12 .175 C1
  Childrey OX12 ....213 B2
  Chinnor OX39 ....168 B4
  Chipping Norton OX7 ...42 C2
  Clifton Hampden OX14 .181 B2
  Cropredy OX17 ....4 C1
  Croughton NN13 ....36 B4
  Cuddesdon OX44 ......144 A1
  Culham OX14 ....180 A2
  Cumnor OX2 ....139 B3
  Deddington OX15 ....33 C2
  Didcot OX11 ....218 C4
  Dorchester OX10 ......182 B1
  Drayton OX14 ....179 A1
  Drayton St L OX10 .....183 A3
  East Hendred OX12 ....216 C3

High St continued
  Eweline OX10 ....204 C2
  Eynsham OX29 ....120 C4
  Fernham SN7 ....193 A2
  Fifield OX7 ....69 A1
  Finstock OX7 ....88 A3
  Goring RG8 ....249 B3
  Great Rollright OX7 .....29 A2
  Haddenham HP17 .....130 C3
  Harwell OX11 ....217 C4
  Highworth SN6 ....190 A3
  Hinton Waldrist SN7 ...155 C1
  Hook Norton OX15 ......30 B4
  Islip OX5 ....93 C1
  Kidlington OX5 ....92 C1
  Lechlade GL7 ....150 B2
  Lewknor OX49 ....187 A4
  Little Milton OX44 .....163 C4
  Long Crendon HP18 ....129 B3
  Long Wittenham OX14 ..201 B4
  Ludgershall HP18 ....98 A4
  Middleton Cheney OX17 ..17 C4
  Milton OX14 ....199 B3
  Milton-u-W OX7 ....42 A4
  Nettlebed RG9 ....224 B1
  North Moreton OX11 ...220 A4
  Oxford OX1,OX4 ....123 B1
  Pangbourne RG8 ......256 B3
  Ramsden OX7 ....88 A2
  Ratley OX15 ....2 A2
  Shipton-u-W OX7 ....85 B4
  Shrivenham SN6 ......209 B3
  Shutford OX15 ....14 A3
  Sonning RG4 ....260 B2
  Souldern OX6 ....35 C2
  South Newington OX15 ..31 C4
  Standlake OX29 ....137 B2
  Stanford in the V SN7 ..194 C4
  Steventon OX13 ....199 A2
  Stonesfield OX29 ....89 B4
  Streatley RG8 ....249 A3
  Sutton Courtenay OX14 .200 A4
  Tetsworth OX9 ....166 A4
  Thame OX9 ....129 C1
  Uffington SN7 ....211 B4
  Upper Heyford OX25 ....48 C1
  Upton OX11 ....218 B1
  Wallingford OX10 .....221 B4
  Wargrave RG10 ....191 B3
  Watchfield SN6 ....191 B1
  Watlington OX49 ......186 A1
  Wheatley OX33 ....144 A4
  Whitchurch RG8 ....256 B4
  Witney OX28 ....118 B4
  Woodstock OX20 ....91 A3
  Wootton OX25 ....75 C2
High View OX12 ......214 A2
Highbridge Cl RG4 ...259 C3
Highclere Gdns
  Banbury OX16 ....15 C3
  Wantage OX12 ....214 B3
Highdown Ave RG4 ...259 A3
Highdown Hill Rd RG4 .259 A3
Highdown Sch RG4 ...259 A3
Highfield HP18 ....129 A3
Highfield Ave OX3 ...124 B1
Highfield Cl OX9 .....147 B4
Highfield Pk RG10 ...255 C1
Highfield Rd RG31 ...257 B2
Highlands OX16 ....9 A1
Highlands Sch The
  RG31 ....257 B1
Highmoor Rd RG4 ....258 C2
Hightown Gdns OX16 ..16 B2
Hightown Leys OX16 ...16 B2
Hightown Rd OX16 .....16 B2
Highworth Pl OX28 ...118 A4
Highworth Rd
  Faringdon SN7 ....172 C1
  Shrivenham SN6 ......209 A4
**Highworth Warneford Comp
  Sch** SN6 ....190 A2
Highworth Way RG31 ..257 A1
Hikers Way HP18 .....129 C2
Hill Bottom Cl RG8 ...250 C2
Hill Cl Charlbury OX7 ..73 B2
  Chipping Norton OX7 ...42 C1
  East Challow OX12 .....214 A2
Hill Cres OX7 ....88 B3
Hill Farm Cl OX39 ....168 B3
Hill Farm La OX25 .....47 B3
Hill Gdns RG8 ....249 A3
Hill La OX18 ....152 B4
Hill Lands RG10 ......255 B1
Hill Piece OX11 ....218 A1
Hill Prim Sch The RG4 .259 B3
Hill Rd Chinnor OX39 .168 B3
  Lewknor OX49 ....187 A4
  Lewknor OX49,HP14 ...187 B3
  Watchfield SN6 ....191 B1
  Watlington OX49 ......206 C4
Hill Rise
  Great Rollright OX7 .....29 A2
  Horspath OX33 ....143 B3
  Sandford-on-O OX25 ....91 A4
Hill The Aynho OX17 ...35 B4
  Bourton SN6 ....209 A2
  Burford OX18 ....100 C2
  Burford, Westwell OX18 ..99 C1
  Garsington OX44 ......143 C1
Hill Top OX39 ....168 C2
Hill Top Rd OX4 ......142 A4
Hill View Carterton OX18 .115 B2
  Kingston Lisle OX12 ....212 A2
  Oxford OX3 ....125 A2
  Uffington SN7 ....211 B4
Hill View Cres OX16 ...16 A4

Hill View La OX1 ....159 A4
Hill View Prim Sch OX16 ..16 A4
Hillary Dr OX11 ....218 C4
Hillary Way OX33 ....144 B4
Hillcraft Rd OX33 ....125 B4
Hillcrest La RG9 ....252 C4
Hilliard Ho OX14 ....179 C3
Hilliat Fields OX14 ......179 A1
Hilliers Cl OX14 ....200 A4
Hillsborough Cl 7 OX4 .142 A2
Hillsborough Rd OX4 ...142 A2
Hillside Cumnor OX2 .....140 A3
Harwell OX11 ....217 A2
Whitchurch RG8 ....256 B4
Hillside Cl Banbury OX16 ..16 C2
Upper Arncott OX25 ....96 C4
Hillside Rd OX7 ....46 C1
Hilltop HP18 ....129 B3
Hilltop Ct OX4 ....142 A4
Hilltop Gdns OX5 ....93 C1
Hilltop Rd RG4 ....258 B3
Hillview Cl RG31 ....257 A1
Hillview Rd
Abingdon OX14 ....159 C1
Oxford OX2 ....123 A1
Hillwerke OX39 ....168 B3
Hilly Lawn Ct OX7 ....42 C2
Hillyard Barns OX14 ....200 A4
Hilton Rd OX16 ....16 A3
Hinksey Bsns Ctr OX2 ...122 B1
Hinksey Hill OX1 ....141 A2
Hinksey Hill Intc OX1 ...141 B2
Hinton Hill SN4 ....227 A2
Hinton Rd OX13 ....156 A2
Hinton Springs SN4 .....227 A2
Hirstwood RG30 ....257 C1
Hiskins OX12 ....214 A3
Hitchman Dr OX7 ....42 C2
Hithercroft Cholsey OX10 .220 B3
South Moreton OX11 .....220 B3
Hithercroft Ct OX10 .....221 A3
Hithercroft Ind Est
OX10 ....221 A4
Hithercroft Rd OX10 ....221 A4
Hive Mews 4 OX14 ......179 C3
Hixet Wood OX7 ....73 A2
HM Prison (Bullingdon)
OX25,HP18 ....97 A4
Hobbs Cl OX14 ....180 A4
Hobby Ct OX4 ....142 C1
Hobbyhorse La OX14 ....200 A4
Hobson Rd OX2 ....123 A4
Hocker Bench SN6 ......227 B2
Hocketts Cl RG8 ....250 C2
Hockmore St OX4 ....142 B2
Hodge Ct OX1 ....141 B4
Hodgson Cl OX27 ....49 C4
Hogarth Pl OX14 ....179 C3
Hogg End Bloxham OX15 ...21 C2
Chipping Warden OX17 ......5 C3
Holborn Hill OX12 ......231 B4
Holcombe La OX10 ......183 B3
Holford Rd OX28 ....117 C4
Holis Cl OX28 ....118 B4
Holkham Cl RG30 ....257 C1
Holland Cl OX39 ....168 B4
Holland Pl OX3 ....142 C4
Holland Rd OX14 ....160 A1
Hollandridge La OX49,
RG9 ....207 B2
Hollands Rise OX17 ......23 C2
Holley Cres OX3 ....124 C2
Holliers Cl
Sydenham OX39 ....167 B4
Thame OX9 ....147 C4
Holliers Cres OX7 ....60 C4
Hollies Ct The 18 OX16 ...16 B3
Hollington HP18 ....129 A4
Hollow Furlong OX29 ...107 B1
Hollow Way Aynho OX17 ...35 B4
Childrey OX12 ....213 B2
Oxford OX3,OX4 ....142 B3
Holloway Hill OX15 ....12 A1
Holloway La
Compton Wynyates OX15 ...12 A1
Northend RG9 ....207 C3
Holloway Rd OX33 ......144 A4
Holloway Rd The SN7 ...192 A4
Holloway The
Harwell OX11 ....217 C3
Mollington OX17 ....4 A2
Holloway Way OX11 .....218 B1
Holly Cl Bicester OX26 .....65 C3
Kidlington OX5 ....108 C4
Rotherfield Peppard RG9 ..242 C3
Holly Ct OX4 ....142 C2
Hollybush Rd
Carterton OX18 ....115 B1
Hook Norton OX15 ....30 A4
Hollybush Row OX1 .....123 A1
Holm Sq OX26 ....65 C3
Holm Way OX26 ....65 C3
Holme Park Farm La
RG4 ....260 B1
Holmemoor Dr RG4 .....260 C1
Holmlea Rd RG8 ....249 B3
Holoway Rd OX28 ....118 A4
Holt The
4 Abingdon OX14 ....179 C4
Mollington OX17 ....3 C2
Purley on T RG8 ....257 B2
Holt Weer Cl OX2 ....109 A1
Holy Trinity RC Sch OX7 ..42 C2
Holyoake Rd OX3 ....124 B2
Holyrood Cl RG4 ....259 B3
Holywell Bsns Ctr OX2 ..141 A4
Holywell Cl OX14 ....160 B1
Holywell St OX1 ....123 B1
Home Cl Carterton OX18 ..115 B1
Cutteslowe OX2 ....122 B4
Kidlington OX5 ....92 C1
Shabbington HP18 ....128 B2
Wootton (Oxford) OX13 ...159 A3
Home Croft RG31 ....257 A1
Home Farm OX10 ....221 C4
Home Farm Barns OX18 .133 A3
Home Farm Cl
Ambrosden OX25 ....81 B2
East Hendred OX12 ......216 B4
Shipton-u-W OX7 ....85 B4
Home Farm Cotts OX29 .102 C4
Home Farm Ct OX17 .....23 A2
Homefield Cl HP14 ......188 C2
Homelands Way RG9 ....244 B1
Homeleaze Rd SN6 ......209 C4
Homestall Cl OX2 ....122 A1
Homestead Cres OX25 ....63 A4
Homestead Rd OX16 .....16 C1
Homestead The
Bladon OX20 ....91 B2
Kidlington OX5 ....108 B4
Shiplake RG9 ....254 A1
1 Thame OX9 ....129 C1
Hone Ct OX7 ....73 A2
Honey La OX10 ....220 C1
Honey Meadow Rd RG4 .259 C1
Honeybottom La OX13 ..159 A3
Honeyham Cl OX18 ......116 B2
Honeysuckle Cl OX26 ....65 C3
Honeysuckle Gr OX4 ....143 A1
Honor Cl OX5 ....108 C4
Hook End La RG8 ....249 A1
Hook Norton CE Sch
OX15 ....30 A4
Hook Norton Rd
Great Rollright OX7 ....29 A2
Sibford Ferris OX15 ....19 A4
Hookend La RG8 ....251 B4
Hooks Cl GL7 ....132 C1
Hop Gdns RG9 ....244 B1
Hopcraft Cl OX25 ....96 C4
Hopcraft La OX15 ....33 C2
Hopkins Ct OX4 ....142 B3
Hopton Rd OX9 ....130 A1
Hordern Cl HP17 ....130 C3
Horley Path Rd OX15 ......8 A1
Horn Hill OX15 ....32 C3
Horn Hill Rd OX17 ....22 C2
Horn La Adlestrop GL56 ....40 A3
East Hendred OX12 ......216 B3
Hornbeam Cl
Banbury OX16 ....16 A3
Purley on T RG8 ....257 B3
Hornbeam Dr OX4 ......143 A1
Hornbeam Rd OX26 ......65 C3
Horne OX27 ....66 A4
Hornsea Cl RG30 ....257 C1
Hornton Hollow OX15 ....21 B2
Horse Cl The RG4 ....259 B2
Horse Close Cotts OX44 .164 B4
Horse Fair Banbury OX16 ..16 B3
Chipping Norton OX7 ....42 C2
Deddington OX15 ....33 C2
Horse Shoe La OX7 ....72 A4
Horsecroft SN7 ....194 C4
Horseman Cl OX3 ....124 A3
Horsemere La OX29 .....107 B1
Horsepond Rd RG4 .....252 A3
Horseshoe La OX20 ....75 C2
Horseshoe Pk RG8 ....256 B3
Horseshoe Rd
Bledlow Ridge HP14 ......189 B4
Pangbourne RG8 ....256 B3
Horseshoes Cl OX13 ....158 A4
Horseshoes La OX10 ....203 C2
Horseshoes Pl OX9 .....148 A4
Horsham Cl OX16 ....8 C1
Horspath CE Prim Sch
OX33 ....143 B4
Horspath Driftway OX4 .142 C4
Horspath Rd OX4 ....142 C3
Horspath Rd Ind Est
OX4 ....142 C3
Horton Ave OX9 ....148 A4
Horton Cl OX9 ....148 A4
Horton General Hospl
OX16 ....16 B2
Horton La OX15 ....21 A1
Horton View OX16 ....16 B2
Horwood Cl OX3 ....124 B2
Hosker Cl OX3 ....125 A2
Hound Cl OX14 ....160 B1
Howard Ave OX12 ....196 C1
Howard Cornish Rd
OX13 ....178 B4
Howard Rd OX16 ....16 C3
Howard St OX4 ....142 A4
Howbery Farm OX10 ....221 C4
Howe Cl OX33 ....144 A4
Howe Rd OX49 ....206 B4
Howes La OX26 ....65 A2
Howgate Dr RG8 ....249 B4
Howland Rd OX9 ....148 A4
Hoyle Cl OX28 ....104 A2
Huckleberry Cl RG8 .....257 B2
Hudleston Ave OX10 ....204 B1
Hudson Ct OX15 ....33 C2
Hudson St Bicester OX26 ..65 B2
Deddington OX15 ....33 C2
Hugh Allen Cres OX3 ....123 C2
Hugh Price Ho OX4 ......142 A4
Hughes Cl OX7 ....73 B1
Hughes Cres SN7 ....192 B2
Hughes Ho OX4 ....141 C4
Humber Cl Didcot OX11 ..201 A1
Wantage OX12 ....214 C3
Humber St OX15 ....21 C2
Humber Wlk OX16 ....15 C4
Humfrey Rd OX3 ....124 C2
Humphries Cl OX18 .....115 C2
Hunder Ct OX1 ....141 B1
Hundred Acre Cl OX3 ...142 C4
Hungerford Rd OX13 ....199 A1
Hunsdon Rd OX4 ....142 A2
Hunt Cl OX26 ....65 C1
Hunt Rd OX9 ....148 A4
Hunt's Cl OX29 ....89 B4
Hunter Cl Abingdon OX14 .160 A2
Oxford OX4 ....142 C3
Huntercombe End La
RG9 ....224 A2
Hunters Chase RG4 .....258 C3
Hunters Cl OX12 ....196 B1
Hunters Field SN7 ......194 C4
Hunters Piece SN6 ......209 A1
Hunters Point OX39 .....168 B3
Hunts Cl OX18 ....100 C2
Hurdeswell OX29 ....90 A1
Hurdlers Gn OX49 ....186 A1
Hurst Cl OX10 ....221 B3
Hurst La Cumnor OX2 ....140 A3
Freeland OX29 ....106 A4
Hurst Rise Rd OX2 ......140 B4
Hurst St OX4 ....141 C4
Huscarle Way RG31 .....257 B2
Hutchcomb Rd OX2 .....140 B4
Hutchcombe Farm Cl
OX2 ....140 B4
Huxley Cl Bicester OX26 ...65 B2
Wootton (Oxford) OX13 ...159 A3
Hyacinth Wlk OX4 ......161 C4
Hyde Copse OX13 ....178 B4
Hyde Gr OX15 ....21 B2
Hyde Pl OX14 ....179 B3
Hyde Rd OX12 ....196 A3
Hyde The OX14 ....179 B3
Hydes The RG31 ....257 B2
Hydrangea Wlk OX16 ......9 A1
Hythe Bridge St OX1 ....123 A1

I

Ian Mikardo Way RG4 ...259 B1
Ibstone Ave RG4 ....259 C3
Ibstone Rd HP14 ....188 B2
Ickford Comb Sch HP18 .128 A2
Ickford Rd
Shabbington HP18 ....128 B1
Tiddington OX9 ....145 C4
Worminghall HP18 ....127 C3
Ickleton Rd OX12 ....214 A2
Icknield Cl Chinnor OX39 .168 A2
Didcot OX11 ....200 B1
Icknield Com Sch OX49 .186 A1
Icknield Cotts RG8 ......249 A3
Icknield La OX12 ....214 C2
Icknield Pl RG8 ....249 B4
Icknield Rd RG8 ....249 B4
Icknield Way SN6 ....227 B2
Idbury Cl OX28 ....117 B4
Idstone Hill SN6 ....228 A2
Idstone Rd SN6 ....228 A3
Iffley Mead Sch OX4 ....141 C3
Iffley Rd OX4 ....141 C4
Iffley Turn OX4 ....142 A3
Ilchester Mews RG4 ....259 C3
Ilex Cl RG4 ....252 C2
Ilges La OX10 ....221 A1
Ilkley Rd RG4 ....258 C2
Illingworth Ave RG4 ....259 C3
Ilsley Cl RG4 ....252 C3
Imperial Ct RG9 ....244 C1
Independent Bsns Pk
HP14 ....188 B3
Ingham La OX49 ....186 A1
Ingle Cl OX3 ....124 A2
Inglewood Cl RG4 ......252 C3
Ingrebourne Way OX11 ..200 C2
Inkerman Cl OX14 ......159 B1
Innsworth Rd OX18 .....115 C2
Inott Furze OX3 ....142 B4
Insall Rd OX7 ....42 C2
Inst Of Virology &
Experimental Microbiology
OX1 ....123 B1
Ireton Cl OX44 ....184 B3
Ireton Ct OX9 ....129 C1
Iron Down Hill
Barford St M OX7,OX15 ....32 B2
South Newington OX7,OX15 .31 C2
Ironside Dr SN6 ....191 B1
Ironstone Hollow OX15 ...30 B4
Ironstones OX16 ....16 A4
Ishree Cotts RG9 ....242 A3
Isis Ave OX26 ....65 A1
Isis Bsns Ctr OX4 ....142 C3
Isis CE Mid Sch OX4 ....141 C3
Isis Cl Abingdon OX14 ....160 B1
Long Hanborough OX29 ...106 A4
Islip Rd Bletchingdon OX5 ..93 A4
Cutteslowe OX2 ....123 A4
Islip Sta OX5 ....93 C1
Islsley Rd OX3 ....124 C2
Itchen Ct OX11 ....201 A2
Ivatt Wlk OX16 ....16 C4
Ivy La Mollington OX17 ......4 A2
Oxford OX3 ....124 B2
Shutford OX15 ....14 A3
Ivybank RG31 ....257 B1
Ivydene Rd RG30 ....258 B1

J

Jack Argent Cl 22 OX4 ..142 C1
Jack Straw's La OX3 ....124 A2
Jackdaw La OX4 ....141 C4
Jackies La OX33 ....144 B4
Jackman Cl OX14 ....180 A4
Jackson Cl OX18 ....115 B1
Jackson Cole Ho 5
OX1 ....123 A1
Jackson Dr OX1 ....141 B1
Jackson Rd
Bledington OX7 ....54 B1
Cutteslowe OX2 ....109 A1
Jacobs Cl OX28 ....104 A1
Jacobs Yd OX7 ....60 C4
James Ct OX18 ....152 C4
James St OX4 ....141 C4
James Wolfe Rd OX4 ...142 C4
Janaway OX4 ....142 A1
Jane Morbey Rd OX9 ...148 A4
Jane Seaman Ct OX4 ...143 A1
Japonica Cl OX26 ....65 C3
Japonica Wlk OX16 ....9 A1
Jarn Way OX1 ....140 B1
Jarvis La OX26 ....66 A1
Jasmine Cl OX4 ....142 C2
Jasmine Pl OX26 ....65 C3
Jasmine Wlk OX16 ....9 A1
Javelin Way OX10 ....204 B2
Jay Cl OX26 ....81 A4
Jaynes Cl OX16 ....16 B1
Jeff's Terr OX7 ....73 A2
Jefferson Cl RG4 ....259 B4
Jefferson Way OX9 .....148 A4
Jeffersons Piece OX7 ....73 B3
Jemmetts Cl OX10 ......182 B1
Jennings La OX11 ....217 C4
Jenyns Ct OX14 ....179 B3
Jericho St OX2 ....123 A2
Jerome Way OX5 ....92 B3
Jersey Dr OX16 ....9 A1
Jersey Rd OX4 ....142 A2
Jervis Cl OX7 ....60 C4
Jespers Hill SN7 ....173 A2
Jesse's La HP18 ....129 B3
Jessops Cl Marston OX3 ..123 C3
Oxford OX3 ....124 A3
Jesus Coll OX1 ....123 B1
Jethro Tull Gdns OX10 ..221 C4
Jetty The OX17 ....5 C1
Jeune Hall 2 OX4 ......141 C4
Jeune St OX4 ....141 C4
Joan Lawrence Pl OX3 ..124 C1
John Blandy Prim Sch
OX13 ....156 C1
John Buchan Rd OX3 ...124 A3
John Garne Way OX3 ...124 A1
John Hampen Prim Sch
OX9 ....148 A4
John Kallie Ho OX4 .....142 A3
John Lopes Rd OX29 ....120 C4
John Mason Sch
OX14 ....179 C4
John Mason Rd OX14 ...180 A4
John Morris Rd OX14 ...179 C3
John Piers La OX1 ......141 B3
John Radcliffe Hospl
OX3 ....124 A2
John Smith Dr OX4 .....142 B2
John Snow Pl OX3 ......124 C2
John Towle Cl OX1 .....141 B3
John Watson Sch OX33 .126 A1
Johnson Cl OX44 ....143 B1
Johnston's Way OX7 .....42 C1
Johnstone Pl 19 OX10 ...221 B4
Johnstones SN7 ....195 A2
Jordan Cl Didcot OX11 ...201 A1
Reading RG4 ....259 C3
Jordan Hill OX2 ....109 A1
Jordans Cl OX7 ....88 A2
Josca's Prep Sch OX13 ..178 A4
Josey Cl RG4 ....252 C3
Jourdain Rd OX4 ....142 C2
Jowett Wlk OX1 ....123 B1
Joyce's Rd SN7 ....194 B4
Jubilee Cl OX25 ....62 A4
Jubilee Cotts OX12 .....215 C3
Jubilee Ct OX16 ....16 B3
Jubilee Rd HP14 ....188 C2
Jubilee Terr OX1 ....141 B4
Jubilee Way OX11 ....219 A4
Jubillee La OX7 ....85 A4
Judd's Cl OX28 ....118 B4
Judges Cl OX5 ....108 C4
Judges Rd RG8 ....241 C2
Junction Rd
Banbury OX16 ....16 C3
Churchill OX7 ....55 C2
Oxford OX4 ....142 B3
Juniper Cl OX16 ....9 A1
Juniper Ct
Abingdon OX14 ....179 B4
13 Banbury OX16 ....16 B3
Juniper Dr OX4 ....142 C1
Juniper Gdns OX26 ......65 C3
Juniper Way RG31 ......257 B1
Juxon St OX2 ....123 A2

K

Kames Cl OX4 ....142 A3
Katchside OX14 ....199 C3
Katherine's Wlk GL7 ....150 B2
Keats Cl 4 OX26 ....65 B2
Keats Rd OX16 ....16 A2
Keble Cl GL7 ....150 B3
Keble Coll OX1 ....123 B1
Keble Rd Bicester OX26 ....65 C2
Oxford OX1 ....123 B2
Kedleston Rise OX16 .....16 C1
Keene Cl OX4 ....161 A4
Keens Cl OX7 ....58 C3
Keens La OX39 ....168 B3
Keeys Cl OX27 ....50 B2
Kelburne Rd OX4 ....142 A2
Kelham Hall Dr OX33 ...144 A4
Kelly's Rd OX33 ....143 C4
Kelmscott Cl RG4 ....258 C2
Kelmscott Manor Ho★
GL7 ....151 C1
Kelso Mews RG4 ....259 C3
Kelvedon Way RG4 ......258 C3
Kemps Rd OX17 ....23 A3
Kempson Cres OX4 .....142 A1
Kempster Cl OX14 ....180 A4
Kendal Ave RG4 ....259 C3
Kendal Cres OX2 ....109 A1
Kendal Piece OX7 ....73 B2
Kenhill Rd OX15 ....6 C1
Kenilworth Ave OX4 .....142 A4
Kenilworth Ct OX4 ......142 A4
Kenilworth Rd OX2 ......139 C2
Kenilworth Way OX16 ....15 C3
Kenley Ave OX18 ....115 C2
Kennedy Cl OX4 ....142 C4
Kennedy Cres OX10 .....220 C1
Kennedy Dr RG8 ....256 C3
Kennedy Ho OX16 ....16 A3
Kennedy Rd OX26 ....65 B1
Kennel La
Chipping Norton OX7 ....42 A1
Steventon OX13 ....199 A3
Kennet Cl
Berinsfield OX10 ....182 B2
Bicester OX26 ....65 B1
Grove OX12 ....196 B1
Kennet Rd
Abingdon OX14 ....160 A1
Harwell OX11 ....217 B1
Kennett Rd OX3 ....124 B1
Kennetts Hos OX15 ....21 B2
Kennington Rd
Kennington OX1 ....141 C1
Kennington OX1 ....160 C3
Radley OX14 ....160 C3
Kennington Rdbt OX1 ...141 B2
Kennylands Rd RG4 .....253 A2
Kensington Cl
Abingdon OX14 ....179 C2
Kings Sutton OX17 ....23 C3
Kent Cl Abingdon OX14 ...180 A4
Oxford OX4 ....142 C2
Kentons La RG10 ....255 B4
Kentwood Cl
Cholsey OX10 ....220 C1
Reading RG30 ....257 C1
Kentwood Hill RG31 .....257 C1
Kenville Rd OX1 ....141 B1
Kernham Dr RG31 ....257 B2
Kerry Cl OX16 ....9 A1
Kersington Cres OX4 ....142 B2
Kerwood Cl OX20 ....91 A4
Keston Cl RG4 ....259 B1
Kestrel Cl OX18 ....115 B2
Kestrel Cres OX4 ....142 B1
Kestrel Pl OX4 ....142 B1
Kestrel Way OX26 ....81 A4
Kestrels The OX12 ......196 B1
Ketchmere Cl HP18 .....129 B3
Kew Win OX11 ....201 A1
Keydale Rd OX33 ....143 C4
Keyser Rd OX15 ....22 C4
Keyte's Cl OX17 ....23 A2
Kibble Cl OX11 ....219 A4
Kiddington Rd OX7 ....60 C4
Kidlington Ctr OX5 ....92 C1
Kidlington Rd OX5 ....93 C1
Kidmore End CE Prim Sch
RG4 ....252 B2
Kidmore End Rd RG4 ...259 A4
Kidmore La RG4 ....252 C2
Kidmore Rd RG4 ....258 C3
Kilbale Cres OX16 ....16 B2
Kildare Gdns RG4 ....259 B2
Kilkenny La OX18 ....115 C3
Kiln Cl Aston OX18 ......135 B2
Sandford-on-T OX4 ....161 B4
Kiln La Garsington OX44 ..143 B1
Oxford OX3 ....124 C1
Shiplake RG9 ....254 B1
Wheatley OX33 ....144 A4
Kiln Rd RG4 ....259 B4
Kiln Terr SN7 ....173 A2
Kimbells Cl HP18 ....128 B1
Kimber Cl OX33 ....144 A4
Kimber Rd OX14 ....179 B4
Kimberley Villas 21 OX16 .16 B3
Kimbers Cl OX12 ....196 A2
Kinecroft OX10 ....221 B4
Kineton Rd OX1 ....141 B4
King Alfred Dr OX11 ....200 C1
King Alfred's Sch OX12 .214 B2
King Alfred's Sch E
OX12 ....214 C2
King Alfred's Sch W
OX12 ....214 A2
King Edward St OX1 ....123 B1
King James Way RG9 ...254 B4
King St OX2 ....123 A2
King Wlk OX11 ....200 C1

King's Ave OX26 ....65 B1
King's Cl OX9 ....147 C4
King's Cross Rd OX2 .....123 A4
King's End OX26 ....65 B1
King's Head La OX5 ....93 C1
King's Head Mews OX7 ....42 C2
King's La SN7 ....192 B2
King's Mill La OX3 ....123 C1
King's Rd Banbury OX16 ...16 A3
  Henley-on-T RG9 ....244 B1
  Thame OX9 ....148 A4
King's Sch The OX29 ....104 B2
King's Sutton Sta OX17 ...23 C3
Kingfisher Cl OX14 .....179 C3
Kingfisher Dr
  Banbury OX16 ....16 C2
  Witney OX28 ....118 A3
Kingfisher Gn OX4 .....142 C1
Kingfisher Sch OX14 ....179 C3
Kingfisher Way OX26 .....81 A4
Kingfishers OX12 ......214 C4
Kingham Dr OX18 ......115 B1
Kingham Hill Sch OX7 ....41 A1
Kingham Rd OX7 ....55 C3
Kingham Sta OX7 ....54 C1
Kings Ave Highworth SN6 190 A3
  Marcham OX13 ....178 B4
Kings Cl Ashbury SN6 ...228 A4
  Henley-on-T RG9 ......244 B1
  Lecombe Bassett OX12 .214 A1
  Worminghall HP18 .....127 B3
Kings Farm La RG9 .....253 C3
Kings La Harwell OX11 ..217 C4
  Kencot GL7 ....132 B2
Kings Meadow Ind Est
  OX2 ....140 C4
Kings Meadow Prim Sch
  OX26 ....65 A2
Kings Orch OX10 ......202 C2
Kings Rd Bloxham OX15 ..21 B2
  Reading RG4 ....259 B1
Kings Stile OX17 ....10 C1
Kings Way Dr OX5 ......109 A4
Kingsclere Rd OX26 ......65 B1
Kingsey Rd OX9 ....148 A4
Kingsholme Cl OX11 ....218 C3
Kingsley Rd ⑤ OX26 .....65 B2
Kingsmead GL7 ....150 B3
Kingston Cl OX14 ......179 C4
Kingston Ct OX2 ....123 A2
Kingston Hill OX39,HP14 188 A4
Kingston Hts OX29 .....105 A4
Kingston Rd OX2 ....123 A2
Kingston Bagpuize Ho*
  OX13 ....176 C4
Kingsway Banbury OX16 ..16 A3
  Reading RG4 ....259 C3
Kingsway Cotts OX18 ...135 B1
Kingswood La HP18 ......98 C3
Kinson Rd RG30 ....258 A1
Kipling Cl OX26 ....65 B2
Kirby Cl Middleton OX7 ..60 C4
  South Moreton OX11 ..219 C3
Kirby Pl OX4 ....142 B3
Kirby Rd GL54 ....68 A2
Kirk Cl Cuttleslowe OX2 109 A1
  Kennington OX1 ......160 C4
Kirkfell Cl RG31 ......257 B1
Kirkham Cl RG4 ....259 C3
Kirlington CE Prim Sch
  OX5 ....78 A2
Kirtlington Rd OX25 ....63 A4
Kit La RG9,OX10 ....241 B3
Knapp Cl OX14 ....179 B4
Knappe Cl RG9 ....254 B4
Knapton's Croft OX25 ...62 B3
Knighton Cl RG4 ......259 A4
Knighton Hill SN6 .....210 C1
Knights Cl OX26 ....124 C1
Knights Ct OX13 ......199 A2
Knights Way OX4 ......259 A3
Knightsbridge La OX49 186 A3
Knoll Cl OX12 ....231 C4
Knoll The RG31 ....257 A1
Knolles Rd OX4 ....142 B3
Knollys Cl OX14 ......160 A2
Knott Oaks OX29 ....89 C3
Knowlands SN6 ....190 A4
Knowle Cl RG4 ....258 B2
Knowle La OX25 ....79 A1
Knowsley Rd RG31 .....257 B2
Kybald St OX1 ....123 B1
Kyetts Cnr OX17 ....4 C1
Kynaston Rd OX11 .....218 C4
Kysbie Cl OX14 ....159 C2

L

Laburnum Ave OX13 ....159 B1
Laburnum Cl OX25 .....81 B2
Laburnum Cres OX5 ....108 C3
Laburnum Gr
  Banbury OX16 ....16 B1
  Didcot OX11 ....218 C4
Laburnum Rd OX2 .....140 B4
Lacemakers
  Chinnor OX39 ....168 B3
  Long Crendon HP18 ...129 B4
Lacey Dr OX9 ....148 A4
Lackmore Gdns RG8 ...250 C4
Ladburn La OX18 ......115 A3
Ladder Hill OX33 .....144 A4
Ladenham Rd OX4 .....142 C2

Ladman Villas SN7 .....173 C4
Lady Gr OX11,OX14 .....201 A2
Lady Jane St RG4 .....259 A2
Lady Wlk SN7 ....211 B4
Ladygrove Cl OX14 ....179 B3
Ladygrove Paddock
  OX14 ....179 B3
Ladywell Cl OX29 .....105 B3
Laggots Cl SN7 ....155 C1
Lake Rd
  East Hagbourne OX11 .218 C3
  Shrivenham SN6 ......209 B4
Lake St OX1 ....141 B3
Lake View NN13 ....38 A2
Lake Wlk OX17 ....23 A2
Lakefield Rd OX4 .....142 A1
Lakeside Cuttleslowe OX2 108 C1
  Witney OX28 ....118 A3
Lakeside Ind Est OX29 137 C4
Lakesmere Cl OX5 ......92 B1
Lamarsh Rd OX2 ......122 C1
Lamb La OX20 ....91 A1
Lamb's Cres OX16 ......16 C2
Lamb's La OX20 ....75 C2
Lambe Ave OX14 ......199 B2
Lambert Wlk OX9 .....129 C1
Lamborough Hill OX13 159 A3
Lambourn Rd OX4 .....142 B1
Lambourne Cres OX26 ..65 C1
Lambourne Rd RG4 ....252 C3
Lambourne Way OX17 ...23 A2
Lambridge La RG9 ....244 B2
Lambridge Wood Rd
  RG9 ....244 A2
Lambs Cl OX5 ....92 C1
Lambton Cl OX44 .....142 C3
Lambwath Stream
  OX11 ....200 C2
Lammas Cl OX14 ......159 C1
Lamorna Cres RG31 ...257 B1
Lampitts Gn OX15 ......15 A4
Lancaster Ave OX10 ..204 B2
Lancaster Cl OX26 ......66 A2
Lancaster Dr GL54 ......68 A2
Lancaster Pl OX18 ....115 C1
Lanchester Dr OX16 ....15 C4
Lancott La OX29 ......137 B2
Lancut Rd OX28 ......103 C1
Landells OX18 ....134 C2
Landseer Wlk OX14 ...179 C3
Lane Cl Horley OX15 .....8 A2
  Kidlington OX5 ......108 B4
Lane End OX10 ....222 A4
Lane The
  Bishopstone SN4 ....227 A2
  Chastleton GL56 ......40 B4
  Chilton OX11 ....235 C4
  Cuddesdon OX44 .....144 A1
  Deddington OX15 ......33 A2
  Fritwell OX27 ....49 C4
  Great Tew OX7 ....45 B4
  Lower Heyford OX25 ..62 B3
  Uffington SN7 ......211 B4
Lanes End OX26 ....66 C1
Lanes The OX18 ......134 C2
Langdale Ct OX28 .....118 A4
Langdale Gate OX28 ..118 A4
Langdale Rd OX9 .....148 A4
Langford Cl RG4 .....259 B3
Langford Gdns OX26 ..66 A1
Langford La
  Kidlington OX5 ....92 A1
  Wendlebury OX25 ......80 B3
Langford Village Prim Sch
  OX26 ....81 A4
Langhams Way RG10 ..255 C1
Langley Cl OX3 ......124 B1
Langley La OX18 ......152 B3
Langley Rd
  Abingdon OX14 ......159 C1
  Chalgrove OX44 .....184 B3
Langley's La OX7 .....137 B1
Langston Cl OX7 ....55 C3
Langston Priory Workshops
  OX7 ....54 C1
Langton Ave OX25 ......81 B2
Langtree Sch RG8 ....240 C1
Lanham Way OX4 .....142 A1
Lansdown Cl OX16 ......16 C1
Lansdowne Rd SN7 ...173 A2
Lansdowne Rd OX13 ..159 A3
Lapwing Cl OX26 ....81 A4
Lapwing La OX10 .....221 A1
Larch Cl ⑧ Bicester OX26 65 C2
  Kingston Bagpuize OX13 156 C1
  N Hinksey Village OX2 140 B4
Larch Ct RG4 ....259 A2
Larch End OX44 ......143 B1
Larches The
  Carterton OX18 ......115 B1
  Oxford OX3 ....125 A2
Lardon Cotts RG8 ....249 A3
Larissa Cl RG31 .....257 C1
Lark Hill OX12 ....214 C1
Larkdown OX12 ......214 C2
Larkfield OX11 ....221 A1
Larkfields OX3 ....124 C1
Larkhill Pl OX14 .....179 B4
Larkhill Rd OX14 .....179 C4
Larkins La OX3 ....124 B2
Larkmead Sch OX14 ..179 B4
Larkrise Fst Sch OX4 ..142 A3
Larksfield Cl OX18 ...133 B4
Larksfield Rd OX16 ....16 B1
Larkspur Sq OX26 ......65 C2
Larkswood Cl RG31 ...257 B2
Larsen Rd OX25 ....63 B4

Lashbrook Mead RG9 ..255 A2
Lashbrook Rd RG9 ....255 A2
Lashford La OX13 .....158 C4
Lashlake Rd OX9 .....129 C1
Latchford La OX44 ....164 C4
Lathbury Rd OX2 .....123 A3
Latimer Grange OX3 ..124 B1
Latimer Rd
  Carterton OX18 ......115 C1
  Oxford OX3 ....124 B1
Latton Cl Chilton OX11 235 C4
  Kingston Bagpuize OX13 156 B1
Laud's Cl RG9 ....244 B1
Laughton Hill OX29 ....89 B4
Launceston Ave RG4 .259 C3
Laundry Cotts GL56 ....40 B1
Laundry La OX18 .....135 B2
Launton Bsns Ctr OX26 ..66 A1
Launton CE Prim Sch
  OX26 ....66 B2
Launton CE Sch OX26 .66 B1
Launton Rd Bicester OX26 66 A1
  Stratton Audley OX27 ..66 B4
Laurel Cl Banbury OX16 ..16 B1
  Carterton OX18 ......115 B2
  Chalgrove OX44 .....184 B4
Laurel Cres OX12 ....214 C4
Laurel Ct OX4 ....142 A4
Laurel Dr OX13 ......156 C1
Laurel Farm Cl OX12 124 B2
Laurels The
  Fringford OX27 ....52 B3
  Great Coxwell SN7 ...192 B4
  Pangbourne RG8 .....256 B3
  Tetsworth OX9 ......166 A4
Laurence Allison Mews
  RG4 ....258 C1
Lavender Cl OX16 ......9 A1
Lavender Pl
  Bampton OX18 ....134 C2
  Carterton OX18 .....115 B1
Lavender Sq OX18 ....134 C2
Lawn Upton CE Mid Sch
  OX4 ....142 A1
Lawns The HP18 ....98 A1
Lawrence Cl OX12 ....213 B2
Lawrence Fields OX25 ..62 A4
Lawrence La OX29 .....88 B3
Lawrence Leys OX15 ...21 C3
Lawrence Rd OX4 .....142 B3
Lawrence Way OX26 ....65 B1
Lawson Dr RG4 ....258 C3
Lawson La OX11 .....235 C4
Lawson Rd RG9 ......254 C4
Lawton Ave OX18 ....115 B1
Lay Ave OX10 ....182 B3
Laytm Rise RG31 .....257 B2
Lea Gr OX11 ....200 C1
Lea Rd OX16 ....16 C2
Lea Rd RG4 ....252 C2
Leabrook Cl OX16 .....16 B1
Leach Rd
  Berinsfield OX10 ....182 B3
  Bicester OX26 ....65 B1
Leafield Cl OX29 ......86 C2
Leafield Rd
  Crawley OX29 ....103 C3
  Oxford OX4 ....142 B3
  Shipton-u-W OX7,OX29 84 C4
Leamington Dr SN7 ...172 C1
Leaver Rd RG9 ......244 B1
Lechlade Rd Buscot SN7 171 B4
  Faringdon SN7 ......172 B3
  Highworth SN6 ......190 A4
  Langford GL7 ......132 B1
Leckford Pl OX2 .....123 A2
Leckford Rd OX2 .....123 A2
Ledbury Cl RG30 .....258 B1
Ledgers Cl OX4 ....142 B1
Lee Ave OX14 ....160 A4
Lee Cl Charlbury OX7 ..73 B2
  Kidlington OX5 ....92 B1
Lee Ct OX9 ....147 C4
Lee Rd HP27 ....169 C3
Lees Hts OX7 ....73 B2
Lees The OX7 ....172 C2
Leicester Cl RG9 ....244 B2
Leiden Rd OX3 ......142 C4
Leigh Cl OX29 ....105 A3
Leigh Croft OX13 ....159 A4
Leigh Gr OX16 ....16 B3
Lely Ct OX14 ....179 C3
Lennox Gdns OX16 ....16 A2
Lenthal Rd OX5 ....93 A4
Lenthall Rd
  Abingdon OX14 .....179 C4
  Oxford OX4 ....141 C2
Lenton Rd OX16 ......16 B1
Leoline Jenkins Ho
  OX4 ....142 A4
Leon Cl OX4 ....141 C4
Leopold St OX4 .....142 A4
Lerwick Croft OX26 ...66 A2
Lester Cl OX17 ....23 A3
Lester Way OX10 ....221 A4
Letcombe Cl OX12 ....214 C2
Letcombe Ct OX12 ....214 C2
Letcombe Hill OX12 ..214 B2
Letcombe Rd OX12 ..214 B2
Letcombe Wlk OX12 ..196 B1
Letts Alley OX49 ......186 A4
Levenot Cl OX16 ....16 C3
Leverkus Ho OX39 ...168 B3
Levery Cl OX14 ......180 A4
Lewell Ave OX3 ......123 C2
Lewin Cl ⑪ OX4 ......142 C1
Lewington Cl OX44 ..164 B4
Lewis Cl OX3 ....125 A1

Lewis Rd OX7 ....42 B1
Lewknor CE Sch OX49 187 A4
Lewknor Cl OX49 .....187 A4
Ley The OX20 ....91 B3
Leybourne Gdns OX39 168 B4
Leyes The OX15 ....33 C2
Leyesland Ct OX16 .....16 B2
Leys App OX7 ....42 C1
Leys Cl OX15 ....15 A4
Leys Ho OX16 ....16 B3
Leys Pl OX4 ....142 A4
Leys Rd OX2 ....139 B3
Leys The Adderbury OX17 ..22 C2
  Chipping Norton OX7 ..42 B1
  Salford OX7 ....41 C3
Leys View GL7 ....132 C1
Leys Villas OX28 ....118 A4
Leyshon Rd OX13 ....144 B4
Library Ave OX11 ....217 A1
Liddell Rd OX4 ......142 B2
Lidderdale Rd GL54 ...68 A2
Liddiard Cl
  Kennington OX1 .....160 C4
  Wantage OX12 ......214 B3
Liddiard's Row OX11 172 C2
Lidon Rd OX44 ......184 B3
Lido Rd OX11 ....234 C4
Lidsey Rd OX16 ....16 A3
Lilac Cl RG8 ....257 B3
Lily Cl OX26 ....65 B3
Limborough Rd OX12 214 B3
Lime Ave Banbury OX16 ..16 C2
  Stoke Row RG9 ......242 A1
Lime Cres OX26 ......65 C3
Lime Gr Chinnor OX39 168 B3
  Kingston Bagpuize OX13 156 B1
Lime Kiln Rd OX5 ......77 B3
Lime Rd OX14 ....160 B4
Lime Tree Cl OX18 ..115 B2
Lime Tree Rd RG8 ...249 A3
Lime Wlk OX3 ....124 B1
Limes The
  Dorchester OX10 ...182 B1
  Stratton Audley OX27 ..52 B1
Limes Way HP18 ....128 B1
Limetree Cl OX12 ...196 B1
Limetrees OX11 .....217 C1
Linacre Cl OX11 .....219 A4
Linacre Coll OX1 ....123 B1
Linca La OX5 ....77 C1
Linch Hill L Pk* OX29 138 A3
Lincoln Cl Banbury OX16 ..16 A3
  Bicester OX26 ....66 A2
Standlake OX29 ....84 B1
Upper Rissington GL54 ..68 A2
Lincoln Cott OX1 .....123 B1
Lincoln Pl OX9 ....147 C4
Lincoln Rd OX1 ......141 B3
Lincombe La OX1 ....159 C4
Lincraft Cl OX5 ......108 C4
Linden Cl RG8 ....250 C1
Linden Cres OX12 ...124 B2
Linden Ct OX3 ......124 B2
Linden Gate OX11 ...217 C4
Linden Rd OX26 ......65 C1
Lindsay Dr OX14 ....160 A1
Link The Banbury OX16 ..16 A3
  Marston OX3 ....123 C2
  Oxford OX3 ....124 C2
Links Rd OX1 ....160 C4
Links The OX10 .....221 C4
Linkside Ave OX2 ...108 C1
Linkwood Rd OX4 ...103 B1
Linnet Cl
  Clifton Hampden OX14 182 A2
  Oxford OX4 ....142 B1
Linton Rd OX2 ......123 B3
Lion Mdw RG9 ......224 B3
Lipscombe Pl OX18 ...115 B2
Lister Cl RG8 ....257 B3
Litchfield Cl OX7 .....58 C3
Lithgow Rd GL54 ......68 A2
Little Acreage OX3 ..123 C3
Little Baldon Farm Cotts
  OX44 ....162 A1
Little Blenheim OX5 108 A3
Little Bowden La RG8 256 A2
Little Brewery St OX4 123 C1
Little Bridge Rd OX15 ...21 B2
Little Bury OX44 .....143 A1
Little Clarendon St OX1 123 B1
Little Croft Rd RG8 ...249 B3
Little Glebe RG4 .....260 C2
Little Green OX15 .....22 B2
Little Ground OX15 ...22 B2
Little Howe Cl OX14 160 C2
Little La Aynho OX17 ...35 B4
  Milton OX14 ....199 B3
Little Lees OX7 ....73 B2
Little Milton CE Prim Sch
  OX44 ....163 C3
Little Wittenham Nature
  Reserve* OX14 ......202 B3
Littlebrook Mdw OX7 ..70 B1
Littlegate St OX1 ....141 B4
Littlehay Rd OX4 ....142 A3
Littlejohns La RG30 258 B4
Littlemore Hospl OX4 142 A1
Littlemore Rd OX4 ..142 B2
Littlemore Rdbt OX4 142 A2
Littlestead Cl RG4 ...259 C3
Littlewood HP14 ....188 C3
Littleworth OX33 ....126 C4

Littlemore Bsns Ctr
  OX33 ....143 C4
Littleworth Hill OX12 ..214 B3
Littleworth Ind Est
  OX33 ....143 C4
Littleworth Rd
  Benson OX10 ......203 C2
  Wheatley OX33 .....144 A4
Lobelia Rd OX4 .....142 C1
Lock Cres OX5 ......108 C3
Lockhart Cres OX4 ..142 B2
Lockheed Cl OX16 ....16 A2
Lockinge Ct OX11 ...218 C4
Locks La OX12 ......214 B2
Lockstile Mead RG8 ..249 B3
Lockstile Way RG8 ..249 B3
Lockway OX14 ......199 A4
Lococme Hill GL7 ...131 A4
Loddon Ave OX10 ...182 B3
Loddon Cl
  Abingdon OX14 ....160 A1
  Bicester OX26 ....65 B1
Loddon Dr Didcot OX11 201 A4
  Wargrave RG10 .....255 A1
Loder Rd OX11 .....217 C4
Lodersfield GL7 .....150 B2
Lodge Cl Banbury OX16 ..16 B2
  Bicester OX26 ....65 B1
  Marston OX3 ....123 C4
Lodge Hill Intc OX14 160 A3
Lodge Rd OX29 ....90 C1
Lodge Terr OX7 ......42 C2
Logic La OX1 ....123 B1
Lombard St
  ⑥ Abingdon OX14 ...179 C4
  Eynsham OX29 .....120 C4
Lombard Way OX16 ..17 A3
Lomond Ave RG4 ....259 C3
London Ct OX3 .....124 B1
London La OX7 ....71 B1
London Pl OX4 ......123 C1
London Rd Bicester OX26 ..80 C4
  Blewbury OX11 .....236 C4
  Chipping Norton OX7 ..43 A2
  Oxford OX3 ....124 B2
  Sonning RG5,RG6 ...260 B1
  Tiddington OX9 .....145 C3
  Wheatley OX33 .....144 B4
London St SN7 ......173 C3
London Yd ⑧ OX16 ...16 B3
Long Alley OX14 .....179 C3
Long Barrow OX17 .....5 C4
Long Cl
  N Hinksey Village OX2 122 A1
  Oxford OX3 ....142 C4
Long Crendon Ind Est
  HP18 ....128 B2
Long Crendon Rd HP18 128 B2
Long Crendon Sch
  HP18 ....129 B4
Long Ford Cl OX1 ...141 B4
Long Furlong HP17 ..130 C3
Long Furlong Prim Sch
  OX14 ....160 A2
Long Furlong Rd OX13 159 B2
Long Ground OX4 ...142 C1
Long La Central OX4 142 B2
  Purley on T RG31 ...257 A2
  Reading RG31 ......257 A2
Long Lane Prim Sch
  RG8 ....257 A2
Long Toll RG8 ......251 A3
Long Tow OX13 .....159 B1
Long Wall HP17 .....130 C3
Long Wittenham Rd
  OX11 ....220 A4
Longcot & Fernham CE Prim
  Sch SN7 ....192 B1
Longcot Rd Longcot SN7 192 A1
  Shrivenham SN6 ....209 B2
Longelandes Cl OX16 ..16 A4
Longelandes Way OX16 16 A4
Longfellow Cl ⑧ OX26 ..65 B2
Longfellow Dr OX14 ..179 B3
Longfield Cl OX26 ....65 A2
Longfields Bicester OX26 ..65 C1
  Marcham OX13 .....178 B4
Longfields Ct OX26 ...65 C1
Longford Way OX11 200 C1
Longhurst Cl RG4 ....259 B2
Longlands Rd OX4 ...142 C2
Longleat Cl OX16 ......16 C1
Longleat Dr RG31 ....257 A2
Longmead GL7 ....150 B2
Longmore Ave GL54 ..68 A2
Longore OX29 ....89 B4
Longore Ct OX29 .....89 B4
Longwall OX4 ......142 A2
Longwall St OX1 ....123 B1
Longworth Cl OX16 ..16 C4
Longworth Prim Sch
  OX13 ....156 A2
Longworth Rd
  Charney Bassett OX12 176 A2
  Oxford OX2 ....123 A2
Lonsdale Rd OX2 ....123 A4
Lord Cl OX18 ....115 B1
Lord William's Lower Sch
  OX9 ....148 A4
Lord William's Upper Sch
  OX9 ....147 B4
Lords Piece Rd OX7 ...42 B1
Lostock Pl OX11 ....200 C1
Lovatt Cl OX18 .....115 B3
Love La OX49 ......186 A1
Lovegrove's La RG8 241 B2

Lovelace CI OX14 ....160 A2
Lovelace Dr OX5 ....109 A4
Lovelace Rd OX2 ....109 A1
Lovelace Sq 8 OX2 ....109 A1
Lovell CI
  Ducklington OX29 ....118 A2
  Henley-on-T RG9 ....254 B4
  Minster Lovell OX18 .....102 C1
Loverock Rd RG30 ....258 B1
Lowell PI OX28 ....118 A4
Lower Armour Rd RG31 ....257 B1
Lower Cherwell St OX16 ....16 B3
Lower Church St HP14 .....188 C3
Lower CI OX15 ....22 C4
Lower Comn SN7 ....211 B4
Lower Cres OX29 ....102 C2
Lower Elmstone Dr
  RG31 ....257 B1
Lower End
  Great Milton OX44 ....145 A2
  Piddington OX7 ....97 C4
  Salford OX7 ....41 C2
  Shutford OX15 ....14 A3
Lower Farm CI HP18 ....128 B2
Lower Farm La OX17 ....3 C2
Lower Hades Rd OX5 ....77 A3
Lower Henley Rd RG4 .....259 B2
Lower Heyford Rd OX25 ....63 A3
Lower High St OX10 ......100 C3
Lower Icknield Way
  OX39 ....168 B4
  Islip OX5 ....93 C1
Lower Rd
  Aston Rowant OX9 ....166 C2
  Blackthorn OX25 ....82 A2
  Chilton OX11 ....235 B4
  Chinnor OX39 ....168 B4
  Long Hanborough OX29 ....90 C1
Lower St
  Barford St M OX15 ....32 C3
  Islip OX5 ....93 C1
Lower Wharf OX10 ....221 B4
Lower Whitley Rd OX2 ....139 B4
Lowes CI Shiplake RG9 ...255 A2
  Stokenchurch HP14 ......188 B3
Lowfield Gn RG4 ....259 C2
Lowfield Rd RG4 ....259 B3
Loyd CI OX14 ....160 A2
Loyd Rd OX11 ....218 B3
Lucas PI OX14 ....141 C3
Lucca Dr OX14 ....179 B3
Lucerne Ave OX26 ....65 B2
Lucerne Dr OX44 ....163 B1
Lucerne Rd OX2 ....123 B4
Lucey CI RG31 ....257 A2
Lucky La OX16 ....16 B3
Ludford Gdns OX15 ....21 B2
Ludgershall Rd OX25 .....97 C4
Ludlow Dr Banbury OX16 ...15 C4
  Thame OX9 ....148 A4
Ludsden Gr OX9 ....148 A4
Luker Ave RG9 ....244 B2
Lumberd Rd OX14 ....160 A1
Lune CI OX11 ....201 A1
Lupton Rd Thame OX9 .....148 A4
  Wallingford OX10 ....221 A4
Luscombe CI RG4 ....259 B1
Luther Ct 15 OX1 ....141 B4
Lych Gate La OX44 ....145 A1
Lycroft CI RG8 ....249 B4
Lydalls CI OX11 ....200 C1
Lydalls Rd OX11 ....200 C1
Lydia CI OX3 ....124 C2
Lydsee Gate OX12 ....214 A3
Lye Valley OX3 ....142 B4
Lyefield Ct RG4 ....259 A3
Lyford CI OX14 ....179 A1
Lyford Way OX14 ....160 A1
Lymbrook CI OX29 ....119 B3
Lyme Gr RG31 ....257 B1
Lymington Gate RG4 ......258 C3
Lynch The OX12 ....216 B3
Lyndene Rd OX11 ....200 B2
Lyndhurst Rd
  Goring RG8 ....249 B3
  Reading RG1 ....258 A1
Lyndworth CI OX3 ....124 C2
Lyndworth Mews OX3 ......124 C2
Lyne Rd OX5 ....92 B1
Lyneham CI
  Carterton OX18 ....115 C2
  Witney OX28 ....103 C1
Lyneham Rd
  Bicester OX26 ....66 A2
  Milton-u-W OX7 ....70 A2
Lympes CI OX14 ....160 A1
Lynmouth Ct RG1 ....259 A1
Lynmouth Rd
  Didcot OX11 ....218 C4
  Reading RG1 ....259 A1
Lynn CI OX3 ....123 C2
Lynt Farm Cotts SN6 ....170 A3
Lynt Rd SN6 ....170 A3
Lynton La OX29 ....107 B1
Lyon CI OX14 ....160 A1
Lysander CI 8 OX26 .....66 A2
Lytham End RG31 ....257 A2
Lytton Rd OX4 ....142 A3

M

Mabel Prichard Sch
  OX4 ....142 A1
Maberley CI OX14 ......179 B3
Mably Gr OX12 ....214 B3
Mably Way OX12 ....214 B4
Macaulay CI 18 OX26 ...65 B2
Macdonald CI OX11 ....200 B1

MacKenzie Ave OX14 ....199 B2
Mackenzie CI 16 OX26 ..65 B2
Mackley CI OX15 ....33 C2
Macray Rd OX29 ....118 A2
Mafeking Row OX49 .....186 C2
Magdalen CI OX26 ......65 C2
Magdalen Coll OX1 .....123 C1
Magdalen Coll Sch OX4 .141 C4
Magdalen Ct OX11 .....219 A4
Magdalen PI OX18 .....115 B1
Magdalen Rd OX4 ......142 A4
Magdalen St OX1 ......123 B1
Magnette CI OX14 .....179 C4
Magnolia CI OX5 ......108 C4
Magnolias The
  Banbury OX16 ....9 A1
  Bicester OX26 ....65 C3
Magpie La OX1 ....123 B1
Maidcroft Rd OX4 .....142 B3
Maiden's CI SN6 ......191 B1
Maidley CI OX28 ......104 B1
Main Ave OX4 ....161 B4
Main Rd Appleford OX14 .200 C4
  Broughton OX15 ....15 B1
  Curbridge OX29 ......117 B3
  East Hagbourne OX11 ..218 C3
  Fyfield OX13 ....197 B1
  Long Hanborough OX29 ..90 B1
  Middleton Cheney OX17 .17 C4
Main St Adlestrop GL56 ..40 B2
  Bledington OX7 ....54 B1
  Chilton OX11 ....235 B4
  Clanfield OX18 ......152 C4
  Claydon OX17 ....1 B1
  Duns Tew OX25 ....47 B3
  East Hanney OX12 ....197 A3
  Finstock OX7 ....88 C4
  Fringford OX27 ......52 B3
  Grove OX12 ....196 C1
  Hanwell OX17 ....8 C2
  Hethe OX27 ....52 A4
  Letcombe Bassett OX12 .214 A1
  Mollington OX17 ....4 C2
  North Newington OX15 ..15 A2
  Over Norton OX7 ......42 C3
  Shalstone MK18 ......25 C3
  Sibford Gower OX15 ....19 A4
  Tadmarton OX15 ......20 B4
  Turweston NN13 ......24 B4
  West Hagbourne OX11 ..218 B2
  West Hanney OX12 ....196 C3
  Westbury NN13 ....25 A2
  Wroxton OX15 ....15 A4
Maisonettes The RG8 ...249 B4
Majors Rd SN6 ....191 C1
Makins Rd RG9 ....254 A4
Malet CI HP14 ....188 C3
Malford Rd OX3 ......124 C2
Mall The SN6 ....209 C4
Mallard CI OX4 ......142 B1
Mallard Way OX12 ....196 B1
Mallards Way OX26 ....66 A1
Mallins La SN7 ....192 B2
Mallinson Ct OX2 ....123 A1
Mallory Ave RG4 .....259 B3
Maltfield Rd OX3 ....124 A3
Malthouse SN6 ......228 A4
Malthouse La
  Bodicote OX15 ....22 B4
  Dorchester OX10 ....182 B1
  Long Compton CV36 ...27 C3
  Shutford OX15 ......14 A3
Malthouse Paddock
  SN7 ....174 C4
Malthouse Wlk 8 OX16 ..16 B3
Malthouses The SN6 ..228 A4
Maltings CI OX11 ....211 B2
Maltings The RG20 ...235 A1
Maltsters OX29 ......89 B4
Malvern CI Banbury OX16 .16 B1
  Didcot OX11 ....200 B1
Malyns CI OX39 ......168 B4
Manchester Coll OX1 .123 B1
Manchester Terr 18
  OX26 ....65 C1
Mandarin PI OX12 ....196 B1
Mandeville CI OX14 ..160 A1
Mandhill CI OX12 ....214 C4
Mandlebrote Dr OX4 ..142 A1
Manning CI OX15 .....21 C1
Mannings CI OX15 ....19 A4
Manor Ave RG4 ......259 A3
Manor Ct Appleford OX14 .200 C4
  Aston OX18 ....135 C1
  Cassington OX29 ....107 B1
  Chilton OX11 ....217 C1
  Drayton OX14 ....179 A1
  Enstone OX7 ....58 C3
  Great Bourton OX17 ..9 B4
  Shrivenham SN6 .....209 A4
  West Hagbourne OX11 .218 B2
Manor Cotts OX15 ....13 B3
Manor Court Yd OX33 .127 A1
Manor Cres Didcot OX11 .200 B1
  Standlake OX29 .....137 B2
  Stanford in the V SN7 .194 C4
Manor Ct Abingdon OX14 .179 C3
  Banbury OX16 ....16 C4
  Bladon OX20 ....91 B4
  Chadlington OX7 ....73 A2
  Chipping Norton OX7 ..42 C2

Manor Farm CI
  Fernham SN7 ....193 A2
  Kingham OX7 ....54 C3
  Merton OX25 ....95 B4
Manor Farm Cotts OX13 .177 B3
Manor Farm Ct OX20 ..75 C2
Manor Farm La RG8 ...256 B1
Manor Farm Rd
  Dorchester OX10 ....182 B1
  Horspath OX33 ......143 B3
Manor Field OX12 ....214 A1
Manor Gdns GL7 .....150 B2
Manor Gn Harwell OX11 .217 C2
  Stanford in the V SN7 .194 C4
Manor Gr OX1 ....160 C4
Manor La Clanfield OX18 .152 C4
  East Hendred OX12 ..216 A3
  Shrivenham SN6 ....209 A3
Manor Orch OX15 ....8 A2
Manor Pk OX17 ......1 B1
Manor PI OX1 ....123 C1
Manor Prep Sch OX13 .159 B1
Manor Prim Sch OX11 .200 B1
Manor Rd Adderbury OX17 .22 C2
  Bladon OX20 ....91 B4
  Brize Norton OX18 ..116 A2
  Carterton OX18 ....115 B3
  Ducklington OX29 ..118 A2
  Fringford OX27 ....52 B4
  Goring RG8 ....249 A3
  Great Bourton OX17 ..9 B4
  Henley-on-T RG9 ...254 B4
  Middle Barton OX7 ..46 B1
  Oxford OX1 ....123 C1
  South Hinksey OX1 ..141 A3
  Wantage OX12 .....232 B3
  Whitchurch RG8 ....256 B4
  Woodcote OX4 .....91 A4
Manor View OX18 ....134 C2
Manor Way OX5 .....92 C1
Manor Wood Gate RG9 .255 A2
Mansfield CI OX29 ....106 B3
Mansfield Coll OX1 ..123 B1
Mansfield Gdns OX11 .219 A4
Mansfield Rd OX1 ...123 B1
Mansion Hill OX17 ..17 C4
Mansmoor Rd OX5 ...94 C4
Manston CI OX26 ....66 A2
Manzel Rd OX27 ....66 A3
Manzil Way OX4 ....142 A4
Maple Ave OX5 ....108 C4
Maple CI Banbury OX16 .16 C1
  N Hinksey Village OX2 .140 B4
  Sonning Common RG4 .253 A2
Maple Cotts St Goring RG8 .249 A3
Maple Dr OX5 ....108 C4
Maple PI 5 Bicester OX26 .65 C1
  Faringdon SN7 .....172 C2
  Thame OX9 ....147 B4
Maple Well OX29 ...89 B4
Maplene Rd OX4 ...258 C2
Mapledurham Dr RG8 .257 B3
Mapledurham Ho*
  RG4 ....257 C3
Mapledurham View
  RG8 ....257 B1
Maples The
  Carterton OX18 ....115 B1
  Grove OX12 ....196 B1
Maplewall Ho OX29 ..89 B4
March Rd OX17 ......1 B1
Marcham CE Prim Sch
  OX13 ....178 B3
Marcham Rd
  Abingdon OX14,OX13 .179 A4
  Drayton OX14 ......179 A1
Marchwood Ave RG4 .259 B4
Mardy RG4 ....258 C3
Margaret Ct Banbury OX16 .16 A3
  Bicester OX26 .....65 B2
Margaret Rd
  Adderbury OX17 ....23 A3
  Oxford OX4 ....124 C1
Maria Cres OX12 ....214 C3
Marie CI OX27 ......67 C4
Marigold CI 10 OX14 .142 C1
Marigold Wlk OX26 ..65 C3
Maries Dr SN7 .....172 C1
Mariot Ct 11 OX26 ..65 B2
Marjoram Ct OX44 ..143 A1
Mark Rd OX3 ....124 C1
Market End Way OX26 .65 B2
Market PI
  18 Abingdon OX14 ..179 C4
  Banbury OX16 .....16 B3
  Deddington OX15 ..33 C2
  Faringdon SN7 ....172 C2
  Henley-on-T RG9 ..254 B4
  Highworth SN6 ....190 A3
  Lechlade GL7 .....150 B2
  18 Wallingford OX10 .221 B4
  Wantage OX12 ....214 B2
Market Sq
  Bampton OX18 ....134 C2
  Bicester OX26 ....65 C1
  Chipping Norton OX7 .42 C2
Market St Charlbury OX7 .73 A2
  Chipping Norton OX7 ..42 C2

Market St continued
  Oxford OX1 ....123 B1
  Woodstock OX20 ....91 A3
Marlborough Ave OX5 ..92 B1
Marlborough CE Sch
  OX28 ....91 B3
Marlborough CI
  Carterton OX18 ....115 C1
  Eynsham OX29 .....120 C1
  Faringdon SN7 ....172 C2
  Kidlington OX5 ....92 B1
  Kings Sutton OX17 .23 C3
  Oxford OX4 ....142 A1
Marlborough Cr OX20 ..91 A4
Marlborough Cres
  Eynsham OX29 ....106 A4
  Long Hanborough OX29 .90 C1
  Woodstock OX20 ...107 B1
Marlborough Gdns SN7 .172 C1
Marlborough La
  Stanford in the V SN7 .194 C4
  Witney OX28 ....118 A4
Marlborough PI
  10 Banbury OX16 ..16 B3
  Charlbury OX7 .....73 A2
  Eynsham OX29 ....120 C4
  Faringdon SN7 ....172 C1
Marlborough Rd
  Banbury OX16 .....16 B3
  Chipping Norton OX7 .42 C2
  Oxford OX1 ....141 B4
Marley CI OX29 .....120 C1
Marley Ind Est OX16 .16 B4
Marley La OX44 .....184 B4
Marley Way OX16 ..16 C1
Marling CI RG31 ....257 B1
Marlow CI OX10 ....221 A4
Marlow Rd RG9 ....244 C2
Marlow CI OX16 ...15 C3
Marmyon Ho RG9 ..244 C2
Marns Hey OX12 ...214 B3
Marriott CI
  Cuttleslowe OX2 ..109 A1
  Woodstock OX20 ..76 A2
Marriotts CI HP17 ..130 C3
Marriotts La HP17 ..130 C3
Marriotts Way HP17 .130 C3
Marsack St RG4 ...259 B1
Marsh Baldon CE Prim Sch
  OX44 ....162 A2
Marsh CI OX5 .....108 B3
Marsh End OX9 ...179 C4
Marsh End OX9 ..147 A1
Marsh Gibbon CE Sch
  OX27 ....67 C2
Marsh La Clanfield OX18 .152 C4
  East Challow OX12 .213 C4
  Fyfield OX13 ......197 A2
  Marston OX3 ......124 A3
Marsh Rd Oxford OX4 .142 B3
  Shabbington HP18 .128 B2
  Marsh Way SN7 ...211 A3
Marston Ferry Ct OX2,
  OX3 ....123 B3
Marston Ferry Rd OX2,
  OX3 ....123 C2
Marston Mid Sch OX3 .123 C3
Marston Rd
  Oxford OX3,OX4 ...123 C2
  Thame OX9 ....130 A1
Marten Gate OX16 ...16 B2
Marten PI RG31 ....257 A2
Martens CI SN6 .....209 A3
Martens Lake OX13 .156 B1
Martens Rd SN6 ....209 A3
Martin CI OX26 ....80 C4
Martin Ct OX2 .....123 A4
Martin's La OX10 ..182 B1
Martyn's Way OX10 .204 C1
Mary Towerton Sch The
  HP14 ....189 B2
Mary Whipple Ct OX12 .214 B2
Maryfield OX12 ....214 C2
Marygreen OX12 ...214 B4
Marylands Gn OX44 .162 B3
Marymead OX11 ...220 C1
Mascall Ave OX3 ..142 C4
Mascord CI OX16 ..16 A3
Mascord Rd OX16 ..16 A3
Masefield CI 11 OX26 .65 B2
Masefield Cres OX14 .179 B3
Masefield Rd OX16 ..16 A2
Masey CI OX3 .....124 B1
Masons' Rd OX3 ..124 B1
Mathematical Inst OX1 .123 B1
Mather Rd OX4 ...124 C3
Matlock Way OX13 .159 B3
Matlock Rd RG4 ..258 C2
Matson Dr RG9 ...244 C1
Matthew Arnold Sch
  OX2 ....140 B4
Mattock Way OX14 .160 A2
Mattock's CI OX14 .142 B1
Maud CI OX26 ....65 B2
Maud Ho OX17 ....214 C3
Maule CI OX15 ....21 C1
Maunds The OX15 ..33 C2
Mavor CI OX20 ....91 A4
Mawle Ct 11 OX16 .16 C1
Mawles La OX7 ...85 B4
Maxwell Ave OX11 .217 A3

May's CI OX27 .....49 C4
Maycroft 4 OX26 ..65 C2
Mayfair Rd OX4 ...142 A2
Mayfield Ave OX12 ..196 C1
Mayfield CI
  Carterton OX18 ..115 B1
  Chalgrove OX44 ..184 B3
Mayfield Dr RG4 ..259 B2
Mayfield Rd Banbury OX16 .16 B1
  Cumnor OX2 ......121 A1
  Cutteslowe OX2 ..123 A4
Mayott's Rd 6 OX14 .179 C4
Mc Mullan CI OX10 .221 B4
McCrae's Wlk RG10 .255 B1
McKay Trad Est OX26 .80 C4
McKee Sq OX10 ..204 B1
Mdws The OX29 ..186 A1
Mead La Longcot SN7 .192 B1
  Lower Basildon RG8 .249 C1
Mead Platt HP14 ..188 B3
Mead Rd
  Barford St M OX15 .32 C4
  Yarnton OX5 ......108 B2
Mead The OX17 ...3 C2
Mead Way OX5 ...92 C1
Meaden Hill OX3 ..124 A3
Meadow Bank SN7 .172 C2
Meadow CI Cumnor OX2 .121 A2
  Goring RG8 ....249 B3
  Grove OX12 ....196 C1
  Moulsford OX10 ...238 C2
  Shipton-u-W OX7 .70 B1
Meadow Dr OX18 ..100 C3
Meadow La
  Crowmarsh G OX10 ..222 A2
  Fulbrook OX18 ...100 C3
  Long Crendon HP18 .129 C2
  Oxford OX4 ......141 C4
  Shipton-u-W OX7 .70 B1
Meadow PI OX7 ..55 B3
Meadow Prospect OX2 .122 B4
Meadow Rd
  Chinnor OX39 .....168 B3
  Henley-on-T RG9 ..244 C1
  Reading RG1 .....258 C1
  Watchfield SN6 ...191 C1
Meadow View
  Adderbury OX17 ..23 A2
  Banbury OX16 ...16 C2
  Cutteslowe OX2 ..123 B4
  Kidlington OX5 ...92 C1
  Long Crendon OX29 .79 C2
  Wendlebury OX25 ..79 C2
  Witney OX28 .....118 B4
Meadow View Rd OX1 .160 C4
Meadow Way
  Didcot OX11 .....218 B4
  Faringdon SN7 ...172 C1
  Kingham OX7 .....54 C2
  8 Thame OX9 ....129 C1
  Yarnton OX5 ......108 B3
Meadowbank CI
  Ascott-u-W OX7 ..71 A1
  Long Crendon HP18 .129 B4
Meadowside
  Abingdon OX14 ...179 C3
  Reading RG31 ....257 A1
Meadowside CI 11
  OX14 ....179 C3
Meadowside Rd RG8 .256 B3
Meads CI OX14 ...179 C2
Meads The OX12 ..196 C4
Meadside OX10 ...202 C4
Meashill Way OX11 .234 C4
Medcroft Rd OX5 ..107 B1
Medhill CI RG8 ...250 C4
Medina CI OX11 ..201 A1
Medina Gdns OX26 .65 A1
Mediar Rd SN6 ...209 B4
Medlicott Dr OX14 .179 A1
Medlock Gr OX11 ..200 C2
Medway OX11 ....197 A3
Medway CI OX13 ..159 B2
Medway Rd OX13 .159 B2
Meer The OX10 ...204 A3
Melbourne CI OX16 .16 C2
Melford Gn RG4 ..259 C3
Melton Dr OX11 ..200 C1
Melville CI OX26 ..65 A1
Membury Way OX12 .214 B4
Memorial Ave RG9 ..254 C1
Mendip Hts OX11 ..200 B1
Menmarsh Rd HP18 .127 C2
Menpes Rd RG31 ..257 B2
Mercury CI OX18 ..134 C2
Mercury Rd OX4 ..143 A2
Mere Dyke Rd OX13 .198 C3
Mere Rd Cutteslowe OX2 .122 C4
  Finmere MK18 ...39 B3
Meredith CI OX26 ..65 B2
Mereland Rd OX11 .218 C4
Merewood Ave OX3 .125 A2
Merganser Dr OX26 ..81 A4
Meriden CI OX10 ..202 B3
Merivale CI Benson OX10 .204 A1
Merlin CI Abingdon OX14 .160 A1
  Oxford OX4 ......142 C1
Merlin Way OX26 ...81 A4
Merritt Rd OX11 ..200 B1
Merrivale's La OX15 .21 C2
Merrymouth Rd OX7 .69 A1

Mersey Way OX11 . . . . .201 A2
Merthyr Vale RG4 . . . . .259 A3
Merton CI Didcot OX11 . . . .219 A4
  Eynsham OX29 . . . . .120 B4
Merton Coll OX1 . . . . .123 B1
Merton Ct OX2 . . . . .123 A2
Merton Gr OX1 . . . . .123 B1
Merton Rd OX25 . . . . .81 B2
Merton St Banbury OX16 . . .16 C3
  Oxford OX1 . . . . .123 B1
Merton Way OX5 . . . . .108 A3
Merton Wlk ⁊ OX26 . . . . . .65 C2
Metcalf CI OX14 . . . . .179 C2
Metcalfe CI OX15 . . . . .15 B4
Meteor CI OX26 . . . . .66 A2
Mewburn Rd OX16 . . . . .16 A3
Mews The Baydon SN8 . . . .245 A3
  Highworth SN6 . . . . .190 A3
  Warborough OX10 . . . . .203 A3
  Watchfield SN6 . . . . .191 B1
Meyseys Rd OX3 . . . . .142 C4
Micklands Cty Prim Sch
  RG4 .259 B2
Micklands Rd RG4 . . . . .259 C2
Mickle Way OX33 . . . . .125 C2
Middi Haines Ct SN6 . . . . . .190 A3
Middle Aston La OX25 . . . . .48 A3
Middle Barton Cty Prim Sch
  OX7 . . . . .61 A4
Middle Furlong OX11 . . . . . .201 A1
Middle Hill OX15 . . . . .30 A4
Middle La Shotteswell OX17 .8 B4
  Wroxton OX15 . . . . .14 B4
Middle Orch OX7 . . . . .54 B1
Middle Rd Burford OX18 . . .99 A3
  Stanton St John OX33 . . . . .125 B4
Middle Row
  Chipping Norton OX7 . . . . . .42 C2
  Great Rollright OX7 . . . . .29 A3
Middle Springs RG8 . . . . . . .249 B4
Middle St OX5 . . . . .93 C1
Middle Way
  Chinnor OX39 . . . . .168 A3
  Cutteslowe OX2 . . . . .123 A4
  Islip OX5 . . . . .93 C1
Middleton Cheney Com Prim
  Sch OX17 . . . . .17 C4
Middleton CI OX16 . . . . .17 A4
Middleton Rd
  Banbury OX16, OX17 . . . . . . .16 C4
  Bucknell OX27 . . . . .64 C4
  Chacombe OX17 . . . . .10 C2
Middleton Stoney Rd
  OX26 .65 B1
Middleway Bottom
  OX12 . . . . .213 B1
Midget CI OX14 . . . . .179 B3
Midsummer Mdw RG4 . . . . .258 C3
Midway OX17 . . . . .11 A1
Midwinter Ave OX14 . . . . . . .199 B2
Miles Dr OX12 . . . . .214 C4
Milestone CI HP14 . . . . .188 C3
Milestone Rd OX18 . . . . .115 B1
Milestone View Ct RG4 . . .259 C2
Milestone Way RG4 . . . . . . .259 B3
Mileway Gdns OX3 . . . . .124 B1
Milford Rd Reading RG1 . . .258 C1
  Wootton OX20 . . . . .76 A2
Milham Ford Cty Girls Upper
  Sec Sch OX3 . . . . .124 A2
Milking La OX28,OX29 . . . .104 A2
Mill CI Bix RG9 . . . . .243 C4
  Chadlington OX7 . . . . .57 A1
  Charlton-on-O OX5 . . . . .95 A3
  Deddington OX15 . . . . .33 C2
Mill End OX5 . . . . .93 A1
Mill Gn Bampton OX18 . . . .134 C1
  Reading RG4 . . . . .259 B1
Mill Green CI OX18 . . . . . . .134 C1
Mill La Adderbury OX17 . . . .23 A2
  Alvescot OX18 . . . . .133 B3
  Ascott-u-W OX7 . . . . .71 B1
  Benson OX10 . . . . .203 C2
  Black Bourton OX18 . . . . . .133 C3
  Brackley NN13 . . . . .24 A3
  Chalgrove OX44 . . . . .184 B3
  Chinnor OX39 . . . . .168 A4
  Chipping Warden OX17 . . . . .5 C3
  Clanfield OX18 . . . . .152 C4
  Croughton NN13 . . . . .36 B4
  Drayton (Banbury) OX15 . . .15 B4
  East Hendred OX12 . . . . . . .216 B3
  East Hendred, West Hendred
  OX12 . . . . .216 A3
  Great Haseley OX44 . . . . . .164 B4
  Grove OX12 . . . . .214 C4
  Henley-on-T RG9 . . . . .254 C4
  Horton-cum-S OX33 . . . . . .112 A3
  Kidmore End RG4 . . . . .252 B1
  Kings Sutton OX17 . . . . .23 C2
  Kirtlington OX5 . . . . .77 C2
  Lechlade GL7 . . . . .150 C2
  Lower Heyford OX25 . . . . . . .62 B3
  Marston OX3 . . . . .123 C4
  Middle Barton OX7 . . . . .60 C4
  Milton OX14 . . . . .199 B3
  Oxford OX4 . . . . .141 C2
  Shiplake RG9 . . . . .255 A1
  South Moreton OX11 . . . . . .220 A3
  Stokenchurch HP14 . . . . . . .188 B3
  Sutton Courtenay OX14 . . .199 B3
  Upper Arncott OX25 . . . . . . .96 C4
  Upper Heyford OX25 . . . . . . .48 C1
  Wallingford OX10 . . . . .221 B4

Mill La continued
  Westbury NN13 . . . . .25 A2
  Weston-on-the-G OX25 . . . .79 A3
  Wootton OX20 . . . . .75 C2
Mill Lane Cty Prim Sch
  OX29 . . . . .168 A4
Mill Orch OX12 . . . . .197 A3
Mill Paddock
  ⑧ Abingdon OX14 . . . . .179 C3
  Letcombe Bassett OX12 . . .214 A1
Mill Rd Abingdon OX14 . . . .179 B3
  Cutteslowe OX2 . . . . .122 B4
  Goring RG8 . . . . .249 B4
  Marcham OX13 . . . . .178 B3
  Nettlebed RG9 . . . . .224 C2
  Reading RG4 . . . . .259 B1
  Shiplake RG9 . . . . .255 A2
  Stokenchurch HP14 . . . . . . .188 B3
  Stratton Audley OX27 . . . . . .52 C1
Mill St Eynsham OX29 . . . . .120 C4
  Islip OX5 . . . . .109 C4
  Kidlington OX5 . . . . .92 C1
  Oxford OX2 . . . . .123 A1
  Stanton St John OX33 . . . . .125 C4
  Steventon OX13 . . . . .198 C2
  Wantage OX12 . . . . .214 B3
  Witney OX28 . . . . .104 A1
Mill St Mews OX29 . . . . .120 C4
Mill The OX7 . . . . .42 B1
Mill View OX49 . . . . .185 B2
Millaway La SN7 . . . . .195 B3
Millbank OX2 . . . . .141 A4
Millbrook CI
  Blewbury OX11 . . . . .219 A1
  Wallingford OX10 . . . . .221 B4
Millbrook Cty Prim Sch
  OX14 . . . . .199 B3
Millbrook Sq OX12 . . . . .196 C1
Milldown Ave RG8 . . . . .249 B4
Milldown Rd RG8 . . . . .249 B4
Miller Ho OX16 . . . . .16 A3
Miller Rd Banbury OX16 . . . .16 A3
  Wheatley OX33 . . . . .144 B4
Miller's Acre ⒈ OX2 . . . . . .109 A1
Millers CI
  Chalgrove OX44 . . . . .184 B4
  Goring RG8 . . . . .249 A4
Millers Ct RG4 . . . . .259 B1
Millers La OX15 . . . . .7 B4
Millers Mews OX28 . . . . . . .104 A1
Millers Turn OX33 . . . . .168 A3
Millers Farm Cotts
  OX13 . . . . .177 B3
Millfield Ave OX27 . . . . .67 C2
Millfield CI OX27 . . . . .67 C2
Milham The OX12 . . . . .216 A3
Millmoor Cres OX29 . . . . . .120 C4
Mills La OX15 . . . . .15 A4
Millstream Ct OX2 . . . . .122 B4
Millview OX7 . . . . .42 C1
Millway Cl OX2 . . . . .122 C4
Millway La OX13 . . . . .157 C3
Millwood End OX29 . . . . .90 A1
Millwood Farm Barns
  OX29 .90 A1
Millwood Vale OX29 . . . . .90 A1
Millwright CI ⑶ OX16 . . . . .16 A3
Milne PI OX3 . . . . .124 A3
Milton Bsns & Tech Ctr
  OX13 . . . . .199 A1
Milton CE Prim Sch
  OX13 . . . . .199 B2
Milton CI ⑴ Bicester OX26 .65 B2
  Henley-on-T RG9 . . . . .244 B1
Milton Cres OX33 . . . . .125 C2
Milton Hill OX14 . . . . .199 A3
Milton La OX13 . . . . .199 A3
Milton Manor Dr OX44 . . . .163 C3
Milton Manor Ho*
  OX14 . . . . .199 B3
Milton Park Est OX14 . . . . .199 C2
Milton Rd Bloxham OX15 . . .22 C2
  Didcot OX11 . . . . .200 A2
  Milton (Banbury) OX15 . . . . .22 B1
  Oxford OX4 . . . . .142 A3
  Shipton-u-W OX7 . . . . .70 B1
  Sutton Courtenay OX14 . . .199 C3
Milton St OX16 . . . . .16 B3
Milvery Way OX4 . . . . .142 A2
Minchery Farm Cotts
  OX4 . . . . .142 B1
Minchery Rd OX4 . . . . .142 B2
Minchins Cl OX14 . . . . .180 B4
Minnow La OX18 . . . . .99 B3
Minns Rd OX12 . . . . .196 C1
Minster Ind Pk OX29 . . . . . .103 A1
Minster Lovell Hall*
  OX29 . . . . .103 A2
Minster Rd
  Brize Norton OX18 . . . . .116 A3
  Oxford OX4 . . . . .142 A4
Minster Riding OX29 . . . . . .103 A2
Mint The ⑶ OX10 . . . . .221 B4
Minton CI RG30 . . . . .257 C1
Minty CI OX18 . . . . .115 B1
Mirfield Rd OX18 . . . . .117 C4
Mistletoe Gn OX4 . . . . .142 C1
Mitchell CI Thame OX9 . . . .147 C4
  Wootton (Oxford) OX13 . . . .159 A4
Mixbury NN13 . . . . .38 B4
Moat Cl OX18 . . . . .116 A2
Moat La OX27 . . . . .67 C1
Moat The OX7 . . . . .54 C3
Moat's Cres OX9 . . . . .148 A4
Mobbs La OX15 . . . . .30 A4
Moberly Cl OX4 . . . . .141 C4

Moir Ct OX12 . . . . .214 B3
Mold Cres OX16 . . . . .16 A3
Mole PI ⒗ OX4 . . . . .142 C1
Mollington La OX17 . . . . .3 A2
Mollington Rd OX17 . . . . .9 B4
Molyneux Dr OX15 . . . . .22 C4
Molyns Ho RG9 . . . . .244 C2
Monarchs Ct OX10 . . . . .9 A1
Monard Terr ⒑ OX4 . . . . . .141 C4
Monet La OX12 . . . . .196 A1
Monkey Ct ⒌ RG4 . . . . .259 B1
Monks CI
  Dorchester OX10 . . . . .182 C1
  Oxford OX4 . . . . .142 B1
  West Hanney OX12 . . . . .196 C3
Monks Lode OX11 . . . . .200 C2
Monks Mead OX10 . . . . .202 C1
Monks Wlk GL7 . . . . .150 C2
Monmouth Ct ⒗ RG1 . . . . .259 A1
Monmouth Rd OX1 . . . . .141 B3
Mons Way OX14 . . . . .159 B1
Montabaur Rd NN13 . . . . . . .24 A4
Montagu Rd OX2 . . . . .140 B4
Montague St RG4 . . . . .259 B1
Montgomery Rd OX27 . . . . . .66 A4
Montpelier Dr RG4 . . . . .259 B3
Montrose Way OX9 . . . . . . .148 A4
Monument Ind Pk OX44 . . .184 C2
Monument Rd OX44 . . . . . . .184 C3
Monument St OX16 . . . . .16 B3
Moody Rd OX3 . . . . .123 C2
Moor Ave OX28 . . . . .103 A1
Moor La OX15 . . . . .31 C4
Moor Pond CI OX26 . . . . .65 C1
Moorbank OX4 . . . . .142 C2
Moorbrook OX11 . . . . .200 B2
Moorend La Thame OX9 . . .129 C1
  Thame OX9 . . . . .130 A1
Moorfield CI OX16 . . . . .16 C3
Moorgate GL7 . . . . .150 A2
Moorhen Wlk OX44 . . . . . . .142 C1
Moorland CI OX28 . . . . .103 C1
Moorland Rd OX28 . . . . .117 C4
Moorlands The
  Benson OX10 . . . . .204 A2
  Kidlington OX5 . . . . .92 C1
Moors CI OX29 . . . . .89 C3
Moors Drive The OX17 . . . . .17 C4
Moors The Kidlington OX5 . .92 B1
  Pangbourne RG8 . . . . .256 B3
Moreton Ave OX10 . . . . .221 A4
Moreton La
  Northmoor OX8 . . . . .156 C4
  Thame OX9 . . . . .147 C4
Moreton Rd
  Aston Tirrold OX11 . . . . .219 C1
  Cutteslowe OX2 . . . . .123 A3
Morecambe Ave RG4 . . . . . .258 C3
Moreton Ave OX10 . . . . .221 A4
Morland Rd OX14 . . . . .142 A4
Morlais RG4 . . . . .259 A3
Morland CI OX33 . . . . .144 A4
Morland Rd OX13 . . . . .178 B3
Morlands OX12 . . . . .197 A4
Morrell Ave OX4 . . . . .142 A4
Morrell CI OX25 . . . . .108 B4
Morrell Cres OX4 . . . . .142 A2
Morrells CI OX11 . . . . .200 B1
Morris Cres OX4 . . . . .142 A2
Morris Dr OX16 . . . . .15 C4
Morris Ho OX4 . . . . .142 A2
Morse Rd OX11 . . . . .218 B3
Mortimer Dr OX3 . . . . .123 C2
Mortimer Rd OX4 . . . . .141 C2
Morton Ave OX5 . . . . .108 C4
Morton CI Abingdon OX14 .180 B4
  Kidlington OX5 . . . . .108 C4
Morton King CI HP18 . . . . . .128 B2
Mosquito La OX10 . . . . .204 B1
Moss CI RG4 . . . . .259 A3
Motte The OX14 . . . . .179 C4
Moulsford Prep Sch
  OX10 . . . . .239 A3
Mount Owen Rd OX18 . . . . .35 A2
Mount PI OX2 . . . . .123 A1
Mount Pleasant
  Bishopstone SN6 . . . . .227 B2
  Lechlade GL7 . . . . .150 B2
  Wardington OX17 . . . . .5 B4
Mount Pleasant Cotts
  OX12 . . . . .216 B3
Mount St OX2 . . . . .123 A1
Mount The Reading RG4 . . .258 C2
  Streatley RG8 . . . . .248 C4
Mount View OX29 . . . . .244 B1
Mount View Ct RG9 . . . . . . .244 B1
Mountfield RG8 . . . . .249 B4
Mountfield Rd OX28 . . . . . . .117 C4
Mousey La ⒕ OX10 . . . . . . .221 B4
Mowbray Dr RG30 . . . . .258 A1
Mowbray Rd OX11 . . . . .218 C3
Moworth CI RG4 . . . . .240 C1
Mulberries The OX12 . . . . . .197 A3
Mulberry Bush Sch The
  OX29 . . . . .137 B1
Mulberry Ct OX23 . . . . .123 A4
Mulberry Dr
  Bicester OX26 . . . . .65 C3
  Wheatley OX33 . . . . .144 A4
Mulcaster Ave OX5 . . . . .108 B4
Mullard Way OX14 . . . . .179 C4
Mullein Rd OX26 . . . . .65 C3
Mullens Terr RG4 . . . . .258 B4
Mumbery Hill RG10 . . . . . . .255 C1
Murcott Rd OX5 . . . . .93 B3
Murdock CI OX15 . . . . .33 C2
Murdock Rd OX26 . . . . .66 A1
Murray Ct OX2 . . . . .123 B2

Murren The OX10 . . . . .221 B3
Mus Of Modern Art*
  OX1 . . . . .123 B1
Mus Of Oxford* OX1 . . . . . .123 B1
Museum Rd OX1 . . . . .123 B1
Musgrave Rd OX9 . . . . .168 B4
Musson CI ⒑ OX14 . . . . . . .179 C3
Mustard La RG4 . . . . .260 C1
Myrtle CI
  Long Hanborough OX29 . . . .90 A1
  Reading RG31 . . . . .257 B2

N

Naldertown OX12 . . . . .214 B3
Napier Ct OX14 . . . . .180 A4
Napier Rd OX4 . . . . .142 B3
Nappins CI HP18 . . . . .129 B3
Narrowby Ct OX16 . . . . .16 B1
Naseby Ct OX16 . . . . .16 B1
Nash Dr OX14 . . . . .179 C3
Nash La OX29 . . . . .106 A4
National Herb Ctr The*
  OX17 . . . . .4 A2
Navigation Way OX2 . . . . . . .123 A3
Neal's La RG9 . . . . .242 A1
Needlemakers HP18 . . . . . . .129 B4
Neithrop Ave OX16 . . . . .16 A4
Neithrop CI OX16 . . . . .16 A4
Neithrop Inf Sch OX16 . . . . .16 A3
Neithrop Jun Sch OX16 . . . .16 A3
Nell Hill SN6 . . . . .227 B2
Nelson CI OX10 . . . . .221 B4
Nelson Rd RG4 . . . . .259 B1
Nelson St Oxford OX2 . . . . .123 A1
  Thame OX9 . . . . .147 C4
Nene Gr OX13 . . . . .201 A1
Nene Rd OX13 . . . . .159 B1
Nether CI NN13 . . . . .24 A4
Nether Dunford CI OX3 . . . .142 C4
Netheravon CI OX18 . . . . . .115 B1
Nethercote La OX49 . . . . . . .167 A1
Nethercote Rd OX5 . . . . .77 B3
Netherton La OX13 . . . . .157 B2
Netherton CI OX11 . . . . .217 A1
Netherwoods Rd OX3 . . . . .124 C1
Netherworton Rd OX15 . . . . .32 C3
Netley CI RG4 . . . . .259 C3
Netting St OX15 . . . . .30 A4
Nettlebed Com Prim Sch
  RG9 .224 B2
Nettlebed Mead OX4 . . . . . .142 C1
Neunkirchen Way OX26 . . . . .65 B4
Neville Way OX7 . . . . .194 C4
Nevis Rd RG31 . . . . .257 B2
New Bldgs SN7 . . . . .211 B4
New Close La OX28 . . . . . . .117 C3
New Coll OX1 . . . . .123 B1
New Coll Sch OX1 . . . . .123 B1
New College La OX1 . . . . . .123 B1
New College Sq OX25 . . . . .48 C1
New Cross Rd OX3 . . . . .124 C2
New High St OX3 . . . . .124 B2
New Hill RG8 . . . . .257 B3
New Hinksey CE Fst Sch
  OX1 .141 B3
New Inn Hall St OX1 . . . . . .123 B1
New Inn Rd OX3 . . . . .111 A1
New Marston Fst Sch
  OX3 .124 A3
New PI OX17 . . . . .17 C2
New Pond La OX29 . . . . .95 A3
New Rd Adderbury OX17 . . .22 C2
  Bampton OX18 . . . . .134 C2
  Banbury OX16 . . . . .16 B3
  Bledington OX7 . . . . .54 B2
  Bletchingdon OX5 . . . . .93 A4
  Charney Bassett OX12 . . . .175 C1
  Childrey OX12 . . . . .213 B3
  East Hagbourne OX11 . . . . .218 A3
  Great Tew OX7 . . . . .45 B4
  Hailey OX29 . . . . .104 A3
  Kingham OX7 . . . . .54 C2
  Long Hanborough OX29 . . . .90 A1
  Marcham OX13 . . . . .178 B3
  Milcombe OX15 . . . . .21 A1
  Oxford OX1 . . . . .123 B1
  Radley OX14 . . . . .160 C1
  Ratley OX15 . . . . .2 A3
  Shiplake RG9 . . . . .255 A1
  Shotteswell OX17 . . . . .8 B4
  Shrivenham SN6 . . . . .209 C2
  Stokenchurch HP14 . . . . . . .188 C3
  Wallingford OX10 . . . . .221 B4
  Warborough OX10 . . . . .203 A3
  Watlington OX49 . . . . .186 A1
  Woodstock OX20 . . . . .91 A3
  Wootton OX20 . . . . .75 B4
New Row Ambrosden OX25 .81 B2
  Bucknell OX27 . . . . .64 C4
New St Abingdon OX14 . . . .179 C4
  Chipping Norton OX7 . . . . . .42 C2
  Deddington OX15 . . . . .33 C2
  Henley-on-T RG9 . . . . .244 B1
New Town Cotts SN6 . . . . .227 B2
New Town La SN6 . . . . .227 B2
New Yatt La OX29 . . . . .104 C4
New Yatt Rd OX28,OX29 . .104 B4
Newalls Rise RG10 . . . . .255 C1

Newcombe CI OX15 . . . . .21 A1
Newells CI OX44 . . . . .163 B1
Newfield Rd RG4 . . . . .252 C3
Newgate Rd OX5 . . . . .95 C3
Newington Rd OX44 . . . . . . .163 B1
Newland OX28 . . . . .104 B1
Newland CI OX29 . . . . .120 C4
Newland Mill OX28 . . . . .104 B1
Newland PI OX16 . . . . .16 B3
Newland Rd OX16 . . . . .16 B3
Newland St OX29 . . . . .120 C4
Newlands Ave
  Didcot OX11 . . . . .218 C4
  Reading RG4 . . . . .259 A2
Newlands Dr OX12 . . . . .196 B1
Newlands La RG9 . . . . .242 A2
Newlin CI OX4 . . . . .141 C2
Newman Ct Oxford OX4 . . .123 C1
  Witney OX29 . . . . .103 B1
Newman La OX14 . . . . .179 A1
Newman Rd OX4 . . . . .142 A2
Newmans CI OX11 . . . . .218 B2
Newmill La OX29 . . . . .103 C1
Newnham Gn OX12 . . . . . . .221 C4
Newnhamhill Bottom
  RG9 .242 A3
Newport CI OX5 . . . . .108 B4
Newport Rd RG1 . . . . .259 A1
Newport Terr ⒑ OX26 . . . . . .65 C1
Newtec PI OX4 . . . . .141 C4
Newton Ave RG4 . . . . .259 B3
Newton Rd OX1 . . . . .141 B4
Newton Way OX10 . . . . .204 A3
Newton Rd OX1 . . . . .240 B4
Newtown Gdns RG9 . . . . . .254 C4
Newtown Rd RG9 . . . . .254 C4
Nicholas Ave OX3 . . . . .123 C2
Nicholas Rd RG9 . . . . .254 A4
Nicholson Rd OX3 . . . . .123 C2
Nigel Ct NN13 . . . . .24 A4
Nightingale Ave OX4 . . . . . .142 C1
Nightingale La SN6 . . . . . . .208 A3
Nightingale PI OX26 . . . . .81 A4
Nine Acres CI OX7 . . . . .73 A2
Nine Acres La OX7 . . . . .73 A2
Nineteenth St OX11 . . . . . . .217 A1
Ninety Cut Hill OX18 . . . . . .102 A2
Ninth Ave OX3 . . . . .142 C4
Ninth St OX11 . . . . .217 A1
Nire Rd RG4 . . . . .259 C1
Nixon Rd OX4 . . . . .141 C3
Nizewell Head OX25 . . . . . . .62 A4
Noble Rd RG9 . . . . .254 C4
Nobles CI Grove OX12 . . . .196 B1
  N Hinksey Village OX2 . . . .140 A4
Nobles La OX2 . . . . .140 A4
Nor Brook CI OX14 . . . . .160 B3
Norcot CI RG30 . . . . .258 A1
Norcotts Kiln Cotts HP18 . .98 A1
Norfolk CI OX14 . . . . .160 C1
Norfolk St OX1 . . . . .141 B4
Norham End OX2 . . . . .123 B2
Norham Gdns OX2 . . . . .123 B2
Norham Rd OX2 . . . . .123 B2
Norman Ave
  Abingdon OX14 . . . . .160 A3
  Henley-on-T RG9 . . . . .244 C1
Norman PI RG1 . . . . .259 A3
Norman Rd RG4 . . . . .259 B2
Norman Smith Rd ⒛
  OX4 . . . . .142 C2
Norman Way OX10 . . . . .221 B4
Normandy Cres OX4 . . . . . .142 C2
Norreys Ave OX1 . . . . .141 B3
Norreys CI OX11 . . . . .218 B4
Norreys Rd Cumnor OX2 . .139 C2
  Didcot OX11 . . . . .218 B4
Norries Dr OX10 . . . . .203 B1
Norris CI Abingdon OX14 . .160 B3
  Adderbury OX17 . . . . .22 C1
Norris Rd OX25 . . . . .96 C4
North Aston Rd OX25 . . . . . .47 B3
North Ave OX14 . . . . .160 A3
North Bar PI OX16 . . . . .16 B3
North Bar St OX16 . . . . .16 B3
North Bush Furlong
  OX11 . . . . .218 C3
North CI OX9 . . . . .145 C4
North Croft OX11 . . . . .218 C3
North Dr Grove OX12 . . . . . .196 C2
  Harwell OX11 . . . . .217 B2
North Gn OX12 . . . . .196 C4
North Hill HP18 . . . . .98 A3
North Hinksey CE Prim Sch
  OX2 .140 C4
North Hinksey La OX2 . . . . .140 C4
North Hinksey Village
  OX2 .140 C4
North Kidlington Prim Sch
  OX5 . . . . .92 C2
North La OX25 . . . . .79 A3
North Leigh Bsns Pk
  OX29 . . . . .105 B4
North Leigh CE Sch
  OX29 . . . . .105 A1
North Leigh Roman Villa*
  OX29 .89 B2
North Lodge OX42 . . . . .53 A2
North Manor Estate The
  OX44 . . . . .143 C3
North Mill Rd HP27 . . . . . . .149 C2
North Oxfordshire Coll
  OX16 .16 A3
North Parade Ave OX2 . . . .123 B2
North PI OX3 . . . . .124 B2
North Quay OX14 . . . . .179 C2
North Rd Didcot OX11 . . . . .200 B3

North Rd continued
Moulsford OX10 ....238 C2
North Side OX25 ....48 A1
North St Aston OX18 ....135 C2
Banbury OX16 ....16 C4
Bicester OX26 ....65 C2
Fritwell OX27 ....49 C4
Islip OX5 ....93 C1
Marcham OX13 ....178 B3
Middle Barton OX7 ....60 C4
Oxford OX2 ....123 A1
Reading RG4 ....259 A1
Thame OX9 ....129 C1
Watchfield SN6 ....191 B1
North Way
Cutteslowe OX2 ....109 A1
Oxford OX3 ....124 C2
Steventon OX13 ....198 C2
Northampton Rd 141 B3
Northbourne CE Prim Sch
OX11 ....218 C4
Northbourne Rd OX11 ...218 C4
Northbrook Ho OX4 ....142 C1
Northbrook Rd RG4 ....259 B3
Northcot La OX14 ....16 A4
Northcourt La OX14 ....160 A1
Northcourt Rd OX14 ....159 C1
Northcourt Wlk OX14 .....180 A4
Northern By-pass Rd
Cutteslowe OX2 ....108 C1
Oxford OX3 ....124 B3
Northern Ho Sch OX2 ....123 A4
Northfield Ave RG9 ....255 A2
Northfield Cl OX4 ....142 B1
Northfield Ct RG9 ....244 B2
Northfield End RG9 ......244 B2
Northfield Rd
Abingdon OX14 ....160 A2
Oxford OX3 ....124 C2
Reading RG1 ....259 A1
Shiplake RG9 ....259 A1
Northfield Sch OX4 ....142 B1
Northford Cl SN6 ....209 B4
Northford Hill SN6 ....209 B4
Northford Ind Est SN6 ....209 B4
Northmead La OX12 ....196 A4
Northmoor Pk OX29 ....138 B1
Northmoor Rd OX2 ....123 B3
Northolt Rd OX18 ....115 C2
Northumberland Ct 4
OX16 ....16 C3
Northview Cty Prim Sch
SN6 ....190 A4
Northwood Cir OX25 .....115 C2
Northwood Rd OX29 ......103 B1
Norton Cl OX3 ....124 B1
Norton Pk OX7 ....42 C2
Norton Terr OX29 ....102 C2
Norton Way OX18 ....115 C2
Norwood Ave OX13 ....156 C1
Nosworthy Way OX10 ....221 C3
Nottwood La RG9 ....242 A3
Nourse Cl OX3 ....110 A3
Nowell Rd OX4 ....141 C2
Nuffield Cl Bicester OX26 ...65 C3
Didcot OX11 ....219 A4
Nuffield Coll Oxford OX1 ..123 A1
Oxford OX1 ....123 B1
Nuffield Dr OX16 ....16 A4
Nuffield Hill RG9 ....223 B2
Nuffield Ind Est OX4 .....142 B1
Nuffield La OX10 ....222 C3
Nuffield Orthopaedic Ctr
OX3 ....124 B1
Nuffield Rd OX4 ....124 C1
Nuffield Way OX14 ....179 B4
Nun's Acre RG8 ....249 B3
Nuneham Courtenay
Arboretum OX44 ....161 C1
Nuneham Sq OX14 ....179 C4
Nunhide La RG8 ....256 C1
Nunnery Cl OX4 ....142 B1
Nunney Brook OX11 .....200 C2
Nurseries Rd OX5 ....108 B4
Nursery Cl Oxford OX3 ...124 B1
Shiplake RG9 ....255 A2
Nursery Dr OX16 ....16 B4
Nursery Gdns RG8 ....25 C3
Nursery La OX16 ....16 B4
Nursery Rd OX29 ....105 B4
Nursery The OX14 ....200 A4
Nursery View SN7 ....173 A2
Nut Hatch Cotts RG8 ....142 A2
Nuthatch Cl 1 OX4 ....142 C1
Nyatt Rd OX14 ....180 B4
Nye Bevan Cl OX4 ....142 A4

O

O'Connors Rd OX29 ....102 C1
Oak Ave OX14 ....160 C3
Oak Cl OX26 ....65 C2
Oak Dr OX5 ....92 C1
Oak End Way OX39 ....168 B3
Oak Farm Cl OX9 ....166 A4
Oak La Ambrosden OX25 ...81 B2
Stanford in the V SN7 .....194 C3
Oak Rd OX16 ....16 B4
Oak St GL7 ....150 B2
Oak Tree Copse RG31 ...257 C2
Oak Tree Rd RG31 ....257 B1
Oak Tree Wlk RG8 ....257 B3
Oakdale Ct 5 OX10 ......221 B4
Oakdene RG8 ....250 C2
Oakdown Cl OX10 ....206 C3
Oakes La OX2 ....121 B1
Oakey Cl OX4 ....133 B3

Oakfield Ind Est OX29 ...120 B3
Oakfield Pl OX28 ....118 A4
Oakfield Rd OX18 ....115 B1
Oakham Cl RG31 ....257 B1
Oakham Rd GL56 ....27 A1
Oakland Cl OX29 ....105 C4
Oakland Rd OX16 ....16 B1
Oaklands OX2 ....121 A2
Oakley Ho OX13 ....158 B1
Oakley La OX39 ....168 A3
Oakley Rd Chinnor OX39 ..168 B3
Horton-cum-S OX33 ....112 B3
Reading RG4 ....258 C2
Oaks Rd RG9 ....255 A2
Oaksmere OX13 ....158 A3
Oakthorpe Pl OX2 ....123 A3
Oakthorpe Rd OX2 ....123 A3
Oasis Pk OX29 ....120 B3
Oathurst Est OX18 ....134 C2
Oatland Rd OX11 ....218 C4
Oatlands Rd OX2 ....122 C1
Observatory Cl OX10 .....204 A2
Observatory St OX2 ....123 A2
Ock Dr OX10 ....182 B3
Ock Mews OX14 ....179 C4
Ock Mill Cl OX14 ....179 B3
Ock St OX14 ....179 C3
Ockley Brook OX11 ....201 A1
Octavian Way NN13 ....24 A4
Oddley La HP27 ....169 B4
Odiham Ave RG4 ....259 C3
Odiham Cl OX18 ....115 C2
Offas Cl OX10 ....204 A3
Ogbourne Cl OX12 ....214 A3
Old Arncott Rd OX25 ....81 B2
Old Bakery The 2 OX1 ...123 A1
Old Barn Cl Benson OX10 ...204 A2
Reading RG4 ....259 A3
Old Barn Gnd OX3 ....142 C4
Old Bath Rd RG4 ....260 B1
Old Bix Rd RG9 ....243 C4
Old Blackalls Dr OX10 ...221 A2
Old Bldgs 18 OX10 ....221 B4
Old Bourne OX11 ....200 C2
Old Bridge Rd OX15 ....21 C2
Old Burford Rd OX7 ....54 B1
Old Chapel Cl OX5 ....92 C1
Old Coachyard The
OX28 ....104 A1
Old Copse Gdns RG4 ....252 C3
Old Council Hos The
Horley OX15 ....8 A2
South Newington OX15 .....31 C4
Old Croft Cl OX39 ....167 C2
Old Dashwood Hill
HP14 ....189 C1
Old Farm Cl
Abingdon OX14 ....180 B4
Worminghall HP18 ....127 B3
Old Farm Cres RG31 .....257 B1
Old Field OX44 ....164 A4
Old Forge Cl OX7 ....54 B1
Old Forge Rd OX7 ....29 A2
Old Foundry The OX4 ....179 C3
Old George Yd OX18 .....100 C3
Old Glebe OX15 ....20 B4
Old Greyfriars St OX1 ...141 B4
Old Grimsbury Rd OX16 ..16 C4
Old High St OX3 ....124 B2
Old Kiln RG9 ....224 C1
Old Kiln The RG9 ....224 C1
Old London Rd
Benson OX10 ....204 A2
Tiddington OX9 ....145 C2
Wheatley OX33 ....144 A4
Chipping Norton OX7 ....56 B4
Old Luxters Farm Brewery
HP14 ....226 C4
Old Maltings The 2 OX9 ..129 C1
Old Manor Cl OX12 ....214 A1
Old Marston Rd OX3 ......123 C2
Old Mill Cl OX12 ....196 C1
Old Mill The RG8 ....256 B3
Old Moor OX14 ....199 B3
Old Moor Cl OX10 ....221 B4
Old Nursery View OX1 ...141 B2
Old Orch OX39 ....149 C1
Old Parr Cl OX16 ....16 A3
Old Parr Rd OX16 ....16 B3
Old Place Yd OX26 ....65 C1
Old Plough Wlk OX15 .....33 A4
Old Pound The OX13 .....159 A3
Old Rd
East Hendred OX12 ....216 C3
Great Tew OX7 ....43 A4
Oxford OX3 ....124 C1
Ratley OX15 ....2 A2
Wheatley OX33 ....144 A4
Old Reading Rd OX10 ....221 C3
Old Rectory Ct OX25 ....48 C1
Old Rectory Ct OX26 ....80 A2
Old Sawmills Rd SN7 ....172 C1
Old School Cl
Bicester OX27 ....65 C4
Stokenchurch HP14 ....188 C2
Old School End OX15 ......10 C3
Old School Ho The OX7 ....70 A1
Old School La OX12 ......211 C3
Old School Pl OX16 ....16 C3
Old School The OX4 ....142 B3
Old Stables The OX3 .....124 A3
Old Stables Yd OX14 .....214 A1
Old Station Yd OX14 .....179 C4
Old Town NN13 ....24 A4
Old Wallingford Way
OX14 ....200 A4
Old Warehouse Flats The
OX28 ....104 B1

Old Well Ct RG4 ....260 B2
Old Wharf Rd SN7 ....210 B4
Old Windmill Way HP18 ..129 B4
Old Witney Rd OX29 ......120 B4
Oldean Cl RG31 ....257 B1
Oliver Rd OX4 ....142 C3
One End La OX10 ....203 C2
Onley Ct 20 OX1 ....141 B4
Onslow Dr OX9 ....130 A1
Onslow Gdns RG4 ....259 B2
Oracle Parkway RG6 .....260 A1
Orange Cl SN6 ....190 A3
Oratory Prep Sch The
RG8 ....250 B3
Oratory Sch The RG8 ....251 A4
Orchard Ave RG4 ....252 C3
Orchard Cl
Abingdon OX14 ....160 A1
Banbury OX16 ....16 A3
Cassington OX29 ....107 B1
Chalgrove OX44 ....184 B4
Charney Bassett OX12 .....175 C1
Combe OX29 ....90 A2
Didcot OX11 ....200 C1
East Hanney OX12 ....197 A3
East Hendred OX12 ....216 B4
Eynsham OX29 ....120 C4
Henley-on-T RG9 ....244 C1
Lechlade GL7 ....150 B2
Purley on T RG31 ....257 B2
Salford OX7 ....41 C2
Shiplake RG9 ....254 C1
Thame OX9 ....148 A4
Upton OX11 ....218 B1
Wallingford OX10 ....221 B3
Warborough OX10 ....203 A4
Wheatley OX33 ....144 A4
Orchard Combe RG8 .....250 B2
Orchard Cotts OX7 ....57 A1
Orchard Ct OX14 ....142 C4
Orchard Field RG4 ....252 B3
Orchard Field La OX20 ....91 B2
Orchard Furlong OX12 ..213 B2
Orchard Gdns OX12 ......213 B3
Orchard Gr OX Bloxham OX15 ..21 B2
Reading RG4 ....259 C2
Orchard Ground OX7 ......49 B4
Orchard Haven OX10 .....202 B4
Orchard Hill SN7 ....172 C1
Orchard La Cropredy OX17 ..4 C1
East Hendred OX12 ....216 B3
Upper Heyford OX25 ....62 C4
Wootton (Oxford) OX1 .....140 B1
Orchard Meadow Fst Sch
OX4 ....142 C1
Orchard Piece OX17 ....4 A2
Orchard Pl
Upper Heyford OX25 ....62 C4
Westbury NN13 ....25 A2
Orchard Rd Ardley OX27 ....50 A2
Buckland SN7 ....174 C4
Hook Norton OX15 ....30 A4
N Hinksey Village OX2 .....140 A4
Orchard Rise
Burford OX18 ....100 C2
East Challow OX12 ....79 C4
Orchard Row OX18 ....100 C3
Orchard The
Appleton OX13 ....158 A4
East Challow OX12 ....214 A3
Merton OX25 ....95 B4
Oxford OX4 ....4 C1
Orchard View OX17 ....4 C1
Orchard Way
Banbury OX16 ....16 A3
Bicester OX26 ....65 B2
Chinnor OX39 ....168 B3
Kidlington OX5 ....108 C4
Kingham OX7 ....54 C2
Marcham OX13 ....178 B3
Middle Barton OX7 ....46 C1
Oxford OX4 ....142 B2
Wantage OX12 ....214 C2
Witney OX28 ....118 A4
Orchard Wlk OX49 ....186 B1
Orchid Cl OX26 ....65 C1
Orchid Ct OX14 ....180 B4
Orchids The OX11 ....235 B4
Ordnance Rd OX11 ....200 B1
Oregon Ave RG31 ....257 B2
Oriel Coll OX1 ....123 B1
Oriel Ct OX11 ....219 A4
Oriel Sq OX1 ....123 B1
Oriel St OX1 ....123 B1
Oriel Way OX26 ....65 C2
Orkney Cl OX16 ....16 A2
Ormerod Sch OX3 ....117 C4
Ormond Rd Thame OX9 ..130 A1
Wantage OX12 ....214 B4
Orpine Cl OX26 ....65 B3
Orpwood Way OX14 ......179 B3
Orwell Cl RG4 ....258 C2
Orwell Dr OX11 ....201 A2
Osberton Rd OX2 ....123 A4
Osborne Cl Bicester OX26 ..65 B2
Cutteslowe OX2 ....122 C4
Kidlington OX5 ....108 B4
Osiers The OX10 ....183 A3
Osler Rd OX3 ....124 B2
Osney Cl OX15 ....30 A4
Osney La OX1 ....123 A1
Osney Mead OX2 ....141 A4
Osney Mead Ind Est
OX2 ....123 A1
Osney Mews OX1 ....123 A1
Osprey Cl OX4 ....142 C1
Osterley Dr RG4 ....259 C3

Osterley Gr OX16 ....16 A2
Oswestry Rd OX1 ....141 B3
Otmoor La Beckley OX3 ...111 A2
Charlton-on-O OX5 ....95 A2
Otters Reach OX1 ....141 C1
Ottery Way OX11 ....201 A1
Otwell Cl OX14 ....160 A1
Our Lady's Convent Senior
Sch OX14 ....180 A4
Our Lady's RC Fst Sch
OX4 ....142 B3
Ouse Cl OX11 ....200 C2
Ouseley Cl OX13 ....123 C2
Outmoor View OX25 ......105 B4
Outram Rd OX4 ....142 A3
Oval The Bicester OX26 ....65 B2
Didcot OX11 ....200 B1
Oxford OX4 ....142 A2
Over Norton Rd OX7 ....42 C2
Overbrooke Gdns OX4 ...143 A1
Overdale Cl OX4 ....124 C2
Overdown Rd RG31 ....257 B1
Overlanders End RG31 ..257 C2
Overmead OX14 ....179 C2
Overmead Gn OX4 ....142 C1
Overstrand Cl OX26 ....66 A2
Overthorpe Prep Sch
OX17 ....17 B4
Overthorpe Rd OX16 ....16 C3
Overton Dr OX9 ....130 A1
Owlington Cl OX2 ....122 B1
Ox Cl OX14 ....180 A4
Oxen Piece OX44 ....145 B1
Oxeye Ct OX4 ....161 C4
Oxford Brookes Univ
OX3 ....124 A1
Oxford Brookes Univ Sch of
Occupational Therapy
OX3 ....124 B1
Oxford Bsns Ctr The
OX1 ....141 A4
Oxford Bsns Pk OX4 .....109 A1
Oxford Bsns Pk N OX4 ...142 B3
Oxford Bsns Pk S OX4 ...142 B2
Oxford Cl OX5 ....77 C2
Oxford Coll of F Ed OX1 ...141 A4
Oxford Cres OX11 ....218 B4
Oxford High Sch For Girls
OX2 ....123 B3
Oxford Hill OX28,OX29 ..118 B4
Oxford La OX12 ....196 C1
Oxford Rd
Abingdon OX13, OX14 .....160 A3
Adderbury OX17 ....23 A2
Banbury OX15,OX16 ....16 B2
Benson OX10 ....204 B4
Bicester OX25, OX26 ....80 B4
Bletchingdon OX5 ....93 A4
Burford OX18 ....100 C2
Clifton Hampden OX14 ....181 C3
Cumnor OX2 ....109 A2
Cutteslowe OX2 ....109 A2
Deddington OX15 ....33 C1
Dorchester OX10 ....182 B1
Enstone OX7 ....58 C2
Eynsham OX29 ....120 C4
Garsington OX4,OX44 .....143 B1
Hampton Poyle OX5 ....93 A2
Kennington OX1 ....160 A3
Kidlington OX5 ....108 C4
Kirtlington OX5 ....77 A4
Marston OX3 ....123 C2
Middleton Stoney OX25 ....64 A2
North Leigh OX29 ....105 B3
Sonning Common RG4 ....253 A3
Yarnton OX5 ....108 A2
Park Cres OX14 ....179 C3
Park Ct Banbury OX16 ......16 A3
Thame OX9 ....148 A4
Park End Bodicote OX15 ..16 C1
Croughton NN13 ....36 B4
Park End Cl OX15 ....16 C1
Park End Pl OX1 ....123 A1
Park End St OX1 ....123 A1
Park End Works NN13 ....36 B4
Park Hill
Hook Norton OX15 ....30 A4
Wheatley OX33 ....126 A1
Park Hospl For Children
OX3 ....124 B1
Park La Appleton OX13 ....158 A4
Ardington OX12 ....215 B2
Aston Rowant OX39 ....167 C2
Bladon OX20 ....91 B2
Checkendon RG8,RG4 .....251 C3
Croughton NN13 ....36 C4
Long Hanborough OX29 ....90 B1
North Newington OX15 .....15 C2
Stanford in the V SN7 .....195 A3
Stokenchurch HP14 ....188 C3
Stonor RG9 ....225 B3
Swalcliffe OX15 ....19 C4
Woodstock OX20 ....91 A3
Park Rd Abingdon OX14 ...179 C4
Banbury OX16 ....16 A3
Chipping Norton OX7 ....42 C2
Combe OX29 ....90 A3
Didcot OX11 ....218 B4
Faringdon SN7 ....172 C2
Henley-on-T RG9 ....244 C1
Hook Norton OX15 ....30 A4
North Leigh OX29 ....105 A3
Witney OX28 ....103 C1
Park Rise OX25 ....48 C1
Park Side Marcham OX13 ..178 B3
Yarnton OX5 ....108 A1
Park St Bladon OX20 ....91 A1
Charlbury OX7 ....73 A2
Thame OX9 ....148 A4
Woodstock OX20 ....91 A3
Park Terr
Cowley OX4 ....142 C4
Thame OX9 ....148 A4
Park The Cumnor OX2 .....139 C2
Harwell OX11 ....217 C3
Park Town OX2 ....123 B2

Paddock Rd continued
Reading RG4 ....259 B3
Wallingford OX10 ....221 B4
Paddock The
Chilton OX11 ....235 B4
Highworth SN6 ....190 A3
Kennington OX1 ....160 C4
Longworth OX13 ....156 B1
Somerton OX25 ....48 C3
Paddocks The
Bampton OX18 ....134 C1
Deddington OX15 ....33 C2
East Hanney OX12 ....197 A3
Mollington OX17 ....3 C2
Souldern OX6 ....35 C2
Yarnton OX5 ....108 A2
Paddox Cl OX2 ....123 A4
Paddox The OX2 ....123 A4
Page Furlong OX10 ....182 B1
Pages La OX15 ....7 B3
Pages Orch RG4 ....252 C3
Paget Rd OX4 ....142 C3
Pagisters Rd OX14 ....160 B1
Paines Hill OX25 ....62 A4
Painswick Cl OX28 ....103 C1
Painters Cl OX15 ....21 B2
Palmer Ave OX25 ....96 C4
Palmer Pl OX4 ....179 C3
Palmer Pl OX4 ....124 C1
Palmers OX12 ....214 C3
Pampas Cl OX18 ....115 C1
Panbourne Inf Sch RG8 ...256 B3
Pangbourne Coll RG8 ....256 A2
Pangbourne Prim Sch
RG8 ....256 C3
Pangbourne Sta RG30 ...258 A1
Panters Rd OX10 ....221 A1
Paper Mill Cotts OX18 ...99 B3
Paper Mill La OX11 ....220 A3
Papist Way OX10 ....238 C4
Parade The
Kidlington OX5 ....108 C3
Oxford OX3 ....124 B2
Paradise La OX15 ....21 A1
Paradise Mews RG9 ......244 B1
Paradise Rd RG9 ....244 B1
Paradise Sq OX1 ....123 A1
Paradise St OX1 ....123 A1
Paradise Terr OX7 ....42 B1
Park Ave Highworth SN6 ..190 A3
Kidlington OX5 ....92 B1
Shrivenham SN6 ....209 B4
Park Cl Aven Dassett CV47 ...2 C4
Banbury OX16 ....16 B3
Bladon OX20 ....91 A2
Cutteslowe OX2 ....109 A1
Didcot OX11 ....218 B4
Hanwell OX17 ....30 A3
Hook Norton OX15 ....30 A3
Kirtlington OX5 ....77 C2
Middleton Stoney OX25 ....64 A2
North Leigh OX29 ....105 B3

Park View
Crowmarsh G OX10 ...222 A3
Wantage OX12 ...214 C3
Park Wall La RG8 ...249 B1
Park Way OX3 ...123 C4
Park Wlk RG8 ...257 B3
Parker St OX4 ...141 C3
Parkers Cl SN7 ...173 A2
Parkers Hill OX9 ...166 A4
Parkhill Dr RG31 ...257 B1
Parklands Banbury OX16 ...16 A4
Freeland OX29 ...105 C4
Parks Rd OX1 ...123 B1
Parkside
Checkendon RG8 ...241 B2
Cuddesdon OX44 ...144 B2
Henley-on-T RG9 ...244 B1
North Leigh OX29 ...105 B3
Witney OX28 ...118 A3
Parkway Dr RG4 ...260 C2
Parliament Rd OX9 ...129 C1
Parrs Rd HP14 ...188 C2
Parry Cl OX3 ...123 C2
Parslow Ho OX49 ...186 B1
Parson's La OX10 ...204 C2
Parson's St OX ...16 B3
Parsonage Ct OX12 ...215 A3
Parsons Mead OX14 ...159 C1
Parsons Pl OX4 ...142 A4
Parsons St OX17 ...23 A2
Partridge Chase RG26 ...81 A4
Partridge Cl OX12 ...214 C2
Partridge Pl OX5 ...92 B1
Partridge Wlk OX4 ...143 A1
Pascali Pl RG16 ...9 A1
Passey Cres OX10 ...204 A2
Patemore La RG9,OX49 ...206 C3
Paternoster La OX10 ...220 C1
Patrick Haugh Rd OX25 ...96 C4
Patrick Rd RG4 ...259 A1
Patricks Orch SN7 ...211 B4
Pattison Pl OX4 ...142 A2
Paul Kent Hall OX3 ...142 C4
Pauling Rd OX3 ...124 C1
Pauls Way OX49 ...186 A1
Paxmans Pl OX16 ...16 B2
Paynes End OX27 ...65 C3
Peachcroft Ctr OX14 ...160 A1
Peachcroft Rd OX14 ...160 A1
Peacock Rd OX3 ...123 C2
Peaks La OX29 ...89 B4
Pear Tree Cl OX7 ...70 A1
Pear Tree Cotts RG9 ...243 B1
Pearce Ct OX9 ...147 C4
Pearce Dr OX7 ...42 C1
Pearce Way OX9 ...148 A4
Pearces Mdw RG9 ...224 B2
Pearces Orch RG9 ...244 B2
Pearson Rd RG4 ...260 B2
Peartree Cl OX4 ...142 C1
Peartree Intc OX2 ...108 C1
Peascroft HP18 ...129 B3
Peat Moors OX3 ...142 B4
Pebble Ct OX18 ...101 B3
Pebble La NN13 ...24 A4
Pebble Dr OX11 ...219 A4
Peel Cl Ducklington OX29 ...118 A2
Reading RG4 ...259 B1
Peel Pl Carterton OX18 ...115 C1
Oxford OX1 ...141 B3
Pee-p-o-day La OX14 ...179 C2
Peers Upper Sch OX4 ...142 B1
Pegasus Ct RG4 ...141 B4
Pegasus Fst Sch OX4 ...142 C1
Pegasus Rd OX4 ...142 C1
Pegswell La OX44 ...145 A1
Pelham Rd OX9 ...130 A1
Pelican Pl OX9 ...147 C4
Pembroke Coll OX1 ...141 B4
Pembroke Ct 4 OX4 ...141 C4
Pembroke Ho 8 RG4 ...259 B1
Pembroke La OX14 ...199 B3
Pembroke Pl
Bampton OX18 ...134 C2
Reading RG4 ...259 B2
Pembroke Sq 4 OX1 ...141 B4
Pembroke St OX1 ...123 B1
Pembroke Way OX26 ...65 C2
Pemscott Cl OX18 ...133 B3
Pen Way OX16 ...9 B1
Pendennis Ave RG4 ...259 C3
Pendon Mus* OX14 ...201 B4
Penfield OX7 ...42 C3
Penley Cl OX9 ...168 A3
Penn Cl Abingdon OX14 ...160 B1
Reading RG4 ...259 A3
Penn The OX7 ...42 C3
Pennington Pl OX9 ...130 A1
Pennycress Rd OX4 ...143 A1
Pennyfarthing Pl OX1 ...123 B1
Pennygreen La OX10 ...202 C1
Pennyhooks La SN6 ...209 A4
Pennypiece RG8 ...249 B4
Pennyroyal RG8 ...250 C1
Pennyweil Dr OX2 ...109 A1
Penpont Water OX11 ...201 A1
Penrhyn Cl OX16 ...15 C4
Penrose Cl OX16 ...16 A3
Penrose Dr OX16 ...16 A3
Pensclose OX28 ...104 B1
Pensfield OX10 ...203 C2
Penson's Gdns OX44 ...123 C1
Penstones Ct SN7 ...194 C4
Pentagon The OX14 ...180 A4

Peppard CE Prim Sch
RG9 ...253 A4
Peppard Hill RG9 ...252 C4
Peppard La RG9 ...254 C4
Peppard Rd RG4 ...253 A2
Pepper Alley
6 Banbury OX16 ...16 B3
Deddington OX15 ...34 C2
Peppercorn Ave OX3 ...142 C4
Percy St OX4 ...141 C3
Peregrine Rd OX4 ...142 B1
Peregrine Way
Bicester OX26 ...81 A4
Grove OX12 ...196 B1
Perian Cl RG4 ...254 B4
Perimeter Rd OX11 ...217 B1
Periwinkle Pl OX4 ...143 A1
Perkins OX1 ...141 B1
Perpetual Park Dr RG9 ...254 C4
Perrin St OX3 ...124 B1
Perrinsfield GL7 ...150 B3
Perrott Cl OX29 ...105 A4
Perry's Rd SN7 ...194 B4
Perserverance Hill RG9 ...254 A3
Peter's Way OX4 ...142 B2
Peterley Rd OX4 ...142 C3
Pether Rd OX3 ...124 C1
Pethers Piece OX18 ...100 B3
Petre Pl OX5 ...92 C1
Pettiwell OX44 ...162 B4
Pevensey Ave RG4 ...259 C3
Pheasant Wlk OX4 ...142 A1
Phelps Pl OX4 ...123 C1
Phelps The OX5 ...108 B4
Philcote St OX15 ...33 C2
Phillimore Rd RG4 ...259 B4
Phipps Rd OX4 ...142 B2
Phoebe Ct OX4 ...123 A3
Phyllis Court Dr RG4 ...244 C2
Pickett Ave OX3 ...142 C4
Picklers Hill OX14 ...160 A1
Picton Way RG4 ...259 A2
Piddington Rd HP18 ...98 A4
Pieces The OX18 ...134 C2
Pierces Hill RG31 ...257 B1
Pigeon Farm Rd RG9 ...224 A4
Pigeon House La OX29 ...106 B3
Pigeonhouse La OX5 ...95 C2
Piggott's Rd 4 RG4 ...259 B1
Piggy La OX26 ...65 C1
Pike Terr 6 OX1 ...141 B4
Pikeshaw Way RG31 ...257 B1
Pilcher Ct OX4 ...123 C1
Pilgrims Cl SN6 ...191 C1
Pill La GL56 ...26 C1
Pimpernel Cl OX4 ...143 A1
Pine Cl Bicester OX26 ...65 C3
Garsington OX44 ...143 B1
Oxford OX4 ...142 C2
Pine Woods Rd OX13 ...156 A1
Pinecroft OX18 ...115 B1
Pines The SN7 ...172 C2
Pinetree Ct RG4 ...259 A3
Pinewood Dr RG4 ...258 C3
Pinewood Sch SN6 ...209 A1
Pingle Dr OX26 ...80 C4
Pinhill Rd OX16 ...16 A4
Pinkhill La OX29 ...120 C3
Pinnocks Way OX2 ...140 A4
Pinsley Rd OX29 ...106 B4
Pioneer Rd Bicester OX26 ...81 A3
Faringdon SN7 ...172 C1
Piper St OX3 ...124 B1
Pipers Croft OX16 ...16 A2
Pipit Cl OX4 ...142 C1
Pipits Croft OX26 ...81 A4
Pipkin Way OX4 ...142 A3
Pitch The HP14 ...189 B2
Pitreavie Ave OX18 ...115 C2
Pitters Piece HP18 ...129 A4
Pitts Rd OX3 ...124 C2
Pixey Pl OX2 ...122 C4
Pixton Cl OX11 ...218 B4
Plain Rd The OX15 ...14 A3
Plain The OX4 ...141 C4
Plane Tree Way OX20 ...91 B3
Plantation Rd
Chilton OX11 ...234 C4
Oxford OX2 ...123 A2
Plantation The OX17 ...4 C1
Plater Coll OX3 ...124 A1
Platt Dr OX26 ...123 A2
Playfield Rd OX1 ...160 C4
Playford Ct OX4 ...147 C4
Playhatch Rd RG4 ...260 A3
Playing Field Rd NN13 ...25 A2
Pleck La OX39 ...167 C2
Plot Rd OX15 ...14 A3
Plough Cl
Cutteslowe OX2 ...122 C4
Warborough OX10 ...203 A3
Plough Cnr OX39 ...148 C1
Plough La RG9 ...254 C1
Ploughley Cl Ardley OX27 ...50 B2
Kidlington OX5 ...108 B4
Ploughley Rd
Ambrosden OX25 ...81 B2
Upper Arncott OX25 ...96 C4
Plowden Pk OX49 ...167 C2
Plowden Way RG9 ...254 C1
Plum La OX7 ...85 B4
Plumbe Ct OX12 ...214 B3
Pluto Rd OX11 ...234 C4
Plym Dr OX11 ...201 A1
Pochard Pl 10 OX4 ...142 C1
Pococks Cl OX18 ...134 C2

Poffley End Hos OX29 ...104 A3
Poffley End La OX29 ...104 A3
Polecat End La OX33 ...125 C2
Pollocks La OX10 ...221 C1
Polstead Rd OX2 ...123 A2
Polsted Rd RG31 ...257 B1
Pond Cl
Farnborough (Berks)
OX12 ...233 C1
Didcot OX11 ...125 A2
Pond End Rd RG4 ...253 A3
Pond Hill OX9 ...89 B4
Pond La RG4 ...257 C4
Ponds La OX3 ...123 C3
Pool Cl RG4 ...254 B4
Pool Cl GL56 ...26 C1
Pool Close Cotts GL56 ...26 C1
Pooles La OX7 ...73 A2
Poolside Cl OX16 ...16 A3
Popes Acre HP17 ...130 C3
Popes Piece OX28 ...103 C1
Poplar Cl Banbury OX16 ...16 C1
Garsington OX44 ...143 B1
Kidlington OX5 ...108 C4
Poplar Farm Cl OX7 ...70 A1
Poplar Farm Rd OX44 ...184 B4
Poplar Gr OX1 ...160 C4
Poplar Rd OX2 ...122 B1
Poplars The OX26 ...66 B1
Poppylands OX26 ...65 B2
Port Hill Rd OX3 ...224 A1
Port Hill Rd OX10 ...203 C3
Port Way
Crowmarsh G OX10 ...221 C2
Kirtlington OX5 ...78 A4
Wantage OX12 ...215 A3
Portal Dr OX25 ...63 B4
Portal Dr N OX25 ...63 B4
Portal Dr S OX25 ...63 B4
Portland Pl OX7 ...42 C2
Portland Rd
Cutteslowe OX2 ...123 A4
Milcombe OX15 ...21 A1
Portman Ctr The RG30 ...258 B1
Portman Rd RG30 ...258 B1
Portway Aynho OX17 ...35 B4
Banbury OX16 ...16 A4
Croughton NN13 ...36 C4
Didcot OX11 ...218 B4
Faringdon SN7 ...172 C2
Wantage OX12 ...214 B2
Portway Cres NN13 ...36 C4
Portway Dr NN13 ...36 B4
Portway Gdns OX17 ...35 B4
Portway Mews OX12 ...214 B2
Post Office La
Letcombe Bassett OX12 ...214 A1
6 Wantage OX12 ...214 B2
Potenger Way OX14 ...179 B3
Potkiln La RG8 ...250 C4
Pott's Cl OX44 ...145 A2
Potters La OX10 ...205 A1
Pottery Fields RG9 ...224 C1
Pottery Piece OX4 ...142 C1
Pottery Rd RG30 ...257 C1
Pottle Cl OX12 ...214 A2
Poultney Pl OX18 ...115 B2
Poulton Pl OX4 ...142 C2
Pound Cl
Ducklington OX29 ...118 A2
Pound Cl OX5 ...77 C2
Yarnton OX5 ...108 A3
Pound Cotts RG8 ...249 A3
Pound Croft OX12 ...214 B4
Pound Ct OX15 ...33 C2
Pound Field Cl OX3 ...124 C3
Pound Hill OX7 ...73 A2
Pound La
Cassington OX29 ...107 B1
Cholsey OX10 ...220 C1
Clanfield OX18 ...133 C1
Sibford Gower OX15 ...13 A1
Sonning RG4 ...260 C1
Stanton St John OX33 ...125 B4
Upton OX11 ...218 B1
Pound Piece SN6 ...228 A4
Pound The Bloxham OX15 ...21 C3
Cholsey OX10 ...220 C1
North Newington OX15 ...15 A2
Wantage OX12 ...215 A3
Pound Way OX4 ...142 B2
Powell Cl OX33 ...125 C2
Powys Gr OX16 ...15 C4
Preachers La OX1 ...141 B4
Prescott Ave OX16 ...15 C3
Prescott Cl OX16 ...16 A3
Prestidge Pl OX5 ...108 C4
Preston Rd OX14 ...179 C2
Prestwick Burn OX11 ...200 C2
Prestwick Pl OX2 ...122 C1
Prew Cotts OX7 ...29 A2
Price Cl OX26 ...65 C2
Prichard Rd OX3 ...124 A2
Priest Cl RG9 ...224 B2
Priest Hill RG4 ...259 A2
Priest Hill La OX3 ...103 C3
Primrose Cl OX18 ...129 C1
Primrose Ct RG8 ...257 B3
Primrose Dr OX26 ...65 C2
Primrose La OX18 ...134 C1
Primrose Pl 8 OX4 ...142 C1
Primsdown Ind Est OX7 ...42 B2
Prince Gr OX14 ...160 A1
Prince William Rd RG31 ...257 B1
Princes Ride OX20 ...91 B3
Princes St OX4 ...141 C4
Princess Gdns OX12 ...214 B4

Princethorpe Dr OX16 ...16 C4
Prior's Forge OX2 ...109 A1
Prior's La SN7 ...155 C2
Priors Wlk GL7 ...150 C2
Priory Ave RG4 ...259 A1
Priory Bank Cotts OX44 ...145 B1
Priory Cl Bicester OX26 ...65 C1
Horton-cum-S OX33 ...112 A3
Priory Copse RG9 ...252 C3
Priory Ct Didcot OX11 ...218 B4
Reading RG4 ...259 A1
Priory Farm Cotts OX27 ...67 C1
Priory Gn SN6 ...190 A3
Priory La Bicester OX26 ...65 C1
Burford OX18 ...100 C3
Lyneham OX7 ...70 B3
Marcham OX13 ...178 B3
Priory Mead SN7 ...192 B1
Priory Mews 2 OX10 ...221 B4
Priory Orch OX12 ...214 B3
Priory Rd Bicester OX26 ...65 C1
Lyneham OX7 ...70 B3
Oxford OX4 ...142 B1
Wantage OX12 ...214 B2
Pritchard Cl OX16 ...16 C4
Pritchard Ct OX1 ...141 B1
Promenade Rd RG4 ...259 A1
Prospect Cl OX29 ...89 B4
Prospect Pl OX49 ...186 A1
Prospect Rd
Banbury OX16 ...16 B3
Upton OX11 ...218 B1
Prospect St RG4 ...259 A1
Prunus Cl OX4 ...142 C2
Puck La OX28 ...104 A1
Puddleduck La SN7 ...192 A4
Puddicote La OX7 ...71 C3
Pudsey Cl OX14 ...179 C2
Pugsden La OX13 ...199 A2
Pulker Cl OX4 ...142 B2
Pullens Field OX3 ...124 A1
Pullens La OX3 ...124 A1
Pulling Cl SN7 ...172 C2
Puma Cl OX10 ...204 B1
Pumbro OX29 ...89 B4
Purcell Rd OX3 ...123 C2
Purfield Dr RG10 ...255 C1
Purland Cl OX4 ...142 B3
Purley Cl Inf Sch RG8 ...257 B3
Purley La RG8 ...257 B3
Purley Rise RG8 ...257 B3
Purley Village RG8 ...257 B3
Purley Way RG8 ...256 C3
Purrants La OX29 ...86 C1
Purslane Dr OX26 ...65 B2
Purslane Rd OX26 ...65 B2
Pusey La OX1 ...123 B1
Pusey St OX1 ...123 B1
Putman Cl OX9 ...148 A4
Putman Pl RG9 ...244 C1
Pye St SN7 ...173 A2
Pykes Cl OX14 ...160 A1
Pym Wlk OX9 ...129 C1
Pyrton La OX49 ...186 A1
Pytenry Cl OX14 ...160 B1
Pytt's La OX18 ...100 C3

Q

Quadrangle The
Bicester OX26 ...65 C1
Cutteslowe OX2 ...122 C4
Woodstock OX20 ...91 B4
Quadrant The OX14 ...180 A4
Quaker La OX10 ...220 C1
Quantock Ave RG4 ...259 B3
Quantock View OX11 ...200 B1
Quarhill Cl OX7 ...42 C3
Quarry Cl Bloxham OX15 ...21 B2
Enstone OX7 ...59 A3
Long Crendon HP18 ...129 B4
Quarry End OX5 ...108 A4
Quarry Gd OX7 ...69 A3
Quarry High St OX3 ...124 C2
Quarry Hollow OX3 ...124 C1
Quarry La Charlbury OX7 ...73 B2
Shiplake RG9 ...255 A2
Quarry Rd
Chadlington OX7 ...57 A1
Oxford OX3 ...124 C1
Sunningwell OX13 ...159 C4
Witney OX28 ...104 A2
Quarry School Pl OX3 ...124 C1
Quartermain Cl OX4 ...142 A3
Quartermain Rd OX44 ...184 B4
Quebec Rd RG9 ...254 C4
Queen James's Sch RG4 ...259 A2
Queen Annes Gate RG4 ...259 B2
Queen Cl RG9 ...244 C1
Queen Eleanor Ct OX29 ...106 A4
Queen Elizabeth Cl
OX14 ...219 A4
Queen Elizabeth Ho
OX1 ...123 B1
Queen Emmas Dyke
OX28 ...117 C4
Queen St Abingdon OX14 ...179 C4
Bampton OX18 ...134 C2
Dorchester OX10 ...182 B1
Eynsham OX29 ...120 C4
Henley-on-T RG9 ...244 C1
Middleton Cheney OX17 ...17 C4
Oxford OX1 ...123 B1
Reading RG4 ...259 A2

Queen's Cres
Clanfield OX18 ...152 C3
Drayton (Banbury) OX15 ...15 B4
The OX28 ...117 C4
Queen's Dyke Cty Prim Sch
OX28 ...117 C4
Queen's La OX1 ...123 B1
Queen's Rd Banbury OX16 ...16 A3
Carterton OX18 ...115 C1
Thame OX9 ...148 A4
Queen's St Ave Bicester OX26 ...65 C1
Highworth SN6 ...190 A3
Kidlington OX5 ...109 A4
Wallingford OX10 ...203 A1
Queens Cl
Dorchester OX10 ...182 B1
N Hinksey Village OX2 ...140 A4
Thame OX9 ...129 C1
Queens Coll OX1 ...123 B1
Queens Ct OX26 ...65 C1
Queens La OX29 ...120 C4
Queens Rd Cholsey OX10 ...220 C1
Reading RG4 ...259 B1
Queens St OX15 ...21 B2
Queens Way OX11 ...219 C4
Queensborough Dr RG4 ...258 C3
Queensway Banbury OX16 ...16 A2
Didcot OX11 ...218 C4
Reading RG4 ...259 B3
Queensway Prim Sch
OX16 ...16 A2
Quickset Cl OX7 ...72 C4
Quintan Ave OX25 ...81 B2

R

Race Farm Cotts OX13 ...176 C4
Rack End OX29 ...137 B2
Radbone Hill OX7 ...42 C3
Radcliffe Hospl OX2 ...123 A2
Radcliffe Rd OX4 ...142 B1
Radcliffe Sq OX1 ...123 B1
Radcot Cl RG5 ...260 C1
Radcot Rd SN7 ...172 C3
Radford Cl OX4 ...141 C2
Radley CE Prim Sch
OX14 ...160 C2
Radley Coll OX14 ...160 B2
Radley Ct OX14 ...160 A1
Radley Ho OX2 ...123 B3
Radley Rd OX14 ...160 B1
Radley Road Ind Est
OX14 ...160 A1
Radley Sta OX14 ...160 C1
Radnage CE Prim Sch
HP14 ...189 B3
Radnage Common Rd
HP14 ...189 B3
Radnage La HP14 ...169 B1
Radnor Cl RG9 ...244 C1
Radnor Rd OX10 ...221 A4
Raghouse La OX27 ...49 C1
Raglan Gdns RG4 ...259 B2
Ragley Mews RG4 ...259 B3
Ragnall's La OX33 ...111 C4
Rahere Rd OX4 ...142 B2
Railway Cotts SN7 ...195 C1
Railway La OX4 ...142 A1
Railway Terr GL7 ...150 B3
Railway View RG8 ...256 B3
Rainbow Way OX14 ...160 A2
Raincliffe Cl OX17 ...35 B4
Raleigh Cres OX28 ...117 B4
Raleigh Park Rd OX2 ...140 C4
Rampion Cl OX4 ...143 A1
Ramsay Rd OX3 ...124 C2
Ramsons Way OX14 ...180 B4
Rand Rd GL54 ...68 A2
Randolph Rd RG1 ...259 A1
Randolph St 8 OX4 ...141 C4
Range Rd OX29 ...103 B1
Ramal Dr OX39 ...168 B3
Rastel Ho 8 OX26 ...16 C3
Rattlecombe Rd OX15 ...6 B1
Rau Ct OX27 ...66 A4
Raven Rd HP14 ...188 C2
Ravencroft OX26 ...81 A4
Ravensbourne Dr RG5 ...260 C1
Ravenscroft Rd RG9 ...244 B1
Ravensmead
Banbury OX16 ...16 A2
Chinnor OX39 ...168 B3
Rawdon Way SN7 ...173 A1
Rawlings Gr OX14 ...179 B4
Rawlins* Cl OX17 ...23 A3
Rawlinson Cl OX7 ...57 A1
Rawlinson Rd OX2 ...123 A3
Raycote Cl OX12 ...201 A1
Ray Ct OX11 ...201 A1
Ray Rd OX26 ...65 B1
Ray View OX5 ...94 C2
Raymond Rd OX30 ...65 B2
Raymund Rd OX3 ...123 C3
Raynham Ct OX13 ...115 C2
Rayson Ho OX3 ...124 A2
Reade Ave OX14 ...180 A4
Reade Cl OX7 ...70 A1
Reade's La RG4 ...252 B2
Reading Blue Coat Sch
RG4 ...260 B2
Reading Ct OX26 ...65 C2
Reading Rd
Aldworth RG8 ...248 A1
Cholsey OX10 ...239 A4
East Hendred OX12 ...216 A4
Goring RG8 ...249 C3

Reading Rd continued
Harwell OX11 ....217 B3
Kidmore End RG4 .....252 A2
Pangbourne RG8 ......256 B3
Streatley RG8 ....249 A3
Wallingford OX10 .....221 B2
Woodcote RG8 ....240 C1
Recreation Rd
Wargrave RG10 ....255 C1
Woodstock OX20 ......91 B3
Rectory Cl
Marsh Gibbon OX27 ...67 C2
Warmington OX17 ......3 A2
Wendlebury OX26 .....80 A2
Rectory Cres OX7 .....60 C4
Rectory Ct OX49 .....187 A4
Rectory Farm Cl OX12 .196 C4
Rectory Gdns OX15 ...15 B4
Rectory Hill RG9 .....206 A1
Rectory La
Aston Tirrold OX11 ....237 C4
Bix RG9 ....225 B1
Fringford OX27 ....52 B3
Kingston Bagpuize OX13 .176 C4
Letcombe Bassett OX12 .231 C4
Lewknor OX9 ....166 C1
Longworth OX13 .....156 A2
Middleton Cheney OX17 .10 C1
Woodstock OX20 ....91 A3
Rectory Mdw OX39 ...168 B4
Rectory Rd
Great Haseley OX44 ...164 C4
Hook Norton OX15 .....30 A4
Oxford OX4 ....141 C4
Reading RG4 ....259 A1
Streatley RG8 ....248 B4
Red Bridge Hollow OX1 .141 B2
Red Copse Rd OX1 ....140 C1
Red Cross Rd RG4 ....259 A1
Red Hill RG9 ....253 C3
Red House Dr RG4 ....253 A3
Red House Rd OX16 ...44 C2
Red La Ewelme RG9,OX49 .206 B1
Woodcote RG8 ....240 B2
Red Lion Dr HP14 ....188 B3
Red Lion Sq OX1 .....123 B1
Red Lion St Cropredy OX17 .4 C1
Kings Sutton OX17 .....23 C3
Red Poll Cl OX16 ......54 A1
Redberry Cl RG4 .....259 B3
Reed Cl OX3 ....124 C1
Redland Rd OX3 ......124 A3
Redlands Cl SN6 .....190 A2
Redmoor Cl OX4 .....142 B1
Redmoor Ct OX26 ....65 B2
Redwing Cl OX4 ......142 B1
Redwood Cl
Kingston Bagpuize OX13 .156 C1
Oxford OX4 ....143 A1
Redwood Way RG31 ...257 B2
Reedmace Cl OX4 ....143 A1
Reedmace Rd OX26 ...65 C2
Reeds Cl OX12 ....214 B3
Reema Hos The SN6 ...190 A1
Regal Ct 15 OX14 .....65 C1
Regal Way SN7 ......172 C2
Regency Hts RG4 ....258 C2
Regent Gdns OX11 ...219 A4
Regent Mall 14 OX12 .214 B2
Regent Mews SN7 ....172 C2
Regent St OX4 ......141 C4
Regents Park Coll OX1 .123 B1
Regents Riverside 15
RG1 ....259 A1
Regis Pl OX12 ....214 A1
Reid Cl OX16 ....16 A3
Reid Pl OX25 ....63 A4
Remenham La RG9 ...244 C2
Remenham Row RG9 ..244 C1
Remus Gate SN13 .....24 A3
Renny Pl OX4 ....141 C3
Renault Ho OX4 .....141 C3
Rest Harrow 17 OX4 ..142 C1
Retford Cl RG5 ......260 C1
Retreat Gdns OX10 ...221 C4
Retreat La RG9 ......169 B1
Rewley Abbey Ct OX1 .123 A1
Rewley Rd OX1 ......123 A1
Reynard Ct 3 OX26 ...65 C1
Reynolds Cl OX7 ......70 B1
Reynolds Way
Abingdon OX14 ......179 C3
East Challow OX12 ....213 C3
Rhigos RG4 ....258 C2
Rhine Cl RG4 ....259 B1
Rhodes Ho OX1 ......123 B1
Richard Gray Ct OX1 .123 A1
Richard Nevill Ct 2
RG4 ....259 B1
Richards La OX2 ......123 A4
Richardson Cl OX4 ...124 C1
Richards OX4 ....124 C1
Richens Dr OX18 .....115 B1
Richfield Ave RG1 ....258 C1
Richman Gdns OX16 ..15 C4
Richmere Rd OX11 ...218 C4
Richmond Rd
Oxford OX1 ....123 A1
Reading RG4 ....258 C2
Richmond St OX17 ...23 C3
Rickyard Cl OX1 .....123 A1
Rickyard The
Arlington OX12 ......215 B3
Chalgrove OX44 .....184 B3
Fulbrook OX18 ......100 C3
Shutford OX15 ....14 A3
Riddell Pl OX7 ......109 A1
Ride The OX13 ......158 A3

Riders Way OX39 .....168 B3
Ridge Cl OX16 ....16 B2
Ridge Hall Cl RG4 ....258 C2
Ridge The RG8 ......249 C1
Ridgefield Rd OX4 ...142 A4
Ridgemont Cl OX2 ...123 A4
Ridgemount Cl RG31 .257 A1
Ridgeway
Wargrave RG10 ......255 C1
Wootton (Oxford) OX1 .140 B1
Ridgeway (YH) The*
OX12 ....232 B3
Ridgeway CE Prim Sch The
OX12 ....213 A2
Ridgeway Cl RG9 .....223 B2
Ridgeway Rd
Didcot OX11 ....218 C4
Oxford OX3 ....124 C2
Ridgeway The
Bloxham OX15 ....21 C2
Nettlebed RG9 ......224 B1
Reading RG4 ....259 A2
Wantage OX12 ......232 B3
Riding La OX29 .....103 B4
Riding The OX9 ......86 C1
Ridings Bglws OX29 ..86 C2
Ridings The Banbury OX16 .16 C4
Kidlington OX5 ......92 B1
Oxford OX3 ....142 B4
Reading RG4 ....259 B4
Stonesfield OX29 ....89 B4
Ridley Rd OX4 ......142 C3
Riely Cl OX4 ....90 B1
Riely Ct OX14 ......179 B3
Riley Dr OX16 ....15 C4
Riley Ho OX4 ....142 B2
Rimes Cl OX13 .....156 C1
Rimmer Cl OX3 .....123 C3
Ringwood Rd
Oxford OX3 ....125 A2
Reading RG30 ......258 A1
Ripley Ave OX29 ....102 C1
Ripley Rd RG30 .....258 A1
Ripon Coll OX44 ....144 A2
Rippington Dr OX3 ...123 C2
Rise The Adderbury OX17 .23 A2
Aston Rowant OX39 ..167 C2
Islip OX5 ....93 C1
Rissington Cl RG31 ..257 C2
Rissington Dr OX28 ..117 C4
Rivacres RG8 ....250 C2
River & Rowing Mus*
RG9 ....244 C1
River Cl OX14 ......179 C3
River Gdns RG8 .....257 B3
River Rd RG4 ....258 B2
River View
Kennington OX1 .....141 C1
Sandford-on-T OX4 ..161 A4
Rivermead Rd OX4 ..141 C2
Rivermead Rehabilitation Ctr
OX1 ....141 C3
Riverside OX16 ......16 C2
Riverside Ct Oxford OX1 .141 B4
15 Reading RG4 .....259 A1
Riverside Gdns OX28 .104 A1
Riverside Rd OX2 ...122 C1
Riverview Rd RG8 ...256 B3
Rivington Glebe GL56 .27 A1
Rivy Cl OX43 ....180 B4
Road Eight OX11 ....217 A1
Road Eighteen OX11 .217 A1
Road Eleven OX11 ...217 A1
Road Fifteen OX11 ..217 A1
Road Five OX11 .....217 A1
Road Four OX11 ....217 A1
Road Nine OX11 ....217 A1
Road One OX11 .....217 A1
Road Six OX11 ......217 A1
Road Thirteen OX11 .217 A1
Road Twelve OX11 ..217 A1
Road Two OX11 .....217 A1
Roadside Cotts SN7 .171 A3
Robert Palmer Cotts The
RG4 ....260 B2
Robert Piggott CE Prim Sch
RG10 ....255 B1
Robert Robinson Ave
OX4 ....142 B1
Robert Sparrow Gdns
OX10 ....222 A3
Roberts Cl OX3 .....125 A2
Robin Hill OX29 ......90 A2
Robin Pl OX4 ....142 C1
Robins Cl
Barford St M OX15 ....32 C3
Great Rollright OX7 ..29 A2
Robins Mead RG8 ...239 B2
Robins Platt OX39 ..168 A3
Robins Way OX26 ....81 A4
Robinson Cl
Blewbury OX11 .....237 A4
Carterton OX18 .....115 B2
Robinswood OX16 ...14 B2
Robsart Pl OX2 .....139 C2
Rochester Ave RG5 .260 C1
Rochester Pl OX7 ....73 B2
Rochester Way OX17 .23 A3
Rochford Gdns OX26 .66 A2
Rock Cl OX18 ....115 B2
Rock Edge OX3 .....124 B1
Rock Farm La OX4 ..161 A4
Rock Hill OX7 ....42 C2
Rock Rd OX18 ......115 B2
Rock The OX15 ......32 C3
Rockbourne Gdns RG30 .258 A1

Rockhill Farm Ct OX7 ...42 C2
Rocky La RG9 ....243 A2
Roding Way OX11 ...201 A1
Rodney Pl OX13 .....156 B2
Rodway Rd RG30 ...257 C1
Roebuck Ct OX11 ...219 A4
Roebuck Rise RG31 .257 B2
Roentgen Ave OX17 ...1 B1
Rofford La OX44 ....164 A2
Roger Bacon La 2 OX1 .141 B4
Roger Dudman Way
OX1,OX2 ....123 A1
Rogers St OX2 ......123 A4
Rokeby Dr RG4 .....258 B4
Rolfe Pl OX3 ....124 A2
Rollright Stones* OX7 .28 A1
Rolls Ct OX12 ......214 B3
Roman Pl OX11 ....200 B1
Roman Rd OX33 ....144 B4
Roman Way Beckley OX3 .111 A2
Bicester OX26 ....65 C1
Brackley NN13 ....24 A4
Lechlade GL7 ....150 B3
Oxford OX4 ....142 C3
Wantage OX12 ......214 B3
Roman Wlk SN6 ....191 C1
Romany Cl RG30 ...258 A1
Romany La RG30 ...258 A1
Romany Rd OX16 ....8 C3
Romsey Rd RG30 ...258 A1
Romulus Way NN13 ..24 A3
Rookery Cl
Abingdon OX14 .....159 A1
Bodicote OX15 ......22 C4
Rookery Ho OX44 ...143 C1
Rookery Way OX26 ..65 B2
Rooks La OX9 ......147 C4
Roosevelt Dr OX3 ..124 B1
Roosevelt Rd OX19 .106 A4
Rope Way OX15 .....30 A3
Rope Wlk OX16 ......16 B3
Roper Rd OX25 .....63 B4
Rosamund Dr OX20 ..91 A4
Rosamund Rd OX2 ..122 C4
Rose Ave OX14 ....159 C2
Rose Cl Bucknell OX27 .64 C4
Carterton OX18 .....115 B1
Rose Cse HP14 .....48 B4
Rose Ct 2 OX4 .....142 A2
Rose Gdns OX2 ....140 B4
Rose Hill OX4 ......142 A2
Rose Hill Fst Sch OX4 .142 A2
Rose La OX1 ....123 B1
Rose Pl OX1 ....141 B4
Rosebay Cres OX12 .214 B4
Rosebery Rd RG4 ..258 B4
Rosedale Ave OX16 ..9 A1
Rosehill Ho RG4 ...259 B4
Rosehill Park RG4 ..259 B4
Rosemary Ct OX4 ..141 C4
Rosemary La OX18 .134 C2
Rosemead Ave RG31 .257 A2
Roses La OX7 ....41 C3
Rosina Wlk OX16 ....9 A1
Ross Rd 16 RG4 ....259 A1
Rossendale Rd RG4 .259 B2
Rotha Field Rd OX2 .109 A1
Rother Garth OX11 .201 A2
Rother Rd OX16 ......6 C1
Rotherfield Rd RG9 .254 C4
Rotherfield Way RG4 .259 A2
Rothwell Gdns RG5 .260 C1
Rothwell Wlk RG4 ..259 B1
Rottweils Cl OX10 ..221 A1
Rotten Row OX10 ..182 B1
Round Close Rd
Adderbury OX17 .....22 C2
Hook Norton OX15 ...30 A4
Roundham Ct OX5 ...92 B1
Roundhead Dr OX9 .129 C1
Roundhill Rd OX17 ...4 A2
Roundhills Mead SN6 .190 A4
Roundtown OX17 ....35 B4
Roundway The OX3 .124 C2
Rouses La GL7 ......150 B2
Rousham Pk* OX25 ..62 A3
Rousham Rd OX5 ....77 B4
Routh Rd OX3 .....124 C2
Roves La SN6 ......208 A4
Row La RG4 ....259 A4
Row The Bletchingdon OX5 .93 A4
Hinton Waldrist SN7 .155 C1
Lechlade GL7 ....150 C4
Lyneham OX7 ....70 B3
Mollington OX17 ......3 C2
Stanton Harcourt OX29 .138 A4
Wootton OX20 ....75 B4
Rowallan Cl RG4 ...259 B3
Rowan Cl Carterton OX18 .115 B2
Kidlington OX5 ......108 B4
Sonning Common RG4 .252 C2
Rowan Gr OX4 .....143 A1
Rowan Rd OX26 .....65 C2
Rowans The OX10 ..220 C1
Rowan Wy OX3 .....92 A1
Rowell Way OX7 ....42 C2
Rowland Cl
Cutteslowe OX2 ....122 C4
Wallingford OX10 ...203 B1
Rowland Rd OX10 ..221 A1
Rowlands Ho OX3 ..125 A2
Rowles Cl OX1 .....141 C1
Rowles Paddock RG20 .235 A1
Rowney Pl OX4 ....142 A2
Rowstock OX11 ....217 A4
Roxburgh Dr OX11 .200 B2

Royal Berkshire Ct
OX11 ....218 C4
Royal Mans RG9 ....244 C1
Royal Military Coll of Science
SN6 ....209 C4
Ruck Keene Cl OX26 .65 B1
Rufus Isaacs Rd RG4 .259 A1
Rugge Furlong OX11 .201 A1
Rumbolds Cl OX10 ..203 C3
Rumsey's La OX11 ..237 A4
Rupert Cl RG9 ......244 C2
Rupert House Sch RG9 .244 C1
Rupert Rd
Chalgrove OX44 ....184 B3
Oxford OX4 ....142 C3
Rupert Way OX9 ...130 A1
Rupert's La RG9 ...244 C2
Ruscote Arc OX16 ...16 A4
Ruscote Ave OX16 ..16 A4
Ruscote Sq OX16 ...16 A4
Rush Common Cty Prim Sch
OX14 ....160 A1
Rush Wlk OX14 ....130 A1
Rushbeds Wood Nature
Reserve* HP18 ......98 B2
Rushmead Copse OX14 .160 B1
Ruskin Ave OX14 ..179 C3
Ruskin Cl OX11 ....219 A4
Ruskin Coll Oxford OX1 .123 A2
Oxford,Headington OX3 .124 B2
Ruskin Rd OX16 .....16 B2
Ruskin Wlk OX26 ...65 C2
Russell Cl OX2 .....123 A2
Russell Jackson Cl
OX10 ....182 B3
Russell Rd RG4 ....258 B4
Russell St OX2 ....123 A1
Russet Ave GL7 ....150 C2
Russet Cl RG4 .....252 C3
Russet Glade RG4 .259 B4
Russet Rd OX27 .....50 B2
Rutherfield Cl OX14 .160 A1
Rutherford Ave OX11 .217 A2
Rutherway OX2 ....123 A2
Rutten La OX5 .....108 A3
Rutters Cl OX5 .....108 B4
Rycote La OX9 .....146 B3
Rycotewood Coll OX9 .129 C1
Rydal Ave RG30 ...257 C1
Ryder Cl OX5 ......108 A3
Rydes Cl OX15 ......22 C4
Rydes The OX15 ....22 C4
Rye Cl OX16 ....8 C1
Rye Grass OX20 .....91 A4
Rye St Antony Sch OX3 .124 A2
Ryecote Chapel* OX9 .146 B3
Ryecroft Cl Sonning RG5 .260 C1
Wargrave RG10 ....255 C1
Rymans Cres OX11 .219 A3
Rymers La OX4 ....142 A3

S

Sackville Cl OX17 .....8 C2
Sacred Heart RC Prim Sch
RG9 ....244 B1
Sadler Wlk OX1 ....141 A4
Sadlers Croft OX44 .143 C1
Sadlers Ct OX14 ...160 A2
Sadlers The RG31 ..257 A1
Saffron Cl OX4 ......65 B3
Saffron Ct OX4 ....180 A4
Sage Rd RG31 .....257 B2
Sage Wlk 18 OX4 ..142 C1
St Alban's Ct 20 OX11 .221 B4
St Aldates OX1 .....123 B1
St Aloysius RC Fst Sch
OX2 ....123 A2
St Amand Dr OX14 .179 C3
St Amand's RC Prim Sch
OX12 ....216 C3
St Andrew's CE Inf Sch
OX39 ....168 B4
St Andrew's CE Prim Sch
Chinnor OX39 ......168 B3
Didcot OX11 ....218 C4
Henley-on-T RG9 ...254 B4
Oxford OX3 ....124 B2
St Andrews CE Prim Sch
OX3 ....124 B2
St Andrews Cl OX14 .160 B1
St Andrews Ho OX39 .168 B3
St Andrews Rd RG4 .258 C2
St Anne's Cl RG9 ..244 B1
St Anne's Coll OX2 .123 A2
St Anne's Rd
Banbury OX16 ....16 B2
Oxford OX3 ....124 B1
St Annes Cl OX26 ...65 C2
St Annes Rd OX14 .219 A4
St Annes RC Prim Sch
OX2 ....123 A1
St Barnabas RG4 ..259 A3
St Barnabas Rd RG4 .259 A3
St Bernard's Rd OX1 .123 A2
St Birinus Ct GL7 ..150 B3

St Birinus Sch
Didcot OX11 ....218 C4
Dorchester OX10 ..182 B1
St Catherine's Coll OX1 .123 C1
St Catherines Ho OX4 .123 C1
St Catherine's CE Fst Sch
OX4 ....142 B3
St Christopher's CE Prim Sch
GL7 ....132 B1
St Christopher's Pl OX4 .142 A3
St Clement's St OX4 .123 C1
St Cristopher Cotts SN7 .172 C2
St Cross Bldg OX1 ..123 B1
St Cross Rd OX1 ...123 B1
St David's Ct NN13 ..24 A4
St Davids Cl RG4 ...258 C3
St Denys Cl SN7 ...194 C4
St Ebbe's CE Fst Sch
OX1 ....141 B4
St Ebbes St 3 OX1 .141 B4
St Edburg's Cl OX26 .65 B1
St Edburg's Prim Sch
OX26 ....65 C1
St Edith's Way OX26 .65 B1
St Edmund's La 5
OX14 ....179 C3
St Edmund's RC Prim Sch
OX14 ....180 A4
St Edward's Ave OX2 .123 A4
St Edwards Ct OX2 .123 A3
St Edwards Sch OX2 .123 A3
St Francis CE Fst Sch
OX4 ....142 C3
St Francis Cl OX3 ..142 C4
St Francis Rd HP14 .189 B2
St Frideswides Ct OX1 .220 C1
St George's Cres OX16 .16 B2
St George's Pl OX1 .123 B1
St George's Rd SN7 .154 B1
St George's Gate 6
OX1 ....123 A1
St Georges Gdn OX10 .203 B1
St Georges Rd OX10 .221 B4
St Giles OX5 ....93 A4
St Giles Cl OX26 ...80 A2
St Giles' OX1 ......123 B1
St Helen's Ave OX10 .203 C2
St Helen's Ct OX14 .204 A2
St Helen's Cl OX14 .179 C3
OX14 ....179 C3
St Helen's Mews 6
OX14 ....179 C3
St Helen's Pas OX1 .123 B1
St Helen's Way OX10 .203 C2
St Helen's Wharf OX14 .179 C3
St Hilda's Cl OX26 ..65 C2
St Hilda's Ct OX14 .141 C4
St Hildas Cl OX11 ..219 A4
St Hugh's Cl
Bicester OX26 ....65 C2
Stokenchurch HP14 .188 C2
St Hugh's Cold OX2 .123 A3
St Hugh's Dr OX16 ..188 C2
St Hugh's Sch SN7 .174 A4
St Hughs OX16 ......16 B2
St Hughs Rise OX11 .219 A4
St Ives La OX12 ....214 C4
St Ives Rd OX12 ...214 C4
St James OX12 .....214 B3
St James Rd OX14 .256 B3
St James Cl OX29 ...89 B4
St James Rd OX4 ..160 A1
St James Ter OX14 .160 C1
St James View OX12 .197 A3
St James' Tutorial Unit
OX4 ....142 A2
St John Fisher RC Prim Sch
OX4 ....142 B2
St John's Cl Didcot OX11 .219 A4
Fyfield OX13 ....157 A1
St John's Coll OX1 .123 B1
St John's Rd
18 Banbury OX16 ...16 B3
Grove OX12 ....196 C1
St John's Gn OX10 .221 B3
St John's Prim Sch
OX10 ....221 B4
St John's RC Prim Sch
OX16 ....16 C2
St John's Rd
Abingdon OX14 ....180 A4
Banbury OX16 ......16 B3
Reading RG4 ....259 B1
Wallingford OX10 ..221 B4
St John's Row OX14 .201 B4
St John's Terr 6 OX11 .221 B4
St John's Way OX15 ..33 A2
St Johns Dr
Carterton OX18 ....115 C2
Kidlington OX5 ....92 C1
St Johns Rd OX5 ....77 B3
St Joseph's RC Fst Sch
OX4 ....124 A2
St Joseph's RC Prim Sch
OX16 ....15 C3
St Joseph's RC Prim Sch
OX9 ....147 C4
St Katherine's Rd RG9 .254 B4

St Kenelm's CE Prim Sch
OX29 . . . . .102 C1
St Kenelm's Cl OX29 . . . .102 C1
St Laurence's CE Prim Sch
OX10 . . . . .203 A4
St Lawrence Cl OX10 . . . .203 A4
St Lawrence Ho OX10 . . .203 A4
St Lawrence Rd
Lechlade GL7 . . . . .150 B2
South Hinksey OX1 . . . . .141 A3
St Lawrence's CE Prim Sch
GL7 . . . . .150 B2
St Leonard's CE Prim Sch
OX16 . . . . .16 C3
St Leonard's Cl OX16 . . . .221 B3
St Leonard's La OX10 . . .221 B4
St Leonard's Rd OX3 . . . .124 B2
St Leonard's Sq [17]
OX10 . . . . .221 B4
St Leonards Cl OX49 . . . .186 A1
St Lucian's La OX10 . . . . .221 B3
St Luke's Rd OX4 . . . . . . .142 B3
St Lukes Ct RG4 . . . . . . .259 A2
St Lukes Way RG4 . . . . . .259 A3
St Margaret's Rd OX2 . . .123 A2
St Mark's Rd RG9 . . . . . .254 B4
St Martin's Rd OX4 . . . . .142 A2
St Martin's St OX10 . . . . .221 B4
St Martins RC Prim Sch
RG4 . . . . .259 C3
St Mary & John CE Fst Sch
OX4 . . . . .142 A4
St Mary's CE Inf Sch
OX28 . . . . .118 A4
St Mary's CE Prim Sch
Banbury OX16 . . . . .16 B3
Chipping Norton OX7 . . . .42 C1
St Mary's Cl
[1] Banbury OX16 . . . . . . .16 B3
Bicester OX26 . . . . .65 B1
Chalgrove OX44 . . . . . . .184 B3
Henley-on-T RG9 . . . . . .254 A4
Kidlington OX5 . . . . .92 C1
Oxford OX4 . . . . .142 A1
St Mary's Ct OX28 . . . . . .118 A4
St Mary's Gn OX14 . . . . .159 C1
St Mary's Ho OX33 . . . . .144 A4
St Mary's La OX7 . . . . . . .30 C2
St Mary's Mead OX28 . . .118 A4
St Mary's RC Prim Sch
OX26 . . . . .65 C1
St Mary's Rd
Adderbury OX17 . . . . .22 C1
East Hendred OX12 . . . . .216 C3
Oxford OX4 . . . . .141 C4
St Mary's Sch OX12 . . . .214 B2
St Mary's St OX10 . . . . . .221 B4
St Mary's Way OX12 . . . .214 B3
St Marys Cl OX33 . . . . . .144 A4
St Michael's Ave
Abingdon OX14 . . . . .179 C4
Highworth SN6 . . . . .190 A3
St Michael's CE Prim Sch
OX13 . . . . .198 C2
St Michael's Cl OX27 . . . .52 B3
St Michael's La OX1 . . . .123 B1
St Michael's Way OX13 . .198 C2
St Michaels CE Fst Sch
OX3 . . . . .123 C1
St Nicholas CE Inf Sch
OX10 . . . . .203 B1
St Nicholas CE Prim Sch
SN8 . . . . .245 C1
St Nicholas Fst Sch
OX3 . . . . .123 C1
St Nicholas Rd
Oxford OX4 . . . . .142 B1
Tackley OX5 . . . . .77 B3
Wallingford OX10 . . . . . .221 B4
St Nicholas' Gn OX14 . . .159 C1
St Nicolas CE Sch OX14 .179 C4
St Omer Rd OX4 . . . . . . .142 C1
St Paul's Cres OX2 . . . . .140 B4
St Pauls Arts Ctr* OX2 . .123 A1
St Peter's CE Prim Sch
OX18 . . . . .133 B3
St Peter's CE Prim Sch
OX29 . . . . .107 B1
St Peter's Cl
Cassington OX29 . . . . . . .107 B1
Stoke Lyne OX27 . . . . . . .51 A3
Wootton (Oxford) OX13 . .159 A3
St Peter's Coll OX1 . . . . .123 B1
St Peter's Cres OX26 . . . .65 A2
St Peter's PI [22] OX16 . . .221 B4
St Peter's Rd
Abingdon OX14 . . . . .160 B1
Brackley NN13 . . . . .24 A4
Cutteslowe OX2 . . . . . . .122 C4
Didcot OX11 . . . . .218 C4
St Peter's St OX10 . . . . . .221 B4
St Peters Ave RG4 . . . . .258 C2
St Peters Cl OX15 . . . . . .31 C4
St Peters Gate NN13 . . . .24 A4
St Peters Hill RG4 . . . . . .258 C2
St Philip & St James CE Fst
Sch OX2 . . . . .123 A2
St Ruald's Cl OX26 . . . . . .65 C2
St Rumbold's Rd OX10 . . .221 B4
St Stephens Cl [6] RG4 . .259 A1

St Swithun's CE Prim Sch
OX1 . . . . .160 C4
St Swithun's Rd OX1 . . . .160 C4
St Thomas Moore RC Sch
OX5 . . . . .108 C4
St Thomas St OX15 . . . . .33 C2
St Thomas' St OX1 . . . . .123 A1
St Thomas's Cl SN7 . . . .155 C1
Salegate La OX4 . . . . . . .142 B3
Salesian Gdns OX4 . . . . .142 B3
Salesian Ho OX4 . . . . . . .142 B3
Salford Rd OX3 . . . . .123 C2
Salisbury Cres OX2 . . . . .123 A4
Sallow Cl OX26 . . . . .65 C3
Salmon Cl OX15 . . . . .21 C3
Salop Cl SN6 . . . . .209 A3
Salt La OX9 . . . . .166 C1
Salter Cl OX1 . . . . .141 B4
Salters La HP18 . . . . .98 B4
Salvia Cl OX16 . . . . .9 A1
Samian Way OX10 . . . . . .202 B4
Samor Way OX11 . . . . . .218 B4
Samphire Rd OX4 . . . . . .142 C1
Samuelson Ct [2] OX16 . .16 B3
Sand Hills SN6 . . . . .209 A4
Sand View SN7 . . . . .172 C1
Sandcroft Rd RG4 . . . . . .258 C3
Sandell Cl OX16 . . . . .16 B3
Sanderling Cl OX26 . . . . .81 A4
Sanderling Wlk OX16 . . . .16 C2
Sandfield Rd OX3 . . . . . .124 A2
Sandfine Rd OX15 . . . . . .15 A1
Sandford Cl
Abingdon OX14 . . . . .160 A1
Woodcote RG8 . . . . .250 C4
Sandford Dr RG5 . . . . . .260 C1
Sandford Gn OX16 . . . . . .16 C1
Sandford La OX1 . . . . . . .160 C4
Sandford Mount OX7 . . . .73 B2
Sandford Pk OX7 . . . . . . .73 B2
Sandford Rd OX4 . . . . . .142 A1
Sandford Rise OX7 . . . . . .73 B2
Sandford St Martin Rd
OX7 . . . . .46 B1
Sandgate Ave RG30 . . . .257 C1
Sandhill Rd OX5 . . . . . . .108 A4
Sandhills Prim Sch OX3 .125 A2
Sandleigh Rd OX13 . . . . .159 A4
Sandpit Cl OX26 . . . . .81 A4
Sandpit Hill MK18 . . . . . .39 C3
Sandpit La RG4 . . . . .259 C4
Sandringham Dr OX11 . .219 A4
Sandringham Rd OX17 . . .23 C3
Sands Cl Bletchingdon OX5 .93 A4
Cumnor OX2 . . . . .139 C3
Sands La OX15 . . . . .31 C4
Sands Rd OX11 . . . . .219 C3
Sands The Benson OX10 .204 B3
Milton-u-W OX7 . . . . .70 A1
Sands Way OX10 . . . . . . .203 C3
Sandy La Beckley OX3 . . .111 A1
Cholsey OX10 . . . . .220 C1
Kingston Bagpuize OX13 .156 C1
Long Crendon HP18 . . . .129 A3
Oxford OX4 . . . . .142 C2
Shrivenham SN6 . . . . . . .209 A3
Stanford in the V SN7 . . .174 B2
Tiddington OX9 . . . . .145 C3
Upper Rissington GL54 . . .68 A2
Wootton (Oxford) OX1 . . .140 A3
Yarnton OX5 . . . . .108 B4
Sandy La W OX4 . . . . . . .142 C2
Sandy Lane Ct GL54 . . . .68 A2
Sandy Lane Est OX9 . . . .145 C4
Sarajac Ave OX12 . . . . . .214 B1
Sarsden Cl OX7 . . . . .57 A1
Sarum Cl OX18 . . . . .115 C2
Satin La OX15 . . . . .33 C2
Satwell Cl RG9 . . . . .243 A2
Saunders Cl OX49 . . . . . .186 A1
Saunders Ct RG8 . . . . . .257 A3
Saunders Rd OX4 . . . . . .142 A3
Saunders Wood Copse
HP14 . . . . .188 C2
Savile Rd OX1 . . . . .123 B1
Savile Way OX12 . . . . . . .196 B1
Saw Cl OX44 . . . . .184 B4
Sawpit Rd OX4 . . . . .142 C2
Sawpits La OX5 . . . . .40 A1
Saxel Cl OX18 . . . . .135 C2
Saxifrage Sq [3] OX4 . . .142 C1
Saxon Cl OX10 . . . . .221 B4
Saxon Ct Benson OX10 . .203 C2
Bicester OX26 . . . . .65 C1
Saxon Orch SN6 . . . . . . .191 B1
Saxon Pl OX12 . . . . .214 A3
Saxon Way Oxford OX3 . .124 A2
Witney OX28 . . . . .118 A4
Saxons Heath OX14 . . . .201 B4
Saxons Way OX11 . . . . . .219 A4
Saxton Rd OX14 . . . . . . .179 C3
Sayers Orch OX11 . . . . . .200 B1
Scafell Cl RG31 . . . . .257 B1
Scampton Cl OX18 . . . . . .66 A2
Schilling St OX25 . . . . .6 A1
Schofield Ave OX28 . . . .104 A2
Schofield Gdns OX28 . . .104 A2
Schofields Way OX15 . . . .21 C3
Scholar Cl SN6 . . . . .191 C1
Scholar Pl OX2 . . . . .140 B4
Scholars Acre OX18 . . . .115 B2
Scholars Cl RG4 . . . . . . .258 C2
Schongau Cl OX14 . . . . .179 B2
School Cl Ickford HP18 . .128 A4
Long Compton CV36 . . . . .27 C3
Longworth OX13 . . . . . . .156 B2
Steventon OX13 . . . . . . .198 C2
School Cotts RG9 . . . . . .243 B1

School End OX17 . . . . . . .35 B4
School Hill
Minster Lovell OX29 . . . .102 C2
Mollington OX17 . . . . .3 C2
Wargrave RG10 . . . . .255 B1
School La
Appleford OX14 . . . . .200 C4
Aston Rowant OX49 . . . .167 C2
Banbury OX16 . . . . .16 B3
Black Bourton OX18 . . . .133 C3
Chilson OX7 . . . . .71 C2
Coleshill SN6 . . . . .191 A4
Great Bourton OX17 . . . . .9 B4
Harwell OX11 . . . . .217 C4
Kingston Bagpuize OX13 .156 C1
Middleton Stoney OX25 . .64 A2
Milton OX14 . . . . .199 B3
Milton, Milton Heights
OX14 . . . . .199 B2
Minster Lovell OX29 . . . .102 C2
North Newington OX15 . . .15 B2
Reading RG4 . . . . .259 A3
Reading, Emmer Green
RG4 . . . . .259 A3
Shabbington HP18 . . . . .128 B2
Stadhampton OX44 . . . . .163 B1
Stoke Lyne OX27 . . . . . . .51 A3
Stoke Row RG9 . . . . .241 C2
Upper Heyford OX25 . . . . .62 C4
Wargrave RG10 . . . . .255 B1
Warmington OX17 . . . . . . .3 A2
School of St Helen & St
Katherine OX14 . . . . . . .179 B4
School Paddock OX27 . . . .64 C4
School Pl OX1 . . . . .141 B3
School Rd
Ardington OX12 . . . . .215 B3
Finstock OX7 . . . . .88 B3
Kidlington OX5 . . . . .92 C1
West Hanney OX12 . . . . .196 C3
School View OX16 . . . . . . .16 C3
School Yd OX44 . . . . .163 B1
Schooler's La OX16 . . . . . .16 B2
Scotland End OX15 . . . . . .30 A4
Scotsgrove Cotts OX9 . . .130 A2
Scott Cl Bicester OX26 . . .65 B2
Kidlington OX5 . . . . .108 B4
Reading RG4 . . . . .259 A3
Scott Rd OX2 . . . . .123 A4
Scotts Cnr NN13 . . . . . . .25 A2
Scotts La OX27 . . . . .67 C1
Scours La RG30 . . . . .258 A1
Scrutton Cl OX3 . . . . . . .124 C2
Seacourt Rd OX2 . . . . . .122 B2
Sealham Rd OX29 . . . . . .118 A2
Second Ave OX11 . . . . . .200 B1
Second St
Croughton NN13 . . . . .36 C3
Harwell OX11 . . . . .217 B2
Sedgefield Cl RG4 . . . . . .252 C3
Sedgemoor Dr OX9 . . . . .130 A1
Sedgewell Rd RG4 . . . . . .252 C3
Seelscheid Way OX26 . . .81 A4
Seeson Way OX12 . . . . . .214 B2
Sefton Pl OX15 . . . . .22 C4
Sefton Rd OX3 . . . . .124 C2
Segsbury Ct OX12 . . . . . .214 A3
Segsbury Rd OX12 . . . . . .214 A3
Selborne Gdns RG30 . . .258 A1
Sellwood Dr OX18 . . . . . .115 C2
Sellwood Rd OX14 . . . . .159 C2
Selwyn Cres OX14 . . . . . .160 C1
Send Rd RG4 . . . . .259 B1
Sermon Cl OX3 . . . . .124 C1
Setler Ho [6] OX16 . . . . . .16 C3
Setts The SN7 . . . . .172 C1
Seven Acres
Long Crendon HP18 . . . .129 A4
Shrivenham SN6 . . . . . . .190 A4
Seventeenth St OX11 . . . .217 A1
Seventh Ave OX11 . . . . . .142 C4
Severalls Cl OX10 . . . . . .203 B1
Severn Cl OX26 . . . . .65 A2
Severn Rd
Abingdon OX13 . . . . .159 B1
Harwell OX11 . . . . .217 A1
Sewell Cl OX14 . . . . .160 B1
Sewell's La OX39 . . . . . .147 C4
Seymour Milward Terr [24]
OX10 . . . . .221 B4
Shackleton Cl [4] OX26 . .66 A2
Shades The OX16 . . . . . . .16 B3
Shadwell Rd OX10 . . . . . .182 B3
Shaftesbury Rd OX3 . . . .124 B2
Shakenoak OX29 . . . . . . .105 B3
Shakespeare Cl RG4 . . . .259 B3
Shakespeare Dr OX26 . . . .65 B2
Shakespeare Rd OX29 . .120 B4
Shannon Cl OX12 . . . . . . .196 A1
Sharland Cl OX12 . . . . . .214 C4
Sharman Beer Ct OX7 . . .147 C4
Sharpey Cotts OX26 . . . . .66 A1
Shaw Cl OX16 . . . . .65 B2
Shaw's Copse OX14 . . . .160 C1
Sheards La SN7 . . . . .194 C4
Shearings The OX5 . . . . . .30 A4
Shearwater Dr OX26 . . . . .81 A4
Sheen Cl OX27 . . . . .65 A3
Sheep St Bicester OX26 . . .65 C1
Burford OX18 . . . . .100 C3
Charlbury OX7 . . . . .73 A2
Highworth SN6 . . . . .190 A3
Sheep Wlk RG4 . . . . .259 A2
Sheepwash La OX13 . . . .199 A3
Sheepway Ct [2] OX4 . . .142 A2
Sheepways La RG4 . . . . .259 A3

Sheerstock HP17 . . . . . . .130 C3
Sheldon Rd HP18 . . . . . .128 A2
Sheldon Way OX4 . . . . . .142 B2
Sheldonian* OX1 . . . . . .123 B1
Sheldons Piece OX49 . . .186 A1
Shelford Pl OX3 . . . . .124 B1
Shelley Cl
Abingdon OX14 . . . . .160 A1
Banbury OX16 . . . . .16 A2
[9] Bicester OX26 . . . . . . .65 B2
Oxford OX3 . . . . .124 C1
Shelley Rd OX4 . . . . .142 B2
Shellingford CE Prim Sch
SN7 . . . . .193 C4
Shenington CE Prim Sch
OX15 . . . . .6 C1
Shenington Kart Club*
OX15 . . . . .6 C1
Shepard Way OX7 . . . . . . .42 C2
Shepherd Gdns OX14 . . .159 C1
Shepherds Cl Grove OX12 .196 B1
Sibford Gower OX15 . . . . .19 A4
Weston-on-the-G OX25 . . .79 A1
Shepherds Hill
Sandford-on-T OX4 . . . . .142 C1
Sonning RG6 . . . . .260 B1
Shepherds La RG4 . . . . .258 B3
Sheraton Dr RG31 . . . . . .257 B1
Sherborne St GL7 . . . . . .150 B2
Sherbourne Rd OX28 . . .117 B4
Sheridan Ave RG4 . . . . . .259 A2
Sheriff's Dr OX2 . . . . . . .122 C4
Sherwood Ave OX14 . . . .180 A4
Sherwood Cl OX26 . . . . . .66 A1
Sherwood Dr OX15 . . . . . .22 B3
Sherwood Gdns RG9 . . . .254 B4
Sherwood Pl RG8 . . . . . .257 A2
Sherwood Rd OX11 . . . . .219 A4
Sherwood Rise RG8 . . . .257 A3
Shifford La OX29 . . . . . . .137 B1
Shilbrook Manor OX18 . .133 C2
Shillbrook Ave OX18 . . . .115 B3
Shilldeane Dr OX18 . . . . .115 B2
Shilson La OX7 . . . . .73 A2
Shilton Rd Burford OX18 .100 C2
Carterton OX18 . . . . .115 B2
Ship St OX1 . . . . .123 B1
Shiplake Bottom RG9 . . .252 C3
Shiplake CE Prim Sch
RG9 . . . . .254 C1
Shiplake Coll RG9 . . . . . .254 C1
Shiplake Sta RG9 . . . . . .255 A2
Shipston Rd CV36 . . . . . . .27 C4
Shipton Cl RG31 . . . . . . .257 B1
Shipton Rd
Ascott-u-W OX7 . . . . .71 A1
Shipton-u-W OX7 . . . . . . .70 A1
Woodstock OX20 . . . . . . .91 B3
Shipton Sta OX7 . . . . .70 C1
Shirburn Rd OX49 . . . . . .186 B3
Shirburn St OX49 . . . . . .186 B1
Shirelake Cl OX1 . . . . . . .141 B4
Shires Bsns Pk The
NN13 . . . . .24 A3
Shires Rd NN13 . . . . .24 A3
Shirley Pl OX2 . . . . .123 A2
Shirvell's Hill RG8 . . . . . .250 C4
Shoe La
East Hagbourne OX11 . . .218 C3
Oxford OX1 . . . . .123 A1
Shooters Hill RG8 . . . . . .256 A3
Short Furlong OX11 . . . . .201 A1
Short St Pangbourne RG8 .256 B3
[1] Reading RG4 . . . . . . .259 A1
Watchfield SN6 . . . . .191 B1
Short The RG8 . . . . .257 B3
Shorte Cl OX3 . . . . .142 C4
Shortlands Hill OX10 . . . .238 B2
Shotover SN7 . . . . .211 B3
Shotover Ctry Pk* OX3 . .125 A1
Shotover Kilns OX3 . . . . .124 C1
Shotover Trad Est OX3 . .124 C1
Shrewsbury Pl OX18 . . . .134 C2
Shrieves Cl OX14 . . . . . . .160 A1
Shrivenham CE Prim Sch
SN6 . . . . .209 A4
Shrivenham Hundred
SN6 . . . . .191 B1
Shrivenham Rd
Highworth SN6 . . . . .190 A2
Longcot SN7 . . . . .192 C4
Shrubbery The GL7 . . . . .150 B2
Shute Ave SN6 . . . . .209 B4
Shutford Rd
North Newington OX15 . . .15 A2
Tadmarton OX15 . . . . . . .20 C4
Sibford Gower Prim Sch
OX15 . . . . .19 A4
Sibford Rd
Hook Norton OX15 . . . . . .30 A4
Shutford OX15 . . . . .13 C2
Sibford Sch OX15 . . . . . . .19 A4
Sideleigh Rd OX15 . . . . . .22 C4
Sidings Ind Est The
NN13 . . . . .24 A4
Sidings Rd OX11 . . . . .55 C3
Sidney St OX4 . . . . .141 C4
Signet Cl OX18 . . . . .100 C2
Signet End OX18 . . . . . . .100 C2
Silkdale Cl OX4 . . . . .142 B3
Silver Birches OX33 . . . .125 C3
Silver La OX12 . . . . .213 B3
Silver Rd OX4 . . . . .142 B4
Silver St Bourton SN6 . . .209 A1
Chacombe OX17 . . . . .10 C2
Fernham SN7 . . . . .193 A2
Tetsworth OX9 . . . . .166 A4
Wroxton OX15 . . . . .15 A4
Silverdale Rd RG10 . . . . .255 C1
Silvermead HP18 . . . . . . .127 B3

Silverthorne Dr RG4 . . . .258 C3
Simms Cl OX33 . . . . .125 B4
Simmonds Wlk OX12 . . . .214 B3
Simmons Rd RG9 . . . . . .244 B2
Simmons Way OX9 . . . . .129 C1
Simon Ho OX3 . . . . .124 B2
Simon's Cl OX33 . . . . . . .144 A4
Simons Cl RG31 . . . . . . .257 B2
Simons La RG4 . . . . .85 B4
Simpsons Way OX1 . . . . .160 C4
Sinclair Ave OX4 . . . . .16 A4
Sinclair Dr OX16 . . . . .16 A4
Singers Cl RG9 . . . . .254 C4
Singers La RG9 . . . . .244 C1
Singletree OX4 . . . . .142 A2
Sinnels Field OX7 . . . . . . .85 C4
Sinodun Cl OX14 . . . . . . .201 C4
Sinodun Rd Didcot OX11 .218 C4
Wallingford OX10 . . . . . .203 B1
Sinodun Row OX14 . . . . .200 C4
Sinodun View OX10 . . . . .203 A4
Sint Niklaas Cl OX14 . . . .179 B2
Sir Georges La OX17 . . . . .23 A2
Sir Mortimer's Terr
OX14 . . . . .199 B3
Sires Hill OX10 . . . . .202 B2
Siskin Rd Bicester OX26 . .81 B1
Upper Rissington GL54 . . .68 A3
Sixpenny La OX44 . . . . . .184 C3
Sixteenth St OX11 . . . . . .217 A2
Sixth St Croughton NN13 . .36 C4
Harwell OX11 . . . . .217 A2
Skarries View RG4 . . . . .258 B4
Skelton Cl OX4 . . . . .123 C1
Skene Cl OX3 . . . . .124 B1
Skerrit Way RG8 . . . . . . .257 B2
Skilton Rd RG31 . . . . . . .257 B2
Skimmingdish La OX27 . . .65 C3
Skimmingdish Rd OX6 . . .66 A2
Skinner Rd OX26 . . . . .66 B1
Skippett La OX7 . . . . .88 A2
Skippon Way [6] OX9 . . .129 C1
Skittle Alley OX7 . . . . .35 B4
Slade Cl OX3 . . . . .124 B1
Slade End OX10 . . . . .202 C2
Slade End Rdbt OX10 . . .203 A1
Slade Farm Cotts OX5 . . .63 A1
Slade Rd Cholsey OX10 . .221 A1
Oxford OX3 . . . . .124 C1
Slade The Charlbury OX7 . .73 B2
Oxford OX3 . . . . .142 C4
Slaters Ct OX29 . . . . .90 A1
Slave Hill HP17 . . . . .130 C3
Slaymaker Cl OX3 . . . . . .124 C1
Sloan Cl RG8 . . . . .249 B3
Slopes The RG4 . . . . . . .259 B1
Small Ho OX15 . . . . .19 B4
Smith Barry Cres OX5 . . . .68 A2
Smith Barry Cres GL54 . . .68 A2
Smith Barry Rd OX5 . . . . .68 A2
Smith Ct RG4 . . . . .252 C3
Smith's Cl OX18 . . . . . . .135 C1
Smith's Hill OX12 . . . . . .231 C3
Smiths Farm La OX11 . . .200 B1
Smiths Rickyard OX12 . . .216 B4
Snakehill La OX15 . . . . . . .33 A2
Snipe Rd GL54 . . . . .68 A2
Snowdon Mede OX3 . . . .124 A2
Snows La OX33 . . . . .144 C2
Snowshill Dr OX28 . . . . . .103 B1
Snowsill Dr OX28 . . . . . .117 B4
Snowswick La SN7 . . . . . .170 C3
Snuff La OX17 . . . . .9 A4
Snuggs La OX12 . . . . . . .197 A4
Soane End RG4 . . . . .259 A4
Soden Pl OX33 . . . . .156 B1
Soden Rd OX25 . . . . .63 B4
Sollershott OX2 . . . . . . .108 C1
Solters Cl HP18 . . . . .129 A4
Somerton Rd Ardley OX27 .50 A2
North Aston OX25 . . . . . . .48 A4
Upper Heyford OX25 . . . . .48 C1
Somerville OX11 . . . . . . .219 A4
Somerville Coll OX2 . . . .123 B2
Somerville Ct OX7 . . . . . . .42 C2
Somerville Dr OX26 . . . . .65 C2
Songers Cl OX2 . . . . .140 A4
Sonning CE Prim Sch
RG4 . . . . .260 B2
Sonning Common Prim Sch
RG4 . . . . .252 C3
Sonning La RG4 . . . . .260 B1
Sonning Mdws RG4 . . . . .260 B1
Soot La OX17 . . . . .3 A2
Sopwith Rd GL54 . . . . . . .68 A3
Sorrel Mead OX26 . . . . . .65 B2
Sorrel Rd OX4 . . . . .143 A1
Sotwell St
Brightwell-cum-S OX10 . .202 C1
Brightwell-cum-S OX10 . .203 A1
South Ave
Abingdon OX14 . . . . .159 C1
Henley-on-T RG9 . . . . . .254 C4
Kidlington OX5 . . . . .108 C3
South Bank RG8 . . . . . . .239 B2
South Bar St OX16 . . . . . .16 B3
South Bridge Row OX1 . .141 B4
South Cl OX5 . . . . .108 C4
South Dr Harwell OX11 . .217 B2
Wroxton OX15 . . . . .15 A4
South End
Great Rollright OX7 . . . . . .29 A2
Haddenham HP17 . . . . . .130 C3
South Gate Cl GL54 . . . . .68 A2
South Hills HP18 . . . . .98 A1
South Leigh Rd OX29 . . .119 A4

South Lodge The 8
OX26 ....65 C1
South Mdw OX25 ....81 B2
South Mere OX18 ....116 B2
South Moreton Sch
OX11 ....219 C3
South Newington Rd
Barford St M OX15 ....32 B3
Bloxham OX15 ....21 A1
South Par OX2 ....123 A4
South Park Ave OX11 ..218 B4
South Park Ct 6 OX4 ..141 C4
South Parks Rd OX1 ....123 B1
South Row OX1 ....235 B4
South Side OX25 ....62 A4
South St Banbury OX16 ..16 C4
Blewbury OX11 ....237 A4
Letcombe Bassett OX12 ..214 A1
Lower Heyford OX25 ....63 A3
Middle Barton OX7 ....60 C4
Oxford OX2 ....141 A4
Reading RG4 ....259 A1
Watchfield SN6 ....191 B1
South Stoke Cty Prim Sch
RG8 ....239 A2
South Stoke Rd RG8 ....240 A1
South View
Great Bourton OX17 ....9 B4
4 Wallingford OX10 ....221 B4
South View Ave RG4 ....259 B1
South View Pk RG4 ......259 B1

Southam Rd
Banbury OX16, OX17 ....9 B2
Mollington OX17 ....A A2
Southampton St SN7 ..172 C2
Southby Cl OX13 ....158 A4
Southcroft OX23 ....123 A4
Southdale Rd OX2 ....123 A4
Southdown Ct SN7 ......194 C4
Southern Rd RG4 ....259 A3
Southend OX44 ....162 C4
Southend Cotts OX5 ......78 A2
Southern By-pass Rd
OX1 ....141 B2
N Hinksey Village OX2 ......140 C4
Oxford OX1,OX4 ....141 C2
South Hinksey OX1 ....141 A2
Southern Rd OX9 ....147 C4
Southerndene Cl RG31 ..257 B1
Southfield Dr OX14 ......199 C4
Southfield La OX27 ....49 C4
Southfield Pk OX4 ....142 A4
Southfield Prim Sch
SN6 ....190 A3
Southfield Rd OX4 ....142 A4
Southlands OX18 ....135 C1
Southlawn OX28 ....104 C1
Southmead Ind Pk
OX11 ....200 B2
Southmoor Pl OX2 ....123 A2
Southmoor Rd OX2 ......123 A2
Southmoor Way OX14 ..179 C4
Southrop CE Prim Sch
GL7 ....131 A2
Southrop Rd OX15 ....30 A3
Southwold 3 OX6 ....65 C1
Southwold Cty Prim Sch
OX26 ....65 C3
Southwood Rd OX29 ....103 B1
Sovereign Cl OX11 ......219 A4
Spa Cl SN6 ....190 A4
Span Hill RG4 ....260 A4
Spareacre La OX29 .....120 C4
Sparsey Pl OX2 ....109 A1
Sparsholt St OX12 ....212 C2
Spears The OX5 ....108 A3
Speedwell Cmb OX4 .....142 A1
Speedwell Fst Sch OX4 .142 A1
Speedwell St OX1 ....141 B4
Spencer Ave OX5 ....108 A4
Spencer Cres OX4 ....142 A2
Spencer Ct 28 OX16 .....16 B3
Spencers Cl SN7 ....194 B4
Spendlove Ctr The OX7 ..73 A2
Spenlove Cl OX14 ....159 C1
Spenser Cl OX26 ....65 B2
Spey Rd OX13 ....159 B2
Speyside Cl OX18 ....115 B3
Spier's La OX27 ....67 C1
Spinage Cl SN7 ....173 A2
Spindleberry Cl OX4 ....142 C1
Spindlers OX5 ....92 C1
Spindleside 1 OX26 ......65 C1
Spinney Bank OX17 ....21 C3
Spinney Cl RG4 ....259 A4
Spinney Cres OX16 ......16 C2
Spinney Field OX4 ....142 C1
Spinney The
Abingdon OX14 ....159 B1
East Hendred OX12 ....216 B3
Launton OX26 ....66 B1
Lechlade GL7 ....150 B2
Spinneys Cl OX14 ....160 C2
Spinneys The OX5 ....58 B3
Spitfire Cl Benson OX10 ..204 A1
6 Bicester OX26 ....66 A2
Spleen The OX5 ....14 A3
Spooner Cl OX3 ....124 C2
Sprigs Holly La HP14 ..189 A4
Spring Cl OX28 ....118 A4
Spring Copse OX1 ....141 A2
Spring Farm OX25 ....47 B3
Spring Farm Mews RG8 .239 B1
Spring Gdns
Abingdon OX14 ....179 B4
Lechlade GL7 ....150 B2
Spring Hill OX13 ....176 B4
Spring Hill Rd OX5 ......107 C4

Spring La
Aston Tirrold OX11 ....237 C4
Great Bourton OX17 ....9 B4
Horspath OX33 ....143 B4
Idbury OX7 ....69 A2
Oxford OX4 ....142 B1
Oxford,Headington Quarry
OX3 ....124 C1
Reading RG4 ....260 A3
Watlington OX49 ....186 B1
Spring Path OX9 ....147 C4
Spring Pl OX7 ....42 C1
Spring Rd OX14 ....179 B3
Spring St OX7 ....42 C2
Spring Terr OX14 ....179 B4
Spring Wlk RG10 ....255 B1
Springdale OX10 ....221 B4
Springfield OX17 ....8 C2
Springfield Ave OX16 ....16 B2
Springfield CE Sch
OX29 ....89 B4
Springfield Dr
Shrivenham SN6 ....209 A3
Watlington OX49 ....186 B1
Springfield Dr OX14 ....179 C4
Springfield Gdns OX35 .168 B4
Springfield Mews RG4 ..259 A2
Springfield Pk OX28 ....103 C1
Springfield Rd
Bicester OX27 ....65 C4
Kidlington OX5 ....108 C4
N Hinksey Village OX2 ......140 A4
Stokenchurch HP14 ....188 A2
Wantage OX12 ....214 C2
Springfield Sch OX28 ...103 C1
Springhill Rd RG8 ....249 B4
Springs The OX28 ....118 A4
Springwell Hill OX5 ....58 A1
Springwell Ho 10 OX16 .16 B3
Springwood La RG9 .....253 A4
Spruce Dr OX26 ....65 C3
Spruce Gdns OX4 ....161 C4
Spruce Rd OX5 ....108 A4
Spur The RG10 ....255 C2
Square Firs OX29 ....90 A3
Square The
12 Abingdon OX14 ....179 C4
Aston OX18 ....135 C2
Aynho OX17 ....35 B4
Eynsham OX29 ....120 C4
Great Tew OX7 ....45 B4
Kings Sutton OX17 ....23 C3
Long Crendon HP18 ....130 A3
Longworth OX13 ....156 A2
N Hinksey Village OX2 ......122 B1
2 Oxford OX4 ....142 B2
Pangbourne RG8 ....256 B3
Squire's Wlk OX10 ....221 B3
Squires Cl OX18 ....116 B2
Squires Rd SN6 ....191 B1
Squitchey La OX2 ....123 A4
Stable Cl [?] Finmere MK18 ..39 B4
Oxford OX1 ....123 B1
Stable Cotts GL56 ....40 B2
Stable Rd OX26 ....65 C2
Staddlestone Cl RG31 ..257 B1
Stadhampton Prim Sch
OX44 ....163 B1
Stadhampton Rd
Drayton St L OX10 ....183 A3
Little Milton OX44 ....163 C3
Stadium Way RG30 ....258 A1
Staffordshire Cl RG30 ....257 C1
Stainer Pl OX3 ....123 C2
Stainfield Rd OX3 ....124 C1
Stainswick La SN6 ....209 B3
Stallpits Rd SN6 ....209 A4
Stanbridge Cl OX16 ....16 A3
Standlake CE Prim Sch
OX29 ....137 B2
Standlake Rd
Ducklington OX29 ....118 B2
Northmoor OX29 ....138 A1
Standon Ct OX3 ....124 B1
Stanford Dr 8 OX14 .....179 C4
Stanford in the Vale CE Prim
Sch SN7 ....194 C4
Stanford Rd SN7 ....173 A2
Stanley Cl OX4 ....142 C1
Stanley Cl OX2 ....140 B4
Stanley Rd OX4 ....141 C4
Stanmore Cres OX18 ......115 C2
Stansfeld Pl OX3 ....124 C1
Stansfeld Cl OX3 ....124 C1
Stanton Cl OX28 ....117 C4
Stanton Cotts OX5 ......125 B4
Swalcliffe OX15 ....19 C4
Stanton Harcourt CE Prim
Sch OX29 ....138 A4
Stanton Harcourt Ind Est
OX29 ....138 A4
Stanton Harcourt Rd
South Leigh OX29 ....119 B3
Witney OX28 ....118 B4
Stanton Rd
Forest Hill OX33 ....125 C2
N Hinksey Village OX2 ......140 C3
Stanville Rd OX2 ....140 A1
Stanway Cl OX28 ....103 B1
Stanway Rd OX3 ....125 A2
Stanwell Cl OX17 ....11 A1
Stanwell Dr OX17 ....11 A1
Stanwell La OX17 ....9 B4
Stanwell Lea OX17 ....11 A1
Stapleton Rd OX3 ....124 B1
Star La SN6 ....191 B1
Star Rd RG4 ....259 B1

Starina Croft OX16 ....9 A1
Starnham Rd OX29 ......118 A2
Starwort Path 4 OX4 ....142 A1
Station App Bicester OX26 .65 C1
Kidlington OX5 ....92 B1
Station Field Ind Est OX5 .92 B1
Station La OX28 ....118 A3
Station Rd Ardley OX27 ..50 B2
Ashbury SN6 ....228 A4
Aynho OX17 ....35 A3
Bampton OX18 ....134 C3
Black Bourton OX18 ....133 C3
Blackthorn OX25 ....82 A2
Bletchingdon OX5 ....93 A4
Brize Norton OX18 ....116 B2
Chinnor OX39 ....168 B3
Chipping Norton OX7 ....42 B1
Cholsey OX10 ....220 C1
Cropredy OX17 ....4 C1
Culham OX14 ....180 C2
Didcot OX11 ....200 C1
Eynsham OX29 ....120 C4
Farringdon SN7 ....172 C2
Goring RG8 ....249 B3
Grove OX12 ....214 C4
Haddenham HP17 ....130 C3
Henley-on-T RG9 ....244 C1
Highworth SN6 ....190 A3
Hook Norton OX15 ....30 B4
Kingham OX7 ....54 C2
Launton OX26 ....66 C2
Lechlade GL7 ....150 B3
Lower Heyford OX25 ....62 B4
Marsh Gibbon OX27 ....67 C2
Pangbourne RG8 ....256 B3
Shiplake RG9 ....255 A2
Shipton-u-W OX7 ....70 C1
Shrivenham SN6 ....209 A3
South Leigh OX29 ....119 B3
Uffington SN7 ....211 B4
Upton OX11 ....218 B1
Wallingford OX10 ....221 B4
Wargrave RG10 ....255 B1
Station Rd Ind Est OX5 ....92 C1
Station Yard Ind Est
Adderbury OX17 ....23 A1
Chipping Norton OX7 ....42 B1
Station Yd
Steventon OX13 ....199 A2
Thame OX9 ....148 A4
Staunton Rd OX3 ....124 A2
Staverton Rd OX2 ....123 A3
Steady's La OX29 ....118 A3
Steep Rise OX3 ....124 B3
Steeple Cl OX15 ....21 C2
Steepness Hill OX15 .....32 C2
Stenton Cl OX14 ....179 C3
Stephen Cl OX15 ....124 B2
Stephen Freeman Prim Sch
OX11 ....200 B1
Stephen Rd OX3 ....124 A2
Stephenson Ho 4 OX1 ..141 B4
Steppingstone La SN6 ..209 A2
Steptoe Cl OX12 ....196 B1
Sterling Cl
7 Bicester OX26 ....66 A2
Kidlington OX5 ....108 C4
Sterling Rd OX5 ....108 C4
Sterling Road App OX5 ..92 C1
Sterling Way RG30 ......258 A1
Stert Rd OX39 ....167 C2
Stert St OX14 ....179 C4
Stevens Cl OX2 ....123 A2
Stevens La RG9 ....252 B4
Stevenson Cl OX26 ......65 B2
Stevenson Dr OX14 ......179 B4
Steventon Rd
Drayton OX13,OX14 ....199 A4
East Hanney OX12,OX13 ..197 C4
Stewart St OX1 ....141 B3
Stile Rd OX3 ....143 A3
Stimpsons Cl OX2 ....122 A1
Stirling Cl
Carterton OX18 ....138 A1
Reading RG4 ....259 B3
Wantage OX12 ....214 C4
Stirling Cl OX15 ....15 C3
Stirlings Rd 4 OX12 ....214 B2
Stockey End OX14 ....160 B1
Stockham Pk OX12 ......214 B3
Stockham Prim Sch
OX12 ....214 B3
Stockham Way OX12 ...214 B3
Stocking La OX15 ....6 B4
Stockleys Rd OX3 ....124 A3
Stockmore St OX4 ....141 C4
Stocks La OX13 ....198 C2
Stocks The OX7 ....57 A1
Stocks Tree Cl OX5 .....108 A3
Stoke Lyne Rd OX27 .....52 B1
Stoke Pl OX3 ....124 B2
Stoke Row CE Prim Sch
RG9 ....241 C3
Stoke Row Rd RG9 ......252 C4
Stokenchurch Inf Sch
HP14 ....188 C2
Stokenchurch Jun Sch
HP14 ....188 C2
Stokes View RG8 ....256 B3
Stone Cl OX2 ....122 A1
Stone Ct 2 Banbury OX16 16 B3
Great Rollright OX7 ....29 A3
Stone Hill Cl OX15 ....20 B1
Stone House Cl OX13 ..156 C1
Stone Quarry La OX4 ..142 B2
Stone St Oxford OX4 .....142 A4
Reading RG30 ....258 A1

Stonebridge Rd OX13 ..198 C3
Stoneburge Cres OX26 ..65 C2
Stonebury Cl OX12 ......214 C3
Stonecrop Leyes OX5 ....65 C3
Stonefield Dr SN6 ....190 A2
Stonefield Way SN6 .....209 B3
Stonegables OX28 ....118 A3
Stonehill La
Abingdon OX14 ....179 B2
Kingston Bagpuize OX13 ..176 B4
Stonehill Wlk OX14 ......179 B2
Stoneleigh Cl OX7 ....57 A1
Stoneleigh Dr OX18 .....115 B3
Stonesfield OX11 ....219 A4
Stonesfield La OX7 ....89 A4
Stonesfield Prim Sch
OX29 ....89 B4
Stonesfield Rd OX29 .....90 C1
Stonesfield Riding OX7 ..74 B1
Stoney La OX9,OX49 ....185 C4
Stonhouse Cres OX14 ..160 C1
Stonor Cl OX11 ....200 C1
Stonor Gr OX18 ....186 A1
Stonor Ho [?] OX49 ....226 A4
Stonor Pl OX3 ....124 A1
Stort Cl OX11 ....200 C2
Stour Cl OX11 ....201 A1
Stoutsfield Cl OX5 ....108 A3
Stow Ave OX28 ....117 B4
Stow Rd Bledington OX7 ..54 B3
Fifield OX7 ....69 A1
Stowford Cl OX3 ....124 C3
Stowford Rd OX3 ....124 C3
Stowhill OX12 ....213 B2
Stowood Cl OX3 ....124 C2
Strachey Cl RG8 ....256 B1
Strafford Way OX9 ....148 A4
Strainges Cl OX29 ....118 A2
Stranks Cl SN6 ....190 A2
Stratfield Rd
Cutteslowe OX2 ....123 A3
Kidlington OX5 ....108 C1
Stratford Dr OX29 ....120 B4
Stratford La OX20 ....76 A1
Stratford Rd
Drayton (Banbury) OX15 ...15 C4
Shenington OX15 ....6 C4
Wroxton OX15 ....14 C4
Stratford St OX4 ....141 C4
Strathmore Cl OX18 ....115 B3
Stratton Audley Manor
OX27 ....52 B1
Stratton Audley Rd
Fringford OX27 ....52 B3
Stoke Lyne OX27 ....51 A3
Stratton Way OX14 ......179 C4
Strawberry Hill OX15 ....21 C2
Strawberry Path OX15 ..142 C1
Strawberry Terr OX15 ....21 C2
Stream Rd OX11 ....218 B1
Streatley & Goring Bridge
RG8 ....249 A3
Streatley Hill RG8 ....248 C3
Streatley Lodge 24 OX1 .141 B4
Streatley CE Sch RG8 ....248 C3
Street The
Crowmarsh G OX10 ....222 A3
Crowmarsh G, N Stoke
OX10 ....221 B1
Ipsden OX10 ....240 B4
Moulsford OX10 ....239 A3
South Stoke RG8 ....239 A2
Stoke Lyne OX27 ....51 A3
Tidmarsh RG8 ....256 B1
Stroud Cl OX16 ....16 C4
Stuart Cl RG4 ....259 A3
Stuart Way OX3 ....130 A1
Stubble Cl OX2 ....140 A4
Stubbs Ave OX3 ....142 C4
Stud Farm Cl OX17 ....9 B4
Studdridge Ct HP14 ....188 B2
Sturges Cl OX13 ....124 B3
Sturt Cl OX7 ....73 B1
Sturt Rd OX7 ....73 B2
Styles Cl OX27 ....67 C1
Styles The OX12 ....217 B4
Sudbury Ct SN7 ....173 A2
Sudbury La OX13 ....156 B2
Suffolk Cl OX27 ....67 C2
Suffolk Ho OX10 ....204 A2
Suffolk Way OX14 ....179 B3
Sugarswell La OX15 ....6 A3
Sugworth Cres OX14 ....160 C3
Sugworth La OX14 ....160 B3
Sulham La RG8 ....256 C4
Summer Fields OX14 ....160 A2
Summer Ley OX15 ....32 C3
Summerfield OX1 ....141 B3
Summerfield Rise RG8 ..249 A4
Summerhill Rd OX2 ......122 A4
Summerside OX17 ....223 A3
Summerside SN7 ....174 C4
Summerton Pl OX7 ....42 C2
Summertown Cl OX23 ...124 A3
Summertown Ho OX3 ...123 A4
Sunderland Ave OX2 ....109 A1
Sunderland Dr OX26 ......66 A2
Sundew Cl OX14 ....143 A1
Summerhall CE Prim Sch
OX13 ....159 C3
Sunningwell
Oxford OX1 ....141 B3
Sunningwell OX13 ....159 C2
Sunningwell Rd OX14 ...143 B3
Sunny Rise OX33 ....143 B3
Sunnymeade Ct 2 OX2 .109 A1
Sunnyside Benson OX10 .203 C3

Sunnyside continued
Oxford OX4 ....142 A3
Wheatley OX33 ....144 B4
Surley Row RG4 ....259 A3
Sussex Dr OX16 ....15 C4
Sutherland Beck OX11 ..200 C2
Sutton Cl OX14 ....179 C4
Sutton Courtenay Rd
OX14 ....199 C3
Sutton La OX29 ....120 A1
Sutton Rd Milton OX14 ..199 C3
Oxford OX3 ....124 B3
Sutton Wick La OX14 ....179 B1
Sutton Way OX14 ....142 C1
Swain Ct OX28 ....118 A3
Swalcliffe Lea OX15 ......14 A1
Swalcliffe Park Sch
OX15 ....19 C4
Swalcliffe Rd OX15 ....20 A4
Swale Dr OX11 ....201 A1
Swallow Cl Bicester OX26 .81 A4
3 Sandford-on-T OX4 ....142 C1
Swan Cl Grove OX12 ....196 B1
Lechlade GL7 ....150 B2
Middleton Cheney OX17 ...17 C4
Swan Close Rd OX16 .....16 B3
Swan Ct 7 Oxford OX1 ..123 A1
Witney OX28 ....118 A4
Swan Gdns OX9 ....166 A4
Swan Ind Est OX16 ....16 B3
Swan La Burford OX18 ..100 C3
Faringdon SN7 ....172 C2
Great Bourton OX17 ....9 A1
Long Hanborough OX29 ....90 A1
Swan Lane Cl OX18 .....100 C3
Swan St Eynsham OX29 .120 C4
Oxford OX2 ....123 A1
Swan Wlk OX9 ....147 C4
Swanhall La OX29 ....104 A3
Swanlands Ho OX29 .....120 C4
Swansea Rd RG1 ....259 A1
Swansea Terr RG31 ......257 A2
Swansfield Bicester OX26 .81 A4
Lechlade GL7 ....150 B3
Swanston Field RG8 .....256 B4
Swarbourne Cl OX11 ....200 C1
Sweeps La OX18 ....100 C3
Sweet Briar OX13 ....178 B3
Sweetmans Rd OX2 ......140 B4
Swerford Rd OX15 ....30 A3
Swift Cl Bicester OX26 ....65 B2
9 Sandford-on-T OX4 ....142 C1
Swift Way OX10 ....204 B2
Swin La OX18 ....101 C3
Swinbourne Rd OX14 ....142 A1
Swinbrook Ct RG31 ......257 B2
Swinbrook Ct OX28 ......118 A4
Swinbrook Rd
Carterton OX18 ....115 B3
Shipton-u-W OX7 ....85 C3
Swinburne Rd
Abingdon OX14 ....179 A3
Oxford OX4 ....141 C2
Swindon Rd SN6 ....190 A3
Swindon St SN6 ....190 A3
Swingburn Pl OX28 ......118 A4
Swinnerton Ho RG9 .....244 C2
Swinstead Ct OX44 ......184 B3
Sworford La OX44 ....144 C3
Sycamore Cl
Abingdon OX13 ....159 B1
Long Crendon HP18 ....129 A3
Sibford Gower OX15 ....19 A4
Watlington OX49 ....186 A1
Witney OX28 ....104 B1
Sycamore Cres OX1,
OX4 ....160 C3
Sycamore Ct RG8 ....256 B3
Sycamore Dr
Banbury OX16 ....16 B1
Carterton OX18 ....115 B2
Sycamore Gdns OX26 ...65 C2
Sycamore Pl OX13 ....144 B4
Sycamore Rd
Ambrosden OX25 ....81 B2
Launton OX26 ....66 B1
N Hinksey Village OX2 ......140 B4
Sycamore Terr OX15 ......21 B2
Sycamore Wlk OX12 .....196 B1
Sycamores The OX3 .....124 C2
Sydenham Gr OX9 ....167 C4
Sylvester Cl OX18 ....100 C3
Sympson Cl 12 OX14 ...179 C3
Syringa Wlk OX16 ....9 A1

T

Tackley CE Prim Sch
OX5 ....77 B3
Tackley Sta OX5 ....77 C3
Tackley Pl OX2 ....123 A2
Tacks La HP17 ....130 C3
Tadmarton Pk OX15 ......21 A3
Tadmarton Rd OX15 ......21 A1
Taggs Gate OX3 ....124 C3
Tailsman Bsns Ctr The
OX26 ....80 C4
Tait Dr OX25 ....63 A4
Talbot Cl Banbury OX16 ..15 C4
Reading RG4 ....259 B1
Talbot Fields OX18 ....100 C3
Talbot Rd OX2 ....109 A1
Talbot Way RG31 ....257 B2

Talisman Rd OX26 . . . . .80 C4
Tamar Cres OX26 . . . . .65 A2
Tamar Way OX11 . . . . .201 A1
Tamarisk Gdns OX26 . . . . . .65 C3
Tamesis PI RG4 . . . . .259 A1
Tangmere Ave OX18 . . . . . .115 C2
Tangmere CI OX26 . . . . .66 A2
Tanner's La OX18 . . . . .100 B3
Tanners Ct OX7 . . . . .73 A2
Tanners La
  Adderbury OX17 . . . . .22 C2
  Eynsham OX29 . . . . .120 C4
  Mapledurham RG4 . . . . . . .258 C4
Taphouse Ave OX28 . . . . . .104 A1
Tarragon Dr OX4 . . . . .142 C1
Tarrant Ave OX28 . . . . . . .104 B1
Taston Rd OX7 . . . . .73 A4
Tatham Rd OX14 . . . . .159 C1
Tatlings Rd OX13 . . . . .198 C3
Taverner PI OX3 . . . . .123 C2
Tavistock Ave OX11 . . . . . .218 B4
Tavy CI OX11 . . . . .200 C2
Tawney St OX4 . . . . .142 A4
Tay Gdns OX26 . . . . .65 B2
Taylor CI OX26 . . . . .65 C3
Taynton OX18 . . . . .100 A4
Tays Gateway OX15 . . . . . . .33 C2
Tchure The OX15 . . . . .33 C2
Teal CI Banbury OX16 . . . . .16 C2
  Grove OX12 . . . . .196 B1
  Sandford-on-T OX4 . . . . . .142 C1
Teale CI OX25 . . . . .96 C4
Teescroft OX11 . . . . .201 A2
Telford Cres RG5 . . . . .260 C1
Telford Rd OX26 . . . . .66 A2
Templar Rd OX2 . . . . .109 A1
Templars CI OX33 . . . . . . .144 A4
Templars Sq OX4 . . . . .142 B3
Temple Cloisters OX4 . . . . .142 B3
Temple Cowley Com Sch
  OX4 . . . . .142 B3
Temple Ho RG9 . . . . .244 C2
Temple Rd OX4 . . . . .142 B3
Temple St Brill HP18 . . . . . .98 A1
  Oxford OX4 . . . . .141 C4
Templeton Ho RG9 . . . . . . .254 C4
Tenby Ave RG4 . . . . .259 B3
Tenlands OX17 . . . . .17 C4
Tennis The OX29 . . . . .107 B1
Tennyson CI OX16 . . . . .16 A2
Tennyson Dr OX14 . . . . . . .179 B3
Tenpenny OX10 . . . . .202 B4
Tenth St OX11 . . . . .217 A2
Tern Wlk OX4 . . . . .142 C1
Terrace The OX7 . . . . .70 A1
Terrington CI OX14 . . . . . .160 A1
Tessa Rd RG1 . . . . .258 C1
Tetbury Dr OX28 . . . . .103 B1
Tetsworth Prim Sch
  OX9 . . . . .166 A4
Tew La OX20 . . . . .75 C3
Tewer The OX29 . . . . .89 B4
Thackley End OX2 . . . . . . .123 A3
Thame La
  Clifton Hampden OX14 . . . .181 A3
  Culham OX14 . . . . .180 B2
Thame Park Rd OX9 . . . . . .148 A3
Thame Plk Bsns Ctr OX9 . . .148 A4
Thame Rd
  Blackthorn OX25 . . . . .82 A2
  Chinnor OX39 . . . . .168 A4
  Great Haseley OX44 . . . . . .164 C4
  Great Milton OX44 . . . . . . .145 B1
  Haddenham HP17 . . . . . . .130 B3
  Little Milton OX44 . . . . . . .164 A4
  Long Crendon HP18,OX9 . . .129 B2
  Piddington OX25,HP18 . . . . .97 B3
  Towersey OX9 . . . . .148 C4
  Warborough OX10 . . . . . . .203 A4
Thames Ave
  Bicester OX26 . . . . .65 A2
  Pangbourne RG8 . . . . .256 B3
  Reading RG1 . . . . .259 A1
Thames Bank RG8 . . . . . . .249 A4
Thames Ct
  Abingdon OX14 . . . . .180 A4
  ■ Oxford OX1 . . . . .141 B4
Thames Dr RG10 . . . . .260 C4
Thames Gdns OX7 . . . . .73 A2
Thames Ho RG9 . . . . .244 C2
Thames Mead OX10 . . . . . .221 C2
Thames Pk OX10 . . . . .221 A4
Thames Rd Goring RG8 . . . .249 A3
  Harwell OX11 . . . . .217 A2
Thames Side
  Henley-on-T RG9 . . . . .244 C1
  ■ Reading RG4 . . . . .259 A1
Thames Side Prom RG1 . . . .259 A1
Thames St
  Abingdon OX14 . . . . .179 C3
  Charlbury OX7 . . . . .73 A2
  Eynsham OX29 . . . . .120 C4
  Lechlade GL7 . . . . .150 B2
  Oxford OX1 . . . . .141 B4
  Sonning RG4 . . . . .260 B2
  Wallingford OX10 . . . . . . .221 B4
Thames Valley Bsns Pk
  RG6 . . . . .260 A1
Thames View OX14 . . . . . . .180 A4
Thames View Ind Pk
  OX14 . . . . .180 A4
Thames View Rd OX14 . . . .141 C2
Thameside Prim Sch
  Abingdon OX14 . . . . .179 B3

Thameside Prim Sch continued
  Reading RG4 . . . . .259 A1
Thameside Reach OX10 . . . .239 A2
Thatchers CI OX15 . . . . .13 A3
The Laurels OX44 . . . . .163 B1
Thelwell Ho OX4 . . . . .142 A4
Thenford Rd OX17 . . . . .11 B1
Theobald Dr RG31 . . . . . . .257 B2
Thesiger Rd OX14 . . . . .179 C4
Thetford Mews RG4 . . . . . .259 B3
Third Acre Rise OX2 . . . . . .140 A4
Third St Croughton NN13 . . . .36 C3
  Harwell OX11 . . . . .217 A1
Thirlmere Ave RG30 . . . . . .257 C1
Thirteenth St OX11 . . . . . . .217 A1
Thistle Dr OX4 . . . . .143 A1
Thistlecroft CI OX14 . . . . . .160 A1
Thistledown RG31 . . . . . . .257 B1
Thomas Mews OX4 . . . . . . .123 C1
Thomas Reade Prim Sch
  OX14 . . . . .180 A4
Thompson Dr OX27 . . . . . . .65 C4
Thomson Ave OX11 . . . . . .217 A2
Thomson Terr OX4 . . . . . . .142 A1
Thornbury Rd OX29 . . . . . .120 B4
Thornbury Rise OX16 . . . . . .15 C3
Thorncliffe Rd OX2 . . . . . . .123 A3
Thorne CI OX5 . . . . .92 B1
Thorney Leys OX28 . . . . . . .117 C4
Thorney Leys Ind Pk
  OX28 . . . . .117 C3
Thornhill OX17 . . . . .10 C2
Thornhill CI OX12 . . . . .214 B3
Thornhill Wlk OX14 . . . . . .159 C1
Thorningdown OX11 . . . . . .235 B4
Thorpe CI OX16 . . . . .16 C3
Thorpe Dr OX16 . . . . .16 C3
Thorpe La OX16 . . . . .16 C3
Thorpe Mead OX16 . . . . . . .16 C3
Thorpe PI OX16 . . . . .16 C3
Thorpe Rd
  Chacombe OX17 . . . . .10 C2
  Wardington OX17 . . . . .10 C2
Thorpe St OX11 . . . . .219 C1
Thorpe Way OX16 . . . . .16 C3
Thorpes Field OX18 . . . . . .133 B3
Three Corners Rd OX4 . . . . .143 A1
Three Fields Rd OX3 . . . . . .142 C4
Three Gables La OX68 . . . . .249 A4
Three Pigeons CI OX14 . . . .214 C2
Thrift PI OX4 . . . . .142 C1
Thrupp La OX14 . . . . .160 B1
Thurne View OX11 . . . . . . .201 A1
Thurston CI ■ OX14 . . . . . .179 C2
Tichborne OX9 . . . . .148 A4
Ticknell Piece Rd OX7 . . . . .73 B2
Tidmarsh La Oxford OX1 . . .123 A1
  Tidmarsh RG8 . . . . .256 A1
Tidmarsh Rd RG8 . . . . .256 B2
Tidmarsh St RG30 . . . . . . .258 A1
Tidmore La RG8 . . . . .240 C1
Tidworth Row OX18 . . . . . .152 C4
Tilbury CI OX4 . . . . .259 B2
Tilbury La OX2 . . . . .122 B1
Tilebarn CI RG9 . . . . .244 B1
Tilebarn La RG9 . . . . .254 A4
Tilehouse CI OX3 . . . . .124 C2
Tilehurst Sta RG31 . . . . . . .257 C2
Tilgarsley Rd OX29 . . . . . . .120 B4
Tilling CI RG31 . . . . .257 A1
Tilsley Rd OX7 . . . . .42 B1
Timber Way OX39 . . . . .168 B3
Timber Yard Cotts OX7 . . . . .74 B4
Timbers La RG9 . . . . .223 B1
Timms Rd OX16 . . . . .16 B1
Timothy Way ■ OX4 . . . . . .142 C1
Tinkerbush La OX12 . . . . . .214 B3
Tinkers La OX17 . . . . .3 C2
Tirrold Way OX12 . . . . .214 C3
Titchener CI OX26 . . . . .65 B2
Tite La OX15 . . . . .30 A4
Tithe Ct OX16 . . . . .16 A3
Tithe La OX15 . . . . .34 B3
Tithings The OX15 . . . . .19 C4
Titup Hall Dr OX3 . . . . .124 C2
Tiverton CI RG5 . . . . .260 C1
Tokers Green Rd RG4 . . . . .258 C4
Tokersgreen La
  Mapledurham RG4 . . . . . . .258 B3
  Reading RG4 . . . . .258 B3
Tollbrook Cnr OX15 . . . . . . .78 B1
Tollgate Rd ■ OX26 . . . . . . .65 C1
Tollgate Rd OX44 . . . . .180 A2
Tollington Ct SN7 . . . . .172 C1
Tolsey Mus* OX10 . . . . . . .100 C3
Tomkin's Almshouses ■
  OX14 . . . . .179 C4
Tompkins La OX27 . . . . .67 C1
Tompkins Terr OX5 . . . . .93 C1
Toot Hill Butts OX3 . . . . . . .124 C2
Top Station Rd NN13 . . . . . .24 A4
Torridge Dr OX11 . . . . .201 A1
Tothill OX7 . . . . .70 B1
Tower CI Abingdon OX14 . . .179 B3
  Marcham OX13 . . . . .178 B3
  Reading RG4 . . . . .259 B2
Tower Cres OX1 . . . . .123 B1
Tower Farm CI OX9 . . . . . . .147 B4
Tower Gdns OX11 . . . . .200 B1
Tower Hill OX28 . . . . .117 C4
Tower Hill Com Sch
  OX28 . . . . .104 A1
Tower Rd OX10 . . . . .182 B3
Tower View SN7 . . . . .172 C1
Towersey Dr OX9 . . . . .148 A4
Towersey Rd OX9 . . . . .148 A4
Town CI Finmere MK18 . . . . .39 B3
  Sutton Courtenay OX14 . . . .200 A4

Town End Rd
  Bledlow Ridge HP14 . . . . . .189 B4
  Faringdon SN7 . . . . .172 C1
Town Furlong
  Appleton OX13 . . . . .158 A4
  Bodicote OX15 . . . . .22 B4
Town Furze OX3 . . . . .142 B4
Town Gn The OX5 . . . . .92 C1
Town Pond La OX13 . . . . . .176 B4
Town Well End OX27 . . . . . .49 C4
Townhill OX5 . . . . .2 A2
Townlands Hospl RG9 . . . . .244 B1
Towns End OX17 . . . . .104 A3
Townsend
  Abingdon OX14 . . . . .179 C3
  Banbury OX16 . . . . .16 A3
  Barford St M OX15 . . . . . . .32 C3
  Harwell OX11 . . . . .217 C4
  Harwell, Chilton OX11 . . . . .217 B1
  Marsh Gibbon OX27 . . . . . .67 C1
Townsend La
  Marsh Gibbon OX27 . . . . . .67 C1
  Middleton Cheney OX17 . . . .11 C3
Townsend Rd
  Aldworth RG8 . . . . .247 C2
  Shrivenham SN6 . . . . .209 A3
  Streatley RG8 . . . . .249 A4
Townsend Sq OX4 . . . . . . .141 C3
Townside HP17 . . . . .130 C3
Toy La OX7 . . . . .42 B1
Toynbee CI OX2 . . . . .140 B4
Trafford Rd Oxford OX3 . . . .124 C2
  Reading RG1 . . . . .258 C1
Traitor's Ford La OX15 . . . . .18 B2
Tramhill HP18 . . . . .98 A1
Tramway Ind Est The
  OX16 . . . . .16 C3
Tramway Rd OX16 . . . . .16 C3
Treadwells SN7 . . . . .194 C4
Treble House Terr
  OX11 . . . . .237 A4
Tredegar Rd RG4 . . . . .259 A3
Tree La OX4 . . . . .142 A2
Treeground PI OX5 . . . . . . .108 C4
Trefoil PI OX4 . . . . .143 A1
Treforgan RG4 . . . . .258 C3
Trelawney Dr OX16 . . . . . . .257 B1
Trenchard Ave OX14 . . . . . .199 B2
Trenchard Circ OX25 . . . . . .49 B1
Trenchard CI OX10 . . . . . . .221 B4
Trendell PI OX14 . . . . .159 C1
Trent Cres OX26 . . . . .65 A2
Trent Rd OX11 . . . . .201 A1
Trenthams CI RG8 . . . . . . .257 A3
Trevor PI OX4 . . . . .142 A3
Trill Mill Ct OX1 . . . . .141 B4
Trinder Rd OX12 . . . . .214 C2
Tring Rd RG31 . . . . .257 B1
Trinity CE Prim Sch
  RG9 . . . . .244 B1
Trinity CI Abingdon OX14 . . .160 A1
  Banbury OX16 . . . . .15 C4
Trinity PI OX11 . . . . .123 B1
Trinity Rd OX3 . . . . .124 C1
Trinity St OX1 . . . . .141 B4
Trinity Way OX17 . . . . .23 B2
Tristram Rd OX29 . . . . .118 A2
Troika CI OX10 . . . . .9 A2
Trot's La OX7 . . . . .85 B4
Troy CI OX3 . . . . .142 C4
Troy La OX5 . . . . .77 C2
Truelocks Way OX12 . . . . . .214 C3
Truemper Gr OX27 . . . . .65 C4
Trust Cnr RG9 . . . . .254 C4
Tubb CI OX26 . . . . .65 B1
Tubbs CI OX12 . . . . .214 B4
Tubbs La OX26 . . . . .80 A4
Tubbs Rd OX26 . . . . .80 A4
Tuck's La OX13 . . . . .156 A2
Tucker Rd OX4 . . . . .142 C2
Tuckers La SN4 . . . . .227 A2
Tuckers Rd SN7 . . . . .173 A2
Tudor CI Banbury OX16 . . . . .16 B1
  Oxford OX4 . . . . .141 C2
Tudor Ct OX2 . . . . .140 A4
Tuer The
  Chadlington OX7 . . . . .57 A1
  Eynsham OX29 . . . . .120 C4
Tullis CI OX14 . . . . .199 C4
Tulwick La OX12 . . . . .197 A1
Tumbledown Hill OX2 . . . . .139 B3
Tumbling Bay Ct OX2 . . . . .123 A1
Tuns La RG9 . . . . .244 C1
Turberville CI OX14 . . . . . .179 C3
Turl St OX1 . . . . .123 B1
Turley La OX29 . . . . .104 A4
Turn Again La ■ OX1 . . . . .141 B4
Turnagain La OX14 . . . . . . .179 C3
Turnberry CI OX26 . . . . .66 A2
Turner CI OX4 . . . . .142 B3
Turner Ct OX5 . . . . .108 C4
Turner Rd OX14 . . . . .179 B3
Turner's Gn OX49 . . . . .205 B4
Turner's Green La
  Britwell Salome OX49 . . . . .205 B4
  Cuxham OX49 . . . . .185 B1
Turners CI OX14 . . . . .160 C1
Turnfields HP18 . . . . .128 A2
Turnpike Rd
  Bicester OX27 . . . . .66 A3
  Cumnor OX2 . . . . .140 A3
  Highworth SN6 . . . . .190 A3
Turnstone Gn OX26 . . . . . . .81 A4
Turret Ho OX2 . . . . .124 B2
Tuscan Ct RG30 . . . . .257 C1
Tweed Cres OX26 . . . . .65 A2

Tweed Dr OX11 . . . . .200 C2
Twelfth St OX11 . . . . .217 A2
Twelve Acre Dr OX14 . . . . .160 B2
Twentieth St OX11 . . . . . . .216 C1
Twin Oaks RG4 . . . . .259 A3
Twitchers Alley ■ OX26 . . . .65 C1
Two Rivers Ind Est
  OX28 . . . . .118 A3
Two Tree Hill RG9 . . . . . . .254 A4
Twyford Ave OX17 . . . . .23 A3
Twyford Gdns OX17 . . . . . . .23 A3
Twyford Gr OX17 . . . . .23 A3
Twyford Mill Ind Est
  OX17 . . . . .23 A1
Twyford Rd OX17 . . . . .23 B4
Twynhams Rd OX5 . . . . .77 B3
Tyburn Glen OX11 . . . . . . .200 C1
Tyler CI RG4 . . . . .258 C3
Tylorstown RG4 . . . . .258 C3
Tyndale PI OX33 . . . . .144 B4
Tyndale Rd OX4 . . . . .141 C4
Tyne Ave OX11 . . . . .200 C1
Tyne Rd OX13 . . . . .159 B1
Tyrell CI SN7 . . . . .194 B4
Tyrrell's Way OX14 . . . . . . .199 C3
Tyrrells CI OX11 . . . . .217 B3
Tyte End OX7 . . . . .29 A2

U

Uffington CE Prim Sch
  SN7 . . . . .211 B4
Uffington Gorse Nature
  Reserve* SN7 . . . . .211 C4
Uffington Trad Est SN7 . . . .193 C1
Ulfgar Rd OX2 . . . . .122 C4
Ullswater Dr RG31 . . . . . . .257 B2
Ulster CI RG4 . . . . .259 A3
Underhill OX10 . . . . .239 A2
Underhill Cir OX3 . . . . .124 C2
Unicorn St OX15 . . . . .21 B2
Union Sq OX20 . . . . .75 C2
Union St Banbury OX16 . . . . .16 A3
  Oxford OX4 . . . . .141 C4
  Woodstock OX20 . . . . .91 A3
Union Way OX28 . . . . .117 C4
Unity CI RG4 . . . . .259 A3
Unity Cres OX16 . . . . .15 C4
University College OX1 . . . .123 B1
Univ Coll Oxford (Annexe)
  OX1 . . . . .123 B2
Univ Mus & Pitt Rivers Mus*
  OX1 . . . . .123 B2
Univ Of Oxford Mathematical
  Inst OX1 . . . . .123 B1
Untons PI SN7 . . . . .173 A2
Upavon Way OX18 . . . . . . .115 B2
Upland Park Rd OX3 . . . . . .124 A4
Uplands Rd RG4 . . . . .258 C3
Uplands Rise OX17 . . . . .9 B3
Upper Barr ■ OX4 . . . . . . .142 B2
Upper Brook Hill OX20 . . . . .91 A3
Upper Campsfield Rd
  OX20 . . . . .91 C3
Upper Comm La SN7 . . . . .211 B4
Upper Cres SN7 . . . . .194 B4
Upper Cres OX29 . . . . .102 C1
Upper Cross La OX11 . . . . .218 C3
Upper End
  Fulbrook OX18 . . . . .100 C4
  Shipton-u-W OX7 . . . . .85 B3
Upper Fisher Row OX1 . . . .123 A1
Upper Gn SN7 . . . . .194 C4
Upper Rd OX1 . . . . .141 C1
Upper Red Cross Rd
  RG8 . . . . .249 B3
Upper Warren Ave RG4 . . . .258 B2
Upper Windsor St OX16 . . . .16 B2
Upper Woodcote Rd
  RG4 . . . . .258 B3
Upperway Furlong
  OX11 . . . . .201 A1
Uppingham Gdns RG4 . . . . .259 B3
Upthorpe Dr OX12 . . . . . . .214 C3
Upton CI Abingdon OX14 . . .160 A1
  Henley-on-T RG9 . . . . .244 C1
  Oxford OX4 . . . . .142 B1
Upton Ct OX16 . . . . .16 B3
Upton Ho* OX15 . . . . .6 B4
Upway Rd OX3 . . . . .124 A3
Upwood Dr OX18 . . . . .115 C2
Urquhart La OX10 . . . . . . .241 A4
Usk Way OX11 . . . . .201 A2
Uxmore Rd RG8 . . . . .241 C2

V

Vale & Downland Mus*
  OX12 . . . . .214 B2
Vale Ave OX12 . . . . .196 C1
Vale Cres RG30 . . . . .257 C1
Vale Rd Harwell OX11 . . . . .217 A2
  Witney OX28 . . . . .117 C4
Valence Cres OX28 . . . . . . .103 C1
Valentia CI OX5 . . . . .92 C4
Valentia Rd OX3 . . . . .124 B1
Valentine Cres RG4 . . . . . . .259 B2
Valetta Way OX10 . . . . .204 B2
Valley CI RG4 . . . . .258 C4
Valley Cotts RG9 . . . . .243 C4
Valley Cres NN13 . . . . .24 A4
Valley Rd Banbury OX16 . . . .16 B2
  Brackley NN13 . . . . .24 A4
  Finmere MK18 . . . . .39 B3

Valley Rd continued
  Henley-on-T RG9 . . . . .254 A4
  Horspath OX33 . . . . .143 C3
Valley Rise NN13 . . . . .24 A4
Valley Road Prim Sch
  RG9 . . . . .254 B4
Valley View
  Great Bourton OX17 . . . . . . .9 B4
  Lower Heyford OX25 . . . . . .62 C3
Van Dieman's SN7 . . . . . . .194 B4
Van Dieman's Rd OX9 . . . . .147 C4
Van Diemens CI OX18 . . . . .134 A3
Van-Dieman's La OX4 . . . . .142 B2
Vanalloys Bsns Pk RG9 . . . .242 A2
Vanbrugh CI OX20 . . . . .91 A4
Vane Rd OX9 . . . . .148 A4
Vanner Rd OX28 . . . . .104 A1
Vastern Rd RG1 . . . . .259 A1
Vauxhall Way OX11 . . . . . . .200 B1
Venables CI OX2 . . . . .123 A2
Venetia CI RG4 . . . . .259 B4
Venners Water OX11 . . . . . .201 A2
Ventfield CI OX33 . . . . .112 A3
Ventnor Rd RG31 . . . . .257 B1
Venvell CI OX7 . . . . .58 C3
Verbena Way ■ OX4 . . . . . .142 C1
Verlam Gr OX11 . . . . .201 A1
Vermont Dr OX20 . . . . .91 A4
Vernon Ave OX2 . . . . .140 C3
Vernon Ave OX12 . . . . .42 C1
Vervain CI OX26 . . . . .65 C3
Vestry CI OX12 . . . . .196 B1
Vetch PI OX4 . . . . .142 C1
Vicarage CI Aston OX18 . . . .135 B2
  Chalgrove OX44 . . . . .184 B4
  Grove OX12 . . . . .196 C1
  Oxford OX4 . . . . .142 A1
Vicarage Ct ■ OX16 . . . . . . .16 B3
Vicarage Flats OX17 . . . . . . .4 C1
Vicarage Gdns OX17 . . . . . . .4 C1
Vicarage Hill OX12 . . . . . . .214 A2
Vicarage La
  Highworth SN6 . . . . .190 A3
  Long Compton CV36 . . . . . .27 C3
  Oxford OX1 . . . . .141 B3
  Piddington OX25 . . . . .97 C3
  Shrivenham SN6 . . . . .209 B3
Vicarage Rd Didcot OX11 . . .218 C4
  Henley-on-T RG9 . . . . .254 A4
  Kidlington OX5 . . . . .92 C1
  Oxford OX1 . . . . .141 B3
  Steventon OX13 . . . . .198 C2
Vicarage Wood Way
  RG31 . . . . .257 A1
Vicars Row ■ OX12 . . . . . . .214 B2
Viceroy Rd GL54 . . . . .68 A3
Vicks CI OX18 . . . . .100 C3
Victor St OX2 . . . . .123 A1
Victoria Cotts OX18 . . . . . .134 C2
Victoria Ct Bicester OX26 . . .65 C1
  Henley-on-T RG9 . . . . .244 C1
  Oxford OX1 . . . . .123 B1
Victoria Gate OX2 . . . . .123 A4
Victoria Hospl OX9 . . . . . . .148 A4
Victoria Mead OX3 . . . . . . .148 A4
Victoria PI Banbury OX16 . . .16 C3
  Chipping Norton OX7 . . . . . .42 C2
Victoria Rd
  Abingdon OX14 . . . . .179 B4
  Bicester OX26 . . . . .65 C1
  Cutteslowe OX2 . . . . .123 A4
  Reading, Tilehurst RG31 . . .257 B1
  Wargrave RG10 . . . . .255 C1
Viking Dr OX11 . . . . .218 A4
Viking Terr OX10 . . . . .204 B2
Village Farm Ct OX25 . . . . . .79 A1
Village Rd OX17 . . . . .3 A2
Villeboys CI OX14 . . . . .180 B4
Villiers Ct ■ OX14 . . . . . . .142 A2
Villiers La OX4 . . . . .142 A2
Villiers Rd OX26 . . . . .65 B1
Vine Cotts Bicester OX26 . . .65 C1
  Cuddesdon OX44 . . . . .144 A1
Vine The HP18 . . . . .128 B2
Viner CI OX28 . . . . .104 B1
Vinery The RG10 . . . . .255 B1
Vines The ■ OX14 . . . . . . .179 C4
Vineyard OX14 . . . . .179 C4
Vineyard CI OX16 . . . . .16 B4
Violet Way OX4 . . . . .161 C4
Virginia Gdns HP14 . . . . . . .189 C4
Virginia Way OX14 . . . . . . .179 B3
Viscount Ind Est
  Bampton OX18 . . . . .134 B4
  Brize Norton OX18 . . . . . . .116 B1
Vivienne Ct OX3 . . . . .124 B1
Volunteer Way SN7 . . . . . . .173 A1
Vorda Rd SN6 . . . . .190 A3

W

Wadard's Mdw OX28 . . . . . .118 B4
Wadham CI OX26 . . . . .65 C2
Wadham Coll OX1 . . . . .123 B1
Waine Rush View OX28 . . . .118 A4
Wainwrights HP14 . . . . .189 B3
Waites CI OX18 . . . . .135 C1
Wales St OX17 . . . . .3 C3
Waleys PI ■ RG4 . . . . .259 B1
Walk The OX5 . . . . .93 C4
Walker Cl OX18 . . . . .134 C1
Walker Dr OX9 . . . . .148 A4
Walker's CI OX18 . . . . .101 C2
Walker's Ht OX7 . . . . .88 B2
Walkers CI OX39 . . . . .106 A3
Wallace CI OX14 . . . . .179 C3

Walled Gdn The RG10 .....255 B1
Walled Gdns The OX26 ....65 C1
Waller Ct RG4 ....259 A1
Waller Dr OX16 ....16 A2
Wallingford Com Hospl OX10 ...221 B3
Wallingford Mus* OX10 ...221 B4
Wallingford Rd
  Cholsey OX10 ....221 A2
  Crowmarsh G OX10 ....221 C1
  Goring OX10,RG8 ......239 B3
  South Stoke OX10,RG8 ..239 B3
  Streatley RG8 ....249 A4
  Warborough OX10 ......203 A3
Wallingford Sch OX10 ....221 B4
Wallingford St OX12 .....214 C2
Walls The SN7 ....194 C4
Walmer Rd RG5 ....260 C1
Walnut Cl Bicester OX26 ..65 C3
  Deddington OX15 ....34 C2
  Long Crendon HP18 ....129 B4
  Sonning Common RG4 ..252 C3
  Witney OX28 ....117 C4
  Wootton OX20 ....75 C2
Walnut Ct SN7 ....172 C2
Walnut Gdns OX17 ......1 B1
Walnut Rise OX25 ......48 C3
Walnut Row OX18 ......94 C3
Walnut Tree Ct RG8 ....249 B3
Walnut Trees Hill SN6 ..228 A4
Walpole Cl ■ OX26 .....65 B2
Walter's Row OX4 .....123 C1
Walterbush Rd OX7 ....42 C1
Waltham Ct RG8 ....249 B4
Waltham Gdns OX16 ...17 A3
Walton Ave
  Adderbury OX17 ......23 A3
  Henley-on-T RG9 .....254 C4
Walton Cl OX15 ....22 C4
Walton Cres OX1 .....123 A1
Walton La OX1 ....123 B1
Walton Manor Ct OX2 ..123 A2
Walton St OX1,OX2 ...123 A1
Walton Well Rd OX2 ..123 A2
Wanbourne La RG9 ...182 B1
Wandhope Way RG31 ..257 B1
Wansbeck Dr OX26 ....65 A2
Wansbeck Wood OX11 ..201 A2
Wantage CE Inf Sch OX12 ...214 B2
Wantage CE Jun Sch OX12 ...214 C3
Wantage CE Prim Sch OX12 ...214 C3
Wantage Hospl OX12 ..214 C3
Wantage Rd Didcot OX11 ..218 B4
  Harwell OX11 ....217 B3
  Streatley RG8 ....248 C4
  Wallingford OX10 .....203 A1
Wapping HP18 ....129 B3
War Meml Pl RG9 .....254 C4
Warbler WlK OX4 .....142 C1
Warborough Rd
  Letcombe Bassett OX12 ..232 A4
  Warborough OX10 .....203 A3
Warbreck Dr RG31 ....257 A2
Warburg Cres OX4 ....142 C2
Warburg Nature Reserve* RG9 ...225 A3
Ward Rd NN13 ....24 A3
Ward's La OX7 ....88 B3
Wardington Rd OX17 ..10 B3
Wardle Ave OX31 .....159 A1
Wards Cres OX15 ....22 C4
Wards Rd OX7 ....42 C2
Ware Leys Cl OX27 ..67 C2
Ware Rd SN7 ....194 B4
Wargrave Hill RG10 ..255 B1
Wargrave Rd
  Cockpole Green RG9 ..255 A4
  Henley-on-T RG9 .....244 C1
Wargrave Sta RG10 ..255 B1
Warkworth Cl OX16 ..115 C4
Warkworth Rd OX17 ..17 C4
Warley Rise RG31 ....257 B2
Warmans Cl OX12 ....214 A3
Warnborough Coll OX1 ..159 C4
Warnborough Rd OX2 ..123 A2
Warneford Hospl OX3, OX4 ...124 A1
Warneford La OX3 ....124 A1
Warneford Rd OX4 ...124 A1
Warner Cres OX11 ...218 B4
Warping House Cotts OX7 ...42 B1
Warren Cres OX3 ....142 B4
Warren Ct RG4 ......258 C1
Warren Hill OX44 ....163 B1
Warren Ho OX4 .....158 C1
Warren House Ct RG4 ..258 C1
Warren Rd RG5 .....260 B1
Warren Row Rd RG10 ..255 C4
Warren The
  Abingdon OX14 ......180 A4
  Reading RG4 ....258 B2
Warriner Comp Sch The OX15 ...21 C3
Warwick Cl
  Abingdon OX14 ......180 A4
  Carterton OX18 ......115 B2
  Stanford in the V SN7 ..194 C4
Warwick Ct ■ OX26 ...66 A2
Warwick Rd OX16,OX17 ..8 C2
Warwick St OX4 .....141 C4
Wasbrough Ave OX12 ..214 B3
Washford Glen OX11 ..201 A1
Washington Rd RG4 ..259 A1

Washington Terr OX7 ...60 C4
Wastie's Orch OX29 ...90 A1
Watchfield Prim Sch SN6 ...191 B1
Watcombe Manor Ind Est OX49 ...186 A1
Watcombe Rd OX49 ...186 A1
Water Eaton La OX5 ..109 A4
Water Eaton Rd OX2 ..123 B4
Water End Rd HP14 ..189 B2
Water La Adderbury OX12 ..23 A2
  Ardley OX27 ....50 A2
  Bloxham OX15 ....21 C3
  Brackley NN13 ......24 A4
  Drayton St L OX10 ..183 A3
  Little Tew OX7 ......45 A3
  Steeple Aston OX25 ..62 A4
Water St OX25 ......48 C3
Watercress Cl OX15 ..22 C4
Waterfowl Sanctuary & Children's Farm* OX15 ...20 A1
Waterloo Cl OX10 ...239 A4
Waterloo Dr OX16 ...16 C3
Waterman Pl RG1 ...259 A1
Waterman's La RG6 ..258 C4
Waterman's Way RG10 ..255 B1
Watermans Reach 20 OX1 ...141 B4
Watermead OX5 .....109 A4
Watermill Way OX3 ..125 A2
Waterperry OX33 ....127 A1
Waterperry Ct ■ OX16 ..16 C3
Waterperry Gdns* OX33 ...127 A1
Waterperry Rd HP18 ..127 B3
Waters La OX17 .....11 A1
Waterside Cotts RG4 ..260 A2
Waterside Dr RG8 ...257 B3
Waterside Villas OX14 ..181 C3
Waterslade Pens HP17 ..130 C3
Watery La Brackley NN13 ..24 A4
  Clifton Hampden OX14 ..181 B2
  Hook Norton OX15 ....30 A4
  Sparsholt OX12 ....212 C2
Wates Way OX16 ....16 C4
Watling La OX10 ....182 B1
Watlington Hill* OX49 ..206 C4
Watlington Hospl OX49 ..186 B1
Watlington Ind Est OX49 ...186 A1
Watlington Rd
  Benson OX10 ....203 C2
  Garsington OX44 .....162 B4
  Lewknor OX49 ....186 C3
  Oxford OX4 ....142 C2
Watlington St RG9 ..244 C2
Watson Cres OX13 ..159 A4
Watsons Cl OX18 ...115 C1
Watt's La OX11 .....237 A4
Watts Way OX5 .....92 C2
Waveney Cl Bicester OX26 ..65 A1
  Didcot OX11 ....201 A1
Waverley Ave OX5 ..109 A4
Wavers Ground OX15 ..115 C2
Waxes Cl OX14 .....160 B1
Wayfaring Cl OX4 ...161 C4
Wayfarings OX26 ...65 C3
Wayland Cres OX11 ..217 B1
Wayland Rd OX12 ..196 B1
Waynflete Rd OX3 ..125 A2
Wayside Gn RG8 ...240 C1
Wayside Ho OX26 ..65 C2
Weald Rise RG30 ..257 C1
Weald St OX18 ....134 C1
Wealden Way RG30 ..257 C1
Wear Rd OX26 .....65 A1
Weaver Croft OX11 ..202 C1
Weavers Cl OX28 ..118 A4
Weavers Cotts CF36 ..27 C1
Weavers Row OX15 ..14 A3
Webb Cl OX10 .....16 C4
Webb Cres OX7 ...42 B1
Webb's Cl OX12 ...202 B1
Webb's Way OX5 ..92 C1
Webbs Cl OX7 ....57 A1
Webster Cl OX9 ...129 C1
Webster's Cl OX29 ..106 A3
Wedgewood Way RG30 ..257 C1
Wedgwood Rd OX26 ..66 A2
Weedon Cl OX10 ..239 A4
Weedon Ct ■ OX10 ..221 B4
Weeping Cross OX15 ..22 C4
Weighbridge Row RG1 ..258 C1
Weir La OX25 .....82 A2
Weirs La OX1 ....141 B3
Welch Way OX28 ..118 A4
Weldon Rd OX3 ..123 C2
Weldon Way OX9 ..148 A4
Welford Gdns OX14 ..160 A1
Well Bank OX15 ..30 A4
Well Hill OX7 ....88 B3
Well La Curbridge OX29 ..117 B3
  Shenington OX15 ...6 C1
  Stonesfield OX29 ...89 B4
Well View RG9 ...241 C2
Welland Ave OX11 ..201 A1
Welland Cl
  Abingdon OX13 ....159 B1
  Reading RG31 .....257 B1
Welland Croft OX26 ..65 A1
Weller Cl OX10 ...204 A4
Wellesbourne Cl OX14 ..180 A4
Wellesley Cl OX16 ..16 C3
Wellington Ave OX16 ..16 C3
Wellington Cl OX26 ..66 A2
Wellington Cotts OX7 ..73 A1
Wellington Pl OX1 ..123 B1

Wellington Rd GL54 ..68 A2
Wellington Sq
  Oxford OX1 ....123 B1
  Watchfield SN6 .....191 B1
Wellington St
  Oxford OX1 ....123 A1
  Thame OX9 ....148 A4
Wellplace Zoo* OX10 ..240 C4
Wellshead La OX11 ..217 C3
Wellsprings OX10 ...202 C1
Wenlock Cl OX11 ...200 B1
Wenman Rd Thame OX9 ..148 A3
  Witney OX28 ....117 C4
Wenric Dr OX29 ...102 C1
Wensum Cres OX26 ..65 A2
Wensum Dr OX11 ..201 A1
Wentworth Rd
  Cutteslowe OX2 ....123 A4
  Thame OX9 ....148 A4
Wesley Cl Bicester OX26 ..65 B2
  Oxford OX4 ....142 C2
Wesley Dr OX16 ...16 A2
Wesley Green Mid Sch OX4 ...142 C1
Wesley La 6 OX26 ..65 C1
Wesley Pl OX17 ...10 C2
Wessex Cl SN7 ...173 A2
Wessex Ind Est OX28 ..118 A3
Wessex Rd Benson OX10 ..204 B2
  Didcot OX11 ....218 C4
Wessex Way
  Bicester OX26 ....65 C1
  Oxford OX2 ....214 B4
  Highworth SN6 .....190 A4
West Allcourt GL7 ..150 B2
West Ave OX14 ...160 A1
West Bar St OX16 ..16 B3
West Chiltern RG8 ..250 C4
West Cotts OX27 ..52 B1
West Croft OX10 ..182 B3
West Ct Banbury OX16 ..16 C3
  Sonning RG4 ....260 C1
West Dr Harwell OX11 ..217 A2
  Sonning RG4 ....260 B1
West Edge OX27 ...67 C1
West End
  Brightwell-cum-S OX10 ..202 B1
  Chipping Norton OX7 ..42 C1
  Cholsey OX10 ....220 C1
  Combe OX29 ....90 A2
  Hornton OX15 ......7 B3
  Kingham OX7 ....54 C2
  Launton OX26 ......66 C2
  Shilton OX18 ....115 A3
  Witney OX28 ....104 A1
  Wootton OX20 ......75 C2
West End Cd OX26 ..66 B1
West End Ind Est OX28 ..104 A1
West End La
  Bishopstone SN6 ..227 B2
  Merton OX25 ......95 A4
West Gr OX2 ......123 A4
West Hawthorn Rd OX25 ..81 B2
West Hill OX12 ....214 B2
West Ilsley Ho OX11 ..235 A1
West Kidlington Cty Prim Sch
  OX5 ....108 C4
West La RG9 ......244 C1
West Oxford Prim Sch OX2 ...123 A1
West Oxon Ind Pk OX18 ..115 C2
West St Banbury OX16 ..65 B2
  Bicester OX26 ......65 B2
  Childrey OX12 .....213 A2
  Chipping Norton OX7 ..42 C1
  Henley-on-T RG9 ..244 B1
  Kingham OX7 ......32 B3
  Oxford OX2 ....123 A1
  Shutford OX15 ....14 A3
  Sparsholt OX12 ...22 C4
West St Helen St OX14 ..179 C3
West View
  5 Oxford OX4 ......142 A2
  Sandford OX25 ....49 A3
West Way Lechlade GL7 ..150 B3
  N Hinksey Village OX2 ..122 B1
West Witney Cty Prim Sch
  OX28 ....117 C4
West Wood Farm Cty Jun &
  Inf Sch RG31 ......257 B2
Westacott Rd OX26 ..81 A3
Westbeech Ct OX16 ..16 B3
Westbourne Ct OX15 ..21 C2
Westbrook
  Faringdon SN7 ....172 C2
  Grove OX12 ....196 C1
Westbrook Gn OX11 ..236 C4
Westbrook Rd OX11 ..236 B1
Westbrook St OX11 ..236 C4
Westbury Cres OX4 ..142 A2
Westbury La RG8 ...257 A3
Westbury Terr OX27 ..67 C1
Westcot La OX12 ..227 A2
Westcote Cl OX28 ..117 B4
Westdene Cres RG4 ..258 C2
Western Ave
  Henley-on-T RG9 ...254 C4
  Sonning RG5 ......260 C1
Western Bsns Pk OX5 ..78 C3
Western By-pass Rd
  Cutteslowe OX2 ...108 C1
  Wytham OX2 ......122 B3
Western Cres OX16 ..16 C2
Western Oaks RG31 ..257 C2
Western Rd
  Henley-on-T RG9 ...254 C4
  Oxford OX1 ....141 B4

Whitehall La RG8 ....241 B2
Whitehills Gn RG8 ...249 B3
Whitehorn Way 图 OX14 ..142 C1
Whitehorns Farm Rd OX12 ...215 A3
Whitehorns Way OX14 ..179 A1
Whitehouse Cl OX13 ..159 B1
Whitehouse La OX7 ..42 C2
Whitehouse Rd
  Oxford OX1 ....141 B4
  Woodcote RG8 .....250 C4
Whitelock Rd OX14 ..159 C1
Whites Forge OX13 ..158 A4
Whiteway OX17 ....3 C2
Whitings La OX29 ..104 A4
Whitley Cres OX26 ..66 A2
Whitley Rd OX26 ..63 B4
Whitley Rd OX10 ..221 A3
Whitson Pl OX4 ...142 A4
Whittall St OX17 ..23 C3
Whittington Pl OX18 ..115 B1
Whittle Rd OX9 ..148 A4
Whittons Cl OX15 ..30 A4
Whitworth Pl OX2 ..123 A1
Wick Cl Abingdon OX14 ..160 B1
  Oxford OX3 ....124 C2
Wick Gn OX12 ....196 B1
Wick Hall OX14 ..180 B4
Wicks Cl OX18 ...152 C4
Widmere La RG4 ..253 A3
Widnell La OX25 ..97 B4
Wigan's La HP27 ..169 B3
Wigginton Rd OX15 ..31 B4
Wigmore La
  Reading RG30 .....258 A1
  Reading RG30 .....258 B1
Wigod Way OX10 ..203 B1
Wilberforce St OX3 ..124 B1
Wilcher Cl OX11 ..218 C3
Wilcote La OX7 ..88 A2
Wilcote Rd OX3 ..124 C2
Wilcote Riding OX7 ..88 B3
Wilcote View OX7 ..105 C3
Wilcox Rd OX7 ...42 C2
Wilder Ave RG8 ..256 C3
Wilding Rd OX10 ..203 B1
Wildmere Cl OX16 ..16 C1
Wildmere Ind Est OX16 ..16 C1
Wildmere Rd OX16 ..16 C1
Wildmoor Gate OX14 ..159 C1
Wilkins Ho OX7 ..42 C1
Wilkins Rd OX4 ..142 B3
Willes Cl SN7 ...172 C2
William Bliss Ave OX7 ..42 C1
William Cl OX16 ..15 C4
William Fletcher Cty Prim Sch OX5 ...108 A3
William Kimber Cres OX3 ...124 C2
William Morris Prim Sch OX16 ...15 C4
William Orchard Cl OX3 ..124 B2
William Smith Cl OX7 ..55 C2
William St OX3 ...123 C2
Williams Mews OX28 ..118 A4
Williamscot Hill OX17 ..10 A3
Williamson Way OX4 ..142 A2
Willis Ct OX7 ....70 B1
Willoughby Rd OX16 ..16 A1
Willow Bank Jun & Inf Sch RG5 ...260 C1
Willow Brook OX14 ..179 B4
Willow Cl
  Garsington OX44 ..143 B1
  Watlington OX49 ..186 A1
  Yarnton OX5 ......108 A3
Willow Cotts OX10 ..238 C3
Willow Court La OX13 ..238 C3
Willow End
  Ambrosden OX25 ..81 B2
  Little Compton GL56 ..27 A1
Willow Gdns RG31 ..257 A1
Willow La Milton OX44 ..199 B3
  Wantage OX12 .....214 B2
  Wargrave RG10 ...255 B2
Willow Mead OX44 ..184 B3
Willow Rd
  Ambrosden OX25 ..81 B2
  Banbury OX16 ....24 A3
  Brackley NN13 ...24 A3
  Chinnor OX39 ....168 B3
  Thame OX9 ....129 C1
Willow Tree Cl OX13 ..159 B1
Willow Way Begbroke OX5 ..92 A1
  Kennington OX1,OX14 ..160 C4
  Oxford OX4 ....142 C1
Willow Wlk OX12 ..214 B3
Willowbrook OX29 ..137 C4
Willows Cl RG8 ...256 B3
Willows Edge OX29 ..120 B4
Willows Gate OX27 ..52 B1
Willows The Grove OX12 ..214 B4
  Highworth SN6 ...190 A3
  Reading RG4 .....259 A1
  Witney OX28 .....104 A4
  Wootton (Oxford) OX1 ..159 A4
Willowside RG5 ...260 C1
Wills Rd OX11 ...200 B1
Wilmot Cl OX28 ..117 C3
Wilmot Way OX12 ..214 A2
Wilmots OX44 ...162 A3
Wilsdon Way OX5 ..92 B1
Wilsham Rd OX14 ..179 C3
Wilson Ave RG9 ..254 C4

Wilson Way OX27 . . . . . . **.65** C4
Winsons CI OX14 . . . . . . **.201** B4
Wilwyne CI RG4 . . . . **.259** B2
Wimble Straw Rd OX10 .**.182** B2
Wimblestraw Rd OX10 .**.182** B3
Wimborn CI OX15 . . . . **.33** C2
Wimborne Ave OX16 . . . . . **.16** A3
Wimborne Gdns RG30 .**.258** A1
Winaway OX11 . . . . **.217** B3
Winchelsea CI OX16 . . . . . . **.8** C1
Winchester CI OX16 . . . . **.16** C4
Winchester Rd OX2 . . . . **.123** A2
Winchester Way OX12 .**.214** B3
Wincroft Rd RG4 . . . . . . **.258** C3
Windale Ave OX4 . . . . . . **.142** C1
Windale Fst Sch OX4 . . **.142** C1
Windale Ho **50** OX4 . . . . **.142** C1
Windbush Mews OX11 . .**.201** A2
Windle Gdns OX26 . . . . **.65** B1
Windmill Ave OX26 . . . . . . **.65** C2
Windmill CI Banbury OX16 .**.16** B2
　Deddington OX15 . . . . **.33** C2
　North Leigh OX29 . . . . **.105** A3
　Towersey OX9 . . . . **.148** C4
Windmill Fst Sch The
　OX3 . . . . **.124** B1
Windmill Hts OX29 . . . . . **.105** A3
Windmill La OX33 . . . . . . **.144** A4
Windmill PI OX12 . . . . . . **.213** C2
Windmill Rd
　Haddenham HP17 . . . . . . **.130** C3
　North Leigh OX29 . . . . **.105** A3
　Oxford OX3 . . . . **.124** B1
　Thame OX9 . . . . **.147** C4
　Towersey OX9 . . . . **.148** C4
Windmill St Brill HP18 . . **.98** A1
　Deddington OX15 . . . . **.33** C2
Windrush OX16 . . . . **.16** A4
Windrush CI
　Bicester OX26 . . . . **.65** B1
　Burford OX18 . . . . **.100** C2
　Grove OX12 . . . . **.196** B1
　Witney OX28 . . . . **.103** C1
Windrush Ct
　Abingdon OX14 . . . . **.179** B4
　Burford OX18 . . . . **.100** C2
Windrush Park Rd OX29 .**.103** B1
Windrush Rd OX10 . . . . **.182** B2
Windrush Twr OX4 . . . . . **.142** C1
Windrush Valley Rd
　OX28 . . . . **.103** C1
Windrush Valley Sch
　OX7 . . . . **.71** B1
Windrush Way
　Abingdon OX14 . . . . **.160** A1
　Standlake OX29 . . . . **.137** B3
Windsor CI
　Carterton OX18 . . . . **.115** B1
　Didcot OX11 . . . . **.219** A4
　Kings Sutton OX17 . . . . . . **.23** C3
Windsor Cotts OX18 . . . **.134** C2
Windsor Cres
　East Hagbourne OX11 . . **.218** C3
　Marston OX3 . . . . **.123** C3
Windsor Ho RG9 . . . . **.254** C4
Windsor St Banbury OX16 . **.16** B3
　Oxford OX3 . . . . **.124** B1
Windsor Terr **24** OX16 . . **.16** B3
Windy Ridge SN7 . . . . . . **.173** A2
Wingate CI OX4 . . . . **.142** C2
Wingfield CI OX10 . . . . . **.204** C2
Wingfield Ct OX4 . . . . . . **.123** C1
Winnyards The OX2 . . . . **.139** C2
Winslet PI RG30 . . . . **.258** A1
Winsmore La **3** OX14 . . **.179** C3

Winston CI OX5 . . . . **.108** C4
Winston Dr OX17 . . . . **.8** C1
Winston Way RG8 . . . . . **.257** A3
Winter La OX12 . . . . **.196** C4
Winter's Field OX10 . . . **.221** C4
Winterberry Way RG4 . **.258** C3
Winterborne Rd OX14 . .**.179** B4
Winterbourne CI OX26 . . **.65** B1
Winterbrook OX10 . . . . **.221** B3
Winterbrook La OX10 . .**.221** B3
Wintergreen La OX10 . .**.221** B3
Winters Way OX15 . . . . . **.21** B2
Wintringham Way RG8 . **.257** B3
Wise Ave OX5 . . . . **.92** B1
Wise CI OX15 . . . . **.22** C4
Wise Cres OX27 . . . . **.52** B3
Wisteria The OX16 . . . . **.9** A1
Witan Way
　Wantage OX12 . . . . **.214** B3
　Witney OX28 . . . . **.118** A4
Wither's Ct OX7 . . . . **.42** C2
Withers Way OX7 . . . . . . **.42** C1
Withington Ct OX14 . . . **.179** C4
Withington Rd OX26 . . . . **.65** C1
Withycombe Dr OX16 . . **.15** C3
Witney Comm Hospl
　OX28 . . . . **.104** A1
Witney Comm Sch OX28 .**.104** A2
　OX28 . . . . **.118** A4
Witney La OX29 . . . . **.86** C2
Witney Rd
　Brize Norton OX18 . . . . . **.116** B3
　Crawley OX29 . . . . **.103** C2
　Ducklington OX29 . . . . . . **.118** A3
　Eynsham OX29 . . . . **.120** B4
　Finstock OX7 . . . . **.88** A3
　Leafield OX29 . . . . **.87** A1
　Long Hanborough OX29 . . **.90** A1
　Standlake OX29 . . . . **.137** A2
Witney St OX18 . . . . **.100** C3
Wittan PК OX28 . . . . **.118** A3
Wittenham CI
　Wallingford OX10 . . . . . . **.203** B1
　Woodcote RG8 . . . . **.250** C4
Wittenham La OX10 . . . **.202** B4
Woburn Ct Banbury OX16 . **.16** C4
　Reading RG4 . . . . **.258** C2
Wolfson Coll OX2 . . . . . . **.123** B3
Wolseley CI OX16 . . . . . . **.16** A4
Wolsely Ho OX4 . . . . **.142** B2
Wolsey CI OX20 . . . . **.91** C2
Wolsey Rd
　Cutteslowe OX2 . . . . **.109** A1
　Reading RG4 . . . . **.259** A1
Wolvercote Fst Sch
　OX2 . . . . **.122** C4
Wolvercote Gn OX2 . . . **.122** C4
Wolvercote Rdbt OX2 . **.108** C1
Wood End OX16 . . . . **.16** C2
Wood Farm Rd OX3 . . . **.124** C1
Wood Gn RG8 . . . . **.250** C4
Wood Green Sch OX28 . **.104** B1
Wood La Hailey OX29 . . **.104** A4
　Kidmore End RG4 . . . . . **.252** B2
　Sonning Common RG4 . . **.252** C3
　Woodcote RG8 . . . . **.250** B4
Wood Lane CI RG4 . . . . **.252** C3
Wood St OX10 . . . . **.221** B4
Wood's Farm Rd OX12 . **.216** B4
Woodberry CI RG4 . . . . **.259** A3
Woodbine PI OX1 . . . . . . **.123** A1
Woodbridge CI OX18 . . **.135** C1
Woodcote Cty Prim Sch
　RG8 . . . . **.240** C1
Woodcote Rd
　Bicester OX27 . . . . **.66** A4
　Reading RG4 . . . . **.258** C2
　South Stoke RG8 . . . . . . **.239** C2

Woodcote Way
　Abingdon OX14 . . . . **.179** C2
　Reading RG4 . . . . **.258** B3
Woodcroft OX1 . . . . **.141** C1
Woodean Ct OX4 . . . . . . **.123** C1
Woodeaton Manor Sch
　OX3 . . . . **.110** A3
Woodfarm Fst Sch OX3 .**.124** C1
Woodfield OX16 . . . . **.16** A4
Woodfield Dr OX7 . . . . . . **.73** B2
Woodfield Rd OX26 . . . . . **.65** C2
Woodford CI Enstone OX7 . **.58** C3
　Reading RG4 . . . . **.258** C2
Woodgate CI OX12 . . . . **.196** B1
Woodgreen OX28 . . . . . **.104** B1
Woodgreen Ave OX16 . . **.16** A3
Woodhall Dr OX16 . . . . . **.16** C2
Woodhill Dr OX12 . . . . . **.214** B4
Woodhill La OX12 . . . . . **.214** A4
Woodhouse Way OX4 . .**.142** A2
Woodland Rise OX29 . . . . **.89** B4
Woodlands
　4 Banbury OX16 . . . . **.16** A3
　Freeland OX29 . . . . **.106** A4
　Kidlington OX5 . . . . **.109** A4
　Standlake OX29 . . . . **.137** B2
Woodlands CI
　Milton-u-W OX7 . . . . **.70** A1
　Oxford OX3 . . . . **.124** A2
Woodlands Ct OX28 . . . **.104** B1
Woodlands Gr RG4 . . . . **.259** C2
Woodlands Rd
　Oxford OX3 . . . . **.124** A2
　Shiplake RG9 . . . . **.254** C2
　Sonning Common RG4 . . **.252** C3
　Witney OX28 . . . . **.104** B1
Woodlands The OX26 . . . **.79** C4
Woodley CI OX14 . . . . . . **.159** C2
Woodpecker CI OX26 . . . **.66** A4
Woodpecker Gn **15** OX4 .**.142** C1
Woodperry Rd OX3 . . . . **.111** A1
Woodpiece Rd OX25 . . . . **.96** C4
Woodrow Ct RG4 . . . . . **.258** C1
Woodruff CI OX4 . . . . . . **.142** C1
Woods Rd RG4 . . . . **.259** C2
Woodside OX29 . . . . **.105** B3
Woodside Dr OX18 . . . . **.114** B3
Woodside La RG4 . . . . . **.252** B3
Woodstock CE Prim Sch
　OX20 . . . . **.91** B3
Woodstock Cl OX2 . . . . **.123** A4
Woodstock Cl Flats
　OX2 . . . . **.123** A4
Woodstock Cl OX2 . . . . **.123** A4
Woodstock Mus* OX20 . . **.91** A3
Woodstock Rd
　Charlbury OX7 . . . . **.73** B1
　Kidlington OX5 . . . . **.91** C2
　Oxford OX2 . . . . **.123** A3
　Stonesfield OX29 . . . . **.89** B4
　Witney OX2,OX5 . . . . **.108** B2
Woodview SN7 . . . . **.172** C2
Woodview Rd RG8 . . . . **.256** B3
Woodville OX39 . . . . **.168** B3
Woodway Rd
　Blewbury OX11 . . . . **.237** A4
　Middle Barton OX7 . . . . . . **.60** C4
　Sibford Ferris OX15 . . . . . **.19** A4
Woolgate OX28 . . . . **.118** A4
Woolstone Rd SN7 . . . . . **.211** A3
Wootten Dr **1** OX4 . . . **.142** A2
Wootten End OX29 . . . . . **.89** B4
Wootton Bsns Pk OX13 .**.158** C4
Wootton CE Prim Sch
　OX20 . . . . **.75** C2

Wootton Rd
　Abingdon OX13,OX14 . . **.159** C1
　Henley-on-T RG9 . . . . . . **.254** B4
Wootton St Peter CE Prim
　Sch OX1 . . . . **.159** A4
Worcester Coll OX1 . . . **.123** A1
Worcester Pk OX11 . . . . **.219** A4
Worcester PI
　Kingston Bagpuize OX13 . .**.156** B1
　Oxford OX1 . . . . **.123** A1
Worcester Rd OX7 . . . . . . **.42** B1
Worcester Road Ind Est
　OX7 . . . . **.42** B2
Worcester St OX1 . . . . . **.123** A1
Wordsworth CI
　6 Bicester OX26 . . . . **.65** B2
　Stanford in the V SN7 . . **.194** B4
Wordsworth Ct RG4 . . . **.259** B4
Wordsworth Rd OX14 . .**.179** B3
Work House Yd OX20 . . . **.75** C2
Workhouse La OX15 . . . . **.21** B3
Wormald Rd OX10 . . . . **.221** B3
Worminghall Rd HP18 . **.127** C2
Wormsley Cres HP14 . . **.188** B2
Wornal Pk HP18 . . . . . . **.127** B4
Worsham Turn OX29 . . **.102** A3
Wortham Rd OX11 . . . . **.200** B1
Worthington Way OX12 . **.214** B3
Worton Rd OX7 . . . . **.46** C1
Worton End HP18 . . . . . . **.98** B4
Wren CI OX33 . . . . **.144** A4
Wren Rd OX2 . . . . **.109** B1
Wrenfield Dr RG4 . . . . . **.258** C3
Wright CI GL54 . . . . **.68** A3
Wright Rd GL54 . . . . **.68** A3
Wrightson CI OX33 . . . . **.143** B3
Wroslyn Rd OX29 . . . . . **.106** A4
Wroxton CE Prim Sch
　OX15 . . . . **.15** A4
Wroxton Coll OX15 . . . . . **.15** A4
Wroxton Ct OX15 . . . . . . **.15** A4
Wroxton Ho OX15 . . . . . **.15** A4
Wyatt Rd OX2 . . . . **.109** A1
Wychcotes RG4 . . . . **.258** C2
Wychwood CE Prim Sch
　OX7 . . . . **.70** B1
Wychwood CI
　Benson OX10 . . . . **.204** A2
　Carterton OX18 . . . . **.115** B3
　Charlbury OX7 . . . . **.73** B2
　Milton-u-W OX7 . . . . **.85** A4
　Sonning Common RG4 . . **.252** C3
　Witney OX28 . . . . **.117** C4
Wychwood Dr OX7 . . . . . **.70** A1
Wychwood Gdns OX16 . **.16** A2
Wychwood La OX3 . . . . **.125** A1
Wychwood Paddocks
　OX7 . . . . **.73** A2
Wychwood Sch OX2 . . **.123** B2
Wychwood View OX29 . **.102** C1
Wycombe Rd HP14 . . . . **.189** B2
Wycombe Way OX18 . . **.115** C1
Wye CI OX26 . . . . **.65** A2
Wyfold Cl RG9 . . . . **.242** A1
Wyfold La RG9 . . . . **.252** B4
Wyfold Rd RG4 . . . . **.252** A3
Wykeham Cres OX4 . . . **.142** A2
Wykeham Gate HP17 . . **.130** C4
Wykeham Pk OX9 . . . . . **.148** A4
Wykeham Rise OX39 . . **.168** B3
Wykeham Way HP17 . . **.130** C3
Wykham Gdns OX16 . . **.16** A2
Wykham La
　Banbury OX15,OX16 . . . . **.16** A1
　Broughton OX15,OX16 . . **.15** C1
Wykham Park (Tudor Hall
　Sch) OX16 . . . . **.22** A4
Wykham PI OX16 . . . . . . **.16** A2
Wyfie CI OX3 . . . . **.124** B1

Wynbush Rd OX4 . . . . . **.142** A2
Wynchway Ho OX15 . . . **.33** C2
Wyncies The SN6 . . . . . . **.227** B2
Wyndale CI RG9 . . . . . . **.244** C1
Wyndham Cres RG5 . . **.260** B1
Wyndham Gdns OX10 . **.221** B3
Wyndham Way OX2 . . **.123** A4
Wyndyke Furlong OX14 . **.179** B4
Wyre Ct RG31 . . . . **.257** B2
Wysdom Way OX18 . . . **.100** C2
Wytham OX29 . . . . **.120** C4
Wytham St OX1 . . . . **.141** B3
Wytham View OX29 . . . **.120** C4

Y

Yare CI OX11 . . . . **.201** A1
Yarnell's Hill OX2 . . . . . **.140** B4
Yarnell's Rd OX2 . . . . . **.140** C4
Yarnton CI RG4 . . . . **.259** B3
Yarnton La OX5 . . . . **.108** C4
Yarnton La OX5 . . . . **.108** B3
Yarnton Rd
　Cassington OX29 . . . . . . **.107** B2
　Kidlington OX5 . . . . **.108** C4
Yatesbury Rd OX18 . . . **.115** C2
Yealm CI OX11 . . . . **.200** C2
Yeates CI OX9 . . . . **.129** C1
Yeats CI OX4 . . . . **.142** C3
Yeftly Dr OX4 . . . . **.142** A1
Yeld Hall Rd OX14 . . . . **.160** A1
Yeomans CI NN13 . . . . . **.24** A4
Yew CI Bicester OX26 . . . . **.65** C3
　Oxford OX4 . . . . **.143** A1
Yew Tree CI OX9 . . . . . . **.166** A4
Yew Tree Ct RG8 . . . . . . **.249** B3
Yew Tree Mews
　Abingdon OX14 . . . . **.179** C4
　Ducklington OX29 . . . . . **.118** A2
Yew Tree Rise NN13 . . . **.36** B4
Yolsum CI HP17 . . . . **.130** C3
York Ave OX3 . . . . **.124** C1
York CI OX26 . . . . **.66** A2
York PI OX4 . . . . **.123** C1
York Rd Carterton OX18 . **.115** C2
　Henley-on-T RG9 . . . . . . **.244** B1
　Oxford OX3 . . . . **.124** C1
　Reading RG1 . . . . **.259** A1
　West Hagbourne OX11 . . **.218** B2
Youens Dr OX9 . . . . **.148** A4
Youghal CI SN6 . . . . **.209** A3
Ypres Way OX14 . . . . . . **.159** B1
Yule Ct **1** OX16 . . . . **.16** A3